Extracanonical Sayings of Jesus

SOCIETY OF BIBLICAL LITERATURE
Resources for Biblical Study

Edited by
Bernard B. Scott

Number 18
Extracanonical Sayings of Jesus

by
WILLIAM D. STROKER

EXTRACANONICAL SAYINGS OF JESUS

By
William D. Stroker

Scholars Press
Atlanta, Georgia

Extracanonical Sayings of Jesus

© 1989
The Society of Biblical Literature

LIBRARY OF CONGRESS
Library of Congress Cataloging-in-Publication Data

Stroker, William.
Extracanonical sayings of Jesus.
  (Sources for Biblical study ; no. 18)
  Includes translations of small fragments of
  Coptic, Greek, and Latin.
  Bibliography: p.
  Includes indexes.
  1. Jesus Christ--words--Extracanonical parallels
I. Title. II. Series.
BT306.S83 1987   232.9'8   86-20211
ISBN 1-55540-055-8 (alk. paper)
ISBN 1-55540-442-1 (alk. paper pbk)

Printed in the United States of America
on acid-free paper

CONTENTS

ABBREVIATIONS

AAA	*Acta Apostolorum Apocrypha*
Adv. haer.	*Adversus haereses*
Apol.	*Apologia*
CG	Cairo Gnostic Library (Nag Hammadi Codices)
CChrSL	Corpus Christianorum Series Latina
Col	Colossians
1 Cor	1 Corinthians
2 Cor	2 Corinthians
CSCO	Corpus Scriptorum Christianorum Orientalium
CSEL	Corpus Scriptorum Ecclesiasticorum Latinorum
Dan	Daniel
De princ.	*De principiis*
De spec. leg.	*De specialibus legibus*
Deut	Deuteronomy
Dial.	Dialogue
Div. inst.	*Divinae institutiones*
Eccl	Ecclesiastes
Eccl. hist.	*Ecclesiasticae historiae*
Eph	Ephesians
EvT	*Evangelische Theologie*
Exc. ex Theod.	*Excerpta ex Theodoto*
Exod	Exodus
Ezek	Ezekiel
Gal	Galatians
Gen	Genesis
GCS	Die Griechischen Christlichen Schriftsteller
GNK	*Geschichte des Neutestamentlichen Kanons*
Haer.	*Haereses*
Heb	Hebrews
Hom	Homily
Hos	Hosea
HTR	*Harvard Theological Review*
Isa	Isaiah
Jam	James
Jer	Jeremiah
Jn	John
JTS	*Journal of Theological Studies*
KlT	Kleine Texte
Lev	Leviticus

vii

LCL	Loeb Classical Library
LSJ	Liddell, Scott, Jones, *Greek-English Lexicon*
Lk	Luke
LXX	Septuagint
Mand.	*Mandate*
Mk	Mark
ms.	manuscript
Mt	Matthew
N.T. Apoc.	*New Testament Apocrypha*
NHS	Nag Hammadi Studies
NPNF	A Select Library of Nicene and Post-Nicene Fathers of the Christian Church
nr.	number
Num	Numbers
P. Eg.	Papyrus Egerton
P. Oxy.	Oxyrhynchus Papyri
PatSy	Patrologia Syriaca
1 Pet	1 Peter
2 Pet	2 Peter
PG	Patrologiae Cursus Completus, Series Graeca
Phil	Philippians
PL	Patrologiae Cursus Completus, Series Latina
Prov	Proverbs
Ps	Psalm
ps.	pseudo
PTS	Patristische Texte und Studien
1QS	*Manual of Discipline*
RB	*Révue Biblique*
RBén	*Révue Bénédictine*
Recog.	*Recognitiones*
Ref.	*Refutationes*
Rev	Revelation
Rom	Romans
1 Sam	1 Samuel
SC	Sources chrétiennes
SD	Studies and Documents
serm.	*sermo,* sermon
TextsS	Texts and Studies
1 Thes	1 Thessalonians
2 Thes	2 Thessalonians
1 Tim	1 Timothy
2 Tim	2 Timothy
TU	Texte und Untersuchungen
var.	variant
Zech.	Zechariah

INTRODUCTION

The importance of "extracanonical sayings of Jesus" and their study has received increased recognition in recent years. This recognition has, at the same time, necessitated a distinct departure from what had been the dominant thrust of many earlier studies.[1] Previously the study of these materials was dominated by a search for "authentic" sayings of Jesus, that is, sayings for which a case might be made that they were spoken by Jesus himself and preserved in sources other than the canonical New Testament. This interest in finding potentially "authentic" sayings of Jesus had the unfortunate result of focusing study on a small number of passages and relegating much of the rest to the periphery. Ironically, as critical study made the number of potentially "authentic" sayings dwindle, the realization increased that the importance of the wider body of material lay in other areas.

Stated quite generally, the importance of the extracanonical sayings is in their role in broadening our understanding of the development and transmission of traditions of Jesus' teachings. A detailed discussion of the ways in which the extracanonical sayings may be studied and the present volume used is beyond the scope of this introduction. The following comments will give some general indications.

The canonical tradition and the sources behind the canonical gospels were neither the only collections nor the sole bearers of the traditions of Jesus' teachings.[2] Thus the question of the earliest stages of the tradition of Jesus' teachings cannot be investigated on the basis of the canonical gospels alone. Extracanonical sayings sometimes preserve a less developed version of a saying and may give us thereby access to a stage of tradition earlier than that of the canonical gospels.[3]

---

[1] The history of research is too extensive for inclusion here. The best bibliography of the older literature is contained in Bernard Pick, *Paralipomena: Remains of Gospels and Sayings of Christ* (Chicago: Open Court, 1908) 126–152. For an assessment of the earlier works, see Alfred Resch, *Agrapha: Aussercanonische Schriftfragmente* (2nd ed.; TU; N.F. 15.3–4; Leipzig: Hinrichs, 1906; reprint, Darmstadt: Wissenschaftliche Buchgesellschaft, 1967) 14–22. For the work since Resch, see Joachim Jeremias, *Unknown Sayings of Jesus* (2nd ed.; London: S.P.C.K., 1964) 4–13, and William D. Stroker, "The Formation of Secondary Sayings of Jesus," (Ph.D. Dissertation, Yale University, 1970) 1–17.

[2] Helmut Koester (in *Synoptische Überlieferung bei den apostolischen Vätern* (TU 65; Berlin: Akademie, 1957) argues convincingly that many of the sayings of Jesus in the Apostolic Fathers are independent of the synoptic gospels. The sayings preserved in *The Gospel of Thomas* are also best viewed as stemming from a collection earlier than the canonical gospels.

[3] For example, the parable of the wicked tenants in *The Gospel of Thomas* 65 (see P11 in this

Analogously, Jesus' sayings were transmitted and redacted independently of the canonical tradition, as well as in dependence upon it. In the extracanonical tradition, as well as in the canonical, sayings were shaped and redacted in large measure to meet the needs of the communities. The processes of redaction of individual sayings and groups of sayings are largely analogous in the canonical and extracanonical tradition. Thus the extracanonical sayings can help us achieve a more complete picture of the transmission and redaction of the sayings of Jesus and the relation of these processes to different groups within early Christianity.

Finally, the extracanonical tradition provides evidence that sayings from other sources have become attributed to Jesus.[4] Again, this is the type of development which took place also within the canonical tradition. Our understanding of the extent to which materials from other sources have become attributed to Jesus would necessitate study of the extracanonical materials.

Study of the extracanonical sayings can thus broaden our understanding of the total picture of the early history of the Jesus tradition by providing additional examples of the ways in which (1) sayings were shaped, collected, and redacted, and (2) sayings from other sources were attributed to Jesus. The present collection has been made with the hope that it might prove to be a useful resource for persons engaged in this study, as well as for those interested solely in the extracanonical sayings themselves.

Since the materials are found scattered throughout a wide variety of writings, a student is largely dependent on collections for access. There has not been a recent comprehensive collection of the materials, particularly one which presents the materials both in original text and in English translation.[5] The present volume makes available to the general student of the New Testament and early Christian literature, as well as to the specialist, a comprehensive collection of the extracanonical sayings of Jesus in original text and English translation, along with appropriate parallel materials.[6]

---

collection) has virtually none of the allegorical elements found in Mark 12:1–12, Matt 21:33–46, and Luke 20:9–19, and is frequently viewed as preserving an earlier version, independent of the synoptic gospels (See, e.g., Crossan, *Parables,* 95).

[4] For example, in *The Gospel of Thomas* 102, the saying about the dog in the manger, known from the Aesopic tradition and Lucian, is attributed to Jesus (see the chapter on Wisdom Sayings, W38). Also, in the *Manichaean Psalm-Book* a saying from an apocryphon of Ezekiel has become attributed to Jesus (see the chapter on I-Sayings, I26, and also William D. Stroker, "The Source of an Agraphon in the Manichaean Psalm-Book," *JTS* n.s. 24/1 [1977] 114–118).

[5] The latest extensive collection of materials in English translation is Pick's *Paralipomena.* Jeremias' *Unknown Sayings* concentrates on a small number of sayings "whose authenticity admits of serious consideration" (44). His survey of the rest of the material remains useful. Jack Finegan's *Hidden Records of the Life of Christ* (Philadelphia: Pilgrim, 1969) contains quotations in original text and translation from a number of apocryphal writings and seventeen individual sayings from the church fathers.

[6] Unless otherwise indicated, the translations from the Greek, Coptic, and Latin are my own.

Initially I had hoped to be able to include a brief discussion of each of the sayings. The amount of material grew to such an extent that it became impossible to include analysis or commentary within a single volume. Even critical notes had to be kept to a minimum. Those notes which are included treat primarily of difficulties present in the original texts as we have them, such as lacunae and other problems related to accurate translation. I have also included some cross references to other sayings in the collection among the notes.

The sayings incorporated in the present volume are grouped in six sections, using the categories developed by Rudolf Bultmann in his *History of the Synoptic Tradition*,[7] apophthegms, parables, prophetic and apocalyptic sayings, wisdom sayings, I-sayings, and community rules. Bultmann's categories are based partly on formal considerations and partly on considerations of content. Some individual sayings could, therefore, be included under more than one category, as he himself indicated.[8] Despite this and some other difficulties, Bultmann's designations have proven useful and have the initial advantage of being comprehensive enough to cover virtually all of the material. Only occasionally has it been necessary to indicate in a note that a specific saying does not really fit one of the six categories. Since this is a collection of the materials rather than a form-critical investigation, an attempt to develop an alternate set of comprehensive categories is inappropriate in this context.

Also, I have not utilized "mixed forms" as sub-categories nor provided lists of the materials in one category which have formal elements in common with another.[9] This, too, would have necessitated a more extensive form-critical investigation than is the purpose of the present volume. The special nature of apophthegms necessitates brief comment. The saying in an apophthegm, if taken alone, could be classified under one of the other headings. The apophthegm is a definite form or genre, however, and is characterized by a saying or teaching placed in a brief context. Within this collection a saying, or even a parable, will be grouped with the apophthegms if it and its context together constitute an apophthegm. Thus Thomas 20 and 21a, in which the parables of the mustard seed and the children in a field are given as Jesus' response to requests of the disciples, are included with the other apophthegms (A22 and A23).

Within each chapter the materials are presented in the chronological sequence of their literary attestation, with the exception that the sayings

---

Materials extant in other languages are given in English translation alone, with the source of the translation indicated. When the English is based on a translation, such as on Wajnberg's German rendering of the Ethiopic *Testament of the Lord in Galilee*, this is also indicated.

[7] New York: Harper & Row, 1963.

[8] Ibid., 4.

[9] References to other sayings in the collection with close parallels in wording or content are, however, indicated in the notes.

from *The Gospel of Thomas* and other Nag Hammadi treatises are grouped together and in the sequence of their occurrence in the volumes of that corpus. These materials occur as the latter part of each chapter. The dating of the various documents and authors, included in the index, is taken from standard works on patrology,[10] the two volumes of Hennecke-Schneemelcher's *New Testament Apocrypha*,[11] and The Nag Hammadi Library.[12] No attempt has been made to do a new assessment of the evidence for dating. Some of the documents are very difficult to date, and the conclusions of scholars vary greatly. Further, the date of a document is not in itself the date of a particular tradition used in it nor of the stage of development of such a tradition. Later documents may preserve earlier materials or earlier versions of materials. The user of this volume should, therefore, not make inferences based solely on the sequence of the materials presented or the dates assigned to the various authors and documents in the index.

The sayings in each section are numbered for purposes of easy reference. Uses of the same or parallel material are given in text and translation under the designation "parallels," except for parallels from the Old and New Testaments which are simply listed in standard reference form. Parallels from the Old Testament Apocrypha are given in text and translation. The sequence of the parallel materials under a particular saying is (1) extra-canonical parallels attributed to Jesus, (2) extracanonical parallels not attributed to Jesus, and (3) canonical parallels. The appendix indicates which of the extracanonical parallels are attributed to Jesus in my judgment, and may be consulted when this is not sufficiently indicated by the citation formula or by the immediate context. The extracanonical parallels are taken primarily from early Christian literature, including apocryphal materials. I have not made an extensive search for parallels in such areas as rabbinic or popular hellenistic literature. In a few instances, examples from these areas have been included, since they have already become part of the general discussion of the sayings in question.

The collection is, to my knowledge, the most extensive which has been published. Nonetheless, some limits on its scope have been necessary. The following comments deal with the types of materials which are included as well as some which it has been necessary to exclude.

The term "extracanonical sayings of Jesus" refers simply to those sayings attributed to Jesus not found in the canonical New Testament. The term here is intended as a designation related to location, not to judgments as to theological or historical value. The question of "authenticity" is not a concern here and plays no role as a criterion for inclusion. Those sayings frequently

---

[10] Berthold Altaner, *Patrology* (Freiburg: Herder, 1960), and Johannes Quasten, *Patrology* (Westminster, MD: Newman, 1951).

[11] Philadelphia: Westminster, 1963, 1965.

[12] Ed., James M. Robinson (San Francisco: Harper & Row, 1977).

called agrapha[13] are included, but also a larger number of parallels to, or varying versions of, canonical sayings found in early Christian literature than is usually treated under the designation agrapha. Thus materials which in the critical literature might be viewed as quotations from memory or as conflations of two or more canonical sayings are included, as are manuscript variants involving a significant addition or difference in meaning. The materials come from the first five centuries of the Christian era. An occasional parallel from a later time has, however, been included.

Though the sources in which the sayings are found are numerous and of wide variety, they may be categorized in the following manner: (1) manuscripts of the New Testament writings, such as Codex Bezae, (2) manuscripts or fragments of manuscripts of noncanonical gospels and other noncanonical writings usually designated New Testament apocrypha, such as the Jewish-Christian gospels, the Oxyrhynchus and Egerton 2 papyri, *The Gospel of Thomas*, etc. and (3) quotations in the works of the church fathers and other early Christian literature.

The following materials have not been included or have been included only in part, as indicated.

(A) The infancy gospels contain some words of Jesus, but these are usually comments on the miraculous deeds narrated and are of a rather different nature from the teaching materials which are our major concern.

(B) The examples of Jesus' sayings in Islamic literature are so numerous as to be virtually a book length collection in themselves. For this reason and because of their late date, they are not included.[14]

(C) The few sayings attributed to Jesus in the Talmudic literature are not included.[15]

(D) The Nag Hammadi corpus presents many challenges to the student of noncanonical sayings. The importance of the sayings in *The Gospel of Thomas* is undisputed and perhaps unsurpassed. They are included in their entirety. So are the sayings in *The Gospel of Philip*. Several tractates of the Nag Hammadi corpus are largely, and sometimes virtually entirely, revelatory

---

[13] The term literally means "unwritten sayings" but has generally been used to designate sayings of Jesus not attested in the canonical gospels. Resch's broader definition, "fragments of extra-canonical scriptures," related to Old Testament materials as well as to New, is seldom used.

[14] E. Sell's and D. S. Margoliouth's "Christ in Mohammedan Literature," in James Hastings, ed., *Dictionary of Christ and the Gospels* (New York: Scribner's, 1906) 2:882–886, remains useful for these materials. See also James Hardy Ropes, "Agrapha," in James Hastings' *Dictionary of the Bible* (New York: Scribner's, 1919), Extra Vol., 350–352. An extensive collection of material was compiled by Michael Asin y Palacos, *Logia et agrapha Domini Jesu apud Moslemicos Scriptores* (Patrologia Orientalis; ed. R. Graffin and F. Nau; Paris: Firmin-Didot, 13.3 [1919], 335–441, and 19.4 [1926], 531–624. Not all of this material is actually attributed to Jesus, however.

[15] Except for the parallel to Matt 5:17 in *b. Shabbath* 116b. See the chapter on I-Sayings (I32). For discussions of sayings attributed to Jesus in the Talmud, see R. Travers Herford, *Christianity in Talmud and Midrash* (reprint, Clifton, NJ: Reference Book Publishers, 1966), and also H. L. Strack, *Jesus, die Häretiker und die Christen* (Leipzig: Hinrichs, 1910).

discourses of Jesus, frequently in the form of dialogues between Jesus and one or more disciples. Treatment of this material and of the analogous treatises in Codices Berolinensis, Brucianus, and Askewianus is impossible within the compass of a single volume. These materials are not included, except for parallels to other sayings and a few other exceptional instances which seem to be justified. The major exceptions are the three parables from *The Apocryphon of James* and the pass words of the soul in its ascent in *The First Apocalypse of James*. The recent English translation of the entire Nag Hammadi Corpus, edited by Robinson, and the reprinting of the texts of *Pistis Sophia, The Two Books of Jeu*, the *Untitled Gnostic Text*, along with English translations,[16] make all of these materials readily available and extensive incorporation in the present collection unnecessary.

(E) There are a few other documents, in addition to those just mentioned, which are largely in the literary form of revelations of Jesus to some of his disciples, such as the *Epistula Apostolorum, The Testament of the Lord*, and the Ethiopic *Apocalypse of Peter*, which are used primarily only as parallels to sayings from other sources. I have, however, included selections of the descriptions of the punishments of the wicked from the Ethiopic version of the *Apocalypse of Peter*, the description of the anti-Christ from *The Testament of the Lord*, and some shorter passages from the *Epistula Apostolorum*.[17]

(F) A few individual sayings, frequently included in other collections, are excluded since it is not sufficiently clear that they are actually given as sayings of Jesus in the document in question. These have been assessed on a case by case basis. I mention an example in order to indicate the kinds of considerations involved. *Barnabas* 6.13 reads, "And the Lord says: See, I make the last things like the first." The Syriac *Didascalia* cites this in fuller form and joins it with a citation of Matt 20:16 par. "For He said: Behold, I make the first things as the last, and the last as the first; and: The last shall be first and the first last."[18] In neither instance is the saying to be viewed as a saying of Jesus. In the *Didascalia*, the saying is joined by "and" to quotations from Isa 43:18–19 and Jer 3:16 as well as to the one from Matt 20:16 par. In *Barnabas* the formula "the Lord says" is used with quotations from the Old Testament but never to cite sayings of Jesus from the synoptic tradition. The saying may be from an apocryphon viewed as scripture, but in neither *Barnabas* nor the *Didascalia* is it to be considered a saying of Jesus.[19]

The pleasant task remains of expressing my gratitude to several people

---

[16] Carl Schmidt & Violet MacDermot, *Pistis Sophia* (NHS 9; Leiden: Brill, 1978), and *The Books of Jeu and the Untitled Text in the Bruce Codex* (NHS 13; Leiden: Brill, 1978).

[17] A complete translation of *Epistula Apostolorum* is available in Hennecke-Schneemelcher, *New Testament Apocrypha*, 1; of the *Testament of the Lord* in James Cooper and Arthur J. Maclean, *The Testament of the Lord* (Edinburgh: T. & T. Clark, 1902).

[18] Trans. from R. Hugh Connolly, *Didascalia Apostolorum* (Oxford: Clarendon, 1929), 234.

[19] See Koester, *Synoptische Überlieferung*, 127.

who have encouraged me in the preparation of this work and to those without whose assistance much would still remain to be done. Professor Nils Dahl first introduced me to the extracanonical sayings during my student days at Yale. His encouragement then and his continued interest in my work over the years is deeply appreciated. I have been fortunate in having two excellent editors during the preparation of these materials for publication, Wayne Meeks of Yale University in the early stages and Bernard Scott of Saint Meinrad Seminary, School of Theology, in the final stages. Their critical reading and suggestions have been of immense value, particularly in my attempts to make the collection more usable for others. I wish to thank Father Ephrem Carr, also of Saint Meinrad, who checked my translations of the Latin rendering of the *Liber Graduum* with the original Syriac. Finally, over the years several students have assisted me in tracking down parallels, typing, proofreading, and preparing indices: Diane Bennett, Bill Dalrymple, Peter Espenshade, Elizabeth Gombach, Ruth Kuo, Patricia Lennon, Cherie Lenzen, Jennifer Marke, Floyd Parker, Kurt Piehler, Shannon Richie, and Sam and Stella Roberts. Their assistance in these crucial tasks is greatly appreciated.

APOPHTHEGMS

A1 / *The Rich Young Man*

It says: The other rich man said to him: Master, what good thing must I do that I may live? He said to him: Man, do what is in the law and the prophets. He answered him: I have done that. He said to him: Go and sell all you possess and distribute it among the poor, and come follow me. But the rich man then began to scratch his head, and it did not please him. And the Lord said to him: How can you say, I have done what is in the law and the prophets? For it is written in the law: Love your neighbor as yourself; and behold, many of your brothers, sons of Abraham, are clothed in filth and die of hunger, while your house is full of many good things, and nothing at all comes out of it for them. And he turned and said to Simon, his disciple, who was sitting by him: Simon, son of Jonah, it is easier for a camel to go through the eye of a needle than for a rich man to enter into the kingdom of heaven.

"dixit, inquit, ad eum alter divitum: magister, quid bonum faciens vivam? dixit ei: homo, legem et prophetas fac. respondit ad eum: feci. dixit ei: vade, vende omnia quae possides et divide pauperibus, et veni, sequere me. coepit autem dives scalpere caput suum et non placuit ei. et dixit ad eum dominus: quomodo dicis: feci legem et prophetas? quoniam scriptum est in lege: diliges proximum tuum sicut teipsum, et ecce multi fratres tui filii Abrahae amicti sunt stercore, morientes prae fame, et domus tua plena est multis bonis, et non egreditur omnino aliquid ex ea ad eos. et conversus dixit Simoni discipulo suo sedenti apud se: Simon, fili Ionae, facilius est camelum intrare per foramen acus quam divitem in regnum caelorum."

> *Gospel of the Nazaraeans* [1], Origen, *Commentary on Matthew* 15.4 (to Matt 19:16ff). Klostermann, *Origenes Werke* 10:389–390.

PARALLELS

Again when he said, If you wish to be perfect, sell your posses-sions and give to the poor, he convicts the one who boasts in having kept all the commandments since his youth. For he had not fulfilled, love your neighbor as yourself.

πάλιν τε αὖ ὅταν εἴπῃ· "εἰ θέλεις τέλειος γενέσθαι, πωλήσας τὰ ὑπάρχοντα δὸς πτωχοῖς," ἐλέγχει τὸν καυχώμενον ἐπὶ τῷ "πάσας τὰς ἐντολὰς ἐκ

νεότητος τετηρηκέναι·" οὐ γὰρ πεπληρώκει τὸ "ἀγαπήσεις τὸν πλησίον
σου ὡς ἑαυτόν."

Clement, *Strom.* 3.6.55. Stählin-Früchtel, *Clemens* 2³: 221.

Mark 10:17–24, Matt 19:16–25, Luke 18:18–25.

A2 / *Baptism of Jesus*

Behold, the mother of the Lord and his brothers said to him: John the Baptist
baptizes for the remission of sins: let us go and be baptized by him. But he
said to them: Wherein have I sinned, so that I should go and be baptized by
him? Unless this very thing which I have said is (a sin of) ignorance.

Ecce mater Domini et fratres ejus dicebant ei: Joannes Baptista baptizat in
remissionem peccatorum: eamus et baptizemur ab eo. Dixit autem eis: Quid
peccavi, ut vadam et baptizer ab eo? Nisi forte hoc ipsum quod dixi, igno-
rantia est.

> *Gospel of the Nazaraeans* [2], Jerome, *Dialogus adversus Pela-
> gianos* 3.2. PL 23: 570–571.

NOTES

A tradition with some similarities is preserved in *De rebaptismate,* ch. 17, of Ps.
Cyprian and attributed there to a work called *Praedicatio Pauli.* Jesus confesses his
sins and is almost compelled to be baptized by Mary, his mother. No words of Jesus
are given. See G. Hartel, *Cypriani opera omnia* 3: 90. Trans. *Ante-Nicene Fathers*
5: 677.

A3 / *Forgive Seventy Times Seven Times*

He said: If your brother has sinned with a word and has made amends with
you, receive him seven times a day. Simon his disciple said to him: Seven
times a day? The Lord answered and said to him: Indeed, I say to you, as
many as seventy times seven times. For in the prophets also, after they were
anointed with the Holy Spirit, a word of sin was found.

Si peccaverit, inquit, frater tuus in verbo, et satis tibi fecerit, septies in die
suscipe eum. Dixit illi Simon discipulus ejus: Septies in die? Respondit
Dominus, et dixit ei: Etiam ego dico tibi, usque septuagies septies. Etenim
in Prophetis quoque postquam uncti sunt Spiritu sancto, inventus est sermo
peccati.

Gospel of the Nazaraeans [3], Jerome, *Dialogus adversus Pelagianos* 3.2.
PL 23: 571.

PARALLELS

The Judaikon[1] has after seventy times seven: For in the prophets
also, after they were anointed by the Holy Spirit, a word of sin was
found.

Τὸ ᾽Ιουδαϊκὸν ἑξῆς ἔχει μετὰ τὸ ἑβδομηκοντάκις ἑπτά· "καὶ γὰρ ἐν τοῖς
προφήταις μετὰ τὸ χρισθῆναι αὐτοὺς ἐν πνεύματι ἁγίῳ εὑρίσκετο ἐν
αὐτοῖς λόγος ἁμαρτίας."
MSS. 566 and 899 to Matthew 18:22. Aland, *Synopsis*, 253.

The one who has not forgiven seventy times seven times is not
worthy of me.

Qui non dimittit septuagies septies, non est me dignus.
Liber Graduum 2.4.6. Kmosko, PatSy 1.3: 34.

Matt 18:21–22, Luke 17:3–4.

NOTES

[1] Term used for the *Gospel of the Nazaraeans* by the copyists of MSS 566 and 899.
"The Jewish Gospel" is an alternate rendering of the word.

A4 / *How Long Will Death Have Power*

When Salome asked, How long will death have power? the Lord said, As long
as you women bear children, not as if life were bad and creation evil, but as
teaching the sequence of nature. For death always follows birth.

τῇ Σαλώμῃ ὁ κύριος πυνθανομένῃ, "μέχρι πότε θάνατος ἰσχύσει;" οὐχ ὡς κακοῦ
τοῦ βίου ὄντος καὶ τῆς κτίσεως πονηρᾶς, "μέχρις ἂν" εἶπεν "ὑμεῖς αἱ γυναῖκες τίκτητε,"
ἀλλ᾽ ὡς τὴν ἀκολουθίαν τὴν φυσικὴν διδάσκων· γενέσει γὰρ πάντως ἕπεται καὶ φθορά.
Gospel of the Egyptians [1a], Clement, *Strom.* 3.6.45. Stählin-Früchtel,
Clemens 2³:217.

PARALLELS

It is probably because the Word had spoken concerning the con-
summation that Salome said, Until when will men die? Scripture
speaks of man in two ways, the visible appearance and the soul,
and again, the one who is being saved and the one who is not. And

sin is said to be the death of the soul. Therefore the Lord answered very carefully, As long as women bear children, that is, as long as the desires are active.

ὅθεν εἰκότως περὶ συντελείας μηνύσαντος τοῦ λόγου ἡ Σαλώμη φησί· "μέχρι τίνος οἱ ἄνθρωποι ἀποθανοῦνται;" ἄνθρωπον δὲ καλεῖ ἡ γραφὴ διχῶς, τόν τε φαινόμενον καὶ τὴν ψυχήν, πάλιν τε αὖ τὸν σῳζόμενον καὶ τὸν μή. καὶ θάνατος ψυχῆς ἡ ἁμαρτία λέγεται. διὸ καὶ παρατετηρημένως ἀποκρίνεται ὁ κύριος· "μέχρις ἂν τίκτωσιν αἱ γυναῖκες," τουτέστι μέχρις ἂν αἱ ἐπιθυμίαι ἐνεργῶσι.

> Gospel of the Egyptians [1b], Clement, Strom. 3.9.64. Stählin-Früchtel, Clemens 2³:255.

And when the Savior says to Salome that there will be death as long as women bear children, he does not speak reproachfully of procreation, for that is necessary for the salvation of believers.

καὶ ὅταν ὁ σωτὴρ πρὸς Σαλώμην λέγῃ μέχρι τότε εἶναι θάνατον, ἄχρις ἂν αἱ γυναῖκες τίκτωσιν, οὐ τὴν γένεσιν κακίζων ἔλεγεν, ἀναγκαίαν οὖσαν διὰ τὴν σωτηρίαν τῶν πιστευόντων.

> Gospel of the Egyptians [1c], Clement, Exc. ex Theod. 67. Stählin-Früchtel, Clemens 3²:129.

The Lord said: The one who is from the truth does not die; the one who is from the woman dies.

ΠΕΧΕ ΠΧΟ
ΕΙC ΧΕ ΠΕΤΕΟΥΕΒΟΛ 2Ν ΤΜΗΕ ΠΕ
ΜΕϤΜΟΥ· ΠΕΤΕΟΥΕΒΟΛ 2Ν ΤΕC2Ι
ΜΕ ΠΕ ϢΑϤΜΟΥ
> Dialogue of the Savior, CG III, 140.11–14.

NOTES

The passages from Clement are generally considered to contain quotations from the Gospel of the Egyptians. See Hennecke-Schneemelcher, N. T. Apoc. 1:166. Only the words, "as long as (you) women bear children," are attributed to Jesus. The explanatory comments are Clement's.

A5 / On Procreation

For when she said, "I have done well then in not having borne children," as if it were improper to engage in procreation, then the Lord answered and said: Eat every plant but do not eat the one which contains bitterness.

φαμένης γὰρ αὐτῆς "καλῶς οὖν ἐποίησα μὴ τεκοῦσα," ὡς οὐ δεόντως τῆς γενέσεως παραλαμβανομένης, ἀμείβεται λέγων ὁ κύριος· "πᾶσαν φάγε βοτάνην, τὴν δὲ πικρίαν ἔχουσαν μὴ φάγῃς.

> *Gospel of the Egyptians* [2], Clement, *Strom.* 3.9.66. Stählin-Früchtel, *Clemens* 2³:226.

A6 / *When the Two Will Be One*

Therefore Cassianus says: When Salome asked when the things would be known that she had inquired about, the Lord said: When you (pl.) have trampled on the garment of shame and when the two become one and the male with the female is neither male nor female.

διὰ τοῦτο τοι ὁ Κασσιανός φησι· "πυνθανομένης τῆς Σαλώμης πότε γνωσθήσεται τὰ περὶ ὧν ἤρετο, ἔφη ὁ κύριος· ὅταν τὸ τῆς αἰσχύνης ἔνδυμα πατήσητε καὶ ὅταν γένηται τὰ δύο ἕν καὶ τὸ ἄρρεν μετὰ τῆς θηλείας οὔτε ἄρρεν οὔτε θῆλυ."

> *Gospel of the Egyptians* [3], Clement, *Strom.* 3.13.92. Stählin-Früchtel, *Clemens* 2³:238.

PARALLELS

For when the Lord himself was asked by someone when his kingdom would come, he said: When the two will be one, and the outside as the inside, and the male with the female neither male nor female.

ἐπερωτηθεὶς γὰρ αὐτὸς ὁ κύριος ὑπό τινος, πότε ἥξει αὐτου ἡ βασιλεία, εἶπεν "Ὅταν ἔσται τὰ δύο ἕν, καὶ τὸ ἔξω ὡς τὸ ἔσω, καὶ τὸ ἄρσεν μετὰ τῆς θηλείας, οὔτε ἄρσεν οὔτε θῆλυ.

> *II Clement* 12.2. Funk-Bihlmeyer, *Die Apostolischen Väter*, 76.

Jesus saw little children being suckled. He said to his disciples: These little children being suckled are like those who enter the kingdom. They said to him: If we are children, shall we enter the kingdom? Jesus said to them: When you make the two one, and when you make the inside as the outside and the outside as the inside and the upper side as the lower side, and when you make the male and the female into a single one so that the male will not be male nor the female be female; when you make eyes in the place of an eye, and a hand in the place of a hand, and a foot in the place of a foot, an image in the place of an image, then you shall enter [the kingdom].

ⲁⲓ̅ⲥ̅ ⲚⲀⲨ Ⲁ2Ⲛ̄ⲔⲞⲨⲈⲒ ⲈⲨⲬⲒ ⲈⲢⲰⲦⲈ ⲠⲈⲬⲀ4 Ⲛ̄

ⲚⲈϤⲘⲀⲐⲎⲦⲎⲤ ϪⲈ ⲚⲈⲈⲒⲔⲞⲨⲈⲒ ⲈⲦϪⲒ ⲈⲢⲰ
ⲦⲈ ⲈⲨⲦⲚ̄ⲦⲰⲚ ⲀⲚⲈⲦⲂⲎⲔ ⲈϨⲞⲨⲚ′ ⲀⲦⲘⲚ̄
ⲦⲈⲢⲞ ⲠⲈϪⲀⲨ ⲚⲀϤ′ ϪⲈ ⲈⲈⲒ ⲈⲚⲞ[1] Ⲛ̄ⲔⲞⲨⲈⲒ ⲦⲚ̄
ⲚⲀⲂⲰⲔ′ ⲈϨⲞⲨⲚ ⲈⲦⲘⲚ̄ⲦⲈⲢⲞ ⲠⲈϪⲈ ⲒⲎ̄Ⲥ̄ ⲚⲀⲨ
ϪⲈ ϨⲞⲦⲀⲚ ⲈⲦⲈⲦⲚ̄ϢⲀⲢ̄ ⲠⲤⲚⲀⲨ ⲞⲨⲀ ⲀⲨⲰ Ⲉ
ⲦⲈⲦⲚ̄ϢⲀⲢ̄ ⲠⲤⲀ ⲚϨⲞⲨⲚ Ⲛ̄ⲐⲈ Ⲙ̄ⲠⲤⲀ ⲚⲂⲞⲖ
ⲀⲨⲰ ⲠⲤⲀ ⲚⲂⲞⲖ Ⲛ̄ⲐⲈ Ⲙ̄ⲠⲤⲀ ⲚϨⲞⲨⲚ ⲀⲨⲰ ⲠⲤⲀ̄
ⲦⲠⲈ Ⲛ̄ⲐⲈ Ⲙ̄ⲠⲤⲀ ⲘⲠⲒⲦⲚ̄ ⲀⲨⲰ ϢⲒⲚⲀ ⲈⲦⲈ
ⲦⲚⲀⲈⲒⲢⲈ Ⲙ̄ⲪⲞ′ⲞⲨⲦ′ ⲘⲚ̄ ⲦⲤϨⲒⲘⲈ Ⲙ̄ⲠⲒⲞⲨⲀ
ⲞⲨⲰⲦ′ ϪⲈⲔⲀⲀⲤ ⲚⲈⲪⲞⲞⲨⲦ′ Ⲣ̄ ϨⲞⲞⲨⲦ′ Ⲛ̄ⲦⲈ
ⲦⲤϨⲒⲘⲈ Ⲣ̄ ⲤϨⲒⲘⲈ ϨⲞⲦⲀⲚ ⲈⲦⲈⲦⲚ̄ϢⲀⲈⲒⲢⲈ
Ⲛ̄ϨⲚ̄ⲂⲀⲖ ⲈⲠⲘⲀ ⲚⲞⲨⲂⲀⲖ′ ⲀⲨⲰ ⲞⲨϬⲒϪ′
ⲈⲠⲘⲀ Ⲛ̄ⲚⲞⲨϬⲒϪ′ ⲀⲨⲰ ⲞⲨⲈⲢⲎⲦⲈ[2] ⲈⲠⲘⲀ
Ⲛ̄ⲞⲨⲈⲢⲎⲦⲈ[2] ⲞⲨϨⲒⲔⲰⲚ′ ⲈⲠⲘⲀ Ⲛ̄ⲞⲨϨⲒⲔⲰ̄
ⲦⲞⲦⲈ ⲦⲈⲦⲚⲀ ⲂⲰⲔ′ⲈϨⲞⲨⲚ [ⲈⲦⲘⲚⲦⲈⲢⲞ]

Gospel of Thomas 22. CG II, 37.20–35.

Concerning these things the Lord said in a mystery: Unless you make the things on the right as those on the left and the things on the left as those on the right and the things above as those below and the things behind as those before, you will not recognize the kingdom.

περὶ ὧν ὁ κύριος ἐν μυστηρίῳ λέγει· Ἐὰν μὴ ποιήσητε τὰ δεξιὰ ὡς τὰ ἀριστερὰ καὶ τὰ ἀριστερὰ ὡς τὰ δεξιὰ καὶ τὰ ἄνω ὡς τὰ κάτω καὶ τὰ ὀπίσω ὡς τὰ ἔμπροσθεν, οὐ μὴ ἐπιγνῶτε τὴν βασιλείαν.

Martyrdom of Peter 9 (*Acts of Peter* 38). Bonnet, *AAA* 1:94.

whence the Lord said in a mystery: Unless you make the right as the left and the left as the right and what is above as what is below and what is before as what is behind, you will not recognize the kingdom of God.

unde dominus in mysterio dixerat: 'Si non feceritis dexteram sicut sinistram et sinistram sicut dexteram, et quae sursum sunt sicut deorsum, et quae ante sicut quae retro, non cognoscetis regnum dei.'

Pseudo-Linus, *Martyrium Petri* 14. Lipsius-Bonnet, *AAA* 1:17.

For the Lord said to me: Unless you make the things below into the things above and the things on the left into the things on the right, you will not enter into my kingdom.

εἶπεν γάρ μοι ὁ κύριος· Ἐὰν μὴ ποιήσητε ὑμῶν τὰ κάτω εἰς τὰ ἄνω, καὶ τὰ ἀριστερὰ εἰς τὰ δεξιά, οὐ μὴ εἰσέλθητε εἰς τὴν βασιλείαν μου.

Acts of Philip 140 (34). Lipsius-Bonnet, *AAA* 2.2:74–75.

He [said]: I have come that I might make [the things below] like the things [above and the things outside] like the things [within. I came to unite] them in [that] place.[3]

[ΠΧΟ]ҐIC [ΠЄΧ]Δ٩
ΧЄ ΔЄI ЄΤΡΔЄI[ΡЄ N̄ΝΔ ΠCΔ M̄ΠIΤ]N̄ N̄
ΘЄ N̄ΝΔ ΠCΔ Ṇ[ΤΠЄ ΔYꞶ N̄ΝΔ ΠCΔ N̄]ΒΟΛ
N̄ΘЄ N̄ΝΔ ΠC̣[Δ N̄ЗΟYΝ ΔЄI ЄΤΡΔЗꞶΤ]
ΡΟY ΜΠΜΔ ЄΤΜ[ΜΔY]³

Gospel of Philip 69. CG II, 67.30–34.

The inside I[4] have made outside and the outside < inside >, and all your fullness has been fulfilled in me. I have not turned back to the things behind but have gone forward to the things before, so that I might not become a reproach.

τὸν ἐντὸς ἐκτὸς πεποίηκα καὶ τὸ ἐκτός < ἐντός >, καὶ πᾶν σου τὸ πλήρωμα ἐν ἐμοὶ ἐπληρώθη. εἰς τὰ ὀπίσω οὐχ ὑπέστρεφα, εἰς δὲ τὰ ἔμπροσθεν προέβην, ἵνα μὴ ὄνειδος γένωμαι.

Acts of Thomas 147. Lipsius-Bonnet, *AAA* 2.2:256.

The internal I have made external, and the external internal; let Thy will be fulfilled in all my members. I have not turned back, and I have not stretched forward; let me not be a wonder and a sign.

Syriac *Acts of Thomas* 147. Trans. of the Syriac from Klijn, *Acts of Thomas*, 144.

He, being the Christ, who was crucified, by whom the [things] that were on the left hand were [placed] on the right hand, and those which were beneath [were] as those which [were] above, and those which [were] behind as those which [were] before, when He rose from the dead, and trod down Sheol, and by death slew Death; . . .

Testament of the Lord 1.28. Trans. of the Syriac from Cooper and Maclean, *The Testament of our Lord*, 88.

If the woman had not separated from the man, she would not die with the man. His separation became the beginning of death. Therefore Christ came to correct the separation which was from the beginning and to unite the two again and to give life to those who died in the separation and to unite them.

ΝЄΜΠЄΤ'
CЗIΜЄ ΠꞶΡΧ ЄΦΟΟYΤ ΝЄCΝΔΜΟY
ΔΝ ΠЄ ΜN̄ ΦΟΟYΤ' ΠЄ٩ΠꞶΡΧ N̄ΤΔ٩'

ϢϢΠΕ Ν̄ΑΡΧΗ Μ̄ΠΜΟΥ ΔΙΑ ΤΟΥΤΟ
ΑΠΕΧΡ̄C ΕΙ ΧΕΚΑΑC ΠΠϢΡΧ Ν̄ΤΑ2
ϢϢΠΕ ΧΙΝ ϢΟΡΠ΄ ΕϤΝΑCΕ2ϢϤ ΕΡΑΤϤ΄
ΠΑΛΙΝ΄ Ν̄Ϥ2ΟΤΡΟΥ Μ̄ΠCΝΑΥ ΑΥϢ ΝΕΝ
ΤΑ2ΜΟΥ 2Μ̄ ΠΠϢΡΧ΄ ΕϤΝΑϯ ΝΑΥ Ν̄ΝΟΥ
ϢΝ2 Ν̄Ϥ2ΟΤΡΟΥ
Gospel of Philip 78. CG II, 70.9–17.

When Eve was in Adam, there was no death. But when she separated from him, death came into being. If she[5] goes in again and he receives her[5] to himself, there will be no death.

Ν̄2ΟΟΥ΄
ΝΕΡΕΕΥ2Α [2Ν] Α[ΔΑ]Μ΄ ΝΕΜΝ̄ ΜΟΥ ϢΟΟΠ΄
Ν̄ΤΑΡΕCΠϢΡΧ [ΕΡ]ΟϤ΄ ΑΠΜΟΥ ϢϢΠΕ ΠΑ
ΛΙΝ ΕϤϢΑ[ΒϢΚ Ε2Ο]ΥΝ Ν̄ϤΧΙΤϤ΄ ΕΡΟϤ ΜΝ̄
ΜΟΥ ΝΑϢϢΠΕ
Gospel of Philip 71. CG II, 68.22–26.

For the man is androgynous, he says, Therefore, according to this conception of theirs, the intercourse of woman with man is shown, in conformity with such teaching, to be an altogether wicked and forbidden matter. For, he says, Attis has been castrated. That is, he has passed over from the earthly parts of the creation below to the eternal substance above, where, he says, there is neither male or female, but a new creature, a new man, which is androgynous.

ἔστι γάρ, φησίν, ἀρρενόθηλυς ὁ ἄνθρωπος. κατὰ τοῦτον οὖν αὐτοῖς τὸν λόγον πάνυ πονηρὸν καὶ κεκωλυμένον κατὰ τὴν διδασκαλίαν ἡ γυναικὸς πρὸς ἄνδρα δεδειγμένη καθέστηκεν ὁμιλία. ἀπεκόπη γάρ, φησίν, ὁ Ἄττις, τοῦτ᾽ ἔστιν ἀπὸ τῶν χοϊκῶν τῆς κτίσεως κάτωθεν μερῶν, καὶ ἐπὶ τὴν αἰωνίαν ἄνω μετελήλυθεν οὐσίαν, ὅπου, φησίν, οὐκ ἔστιν οὔτε θῆλυ οὔτε ἄρσεν, ἀλλὰ καινὴ κτίσις, "καινὸς ἄνθρωπος," ὅ ἐστιν ἀρσενόθηλυς.
Hippolytus, *Ref.* 5.7.14–15. Wendland, *Hippolytus* 3:82

Mark 10:13–16, Matt 19:13–15, 18:3, Luke 18:15–17, John 3:3,5, Mark 10:6–8, Matt 19:4–6, Eph 5:31, Gen 1:27, 2:24–25, 3:7,10, Gal 3:28, Eph 2:14–16, John 17:11, 20–23.

NOTES

See also *Gospel of Thomas* 37, 106 [A25, Pro57].
[1] ΕΕΙ ΕΝΟ = ΕΕΙΕ ΕΝΟ. See Guillaumont, *Thomas*, 16.
[2] ΟΥ is omitted before ΟΥΕΡΗΤΕ, "foot," by haplography.
[3] Completion of the text follows that of Ménard, *L'Évangile selon Philippe*, 78.

⁴ Thomas is speaking.

⁵ In line 25 read ⲈⲤⲰⲀⲂⲰⲔ, "if she goes," instead of ⲈϤⲰⲀⲂⲰⲔ, "if he goes," and ⲚϤⲬⲒⲦⲤ "and he receives her," instead of ⲚϤⲬⲒⲦϤ, "and he receives him."

A7 / *Tribute to Kings*

They came to him to test him with questions, [saying]: Teacher Jesus, we know that you are come [from God], for what you do [testifies] above all the prophets. [Tell] us, [therefore], is it lawful to [give] to kings what pertains to their rule? Shall we [pay] them or not? And Jesus, knowing their thoughts, was moved with indignation and said [to them]: Why do you call me teacher with your mouth and do not hear what I say? Well did I[saiah] prophesy [of] you, when he said: [This people honors] me with their lips, [but] their [heart is far] from [me]; in vain [they worship me], (teaching as doctrines) the precepts (of men).²

$$[\pi\alpha\rho\alpha\gamma\epsilon]^1$$

νόμενοι πρὸς αὐτὸν ἐξ[ετασ-]
τικῶς ἐπείραζον αὐτὸν λ[έγοντες]
διδάσκαλε 'Ιη(σοῦ) οἴδαμεν ὅτι [ἀπὸ θ(εο)ῦ]
ἐλήλυθας ἃ γὰρ ποιεῖς μα[ρτυρεῖ]
ὑπὲρ το[ὺ]ς προφ(ήτ)ας πάντας [λέγε οὖν]
ἡμεῖν· ἐξὸν τοῖς βα(σι)λεῦσ[ιν ἀποδοῦ-]
ναι τὰ ἀν[ή]κοντα τῇ ἀρχῇ ἀπ[οδῶμεν αὐ-]
τοῖς ἢ μ[ή] ὁ δὲ 'Ιη(σοῦς) εἰδὼς [τὴν δι-]
άνοιαν [αὐτ]ῶν ἐμβρειμ[ησάμενος]
εἶπεν α[ὐτοῖς]· τί με καλεῖτ[ε τῷ στό-]
ματι ὑμ[ῶν δι]δάσκαλον· μ[ὴ ἀκού-]
οντες ὃ [λ]έγω· καλῶς 'Η[σ(αΐ)ας περὶ ὑ-]
μῶν ἐπ[ρο]φ(ήτευ)σεν εἰπών· ὁ [λαὸς οὗ-]
τος τοῖς [χείλ]εσιν αὐτ[ῶν τιμῶσιν]
με ἡ [δὲ καρδί]α αὐτῷ[ν πόρρω ἀπέ-]
χει ἀπ' ἐ[μοῦ μ]άτη[ν με σέβονται]
ἐντάλ[ματα

P. Egerton 2, 2r. 43–59. Bell and Skeat, *Fragments of an Unknown Gospel*, 11–13.

Parallels

Mark 12:13–17, Luke 20:20–26, 23:2, Matt 22:15–22, John 3:2, 5:36, 10:24–25, Luke 6:46, Matt 7:21, Isa 29:13 (LXX), Mark 7:6–7, Matt 15:7–9, Ps 78:36–37.

Notes

See also *Thomas* 100 [A36].

¹ The beginning of the work is assumed to have been on the preceding page.
² This last sentence is partly extended in the translation, based on Isaiah 29:13.

A8 / *Jesus and the Lawyers* _____

[And Jesus said] to the lawyers: [Punish] everyone who trangresses [against the law] and not me, [for he (the transgressor) does not know] how he does what he does. [And he turned to the] rulers of the people and spoke this saying: [Search] the scriptures in which you think you have life. These are [the ones which] testify concerning me. Do not think that I have come to accuse [you] to my Father. Moses is [he who] accuses you, on whom you have set your hope. And when they said, We know indeed that God spoke to Moses, but we do not know [where you are from], Jesus answered and said, Now your unbelief is accursed. . . .

[ὁ δὲ]

['Ι(ησοῦς) εἶπεν] τοῖς νομιχο[ῖς· χολά]-
[ζετε πά]ντα τὸν παραπράσσ[οντα]
[παρὰ νό]μον καὶ μὴ ἐμέ· [οὐ γ]ὰ[ρ] ἔ[γ]-
[νωχεν] ὃ ποιεῖ, πῶς ποιε[ῖ]· Προς
[δὲ τοὺς] ἄ[ρ]χοντας τοῦ λαοῦ [στ]ρα-
[φεὶς εἶ]πεν τὸν λόγον τοῦτο[ν]· ἐραυ-
[νᾶτε τ]ὰς γραφάς· ἐν αἷς ὑμεῖς δο
[χεῖτε] ζωὴν ἔχειν· ἐκεῖνα εἰ[σ]ιν
[αἱ μαρτ]υροῦσιν περὶ ἐμοῦ· μὴ δ[ο]-
[χεῖτε ὅ]τι ἐγὼ ἦλθον χατηγο[ρ]ῆσαι
[ὑμῶν] πρὸς τὸν π(ατέ)ρα μου· ἔστιν
[ὁ χατη]γορῶν ὑμῶν Μω(ϋσῆς) εἰς ὃν
[ὑμεῖς] ἠλπίχατε· α[ὐ]τῶν δὲ λε-
[γόντω]ν· ε[ὐ] οἴδαμεν ὅτι Μω(ϋσεῖ) ἐλά-
[λησεν] ὁ θ(εό)ς· σὲ δὲ οὐκ οἴδαμεν
[πόθεν εἶ]· ἀποχριθεὶς ὁ 'Ιη(σοῦς) εἶ-
[πεν αὐτο]ῖς· νῦν χατηγορεῖται
[ὑμῶν ἡ ἀ]πιστεί[α. . . .

P. Edgerton 2, lv. 1–19. Mayeda, *Das Leben-Jesu-Fragment Papyrus Egerton 2*, 8–9, except for lines 4 and 5 where I follow Dodd, *New Testament
Studies*, 27–28.

PARALLELS

John 5:39, 45, 9:29.

A9 / *Lambs in the Midst of Wolves* _____

For the Lord said: You will be as lambs in the midst of wolves. And Peter answered and said to him: If then the wolves tear the lambs? Jesus said to

Peter: Let the lambs have no fear of the wolves after their death; and you, have no fear of those that slay you and can do nothing more to you. Fear, rather, him who after your death has power over body and soul, to cast them into the fiery hell.

λέγει γὰρ ὁ κύριος· "Εσεσθε ὡς ἀρνία ἐν μέσῳ λύκων. ἀποκριθεὶς δὲ ὁ Πέτρος αὐτῷ λέγει· Ἐὰν οὖν διασπαράξωσιν οἱ λύκοι τὰ ἀρνία; εἶπεν ὁ Ἰησοῦς τῷ Πέτρῳ· Μὴ φοβείσθωσαν τὰ ἀρνία τοὺς λύκους μετὰ τὸ ἀποθανεῖν αὐτά· καὶ ὑμεῖς μὴ φοβεῖσθε τοὺς ἀποκτέννοντας ὑμᾶς καὶ μηδὲν ὑμῖν δυναμένους ποιεῖν, ἀλλὰ φοβεῖσθε τὸν μετὰ τὸ ἀποθανεῖν ὑμᾶς ἔχοντα ἐξουσίαν ψυχῆς καὶ σώματος τοῦ βαλεῖν εἰς γέεναν πυρός.
II Clement 5.2–4. Funk-Bihlmeyer, Die Apostolischen Väter, 73.

PARALLELS

He commanded saying, Behold I send you as a sheep in the midst of wolves, but do not fear.

ἐνετείλατο λέγων· ἰδοὺ ἀποστέλλω σε ὡς πρόβατον ἐν μέσῳ λύκων καὶ μὴ φοβηθῇς.
Prochorus, Acts of John. Zahn, Acta Joannis, 83.

O glory of the lamb with one horn which separates the sheep from the goats, as the Lord himself admonishes: Hear me, he said (you) sheep whom I have chosen and do not fear the wolves.

O unicornui gloria agni separare sibi agnos ab haedis, ipso exortante domino: Audite me, inquid, quos elegi agnos et nolite timere lupos.
The Pseudo-Titus Epistle [1]. de Bruyne, "Epistula Titi Discipuli Pauli," 60.

Matt 10:16,28, Luke 10:3, 12:4,5.

A10 / Jesus and the Tax Collector _____

When Zacchaeus, a chief tax-collector—but some say Matthias—heard that the Lord had seen fit to be with him, he said: Look, Lord, I will give half of my belongings as alms, and if I have extorted anything from anyone, I will repay it four times. Then the Lord said: The Son of Man has come today and has found that which was lost.

Ζακχαῖον τοίνυν, οἳ δὲ Ματθίαν φασίν, ἀρχιτελώνην, ἀκηκοότα τοῦ κυρίου καταξιώσαντος πρὸς αὐτὸν γενέσθαι, "ἰδοὺ τὰ ἡμίση τῶν ὑπαρχόντων μου δίδωμι ἐλεημοσύνην" φάναι, "κύριε, καὶ εἴ τινός τι ἐσυκοφάντησα, τετραπλοῦν ἀποδίδωμι." ἐφ' οὗ καὶ ὁ σωτὴρ εἶπεν· "ὁ υἱὸς τοῦ ἀνθρώπου ἐλθὼν σήμερον τὸ ἀπολωλὸς εὗρεν."
Clement, Strom. 4.6.35. Stählin-Früchtel, Clemens 2³:263–264.

PARALLEL

Luke 19:1–10.

NOTES
The material is possibly from the *Traditions of Matthias*, from which Clement quotes in three other passages. See Hennecke-Schneemelcher, *N.T. Apoc.* 1:308–313.

A11 / *The Temple Tax*

And when they came to Capernaum, those who collect the half-shekel tax[1] approached Peter and said: Does your teacher not pay the half-shekel? He said: Yes. And when he came into the house, Jesus spoke to him first, saying: Simon, what do you think? From whom do the kings of the earth collect tribute? From their own sons or from foreigners?[2] He said: From foreigners. Jesus said to him: Are the sons then free? Simon said: Yes. Jesus said: Therefore give as though you were a foreigner to them. And lest we offend them, go to the sea and cast a hook,[3] and take the first fish that comes up, and when you open its mouth, you will find a shekel; take that and give it to them for me and yourself.

Ἐλθόντων δὲ αὐτῶν εἰς Καφαρναοὺμ προσῆλθον οἱ τὰ δίδραχμα λαμβάνοντες τῷ Πέτρῳ καὶ εἶπαν· ὁ διδάσκαλος ὑμῶν οὐ τελεῖ δίδραχμα; λέγει· ναί. καὶ ἐλθόντα εἰς τὴν οἰκίαν προέφθασεν αὐτὸν ὁ Ἰησοῦς λέγων· τί σοι δοκεῖ, Σίμων; οἱ βασιλεῖς τῆς γῆς ἀπὸ τίνων λαμβάνουσιν τέλη ἢ κῆνσον; ἀπὸ τῶν υἱῶν αὐτῶν ἢ ἀπὸ τῶν ἀλλοτρίων; εἰπόντος δὲ ἀπὸ τῶν ἀλλοτρίων, ἔφη αὐτῷ ὁ Ἰησοῦς· ἄρα γε ἐλεύθεροί εἰσιν οἱ υἱοί· ἔφη Σίμων· ναί. λέγει ὁ Ἰησοῦς· δὸς οὖν καὶ σὺ ὡς ἀλλότριος αὐτῶν. ἵνα δὲ μὴ σκανδαλίσωμεν αὐτούς, πορευθεὶς εἰς θάλασσαν βάλε ἄγκιστρον καί τὸν ἀναβάντα πρῶτον ἰχθὺν ἆρον, καὶ ἀνοίξας τὸ στόμα αὐτοῦ εὑρήσεις στατῆρα· ἐκεῖνον λαβὼν δὸς αὐτοῖς ἀντὶ ἐμοῦ καὶ σοῦ.
Codex 713 to Matt 17:24–27.[4] Aland, *Synopsis*, 245.

PARALLELS

And when Simon was gone outside, they that received the didrachma of the tribute, came to Cephas, and said unto him, Doth not your master pay the didrachma? He saith unto them, Certainly. And when Cephas had entered into the house, Jesus anticipated him, saying unto him, What thinkest thou, Simon? the kings of the earth, from whom do they receive toll and tribute? from their sons, or from strangers? Simon said unto him. From strangers. Jesus said unto him, Therefore the sons are free. Simon saith unto him, Yea. Jesus said unto him, Give thou also unto them as if a stranger. And lest it should distress them, go thou to the sea, and cast a hook;

and when thou hast opened the mouth of the fish that first cometh
up, thou shalt find a stater: that take, and give it for me and thee.

> Arabic *Diatessaron* 25. 4–7.[5] Trans. from Hill, *The Earliest Life of Christ*,
> 142.

NOTES

[1] The Greek in Codex 713 has the words double-drachma and stater, which were
the monetary equivalents of the half-shekel and shekel respectively.

[2] See P. Eg. 2r. 43–59 [A7], Thomas 100 [A36], Mark 12:13–17, Matt 22:15–22, Luke
20:20–26.

[3] See Luke 5:4.

[4] The additional material is also contained in Latin MSS. b, ff[1].

[5] Ephrem's commentary indicates that the version of the *Diatessaron* known to him
also had the addition. See Leloir, *Saint Éphrem, Commentaire de l'Évangile Concordant*, 128–129.

A12 / *Who Will See the Coming Kingdom* _____

When the Lord was describing the coming kingdom of the saints to the
disciples, that it would be glorious and wonderful, Judas, being astounded at
the things spoken, said: And who will see these things? The Lord said: Those
who become worthy will see these things.

τοῦ οὖν κυρίου διηγουμένου τοῖς μαθηταῖς περὶ τῆς μελλούσης τῶν ἁγίων βασιλείας
ὡς εἴη ἔνδοξος καὶ θαυμαστή, καταπλαγεὶς ὁ Ἰούδας ἐπὶ τοῖς λεγουμένοις ἔφη· καὶ τίς
ἄρα ὄψεται ταῦτα; ὁ δὲ κύριος ἔφη· "ταῦτα ὄψονται οἱ ἄξιοι γενόμενοι."

> Hippolytus, *Comm. on Daniel* 4.60. Bonwetsch and Achelis, *Hippolytus*
> 1:338.

PARALLELS

> And he (Papias) added saying: These things are indeed believable
> to those who have faith. And when Judas the betrayer did not
> believe and asked how such things would be accomplished by the
> Lord (God), the Lord (Jesus) said: Those who come to these things
> will see.
>
> Et adjecit, dicens: "Haec autem credibilia sunt credentibus. Et
> Juda," inquit, "proditore non credente, et interrogante: Quomodo
> ergo tales geniturae a Domino perficientur?" dixisse Dominum:
> "Videbunt qui venient in illa."
>
> > Papias, in Irenaeus *Adv. Haer.* 5.33.4. Harvey, *Sancti Irenaei* 2:418.

A13 / *The Perishing of Weak Souls*

He (Mani) says in the *Book of Mysteries:* "Since the apostles knew that the souls were immortal, and that in their migrations they array themselves in every form, that they are shaped in every animal, and are cast in the mould of every figure, they asked Messiah what would be the end of those souls which did not receive the truth nor learn the origin of their existence. Whereupon he said: 'Any weak soul which has not received all that belongs to her of truth perishes without any rest or bliss.'"

Mani, *Book of Mysteries* [1]. Trans. from Sachau, *Albiruni's India* 1:54–55.

A14 / *The Inanimate and the Living*

"The apostles asked Jesus about the life of inanimate nature, whereupon he said: 'If that which is inanimate is separated from the living element which is commingled with it, and appears alone by itself, it is again inanimate and is not capable of living, whilst the living element which has left it, retaining its vital energy unimpaired, never dies.'"

Mani, *Book of Mysteries* [2]. Trans. from Sachau, *Albiruni's India* 1:48.

NOTES

The passage may stem from the *Book of Mysteries* but is not so designated by Albiruni.

A15 / *Faith to Move Mountains*

And when the Apostles asked of our Lord, they begged nothing at His hands but this, saying to Him: Increase our faith. He said to them: If there were in you faith, even a mountain would remove from before you. And He said to them: Doubt ye not, lest ye sink down in the midst of the world, even as Simon when he doubted began to sink in the midst of the sea.

Aphrahat, *Demonstration* 1.17, *De fide.* Trans. of the Syriac from Gwynn, NPNF, 2nd ser. 13:351.

PARALLELS

Matt 14:28–31, 17:20, 21:21, Mark 11:23, Luke 17:6, I Cor 13:2.

NOTES

See also *Thomas* 48 [Pro 42].

A16 / *Work on the Sabbath*

On the same day he saw a man working on the Sabbath and said to him: Man, if you know what you are doing, you are blessed. But if you do not know, you are accursed and a transgressor of the law.

τῇ αὐτῇ ἡμέρᾳ θεασάμενός τινα ἐργαζόμενον τῷ σαββάτῳ εἶπεν αὐτῷ· ἄνθρωπε, εἰ μὲν οἶδας τὶ ποιεῖς, μακάριος εἶ· εἰ δὲ μὴ οἶδας, ἐπικατάρατος καὶ παραβάτης εἶ τοῦ νόμου.

Codex D after Luke 6:4. Aland, Synopsis, 66.

A17 / *Jesus in the Temple*

And he took them and brought them into the place of purification itself and walked about in the temple. And a certain Pharisee, a chief priest named Levi, approached and spoke with them and said to the Savior: Who permitted you to walk in this place of purification and to view these holy vessels, without having washed and without your disciples having washing even their feet? On the contrary, while still defiled, you have walked in this temple which is a clean place, in which no one who has not washed himself and changed his clothes walks or dares view these holy vessels. Immediately the Savior stood still, along with the disciples, and answered him: Are you who are here in the temple therefore clean? He said: I am clean, for I have washed in David's pool and have gone down by one stair and come up by the other and have put on clean, white clothes, and then I came and looked at these holy vessels. The Savior answered and said to him: Woe to you blind who do not see. You have washed yourself in these poured-out waters in which dogs and swine have wallowed night and day, and you have washed and wiped the outer skin which harlots and flute girls also anoint, wash, wipe, and beautify for the lust of men, whereas within they are full of scorpions and wickedness of every kind. But I and my disciples, who you say have not washed, have been washed in waters of eternal life[1] which come down from[2] . . . But woe to those who . . .[3]

καὶ παραλαβὼν αὐτοὺς
εἰσήγαγεν εἰς αὐτὸ τὸ ἀγνευτήριον καὶ
περιεπάτει ἐν τῷ ἱερῷ. καὶ προσε[λ]-
θὼν Φαρισαῖός τις ἀρχιερεὺς Λευ[εὶς?]
τὸ ὄνομα συνέτυχεν αὐτοῖς καὶ ε[ἶπεν]
τῷ σω(τῆ)ρι, τίς ἐπέτρεψέν σοι πατ[εῖν]
τοῦτο τὸ ἀγνευτήριον καὶ ἰδεῖν [ταῦ-
τα τὰ ἅγια σκεύη μήτε λουσα[μ]έν[ῳ] μ[ή-
τε μὴν τῶν μαθητῶν σου τοὺς π[όδας βα-
πτισθέντων; ἀλλὰ μεμολυ[μμένος

ἐπάτησας τοῦτο τὸ ἱερὸν τ[όπον ὄντα καθαρόν, ὃν οὐδεὶς ἄ[λλος εἰ μὴ
λουσάμενος καὶ ἀλλά[ξας τὰ ἐνδύματα πατεῖ, οὐδὲ ὁ[ρᾶν τολμᾷ ταῦτα
τὰ ἅγια σκεύη. καὶ σ[τὰς εὐθέως ὁ σω(τὴ)ρ
σ[ὺν τ]οῖς μαθηταῖ[ς ἀπεκρίθη αὐτῷ,
σὺ οὖν ἐνταῦθα ὢν ἐν τῷ ἱερῷ καθα-
ρεύεις; λέγει αὐτῷ ἐκεῖνος, καθαρεύω· ἐλουσά-
μην γὰρ ἐν τῇ λίμνῃ τοῦ Δ(αυεὶ)δ καὶ δι' ἑτέρας κλίμακος κατελθὼν δι' ἑτέρας
ἀ[ν]ῆλθον, καὶ λευκὰ ἐνδύματα ἐνε-
δυσάμην καὶ καθαρά, καὶ τότε ἦλθον
καὶ προσέβλεφα τούτοις τοῖς ἁγίοις
σκεύεσιν. ὁ σω(τὴ)ρ πρὸς αὐτὸν ἀπο-
[κρι]θεὶς εἶπεν, οὐαί, τυφλοὶ μὴ ὁρῶν-
τ[ες] σὺ ἐλούσω τούτοις τοῖς χεομένοις
ὕ[δ]ασιν ἐν οἷς κύνες καὶ χοῖροι βέβλην-
[ται] νυκτὸς καὶ ἡμέρας, καὶ νιψάμε-
[ν]ος τὸ ἐκτὸς δέρμα ἐσμήξω, ὅπερ
[κα]ὶ αἱ πόρναι καὶ α[ἱ] αὐλητρίδες μυρί-
[ζου[σιν κ]αὶ λούουσιν καὶ σμήχουσι
[καὶ κ]αλλωπίζουσι πρὸς ἐπιθυμί-
[αν τ]ῶν ἀν(θρώπ)ων· ἔνδοθεν δὲ ἐκεῖ-
[ναι πεπλ]ήρω <ν> ται σκορπίων καὶ
[πάσης κα]κίας. ἐγὼ δὲ καὶ οἱ
[μαθηταί μου] οὓς λέγεις μὴ βεβα-
[πτίσθαι βεβά]μμεθα ἐν ὕδασι ζω-
[ῆς αἰωνίου τοῖ]ς ἐλθοῦσιν ἀπὸ . . [.]
[. . . . . ἀλ]λὰ οὐαὶ [τ]οῖς [. . .].

P. Oxy. 840. Grenfell and Hunt, *The Oxyrhynchus Papyri* 5:6–7.

PARALLELS

Mark 11:27–28, Matt 21:23, Luke 20:1–2, Mark 7:1–5, Matt 15:1–2,
Matt 23:25–28, Luke 11:39, Matt 23:16, 17, 19, 24.

NOTES

[1] or perhaps "in living water."
[2] This sentence probably ended with words such as "from heaven" or "from the Father." See *OP* 5:10.
[3] The reconstruction of this fragment is relatively certain until the point where it breaks off completely. The last full sentence contains the largest lacunae, but even here the basic sense is clear.

A18 / *Do Not Do What You Hate*

His disciples questioned him. They said to him: Do you want us to fast? And how shall we pray and give alms?[1] And what diet should we observe? Jesus said: Do not lie and do not do what you hate,[2] for all things are revealed before heaven. For there is nothing hidden that will not be revealed, and there is nothing covered that will remain without being uncovered.[3]

ⲁⲩϫⲛⲟⲩϥ ⲛ̄ϭⲓ ⲛⲉϥ'ⲙⲁⲑⲏⲧⲏⲥ
ⲡⲉϫⲁⲩ ⲛⲁϥ ϫⲉ ⲕ'ⲟⲩⲱϣ ⲉⲧⲣⲛ̄ⲣ̄ⲛⲏⲥⲧⲉⲩⲉ
ⲁⲩⲱ ⲉϣ ⲧⲉ ⲑⲉ ⲉⲛⲁϣⲗⲏⲗ ⲉⲛⲁϯ ⲉⲗⲉ
ⲏⲙⲟⲥⲩⲛⲏ ⲁⲩⲱ ⲉⲛⲁⲣ̄ⲡⲁⲣⲁⲧⲏⲣⲉⲓ ⲉⲟⲩ
ⲛ̄ϭⲓⲟⲩⲱⲙ'[4] ⲡⲉϫⲉ ⲓ̄ⲥ̄ϫⲉ ⲙ̄ⲡⲣ̄ϫⲉ ϭⲟⲗ ⲁⲩ
ⲱ ⲡⲉⲧⲉⲧⲙ̄ⲙⲟⲥⲧⲉ ⲙ̄ⲙⲟϥ' ⲙ̄ⲡⲣ̄ⲁⲁϥ ϫⲉ
ⲥⲉϭⲟⲗⲡ' ⲧⲏⲣⲟⲩ ⲉⲃⲟⲗ ⲙ̄ⲡⲉⲙⲧⲟ ⲉⲃⲟⲗ
ⲛ̄ⲧⲡⲉ ⲙⲛ̄ ⲗⲁⲁⲩ ⲅⲁⲣ ⲉϥϩⲏⲡ' ⲉϥⲛⲁⲟⲩ
ⲱⲛϩ ⲉⲃⲟⲗ ⲁⲛ ⲁⲩⲱ ⲙⲛ̄ ⲗⲁⲁⲩ ⲉϥϩⲟⲃ̄ⲥ̄ ⲉⲩ
ⲛⲁϭⲱ ⲟⲩⲉϣⲛ̄ ϭⲟⲗⲡϥ'

Gospel of Thomas 6. CG II, 33.14–23.

PARALLELS

[His disciples] asked him and said: How shall we fast, [and how shall we pray] and how [shall we give alms,] and what [diet] should we observe? Jesus said: [Do not lie and] do not do [what you hate, for all things will be] manifest[5] [before heaven. For there is nothing hidden which will not be revealed.] Blessed is [the one who does not do these things, for all things will be manifest to the Father who is in heaven.]

[ἐξ]ετάζουσιν αὐτὸν ο[ἱ μαθηταὶ αὐτοῦ καὶ]
[λέ]γουσιν· πῶς νηστεύ[σομεν, καὶ πῶς προσ]
[ευξό]μεθα καὶ πῶς [ἐλεημοσύνην ποιή]
[σομεν, κ]αὶ τί παρατηρήσ[ομεν περὶ τῶν βρω]
[μάτω]ν; λέγει Ἰη(σοῦ)ς· [μὴ ψεύδεσθε καὶ ὅ]
[τι μισ]εῖται μὴ ποιεῖ[τε· πάντα γὰρ ἔστ]
[αι πλήρ]ης ἀληθείας ἀν[τὶ τοῦ οὐρανοῦ· οὐ]
[δὲν γάρ ἐστι]ν ἀ[π]οκεκρ[υμμένον ὃ οὐ φανερω]
[<θή>σεται· μα]κάρι[ός] ἐστιν [ὃ ταῦτα μὴ ποιῶν].
[πάντα γὰρ ἐν φαωερ]ῷ ἔστ[αι παρὰ τῷ πατρὶ ὃς]
[ἐν τῷ οὐρανῷ ἐστ]ιν.

P. Oxy. 654.32–42. Fitzmyer,[6] *Essays*, 385.

And he showed them how they should fast and how they should pray and how they should overcome death and how they should destroy sin and that they should teach others as the Lord had taught them.[7]

et ostendit eis, quomodo ieiunarent et quomodo orarent et quomodo superarent mortem et quomodo interficerent peccatum et ipsi alios docerent, sicut ipsos docuit Dominus.
> *Liber Graduum* 20.10. Kmosko, PatSy 1.3:551.

Love the Lord your God with all your heart and other people as yourself, and do not do to your neighbor what is hateful to you, and as you want people to do to you, so also do to them.[8]

Dilige Dominum Deum tuum ex toto corde tuo et homines, ut teipsum; et quod tibi odiosum est, proximo tuo ne facias; et sicuti vis, ut tibi faciant homines, sic et tu fac eis.
> *Liber Graduum* 15.16. Kmosko, ibid., 374–375.

Do to no one what you hate.

καὶ ὃ μισεῖς, μηδενὶ ποιήσῃς.
> Tobit 4:15. Rahlfs, *Septuaginta* 1:1013.

Whatever you wish not to be done to you, do not to another.

πάντα δὲ ὅσα ἐὰν θελήσῃς μὴ γίνεσθαί σοι, καὶ σὺ ἄλλῳ μὴ ποίει.
> *Didache* 1.2. Funk-Bihlmyer, *Die Apostolischen Väter,* 1.

When he went before Hillel, he said to him, "What is hateful to you, do not to your neighbor: that is the whole Torah, while the rest is the commentary thereof; go and learn it.
> *b. Šabb.* 31a. Trans. from Freedman, *Shabbath* 1:31a.

Do not do the things you do not want to happen to you.

ἃ μὴ θέλεις παθεῖν, μὴ ποίει.
> *Sentences of Sextus* 179. Chadwick, *Sentences,* 33.

Mark 4:22, Matt 6:1–18, 7:12, 10:26, Luke 6:31, 8:17, 12:2, Eph 4:25, Col. 3:9, Jam 3:14, Lev 19:11.

NOTES

[1] Similar questions concerning religious observances are also treated in *Thomas* 14 [C33] and *Thomas* 104 [A37].

[2] A sizeable collection of material parallel to "what you hate do not do" is contained in Gotthold Resch, *Das Aposteldecret,* TU 13.3. See also Connolly, "A Negative Form of the Golden Rule in the Diatessaron?" *JTS* 35.

[3] See also *Thomas* 5 [Pro33].

^{not literal}

[4] Perhaps a mistaken writing of **ⲈⲞⲨⳊⲒⲚⲞⲨⲰⲘ**. See Leipoldt, *Das Evangelium nach Thomas*, 26.

[5] Literally, "full of truth."

[6] Text from Fitzmyer, except for περὶ τῶν βρωμάτων in lines 35–36 (from Hofius, *EvT* 20:41) and φανερω < θή > σεται in lines 39–40 (from Marcovich, *JTS* 20:65–66. In line 37, read μισεῖτε instead of μισεῖται. The text is obviously very mutilated, and other restorations are possible. Marcovich (66) considers the beatitude to be the beginning of *Thomas* 7, "Blessed is the lion which the man eats. . . ." Ménard (*L'Evangile selon Thomas*, 87) is in agreement.

[7] An analogous passage concerning Jesus' teaching the disciples to fast and pray occurs in 20.9. See Kmosko, PatSy, 1.3:547, 550.

[8] Other parallels to the "negative form" of the golden rule occur in *Liber Graduum* 7.1 and 30.26. See Kmosko, PatSy, 1.3:146, 922–923.

A19 / *The Authority of James*

The disciples said to Jesus: We know that you will go away from us. Who is it who will be great over us? Jesus said to them: Where(ever) you have come (from), you will go to James the Just, for whose sake heaven and earth came into existence.

> ⲠⲈϪⲈ ⲘⲘⲀⲐⲎⲦⲎⲤ ⲚⲒⲤ ϪⲈ ⲦⲚ
> ⲤⲞⲞⲨⲚ ϪⲈ ⲕⲚⲀⲂⲰⲕ ⲚⲦⲞⲞⲦⲚ ⲚⲒⲘ' ⲠⲈ
> ⲈⲦⲚⲀⲢ ⲚⲞϬ ⲈⳊⲢⲀⲒ ⲈϪⲰⲚ ⲠⲈϪⲈ ⲒⲤ ⲚⲀⲨ
> ϪⲈ ⲠⲘⲀ ⲚⲦⲀⲦⲈⲦⲚⲈⲒ ⲘⲘⲀⲨ ⲈⲦⲈⲦⲚⲀ
> ⲂⲰⲕ' ϢⲀ ⲒⲀⲕⲰⲂⲞⲤ ⲠⲆⲒⲕⲀⲒⲞⲤ ⲠⲀⲈⲒ ⲚⲦⲀ
> ⲦⲠⲈ ⲘⲚ ⲠⲕⲀⳊ ϢⲰⲠⲈ ⲈⲦⲂⲎⲦϤ
>
> Gospel of Thomas 12. CG II, 34.25–30.

Parallels

Mark 9:34, 10:43, Matt 18:1, 20:26, 23:11, Luke 9:46, 22:26.

A20 / *Three Words Spoken to Thomas*

Jesus said to his disciples: Make comparisons; tell me whom I am like. Simon Peter said to him: You are like a righteous angel. Matthew said to him: You are like a wise philosopher. Thomas said to him: Master, my mouth is completely unable to say whom you are like. Jesus said to him: I am not your master, for you have drunk, you have become drunk from the bubbling spring which I have dug.[1] And he took him aside and spoke three words to him. And when Thomas returned to his companions, they asked him: What did Jesus say to you? Thomas said to them: If I speak one of the words which he said to me, you will take up stones and thrown them at me. And fire will come from the stones and consume you.[2]

ΠΕΧΕ Ι͞C
Ν͞ΝΕϤΜΑΘΗΤΗC ΧΕ Τ͞ΝΤϢΝΤ' Ν͞ΤΕΤ͞Ν
ΧΟΟC ΝΑΕΙ ΧΕ ΕΕΙΝΕ Ν͞ΝΙΜ ΠΕΧΑϤ ΝΑϤ'
Ν͞ϬΙ CΙΜϢΝ ΠΕΤΡΟC ΧΕ ΕΚΕΙΝΕ Ν͞ΟΥΑΓ'
ΓΕΛΟC Ν͞ΔΙΚΑΙΟC ΠΕΧΑϤ ΝΑϤ Ν͞ϬΙ ΜΑΘ'
ΘΑΙΟC ΧΕ ΕΚΕΙΝΕ Ν͞ΟΥΡϢΜΕ Μ͞ΦΙΛΟCΟ
ΦΟC Ν͞ΡΜ͞Ν͞2ΗΤ' ΠΕΧΑϤ ΝΑϤ Ν͞ϬΙ ΘϢΜΑC
ΧΕ ΠCΑ2 2ΟΛϢC ΤΑΤΑΠΡΟ ΝΑϢΑΠϤ' ΑΝ
ΕΤΡΑΧΟΟC ΧΕ ΕΚΕΙΝΕ Ν͞ΝΙΜ' ΠΕΧΕ Ι͞ΗC
ΧΕ ΑΝΟΚ' ΠΕΚ'CΑ2 ΑΝ ΕΠΕΙ ΑΚCϢ ΑΚ†2Ε
ΕΒΟΛ 2Ν͞ ΤΠΗΓΗ ΕΤΒ͞ΡΒΡΕ ΤΑΕΙ ΑΝΟΚ'
Ν͞ΤΑΕΙϢΙΤ͞C ΑΥϢ ΑϤΧΙΤϤ ΑϤΑΝΑΧϢΡΕΙ
ΑϤΧϢ ΝΑϤ Ν͞ϢΟΜΤ' Ν͞ϢΑΧΕ Ν͞ΤΑΡΕΘϢ
ΜΑC ΔΕ ΕΙ ϢΑ ΝΕϤ'ϢΒΕΕΡ' ΑΥΧΝΟΥϤ' ΧΕ
Ν͞ΤΑΙ͞C ΧΟΟC ΧΕ ΟΥ ΝΑΚ' ΠΕΧΑϤ' ΝΑΥ Ν͞ϬΙ
ΘϢΜΑC ΧΕ ΕΙϢΑΝΧϢ ΝΗΤ͞Ν ΟΥΑ 2Ν͞ Ν͞ϢΑ
ΧΕ Ν͞ΤΑϤΧΟΟΥ ΝΑΕΙ ΤΕΤΝΑϤΙ ϢΝΕ Ν͞ΤΕ
Τ͞ΝΝΟΥΧΕ ΕΡΟΕΙ ΑΥϢ Ν͞ΤΕΟΥΚϢ2Τ' ΕΙ Ε
ΒΟΛ 2Ν͞ Ν͞ϢΝΕ Ν͞CΡϢ2Κ' Μ͞ΜϢΤ͞Ν

Gospel of Thomas 13. CG II, 34.30–35.14.

PARALLELS

And he (Thomas) began to say: O Jesus, hidden mystery that is revealed to us. You are the one who has revealed many mysteries to us, who took me apart from all my companions and spoke three words to me, with which I am consumed and which I am unable to utter to others.

Καὶ ἤρξατο λέγειν· Ἰησοῦ τὸ μυστήριον τὸ ἀπόκρυφον ὃ ἡμῖν ἀπεκαλύφθη, σὺ εἶ ὁ ἐκφάνας ἡμῖν μυστήρια πάμπολλα, ὁ ἀφορίσας με κατ' ἰδίαν ἐκ τῶν ἑταίρων μου πάντων, καὶ εἰπών μοι τρεῖς λόγους ἐν οἷς ἐγὼ ἐκπυροῦμαι, καὶ ἄλλοις εἰπεῖν αὐτὰ οὐ δύναμαι.

Acts of Thomas 47. Lipsius-Bonnet, *AAA* 2.2:163–164

And Mary answered them: Do not ask me concerning this mystery. If I begin to speak to you, fire will come out of my mouth and consume the whole earth.

Ἡ δὲ Μαριὰμ λέγει αὐτοῖς· <μὴ> ἐρωτᾶτέ με περὶ τοῦ μυστηρίου τούτου, ἐὰν ἄρξωμαι λέγειν ὑμῖν πῦρ ἐκ τοῦ στόματός μου ἐξελεύσεται καὶ καταφλέγει πᾶσαν τὴν οἰκουμένην.

> Questions of Batholomew 2.5. Wilmart and Tisserant, "Fragments Grecs et Latins de L'Évangile de Barthélemy," *RB* 22:322.

And speaking waters touched my lips
From the fountain of the Lord generously.
And so I drank and became intoxicated,
From the living water that does not die.

> *Odes of Solomon* 11.6–7. Trans. of the Syriac from Charlesworth, *The Odes of Solomon,* 52.

Mark 8:27–30, Matt 16:13–16, 23:8, Luke 9:18–21, John 4:10–14, 7:37-38, 8:59, 10:31, 15:15.

NOTES

¹ In 35.7, read , N̄TA̅EIꙎ̅AKTC̅ "I have dug," following the suggestion of Ménard (*L'Évangile selon Thomas,* 58). Without the emendation the phrase would be rendered, ". . . the bubbling spring which I have measured out." In 35:14 read N̄ꝗPⲰK2, "and it (will) consume" (ibid.).

² The passage is mixed in terms of genre. I include it among the apophthegms because of the elements of scholastic dialogue.

A21 / *The Beginning and the End* ─────────────

The disciples said to Jesus: Tell us how our end will be. Jesus said: Have you then discovered the beginning so that you seek the end? For where the beginning is, the end will be. Blessed is the one who will stand at the beginning, and he will know the end and not taste death.¹

ΠΕϪΕ M̄MAΘΗΤΗC N̄IC̅ ϪΕ ϪO
OC ΕPON ϪΕ TN̄2AH ΕCNAꙎⲰΠΕ N̄
Aꙍ N̄2Ε ΠΕϪΕ I̅C̅ ATΕTN̄6ⲰAΠ' ΓAP ΕBOλ
N̄TAPXH ϪΕΚAAC ΕTΕTNAꙎINΕ N̄CA
ΘA2Η ϪΕ 2M̄ ΠMA ΕTΕ TAPXH M̄MAY Ε
ΘA2Η NAꙎⲰΠΕ M̄MAY OYMAKAPIOC
ΠΕTNAⲰ2Ε² ΕPATꝗ 2N̄ TAPXH AYⲰ
ꝗNACOYⲰN Θ2AH AYⲰ ꝗNAϪI †ΠΕ
AN M̄MOY

> *Gospel of Thomas* 18. CG II, 36.9–17.

PARALLELS

But it is not only the washing which is liberating, but also the knowledge of who we were and what we have become, where we

28

were or where we were placed, where we are hastening, from what we are being redeemed, what birth is and what rebirth.

ἔστιν δὲ οὐ τὸ λουτρὸν μόνον τὸ ἐλευθεροῦν, ἀλλὰ καὶ ἡ γνῶσις, τίνες ἦμεν, τί γεγόναμεν· ποῦ ἦμεν, [ἢ] ποῦ ἐνεβλήθημεν· ποῦ σπεύδομεν, πόθεν λυτρούμεθα· τί γέννησις, τί ἀναγέννησις.

Exc. ex Theod. 78. 2. Stählin-Früchtel, *Clemens* 3²:131.

Mark 9:1, Matt 16:28, Luke 9:27, John 8:51–52.

NOTES
    ¹ See also *Thomas* 1 [Pro 30] and *Thomas* 19 [Pro 37].
    ² ℨ is crossed out in the text before ⲰⲆⲈ.

A22 / *The Mustard Seed*

The disciples said to Jesus: Tell us what the kingdom of heaven is like. He said to them: It is like a mustard seed, the smallest of all seeds. But when it falls on the cultivated earth, it produces a large branch and becomes shelter for the birds of heaven.

> ⲠⲈⲬⲈ ⲘⲘⲀⲐⲎⲦⲎⲤ ⲚⲒⲤ ⲬⲈ ⲬⲞⲞⳠ
> ⲈⲢⲞⲚ ⲬⲈ ⲦⲘⲚⲦⲈⲢⲞ ⲚⲘⲠⲎⲨⲈ ⲈⳠ
> ⲦⲚⲦⲰⲚ ⲈⲚⲒⲘ ⲠⲈⲬⲀϤ ⲚⲀⲨ ⲬⲈ ⲈⳠⲦⲚ̄
> ⲦⲰⲚ ⲀⲨⲂⲀ̄ⲂⲒⲗⲈ Ⲛ̄ⳠⲀ̄ⲦⲀⲘ ⳠⲞⲂⲔ̄¹ ⲠⲀ
> ⲢⲀ Ⲛ̄ⳠⲢⲞ6 ⲦⲎⲢⲞⲨ 2ⲞⲦⲀⲚ ⲆⲈ ⲈⳠϢⲀ̄
> 2Ⲉ ⲈⲬⲘ̄ ⲠⲔⲀ2 ⲈⲦⲞⲨⲢ̄ 2ⲰⲂ ⲈⲢⲞϤ ϢⲀϤ
> ⲦⲈⲨⲞ ⲈⲂⲞⲗ Ⲛ̄ⲚⲞⲨⲚⲞ6 Ⲛ̄ⲦⲀⲢ Ⲛ̄ϤϢⲰ
> ⲠⲈ Ⲛ̄ⲤⲔⲈⲠⲎ Ⲛ̄2ⲀⲗⲗⲀⲦⲈ² Ⲛ̄ⲦⲠⲈ

Gospel of Thomas 20. CG II, 36.26–33.

PARALLELS

Mark 4:30–32, Matt 13:31–32, Luke 13:18–19.

NOTES
    ¹ read ⲈⳠⳠⲞⲂⲔ̄ "small(est)." See Guillaumont, *Thomas,* 14.
    ² read Ⲛ̄Ⲛ2ⲀⲗⲗⲀⲦⲈ "for the birds." Ibid.

A23 / *Little Children in a Field*

Mary said to Jesus: Whom are your disciples like? He said: They are like little children who dwell in a field which is not theirs. When the owners of the field come, they will say, Give our field to us. They (will) take off their clothes before them in order to let them have their field and to give it back to them.

ⲡⲉ

ⲭⲉ ⲙⲁⲣⲓⲍⲁⲙ ⲛ̄ⲓⲥ ⲭⲉ ⲉⲛⲉⲕⲙⲁⲑ
ⲧⲏⲥ ⲉⲓⲛⲉ ⲛ̄ⲛⲓⲙ ⲡⲉⲭⲁϥ' ⲭⲉ ⲉⲩⲉⲓⲛⲉ
ⲛ̄ⲍⲛ̄ϣⲏⲣⲉ ϣⲏⲙ ⲉⲩ[ϭ]ⲉⲗⲓⲧ ⲁⲩⲥⲱϣⲉ ⲉⲧⲱ
ⲟⲩ ⲁⲛ ⲧⲉ ⲍⲟⲧⲁⲛ ⲉⲩϣⲁⲉⲓ ⲛ̄ϭⲓ ⲛ̄ⲭⲟⲉⲓⲥ
ⲛ̄ⲧⲥⲱϣⲉ ⲥⲉⲛⲁⲭⲟⲟⲥ ⲭⲉ ⲕⲉ ⲧⲛ̄ⲥⲱϣⲉ
ⲉⲃⲟⲗ ⲛⲁⲛ ⲛ̄ⲧⲟⲟⲩ ⲥⲉⲕⲁⲕ ⲁⲍⲏⲩ ⲙ̄ⲡⲟⲩⲙ
ⲧⲟ ⲉⲃⲟⲗ ⲉⲧⲣⲟⲩⲕⲁⲁⲥ ⲉⲃⲟⲗ ⲛⲁⲩ ⲛ̄ⲥⲉϯ ⲧⲟⲩ
ⲥⲱϣⲉ ⲛⲁⲩ

Gospel of Thomas 21a. CG II, 36.33–37.6.

A24 / *Light Within*

His disciples said: Show us the place where you are, for it is necessary for us to seek it. He said to them: Whoever has ears, let him hear. There is light within a man of light, and it[1] gives light to the whole world. When it[1] does not shine, there is darkness.

ⲡⲉ

ⲭⲉ ⲛⲉϥⲙⲁⲑⲏⲧⲏⲥ ⲭⲉ ⲙⲁⲧⲥⲉⲃⲟⲛ' ⲉⲡⲧⲟ
ⲡⲟⲥ ⲉⲧⲕⲙ̄ⲙⲁⲩ ⲉⲡⲉⲓ ⲧⲁⲛⲁⲅⲕⲏ ⲉⲣⲟⲛ ⲧⲉ
ⲉⲧⲣⲛ̄ϣⲓⲛⲉ ⲛ̄ⲥⲱϥ' ⲡⲉⲭⲁϥ' ⲛⲁⲩ ⲭⲉ ⲡⲉⲧⲉⲩ
ⲛ̄ ⲙⲁⲁⲭⲉ ⲙ̄ⲙⲟϥ ⲙⲁⲣⲉϥ'ⲥⲱⲧⲙ̄ ⲟⲩⲛ̄ ⲟⲩ
ⲟⲉⲓⲛ' ϣⲟⲟⲡ ⲙ̄ⲫⲟⲩⲛ ⲛ̄ⲛⲟⲩⲣⲙ̄ⲟⲩⲉⲓⲛ
ⲁⲩⲱ ϥⲣ ⲟⲩⲟⲉⲓⲛ ⲉⲡⲕⲟⲥⲙⲟⲥ ⲧⲏⲣϥ' ⲉϥⲧⲙ̄
ⲣ̄ ⲟⲩⲟⲉⲓⲛ' ⲟⲩⲕⲁⲕⲉ ⲡⲉ

Gospel of Thomas 24. CG II, 38.3–10.

PARALLELS

> John 14:4–5, 13:36–37, Matt 6:22–23, Luke 11:34–35, John 11:10, Matt 5:14–16.

NOTES
[1] or, "he."

A25 / *Undressing without Shame*

His disciples said: On what day will you be revealed to us and on what day will we see you? Jesus said: When you undress yourselves and are not ashamed and when you take your garments and put them under your feet as little children and tread on them,[1] then [you will see] the Son of the Living One and you will have no fear.

ΠΕΧΕ ΝΕϤΜΑΘΗΤΗС ΧΕ ΑϢ Ⲛ̄
2ΟΟΥ ΕΚΝΑΟΥϢΝ2 ΕΒΟΛ ΝΑΝ ΑΥϢ ΑϢ
Ⲛ̄2ΟΟΥ ΕΝΑΝΑΥ ΕΡΟΚ' ΠΕΧΕ Ⲓ̄С ΧΕ 2Ο
ΤΑΝ ΕΤΕΤⲚ̄ϢΑΚΕΚ ΤΗΥΤⲚ̄ Ε2ΗΥ Ⲙ̄ΠΕ
ΤⲚ̄ϢΙΠΕ ΑΥϢ Ⲛ̄ΤΕΤⲚ̄ϤΙ Ⲛ̄ΝΕΤⲚ̄ϢΤΗΝ
Ⲛ̄ΤΕΤⲚ̄ΚΑΑΥ 2Α ΠΕСΗΤ' Ⲛ̄ΝΕΤⲚ̄ΟΥΕΡΗ
ΤΕ Ⲛ̄ΘΕ Ⲛ̄ΝΙΚΟΥΕΙ Ⲛ̄ϢΗΡΕ ϢΗΜ' Ⲛ̄ΤΕ
ΤⲚ̄ΧΟΠΧⲠ̄' Ⲙ̄ΜΟΟΥ ΤΟΤ[Ε ΤΕΤΝΑΝΑΥ
ΕΠϢΗΡΕ Ⲙ̄ΠΕΤΟΝ2 ΑΥϢ ΤΕΤΝΑⲢ̄
2ΟΤΕ ΑΝ

        Gospel of Thomas 37. CG II, 39.27–40.2.

PARALLELS

His disciples said to him: when will you be revealed to us and
when will we see you? He said: When you undress and are not
ashamed.[2] . . .

        λέγουσιν αὐ
τῷ οἱ μαθηταὶ αὐτοῦ·
πότε ἡμεῖν ἐμφα
νὴς ἔσει καὶ πότε
σε ὀψόμεθα; λέγει·
ὅταν ἐκδύσησθε καὶ
μὴ αἰσχύνθητε
. . .

        P. Oxy. 655.17–23. Fitzmyer, *Essays,* 409.

For this, he says, is the gate of heaven, and this is the house of
God, where the good God dwells alone, where, he says, no
unclean one will enter, no psychic, no fleshly. But it is kept for the
spiritual alone, and those who come there must cast off their
garments and all become bridegrooms, having become male
through the virginal spirit.

αὕτη γάρ, φησίν, ἐστὶν "ἡ πύλη τοῦ οὐρανοῦ" καὶ οὗτος < ὁ > "οἶκος
θεοῦ," ὅπου ὁ ἀγαθὸς θεὸς κατοικεῖ μόνος, εἰς ὃν οὐκ εἰσελεύσεται, φησίν,
ἀκάθαρτος οὐδείς, οὐ ψυχικός, οὐ σαρκικός, ἀλλὰ τηρεῖται πνευματικοῖς
μόνοις, ὅπου δεῖ γενομένους βαλεῖν τὰ ἐνδύματα καὶ πάντας γενέσθαι
νυμφίους ἀπηρσενωμένους διὰ τοῦ παρθενικοῦ πνεύματος.

        Hippolytus, *Ref.* 5.8.44. Wendland, *Hippolytus* 3²:97.

Gen 2:25.

NOTES

¹ See *Gospel of Thomas* 21a [A23] and *Gospel of the Egyptians* 3 [A6].

² In line 19, read ἡμῖν, "to us." The rest of the fragment is totally illegible. Fitzmyer completes it so as to agree with the rest of *Thomas* 37.

A26 / *Tree and Fruit*

His disciples said to him: Who are you that you say these things to us. < Jesus said to them: > From what I say to you, you do not know who I am.¹ But you have become like the Jews, for they love the tree (yet) hate its fruit, and they love the fruit (yet) hate the tree.

ΠΕΧΑΥ ΝΑϥ′ Ν̄ϬΙ ΝΕϥ′ΜΑΘΗΤΗΣ ΧΕ Ν̄ΤΑΚ′
ΝΙΜ′ ΕΚΧⲰ Ν̄ΝΑΪ ΝΑΝ′² 2Ν̄ ΝΕϯΧⲰ Μ̄
ΜΟΟΥ ΝΗΤΝ̄ Ν̄ΤΕΤΝ̄ΕΙΜΕ ΑΝ ΧΕ ΑΝΟΚ′
ΝΙΜ ΑλλΑ Ν̄ΤⲰΤΝ̄ ΑΤΕΤΝ̄ϢⲰΠΕ Ν̄ΘΕ Ν̄
ΝΙΪΟΥΔΑΙΟΣ ΧΕ ϹΕΜΕ Μ̄ΠϢΗΝ ϹΕΜΟϹ
ΤΕ Μ̄ΠΕϥΚΑΡΠΟΣ ΑΥⲰ ϹΕΜΕ Μ̄ΠΚΑΡΠΟϹ
ϹΕΜΟϹΤΕ Μ̄ΠϢΗΝ

> *Gospel of Thomas* 43. CG II, 40.20–26.

PARALLELS

John 8:25.

NOTES

¹ See also *Thomas* 91 [A34].

² ΠΕΧΕ ῙϹ ΝΑΥ ΧΕ, "Jesus said to them," should be in the text here.

A27 / *The New World Is Present*

His disciples said to him: When will the repose of the dead take place and when does the new world come? He said to them: That which you look for has come, but you do not recognize it.

ΠΕΧΑϥ ΝΑϥ Ν̄ϬΙ ΝΕϥΜΑ
ΘΗΤΗϹ ΧΕ ΑϢ Ν̄2ΟΟΥ ΕΤΑΝΑΠΑΥϹΙϹ Ν̄
ΝΕΤΜΟΟΥΤ′ ΝΑϢⲰΠΕ ΑΥⲰ ΑϢ Ν̄2ΟΟΥ
ΕΠΚΟϹΜΟϹ Β̄Β̄ΡΡΕ ΝΗΥ ΠΕΧΑϥ ΝΑΥ ΧΕ
ΤΗ ΕΤΕΤΝ̄ϬⲰϢΤ′ ΕΒΟλ 2ΗΤϹ̄ ΑϹΕΙ ΑλλΑ
Ν̄ΤⲰΤΝ̄ ΤΕΤΝ̄ϹΟΟΥΝ ΑΝ Μ̄ΜΟϹ

> *Gospel of Thomas* 51. CG II, 42.7–12.

PARALLELS

    Luke 17:20-21.

NOTES
  See also *Thomas* 113 and parallels [A38].

A28 / *Concerning the Prophets* _____

His disciples said to him: Twenty-four prophets spoke in Israel and they all spoke concerning (lit. "in") you. He said to them: You have forsaken the living one who is before you and have spoken about the dead.

ПЄΧΑΥ
ΝΑϤ Ñ6Ι ΝЄϤΜΑΘΗΤΗC ΧЄ ΧΟΥΤ ΑϤΤЄ
ΜΠΡΟΦΗΤΗC ΑΥϢΑΧЄ 2Μ ΠΙCΡΑΗΛ'
ΑΥϢ ΑΥϢΑΧЄ ΤΗΡΟΥ 2ΡΑϊ Ñ2ΗΤΚ' ΠЄ
ΧΑϤ ΝΑΥ ΧЄ ΑΤЄΤÑΚϢ ΜΠЄΤΟΝ2 ΜΠЄ
ΤÑΜΤΟ ЄΒΟΛ ΑΥϢ ΑΤЄΤÑϢΑΧЄ 2Λ ΝЄΤ
ΜΟΟΥΤ'

    Gospel of Thomas 52. CG II, 42.12–18.

PARALLELS

    But, he said, when the apostles asked how the Jewish prophets were to be regarded, who were thought to have proclaimed his coming beforehand, our Lord, disturbed that they still held this conception, answered: You have forsaken the living one who is before you and speak about the dead.

    Sed Apostolis, inquit, Dominus noster interrogantibus de Judaeorum Prophetis quid sentiri deberet, qui de adventu ejus aliquid cecinisse in praeteritum putabantur, commotus talia eos etiam nunc sentire, respondit: Dimisistis vivum qui ante vos est, et de mortuis fabulamini.

    Augustine, *C. adv. leg. et proph.* 2.4.14. PL 42:647.

A29 / *The Value of Circumcision* _____

His disciples said to him: Is circumcision of any use or not? He said to them: If it were of any use, their father would beget them from their mother circumcised. But the true circumcision in spirit has found complete usefulness.

ПЄΧΑϤ ΝΑϤ Ñ6Ι ΝЄϤΜΑΘΗΤΗC

ϫⲉ ⲡⲥⲃ̄ⲃⲉ ⲣ̄ⲱⲫⲉⲗⲉⲓ ⲏ ⲙ̄ⲙⲟⲛ ⲡⲉϫⲁϥ′
ⲛⲁⲩ ϫⲉ ⲛⲉϥⲣ̄ⲱⲫⲉⲗⲉⲓ ⲛⲉⲡⲟⲩⲉⲓⲱⲧ′ ⲛⲁ
ϫⲡⲟⲟⲩ ⲉⲃⲟⲗ ϩⲛ̄ ⲧⲟⲩⲙⲁⲁⲩ ⲉⲩⲥⲃ̄ⲃⲏⲩ
ⲁⲗⲗⲁ ⲡⲥⲃ̄ⲃⲉ ⲙ̄ⲙⲉ ϩⲙ̄ ⲡⲛ̄ⲁ̄ ⲁϥϭⲛ̄ ϩⲏⲩ
ⲧⲏⲣϥ′

Gospel of Thomas 53. CG II, 42.18–23.

PARALLELS

The ruler Rufus said to him: If God is so pleased with circumcision, why does the child not come out of the womb circumcised? R. Akiba answered him: Why then does it come out with the umbilical cord connected; doesn't the mother have to cut that off as well? And why is the child not born circumcised? Because God has given the commandments in order to lead Israel to obedience through them.

Tanchuma B 7 (18a). Trans. based on the German in Strack and Billerbeck, *Kommentar zum Neuen Testament aus Talmud und Midrash* 4.1:35.

My heart was pruned and its flower appeared,
Then grace sprang up in it,
And it produced fruits for the Lord.
For the Most High circumcised me by His Holy Spirit,
Then He uncovered my inward being towards Him,
And filled me with His love.
And His circumcising became my salvation,
And I ran in the Way, in His peace,
In the way of truth.

Odes of Solomon 11.1–3. Trans. of the Syriac from Charlesworth, *Odes of Solomon*, 52.

Rom 2:25, 29, 3:1, Phil 3:3, 1 Cor 7:19, Gal 5:6, 6:15, Col 2:11, Deut 10:16, Jer 4:4.

A30 / *The Samaritan and the Lamb*

(They saw) a Samaritan going to Judea carrying a lamb. He said to his disciples: (What will) this one (do) with the lamb?[1] They said to him: (He is carrying it) in order to kill it and eat it. He said to them: While it is alive, he will not eat it, but (only) if he kills it and it becomes a corpse. They said: Otherwise he will not be able to do it. He said to them: You also, seek a place in rest for yourselves, lest you become a corpse and be eaten.

<ⲁⲩⲛⲁⲩ>[2] ⲁⲩⲥⲁⲙⲁⲣⲉⲓⲧⲏⲥ ⲉϥϥⲓ ⲛ̄
ⲛⲟⲩϩⲓⲉⲓⲃ' ⲉϥⲃⲏⲕ' ⲉϩⲟⲩⲛ ⲉϯⲟⲩⲇⲁⲓⲁ ⲡⲉ
ϫⲁϥ' ⲛ̄ⲛⲉϥ'ⲙⲁⲑⲏⲧⲏⲥ ϫⲉ ⲡⲏ ⲙ̄ⲡⲕⲱⲧⲉ
ⲙ̄ⲡⲉϩⲓⲉⲓⲃ' ⲡⲉϫⲁⲩ ⲛⲁϥ ϫⲉⲕⲁⲁⲥ ⲉϥⲛⲁ
ⲙⲟⲟⲩⲧϥ' ⲛ̄ϥⲟⲩⲟⲙϥ' ⲡⲉϫⲁϥ ⲛⲁⲩ ϩⲱⲥ ⲉ
ϥⲟⲛϩ ϥⲛⲁⲟⲩⲟⲙϥ' ⲁⲛ ⲁⲗⲗⲁ ⲉϥϣⲁⲙⲟ
ⲟⲩⲧϥ' ⲛ̄ϥϣⲱⲡⲉ ⲛ̄ⲟⲩⲡⲧⲱⲙⲁ ⲡⲉϫⲁⲩ
ϫⲉ ⲛ̄ⲕⲉⲥⲙⲟⲧ' ϥⲛⲁϣ ⲁⲥ ⲁⲛ ⲡⲉϫⲁϥ ⲛⲁⲩ
ϫⲉ ⲛ̄ⲧⲱⲧⲛ̄ ϩⲱⲧ' ⲧⲏⲩⲧⲛ̄ ϣⲓⲛⲉ ⲛ̄ⲥⲁ ⲟⲩ
ⲧⲟⲡⲟⲥ ⲛⲏⲧⲛ̄ ⲉϩⲟⲩⲛ ⲉⲩⲁⲛⲁⲡⲁⲩⲥⲓⲥ
ϫⲉⲕⲁⲁⲥ ⲛ̄ⲛⲉⲧⲛ̄ϣⲱⲡⲉ ⲙ̄ⲡⲧⲱⲙⲁ ⲛ̄ⲥⲉ
ⲟⲩⲱⲙ' ⲧⲏⲩⲧⲛ̄

Gospel of Thomas 60. CG II, 43.12–23.

NOTES

[1] Though the text would appear to be corrupt, the basic meaning may be sufficiently clear. The disciples' answer, beginning with **ϫⲉⲕⲁⲁⲥ**, "in order to," indicates they have been asked concerning the intent of the Samaritan with the lamb.

[2] ⲁⲩⲛⲁⲩ omitted by haplography.

A31 / *Being Undivided*

Salome said: Who are you, man, and whose son?[1] You have sat upon my couch and eaten from my table. Jesus said to her: I am he who is from him who is undivided; to me were given some of the things of my Father. [Salome said:] I am your disciple. [Jesus said to her:] Therefore, I say, whenever one[2] is undivided, he will be filled with light, but whenever one is divided, he will be filled with darkness.

ⲡⲉϫⲉ ⲥⲁⲗⲱⲙⲏ ⲛ̄ⲧⲁⲕ' ⲛⲓⲙ'
ⲡⲣⲱⲙⲉ ϩⲱⲥ ⲉⲃⲟⲗ ϩⲛ̄ ⲟⲩⲁ ⲁⲕⲧⲉⲗⲟ ⲉϫⲙ̄
ⲡⲁϭⲗⲟϭ ⲁⲩⲱ ⲁⲕ'ⲟⲩⲱⲙ ⲉⲃⲟⲗ ϩⲛ̄ ⲧⲁ
ⲧⲣⲁⲡⲉⲍⲁ ⲡⲉϫⲉ ⲓ̅ⲥ̅ ⲛⲁⲥ ϫⲉ ⲁⲛⲟⲕ' ⲡⲉ
ⲡⲉⲧϣⲟⲟⲡ' ⲉⲃⲟⲗ ϩⲙ̄ ⲡⲉⲧϣⲏϣ ⲁⲩϯ
ⲛⲁⲉⲓ ⲉⲃⲟⲗ ϩⲛ̄ ⲛⲁ ⲡⲁⲉⲓⲱⲧ' ⲁⲛⲟⲕ'ⲧⲉⲕ'
ⲙⲁⲑⲏⲧⲏⲥ ⲉⲧⲃⲉ ⲡⲁⲉⲓ ϯϫⲱ ⲙ̄ⲙⲟⲥ ϫⲉ
ϩⲟⲧⲁⲛ ⲉϥϣⲁϣⲱⲡⲉ ⲉϥϣⲏϥ[3] ϥⲛⲁⲙⲟⲩϩ
ⲟⲩⲟⲉⲓⲛ ϩⲟⲧⲁⲛ ⲇⲉ ⲉϥϣⲁⲛϣⲱⲡⲉ ⲉϥ
ⲡⲏϣ ϥⲛⲁⲙⲟⲩϩ ⲛ̄ⲕⲁⲕⲉ

Gospel of Thomas 61b[3]. CG II, 43.25–34.

PARALLELS

Matt 11:27, Luke 10:22, John 3:35, 13:3.

NOTES

[1] The text is difficult to translate with confidence here. The major problem is whether **OYⲀ** is to be understood as (the) One, or whether the phrase **ⲤⲰⲤ ⲈⲂⲞⲖ 2Ⲛ̄ OYⲀ** represents ὡς ἐκ τίνος, "as from whom," i.e., "whose son." Whether this phrase is to be connected with the preceding or with the following words also poses a problem.

[2] The proper references of the pronouns are difficult to determine. Understanding **ⲈϤ(Ϣ)ⲎϤ**, "empty," to refer to bed or couch results in, "whenever it (the bed) is empty, it will be filled with light," and would probably be a rejection of sexual intercourse (see Leipoldt, *Das Evangelium nach Thomas*, 43). The previous use of **ⲔⲖⲞⳠ**, "bed," in this passage is to an eating couch, however. Most recent translators see a personal reference and translate "he" or "one," following the emendation of **ⲈϤ(Ϣ)ⲎϤ**, "empty" to **ⲈϤ(Ϣ)Ⲏ(Ⲱ)**, "undivided", suggested in Guillaumont (*Thomas*, 34). See Ménard (*L'Évangile selon Thomas*, 66, 162) and Lambdin (in Robinson, *Nag Hammadi Library*, 125). The reference is probably to any disciple or potential disciple, and the contrast with "divided" suggests "undivided" as the appropriate translation here and in line 29. The meaning would be similar to other passages in *Thomas* in which oneness is a positive value and division negative (see e.g., 22, 72, 106).

[3] Probably we have in logion 61 two independent sayings joined by the catch-word **ⲔⲖⲞⳠ**, "bed." The first saying, parallel to Luke 17:34, is probably not to be understood as eliciting the question from Salome concerning Jesus' identity.

A32 / *Jesus Not a Divider*

[A man said] to him: Speak to my brothers, so that they might divide my father's possessions with me. He said to him: O man, who made me a divider? He turned to his disciples (and) said to them: I am not a divider, am I?

[ⲡⲈ⳪]Ⲉ Ⲟ[ⲨⲢⲰⲘⲈ] ⲚⲀϤ ⳧Ⲉ ⳧ⲞⲞⲤ Ⲛ̄ⲚⲀⲤⲚⲎⲨ
ϢⲒⲚⲀ ⲈⲨⲚ[Ⲁ]ⲠⲰϢⲈ Ⲛ̄Ⲛ2ⲚⲀⲀⲨ Ⲙ̄ⲠⲀⲈⲒⲰⲦ'
Ⲛ̄Ⲙ̄ⲘⲀⲈⲒ ⲠⲈ⳪ⲀϤ ⲚⲀϤ ⳧Ⲉ Ⲱ ⲠⲢⲰⲘⲈ ⲚⲒⲘ
ⲠⲈ Ⲛ̄ⲦⲀ2ⲀⲀⲦ' Ⲛ̄ⲢⲈϤⲠⲰϢⲈ ⲀϤⲔⲞⲦϤ̄ Ⲁ'
ⲚⲈϤⲘⲀⲐⲎⲦⲎⲤ ⲠⲈ⳪ⲀϤ ⲚⲀⲨ ⳧Ⲉ ⲘⲎ ⲈⲈⲒ
ϢⲞⲞⲠ' Ⲛ̄ⲢⲈϤⲠⲰϢⲈ

Gospel of Thomas 72. CG II, 46.1–6.

PARALLELS

> "A man said to him: 'Master, my brother (wishes) to share (with me) my father's blessing.' (Jesus) said to him: 'Who set me over you (in order to determine your) share?'"
>
>> 'Abd Al-Jabbar, *Book on the Signs of Muhammed's Prophecy*. Trans. of the Arabic from Pines, *The Jewish Christians of the Early Centuries*, 13.

Luke 12:13–14, Acts 7:27, 35, Exod 2:14.

NOTES
   See *Thomas* 16 [Pro 36].

A33 / *True Blessedness* ———————————————

A woman in the crowd said to him: Blessed is the womb which bore you, and
the breasts which nourished you. He said to her: Blessed are those who have
heard the word of the Father (and) have kept it in truth. For there will be
days when you will say: Blessed is the womb which has not conceived and
the breasts which have not given milk.

ΠΕΧΕ ΟΥСΖΙΜ[Ε] ΝΑϤ 2M̄
ΠΜΗϢΕ ΧΕ ΝΕΕΙΑΤ[C Ν]Θ2Η N̄
ΤΑ2ϤΙ 2ΑΡΟΚ ΑΥΩ N̄ΚΙ[Β]Ε ΕΝΤΑ2
СΑ2ΝΟΥϢΚ ΠΕΧΑϤ ΝΑ[C] ΧΕ ΝΕ
ΕΙΑΤΟΥ N̄ΝΕΝΤΑ2СΩΤM̄ Α:
ΠΛΟΓΟС Μ̄ΠΕΙΩΤ ΑΥΑΡΕ2 ΕΡΟϤ
2N̄ ΟΥΜΕ ΟΥN̄ 2N̄2ΟΟΥ ΓΑΡ ΝΑϢΩΠΕ
N̄ΤΕΤN̄ΧΟΟС ΧΕ ΝΕΕΙΑΤС N̄Θ2Η ΤΑ
ΕΙ ΕΤΕ Μ̄ΠСΩ ΑΥΩ N̄ΚΙΒΕ ΝΑΕΙ ΕΜΠΟΥ
✝ ΕΡΩΤΕ

Gospel of Thomas 79. CG II, 47.3–12.

PARALLELS

   Luke 11:27–28, Mark 3:35, Matt 12:50, Luke 8:21, 1:28 (var), 42,
   48, 23:29, Mark 13:17, Matt 24:19, Luke 21:23.

A34 / *Knowing the Times* ———————————————

They said to him: Tell us who you are so that we may believe in you. He said
to them: You test the face of the heaven and the earth, but you do not know
him who is before you.[1] And you do not know (how) to test this moment.

ΠΕΧΑΥ ΝΑϤ' ΧΕ ΧΟΟС ΕΡΟΝ ΧΕ
N̄ΤΚ ΝΙΜ ϢΙΝΑ ΕΝΑΡΠΙСΤΕΥΕ ΕΡΟΚ' ΠΕ
ΧΑϤ ΝΑΥ ΧΕ ΤΕΤN̄ΡΠΙΡΑΖΕ Μ̄Π2Ο N̄ΤΠΕ
ΜN̄ ΠΚΑ2 ΑΥΩ ΠΕΤN̄ΠΕΤN̄ΜΤΟ ΕΒΟΛ
Μ̄ΠΕΤN̄СΟΥΩΝϤ' ΑΥΩ ΠΕΕΙΚΑΙΡΟС ΤΕ
ΤN̄СΟΟΥΝ ΑΝ N̄ΡΠΙΡΑΖΕ Μ̄ΜΟϤ'

Gospel of Thomas 91. CG II, 48.20–25.

PARALLELS

Matt 16:1–3, Luke 12:54–56.

NOTES
1 See also *Thomas* 43 [A26].

A35 / *Jesus' True Relatives*

His disciples said to him: Your brothers and your mother are standing outside. He said to them: Those here who do the will of my Father are my brothers and my mother. These are they who will enter the kingdom of my Father.

ΠΕΧΕ ⲘⲘⲀⲐⲎⲦⲎⲤ ⲚⲀϤ ϪⲈ ⲚⲈⲔ′ⲤⲚⲎⲨ
ⲘⲚ ⲦⲈⲔⲘⲀⲀⲨ ⲤⲈⲀ2ⲈⲢⲀⲦⲞⲨ 2Ⲓ ⲠⲤⲀ Ⲛ
ⲂⲞⲖ ⲠⲈⲬⲀϤ ⲚⲀⲨ ϪⲈ ⲚⲈⲦⲚ̅ⲚⲈⲈⲓⲘⲀ
ⲈⲦⲢⲈ ⲘⲠⲞⲨⲱⲱ ⲘⲠⲀⲈⲓⲰⲦ′ ⲚⲀⲈⲓ ⲚⲈ
ⲚⲀⲤⲚⲎⲨ ⲘⲚ ⲦⲀⲘⲀⲀⲨ Ⲛ̅ⲦⲞⲞⲨ ⲠⲈ ⲈⲦⲚⲀ
ⲂⲰⲔ′ Ⲉ2ⲞⲨⲚ ⲈⲦⲘⲚ̅ⲦⲈⲢⲞ ⲘⲠⲀⲈⲓⲰⲦ′
     Gospel of Thomas 99. CG II. 49.21–26.

PARALLELS

Furthermore, they deny that he was a man, evidently because of the word the Savior spoke when it was announced to him: Behold your mother and brothers are standing outside, namely: Who are my mother and brothers? And he extended his hand toward the disciples and said: These who do the will of my Father are my brothers and mother and sisters.

πάλιν δὲ ἀρνοῦνται εἶναι αὐτὸν ἄνθρωπον, δῆθεν ἀπὸ τοῦ λόγου οὗ εἴρηκεν ὁ σωτὴρ ἐν τῷ ἀναγγελῆναι αὐτῷ ὅτι "ἰδοὺ ἡ μήτηρ σου καὶ οἱ ἀδελφοί σου ἔξω ἑστήκασιν," ὅτι "τίς μού ἐστι μήτηρ καὶ ἀδελφοί; καὶ ἐκτείνας τὴν χεῖρα ἐπὶ τοὺς μαθητὰς ἔφη οὗτοί εἰσιν οἱ ἀδελφοί μου καὶ ἡ μήτηρ καὶ ἀδελφαὶ οἱ ποιοῦντες τὰ θελήματα τοῦ πατρός μου."
     Gospel of the Ebionites [1], Epiphanius, *Haer.* 30.14.5. Holl, *Epiphanius* 1:351.

For the Lord said: My brothers are these who do the will of my Father.

καὶ γὰρ εἶπεν ὁ κύριος· Ἀδελφοί μου οὗτοί εἰσιν οἱ ποιοῦντες τὸ θέλημα τοῦ πατρός μου.
     II Clement 9.11. Funk-Bihlmeyer, *Die Apostolischen Väter,* 75.

The Lord said: For my brothers and fellow heirs are those who do the will of my Father.

"ἀδελφοί μου γάρ," φησὶν ὁ κύριος, "καὶ συγκληρονόμοι οἱ ποιοῦντες τὸ θέλημα τοῦ πατρός μου."

Clement, *Eclogae propheticae* 20.3. Stählin-Früchtel, *Clemens* 3²:142.

Mark 3:31–35, Matt 12:46–50, Luke 8:19–21, Matt 7:21.

A36 / Tribute to Caesar

They showed Jesus a gold coin and said to him: Caesar's officials demand taxes from us. He said to them: Give Caesar what belongs to Caesar, give God what belongs to God, and give me what is mine.

ΑΥΤСΕΒΕ Ι͞С ΑΥΝΟΥΒ ΑΥⲰ ΠΕΧΑϤ ΝΑϤ'
ΧΕ ΝΕΤΗΠ' ΑΚΑΙСΑΡ' СΕⲰ)ΙΤΕ Μ͞ΜΟΝ Ν͞
Ν͞Ⲱ)ⲰΜ' ΠΕΧΑϤ ΝΑΥ ΧΕ † ΝΑ ΚΑΙСΑΡ'
Ν͞ΚΑΙСΑΡ † ΝΑ ΠΝΟΥΤΕ Μ͞ΠΝΟΥΤΕ
ΑΥⲰ ΠΕΤΕ ΠⲰΕΙ ΠΕ ΜΑΤΝ͞ ΝΑΕΙϤ

Gospel of Thomas 100. CG II, 49.27–31.

PARALLELS

For at that time some came and asked him if it is necesary to pay tribute to Caesar. And he answered: Tell me, whose image does the coin have? And they said, Caesar's. And again he answered them: Therefore give the things of Caesar to Caesar and the things of God to God.

κατ' ἐκεῖνο γὰρ τοῦ καιροῦ προσελθόντες τινὲς ἠρώτων αὐτόν, εἰ δεῖ Καίσαρι φόρους τελεῖν. καὶ ἀπεκρίνατο· Εἴπατέ μοι, τίνος εἰκόνα τὸ νόμισμα ἔχει; οἱ δὲ ἔφασαν· Καίσαρος. καὶ πάλιν ἀνταπεκρίνατο αὐτοῖς· Ἀπόδοτε οὖν τὰ Καίσαρος τῷ Καίσαρι καὶ τὰ τοῦ θεοῦ τῷ θεῷ.

Justin, *Apology* 1.17.2. Goodspeed, *Die ältesten Apologeten*, 38.

Now concerning these words you once said to us, when a stater was brought to you and you saw that it was of silver and copper you asked: Whose image is this? They said: It is the king's. But when you saw that it was silver mixed with copper, you said: Give, therefore, what is the king's to the king, and what is God's to God.

ΕΤΒΕ ΠΕΪ-
Ⲱ)ΑΧΕ ΟΥΝ ΝΤΑΚΧΟΟϤ ΕΡΟΝ Μ͞ΠΙΟΥΟΪⲰ)· Ν͞ΤΕΡΟΥΕΙΝΕ
ΝΑΚ Ν͞†СΑΤΕΕΡΕ ΑΚΝΑΥ ΕΡΟС ΕСΟ Ν͞2ΑΤ 2Ι 2ΟΜΝΤ·

ⲚⲦⲀⲔⲰⲒⲚⲈ ⲬⲈ ⲦⲀⲚⲒⲘ ⲦⲈ ⲦⲈⲒⲌⲒⲔⲰⲚ ⲠⲈⲬⲀⲨ ⲬⲈ ⲦⲀⲠⲢ̄ⲢⲞ
ⲦⲈ· Ⲛ̄ⲦⲈⲢⲈⲔⲚⲀⲨ ⲆⲈ ⲈⲢⲞⲤ ⲬⲈ ⲤⲦⲎⲌ Ⲛ̄ⲌⲀⲦ ⲌⲒ ⲌⲞⲘⲚ̄Ⲧ·
ⲠⲈⲬⲀⲔ ⲬⲈ † Ⲛ̄ⲦⲞ ⲞⲨⲚ Ⲛ̄ⲦⲀⲠⲢ̄ⲢⲞ Ⲙ̄ⲠⲢ̄ⲢⲞ· ⲀⲨⲰ ⲦⲀ-
ⲠⲚⲞⲨⲦⲈ Ⲙ̄ⲠⲚⲞⲨⲦⲈ·

Pistis Sophia 113. Schmidt-MacDermot, *Pistis Sophia*, 292.

Give precisely the things of the world to the world and the things
of God to God.

τὰ μὲν τοῦ κόσμου τῷ κόσμῳ, τὰ δὲ τοῦ θεοῦ τῷ θεῷ ἀκριβῶς ἀποδίδου.
Sentences of Sextus 20. Chadwick, *Sentences*, 14.

Mark 12:13–17, Matt 22:15–22, Luke 20:20–26, 23:2, Rom 13:7,
Prov 24:21 (LXX).

Notes
See also P. Eg. 2, 2ʳ. 43–59 [A7].

A37 / *Fasting and Prayer*

They said to him: Come, let us pray today and let us fast. Jesus said: What
then is the sin that I have committed, or in what have I been overcome? But
when the bridegroom comes out of the bridal chamber, then let them fast
and pray.

ⲠⲈ
ⲬⲀⲨ [ⲚⲀϤ] ⲬⲈ ⲀⲘⲞⲨ Ⲛ̄ⲦⲚ̄ⲰⲖⲎⲖ' Ⲙ̄ⲠⲞⲞⲨ
ⲀⲨⲰ Ⲛ̄ⲦⲚ̄ⲢⲚⲎⲤⲦⲈⲨⲈ ⲠⲈⲬⲈ Ⲓ̄Ⲥ̄ ⲬⲈ ⲞⲨ ⲄⲀⲢ'
ⲠⲈ ⲠⲚⲞⲂⲈ Ⲛ̄ⲦⲀⲈⲒⲀⲀϤ' Ⲏ Ⲛ̄ⲦⲀⲨⲬⲢⲞ ⲈⲢⲞⲈⲒ
ⲌⲚ̄ ⲞⲨ ⲀⲖⲖⲀ ⲌⲞⲦⲀⲚ ⲈⲢⲰⲀⲚⲠⲚⲨⲘⲪⲒⲞⲤ ⲈⲒ
ⲈⲂⲞⲖ ⲌⲘ̄ ⲠⲚⲨⲘⲪⲰⲚ ⲦⲞⲦⲈ ⲘⲀⲢⲞⲨⲚⲎ'
ⲤⲦⲈⲨⲈ ⲀⲨⲰ ⲘⲀⲢⲞⲨⲰⲖⲎⲖ'
Gospel of Thomas 104. CG II, 50.11–16.

Parallels
Mark 2:18–20, Matt 9:14–15, Luke 5:33–35.

Notes
See also *Thomas* 6 [A18] and *Thomas* 14 [C33].

A38 / *The Kingdom Spread Out on the Earth*

His disciples said to him: On what day will the kingdom come? < Jesus
said: > It will not come by watching (for it). They will not say: Lo, here! or

Lo, there! Rather the kingdom of the Father is spread out on the earth, and men do not see it.

ΠΕΧΑΥ

ΝΑϤ Ⲛ̄ϬⲒ ΝⲈϤⲘΑⲐⲎⲦⲎⲤ ϪⲈ ⲦⲘⲚ̄ⲦⲈⲢⲞ
ⲈⲤⲚ̄ⲚⲎⲨ Ⲛ̄Αⲱ Ⲛ̄ⲎⲞⲞⲨ ⲈⲤⲚ̄ⲚⲎⲨ ΑⲚ Ⲍ̄Ⲛ ⲞⲨ
ϬⲰϢⲦ' ⲈⲂⲞⲖ' ⲈⲨⲚΑϪⲞⲞⲤ ΑⲚ ϪⲈ ⲈⲒⲤ ⲎⲎ
ⲦⲈ Ⲙ̄ⲠⲒⲤΑ Ⲏ ⲈⲒⲤ ⲎⲎⲦⲈ ⲦⲎ ΑⲖⲖΑ ⲦⲘⲚⲦⲈⲢⲞ
Ⲙ̄ⲠⲈⲒⲰⲦ' ⲈⲤⲠⲞⲢⲱ' ⲈⲂⲞⲖ ⲎⲒϪⲘ̄ ⲠⲔΑⲎ ΑⲨⲰ
Ⲣ̄ⲢⲰⲘⲈ ΝΑⲨ ΑⲚ ⲈⲢⲞⲤ

Gospel of Thomas 113. CG II, 51.12–18.

PARALLELS

As the Lord said: The kingdom of God is spread out upon the earth, and men do not see it.

ὡς φησιν ὁ κύριος· ἡ βασιλεία τοῦ θεοῦ χαμαὶ ἥπλωται καὶ οἱ ἄνθρωποι οὐκ ἐμβλέπουσιν αὐτήν.

Symeon, Hom. B35. Dörries, Symeon von Mesopotamien, 224, n.3.

Luke 17:20–21.

NOTES

See also *Thomas* 3 and parallels [Pro 31] and *Thomas* 51 [A27].

A39 / *Women Entering the Kingdom*

Simon Peter said to them: Let Mary depart from us, for women are not worthy of the life. Jesus said: Look, I will lead her, so that I may make her male, in order that she too may become a living spirit, like you males. For every woman who makes herself male will enter the kingdom of heaven.

ⲠⲈϪⲈ ⲤⲒⲘⲰⲚ ⲠⲈⲦⲢⲞⲤ

ΝΑⲨ ϪⲈ ⲘΑⲢⲈⲘΑⲢⲒⲎΑⲘ ⲈⲒ ⲈⲂⲞⲖ Ⲛ̄ⲎⲎⲦⲚ̄
ϪⲈ Ⲛ̄ⲤⲎⲒⲞⲘⲈ Ⲙ̄ⲠϢΑ ΑⲚ' Ⲙ̄ⲠⲰⲚⲎ ⲠⲈϪⲈ ⲒⲤ̄
ϪⲈ ⲈⲒⲤ ⲎⲎⲦⲈ ΑⲚⲞⲔ' Ⲧ̄ΝΑⲤⲰⲔ' Ⲙ̄ⲘⲞⲤ ϪⲈ
ⲔΑΑⲤ ⲈⲈⲒΝΑΑⲤ Ⲛ̄ⲎⲞⲞⲨⲦ· ϢⲒΝΑ ⲈⲤΝΑϢⲱ
ⲠⲈ ⲎⲰⲰⲤ Ⲛ̄ⲞⲨⲠⲚ̄Α ⲈϤⲞⲚⲎ ⲈϤⲈⲒⲚⲈ Ⲙ̄
ⲘⲰⲦⲚ̄ Ⲛ̄ⲎⲞⲞⲨⲦ ϪⲈ ⲤⲎⲒⲘⲈ ⲚⲒⲘ' ⲈⲤΝΑΑⲤ
Ⲛ̄ⲎⲞⲞⲨⲦ' ⲤΝΑⲂⲰⲔ' ⲈⲎⲞⲨⲚ̄ ⲈⲦⲘⲚ̄ⲦⲈⲢⲞ
Ⲛ̄Ⲙ̄ⲠⲎⲨⲈ

Gospel of Thomas 114. CG II. 51.18–26.

PARALLELS

> Therefore, the males are drawn together with the logos, but the females, having become men, are united with the angels and go into the pleroma. For this reason, the woman is said to be changed into a man, and the church here on earth into angels.

τὰ οὖν ἀρρενικὰ μετὰ τοῦ λόγου συνεστάλη, τὰ θηλυκὰ δὲ ἀπανδρωθέντα ἑνοῦται τοῖς ἀγγέλοις καὶ εἰς πλήρωμα χωρεῖ. διὰ τοῦτο ἡ γυνὴ εἰς ἄνδρα μετατίθεσθαι λέγεται καὶ ἡ ἐνταῦθα ἐκκλησία εἰς ἀγγέλους.

Clement, *Exc. ex Theod.* 21.3. Stählin-Früchtel, *Clemens* 3²:113.

A40 / Gifts of the True Mother

Because of this a disciple asked the Lord one day for something of the world. He said to him: Ask your mother,[1] and she will give you that which belongs to another.[2]

> ЄТВЄ ПΛЄI ΔYM̄MΔΘΗΤΗΣ P̄
> ΔIΤЄI M̄ПХОЄIС N̄NOY2OOY ЄТВЄ OY
> 2ШВ N̄ТЄ ПKOCMOC ПЄХΔҶ NΔҶ' ХЄ
> ЄPIΔIΤЄI N̄ТЄKMΔΔY ΔYШ CNΔ† NΔK
> ЄВОΛ 2N̄ ΔΛΛОТPION

Gospel of Philip 34b. CG II, 59.23–27.

NOTES

[1] Probably the Holy Spirit. See CG II, 55.23ff for the femininity of the Holy Spirit in Philip.

[2] The sense would seem to be she will give something far superior to things of the world.

A41 / Jesus in the Dye-works

The Lord went into the dye-works of Levi. He took seventy two colors and threw them into the cauldron. He took them all out white and said: Even so came the son of[1] man [as] a dyer.[2,3]

> ΔПХОЄIС ВШK' Є2ОY[N] ЄПMΔ N̄ХШ6Є
> N̄ΛЄГЄI ΔҶҶI ШВЄСNOOYC N̄ХPШMΔ
> ΔҶNOХOY ΔТPO2ТЄ ΔҶN̄ТOY Є2PΔÏ
> ЄYОВШ ТНPOY ΔYШ ПЄХΔҶ ХЄ ТΔЄI
> ТЄ ΘЄ N̄ТΔҶЄI M̄MON N̄6I [П] ШНPЄ· M̄
> ПШНPЄ¹ M̄ПPM[Є ЄҶO] N̄Х6[I]Т'²

Gospel of Philip 54. CG II, 63.25–30.

NOTES

¹ Ⲙ̄ⲡⲱ̄ⲏⲣⲉ "of the son" is repeated by dittography. There are dots above the word in the manuscript.

² I follow Till's reconstruction of the text (*Das Evangelium nach Philippos*, 8). Ménard's reconstruction is analogous (*L'Évangile selon Philippe*, 70), as is the one translated by Isenberg (in Robinson, *Nag Hammadi Library*, 138). Schenke translates "to take away defects" (*Koptisch-gnostische Schriften*, 4). Wilson (*The Gospel of Philip*, 32) does not complete the lacuna. Catanzaro (*JTS* n.s. 13:47) has "Thus came to us the Son of the Son of (dittography?) man . . . the dyers," thus viewing Ⲛ̄ⳬⲓⲧ, "the dyers," as the probable reconstruction but not as a reference to Jesus.

³ See the legend of the child Jesus contained in some versions of the *Infancy Gospel of Thomas* in James, *The Apocryphal New Testament*, 66.

A42 / *Jesus' Love for Mary Magdalene*

And the companion of Christ is Mary Magdalene. [The Lord loved Mary] more than [all] the disciples, [and] kissed her on her [mouth many] times. The other [disciples¹ saw] him [loving Mary]. They said to him: Why do you love her more than all of us? The Savior answered and said to them: Why do I not love you as I do her?

ⲀⲨⲱ [Ⲧ]ⲔⲞⲒ
ⲚⲰⲚⲞⲤ Ⲙ̄ⲡⲉ[ⳉⲤ ⲦⲈ ⲘⲀⲣⲒⲀ ⲦⲘⲀ[ⲄⲆⲀ]
ⲖⲏⲚⲎ ⲚⲈⲣⲉⲡ[ⳉⲞⲈⲒⲤ ⲘⲈ] Ⲙ̄ⲘⲀⲣⲒⲀ Ⲛ]
ⲘⲞⲨⲞ ⲀⲘ̄ⲘⲀⲐⲎ[ⲦⲎⲤ ⲦⲎⲣⲞⲨ ⲀⲨⲱ Ⲁ̄ϥ]
ⲀⲤⲡⲀⳉⲈ Ⲙ̄ⲘⲞⲤ ⲀⲦⲈⲤ[ⲦⲀⲡⲣⲞ Ⲛ̄ⲐⲀⲘ]
Ⲛ̄ⲤⲞⲡ' ⲀⲡⲔⲈⲤⲈⲈⲡⲈ Ⲛ̄[ⲘⲘⲀⲐⲎⲦⲎⲤ¹ ⲀⲨ]
ⲚⲀⲨ] ⲈⲣⲞϥ [ⲈϥⲘⲈ ⲘⲘⲀⲣⲒ]Ⲁ ⲡⲈ ⳉ ⲀⲨ ⳉⲈ
Ⲉ]ⲦⲂⲈ ⲞⲨ ⲔⲘⲈ Ⲙ̄ⲘⲞⲤ ⲡⲀⲣⲀⲣⲞⲚ ⲦⲎⲣ̄Ⲛ Ⲁ̄ϥ'
ⲞⲨⲱ̄ϣⲂ̄ Ⲛ̄ϭⲒ ⲡⲤⲰⲦⲎⲣ' ⲡⲈⳉⲀϥ ⲚⲀⲨ ⲡⲈ
ⳉⲀϥ ⲚⲀⲨ² ⳉⲈ ⲈⲦⲂⲈ ⲞⲨ ϯⲘⲈ Ⲙ̄Ⲙⲱ̄ⲦⲚ̄ ⲀⲚ'
Ⲛ̄ⲦⲈⲤⳉⲈ

Gospel of Philip 55. CG II, 63.32–64.5.

PARALLELS

Peter said to Mary: Sister, we know that the Savior loved you more than other women.

ⲡⲈⳉⲈ ⲡⲈⲦⲣⲞⲤ Ⲙ̄ⲘⲀⲣⲒⳉⲀⲘ ⳉⲈ ⲦⲤⲱ
ⲚⲈ ⲦⲚ̄ⲤⲞⲞⲨⲚ ⳉⲈ ⲚⲈⲣⲈⲡⲤⲱ̄ⲣ̄ ⲞⲨⲀϣⲈ
ⲚⲘⲞⲨⲞ ⲡⲀⲣⲀ ⲡⲔⲈⲤⲈⲈⲡⲈ Ⲛ̄Ⲥ̄ⲦⲒⲘⲈ

Gospel of Mary 10.1–3. Wilson and MacRae in *Nag Hammadi Codices V, 2–5 and VI, 1*, 460.

Surely the Savior knew her very well. For this reason he loved her more than us.

ⲡⲁⲛⲧⲱ'ⲥ'
ⲉⲣⲉⲡⲥⲱⲧⲏⲣ ⲥⲟⲟⲩⲛ ⲙ̄ⲙⲟⲥ ⲁⲥ
ⲫ̇ⲁⲗⲱⲥ ⲉⲧⲃⲉ ⲡⲁï ⲁϥⲟⲩⲟϣⲥ̄ ⲛ̄ϩⲟⲩ
ⲟ ⲉⲣⲟⲛ

Gospel of Mary 18:12–15. Ibid., 468.

For surely, having known her, he (the Savior) doubtlessly loved her.

πάντως γὰρ ἐκεῖνος εἰδὼς αὐτὴν ἀσφ[αλ]ῶ[ς] ἠγάπησεν

Fragment of the *Gospel of Mary* from P. Rylands 463, 22.23–25. Ibid.

John 11:2, 5.

NOTES

1 I follow Till (*Das Evangelium nach Philippos,* 28) in the reconstruction except in reading "disciples" here instead of "women." Ménard (*L'Évangile selon Philippe,* 70) also has "disciples."

2 ⲡⲉϫⲁϥ ⲛⲁⲩ, "he said to them," is repeated by dittography.

PARABLES

P1 / *The Talents* _____

But since the gospel in Hebrew characters which has come down to us directs the threat not against the man who had hidden (the talent) but against the one who had lived dissolutely—for he had three servants; one who squandered the goods of his master with harlots and flute girls, one who increased the profits, and one who hid the talent; accordingly one was received (approvingly), one simply rebuked, and one locked up in prison—I wonder whether in Matthew the threat which is spoken after the saying concerning the one who did nothing may actually refer not to him, but back to the first who had eaten and drunk with the drunken.

ἐπεὶ δὲ τὸ εἰς ἡμᾶς ἧκον Ἑβραϊκοῖς χαρακτῆρσιν Εὐαγγέλιον
τὴν ἀπειλὴν οὐ κατὰ τοῦ ἀποκρύψαντος ἐπῆγεν, ἀλλὰ κατὰ
τοῦ ἀσώτως ἐζηκότος—τρεῖς γὰρ δούλους περιεῖχε, τὸν
μὲν καταφαγόντα τὴν ὕπαρξιν τοῦ δεσπότου μετὰ πορνῶν
καὶ αὐλητρίδων, τὸν δὲ πολλαπλασιάσαντα τὴν ἐργασίαν,
τὸν δὲ κατακρύψαντα τὸ τάλαντον· εἶτα τὸν μὲν ἀποδεχθῆναι,
τὸν δὲ μεμφθῆναι μόνον, τὸν δὲ συγκλεισθῆναι δεσμωτηρίῳ—
ἐφίστημι, μήποτε, κατὰ τὸν Ματθαῖον, μετὰ τὴν συμπλήρωσιν
τοῦ λόγου τοῦ κατὰ τοῦ μηδὲν ἐργασαμένου ἡ ἑξῆς ἐπιλεγομένη
ἀπειλὴ οὐ περὶ αὐτοῦ, ἀλλὰ περὶ τοῦ προτέρου κατ' ἐπανάληψιν
λέλεκται, τοῦ ἐσθίοντος καὶ πίνοντος μετὰ τῶν μεθυόντων.

> *Gospel of the Nazaraeans* [4], Eusebius, *De theophania* 19. Klostermann, *Apocrypha* 2:9.

PARALLELS

Matt 25:14-30, 24:49, Luke 19:12-27, 12:45, 15:13.

P2 / *The Fig-Tree* _____

And ye, receive ye the parable of the fig-tree thereon: as soon as its shoots have gone forth and its boughs have sprouted, the end of the world will come." And I, Peter, answered and said unto him, "Explain to me concerning the fig-tree, [and] how we shall perceive it, for throughout all its days does the fig-tree sprout and every year it brings forth its fruit [and] for its master. What (then) meaneth the parable of the fig-tree? We know it not. "—And the Master answered and said unto me, "Dost thou not understand that the fig-tree is the house of Israel? Even as a man hath planted a fig-tree in his garden and it brought forth no fruit, and he sought its fruit for many years. When he found it not, he said to the keeper of his garden, 'Uproot the fig-tree that our land may not be unfruitful for us.' And the gardener said to God, 'We thy servants (?) wish to clear it (of weeds) and to dig the ground around it and to water it. If it does not then bear fruit, we will immediately remove its roots from the garden and plant another one in its place.' Hast thou not grasped that the fig-tree is the house of Israel? Verily, I say to you, when its boughs have sprouted at the end, then shall deceiving Christs come, and awaken hope (with the words): 'I am the Christ, who am (now) come into the world.' And when they shall see the wickedness of their deeds (even of the false Christs), they shall turn away after them and deny him to whom our fathers gave praise (?), the first Christ whom they crucified and thereby sinned exceedingly. But this deceiver is not the Christ. And when they reject him, he will kill with the sword (dagger) and there shall be many martyrs. Then shall the boughs of the fig-tree, i.e., the house of Israel, sprout, and there shall be many martyrs by his hand: they shall be killed and become martyrs. Enoch and Elias will be sent to instruct them that this is the deceiver who must come into the world and do signs and wonders in order to deceive. And therefore shall they that are slain by his hand be martyrs and shall be reckoned among the good and righteous martyrs who have pleased God in their life."

Apocalypse of Peter 2. Trans. of the Ethiopic from *N.T. Apoc.* 2:668-669.

PARALLELS

> Mark 13:28-29, Matt 24:32-33, Luke 21:29-31, 13:6-9, Mark
> 13:22-23, Matt 24:24, Mark 13:6, Matt 24:5, Luke 21:8.

P3 / *The Date-Palm*

Do not let the kingdom of heaven wither, for it is like a shoot[1] of a date palm whose fruit poured down around it. It put forth leaves, and when they sprouted they made the core[2] dry up. So it is also with the fruit which came forth from this single root. When it had been picked,[3] fruits were produced by many. It (the root) was indeed good, (for) it was now possible to produce new plants for you (and) to find it (i.e., the kingdom).[4]

ⲘⲠⲰⲢ ⲀϨⲰⲔⲘ
ⲚⲦⲘⲚⲦⲢ̄ⲢⲞ ⲚⲘⲠⲎⲨⲈ·
ⲈⲤⲦⲚ̄ⲦⲀⲚⲦ' ⲚⲄⲀⲢ ⲀⲨⲰⲖϨ̄[1] ⲚⲂⲚ
ⲚⲈ ⲈⲚⲦⲀϨⲀⲚⲈϤⲔⲀⲢⲠⲞⲤ ϨⲈ†Ⲉ

46

ⲘⲠⲈϤⲔⲰⲦⲈ ⲀϤⲦⲈⲨⲞ ⲀⲂⲀⲖ Ⲛ̄
ⲐⲈⲚϬⲰⲂⲈ ⲀⲨⲰ Ⲛ̄ⲦⲀⲢⲞⲨ† ⲞⲨⲰ
ⲀⲀⲞⲨⲦⲢⲈⲦⲀⲦⲈ ⲱⲀⲨⲈⲒⲈ ⲦⲈ
ⲈⲒ ⲀⲚ ⲦⲈ ⲐⲈ Ⲙ̄ⲠⲔⲀⲢⲠⲞⲤ Ⲛ̄ⲦⲀⲀ
ⲱⲰⲠⲈ· ⲀⲂⲀⲖ 2Ⲛ̄ †ⲚⲞⲨⲚⲈ Ⲛ̄
ⲞⲨⲰⲦ· Ⲛ̄ⲦⲀⲢⲞⲨⲦⲀⲔⲚϤ³ ⲀⲨ
ⲬⲠⲞ Ⲛ̄2Ⲛ̄ⲔⲀⲢⲠⲞⲤ 2ⲒⲦⲚ̄ 2Ⲁ2
ⲚⲈⲚⲀⲚⲞⲨⲤ ⲘⲘⲈⲚ ⲠⲈ· ⲈⲚⲈ
ⲞⲨⲚ̄ ⲱϬⲀⲘ †ⲚⲞⲨ ⲀⲢ̄ ⲚⲒⲦⲰ
ϬⲈ Ⲃ̄ⲂⲢ̄ⲢⲈ· ⲚⲈⲔ ⲀϬⲚ̄ⲦⲤ·

Apocryphon of James. CG I, 82-35.

NOTES

¹ Read ⲀⲨⲰⲀ2, "a shoot."

² Literally, "the womb," analogous to μήτρα, "womb," used for the core or heart-wood of trees (See LSJ, 1130).

³ Read Ⲛ̄ⲦⲀⲢⲞⲨⲦⲀⲔⲘϤ, "when it had been picked."

⁴ The last sentence is difficult. The antecedents of the pronouns are uncertain. The sentence could also be translated as a condition contrary to fact, "If it were possible to produce new plants now, you would find it." See Malinine, *Epistula Iacobi Apocrypha*, 94, and Williams, in Robinson, *Nag Hammadi Library*, 32.

P4 / *The Grain of Wheat* _____

Be zealous for the word. For the word's first part[1] is faith, the second love, the third works. For life comes from these. For the word is like a grain of wheat. When someone had sown it, he trusted in it; and when it had grown, he loved it because he saw many grains in the place of one. And when he had worked he was saved, because he had prepared it for food. Moreover, he left (some grain) for sowing. So also it is possible for you yourselves to receive the kingdom of heaven. If you do not receive this through knowledge, you will not be able to find it.

      ⲱⲰⲠⲈ Ⲛ̄ⲢⲈϤϬⲈⲠⲎ 2Ⲁ ⲠⲢⲀ
Ⲙ̄ⲠⲖⲞⲄⲞⲤ· ⲠⲖⲞⲄⲞⲤ Ⲛ̄ⲄⲀⲢ ⲱⲀ
Ⲣ̄Ⲡ ⲘⲈⲚ ⲠⲈϤⲀ ⲠⲈ ⲦⲠⲒⲤⲦⲒⲤ
ⲠⲘⲀ2ⲤⲚⲈⲨ ⲠⲈ ⲦⲀⲄⲀⲠⲎ ⲠⲘⲀ2
ⲱⲀⲘⲚ̄Ⲧ ⲠⲈ ⲚⲈ2ⲂⲎⲨⲈ· ⲈⲱⲀϤⲱⲱ
ⲠⲈ ⲄⲀⲢ ⲀⲂⲀⲖ 2Ⲛ̄ ⲚⲈⲈⲒ Ⲛ̄ϬⲒ ⲠⲰⲚ2
ⲠⲖⲞⲄⲞⲤ Ⲛ̄ⲄⲀⲢ ⲈϤⲦⲚ̄ⲦⲰⲚ ⲀⲨ
Ⲃ̄ⲂⲒⲖⲈ Ⲛ̄ⲤⲞⲨⲞ· Ⲡ[Ⲉ]ⲈⲒ Ⲛ̄ⲦⲀⲢⲈⲞⲨ
ⲈⲈⲒ ⲬⲀϤ· ⲀϤⲦⲀⲚ2ⲞⲨⲦϤ· ⲀⲨⲰ Ⲛ̄
ⲦⲀⲢⲈϤⲢⲰⲦ ⲀϤⲘⲢ̄ⲢⲒⲦϤ· ⲈⲀϤⲚⲈⲨ

ⲀⲆⲀⲂ ⲂⲂⲀⲂⲒⲖⲈ· ⲀⲠⲘⲀ ⲚⲞⲨⲈⲒⲈ· ⲀⲨⲰ
ⲚⲦⲀⲢⲈϤⲢ ⲌⲰⲂ· ⲀϤⲞⲨⲬⲈⲈⲒ· ⲈⲀϤ
ⲦⲤⲈⲚⲀϤ ⲚⲚⲞⲨⲌⲢⲈ· ⲠⲀⲖⲒⲚ ⲀϤ
ⲰⲰⲬⲠ ⲀⲬⲞ· ⲦⲈⲈⲒ ⲀⲚ ⲦⲈ· ⲐⲈ
ⲈⲦⲈ ⲞⲨⲚ 6ⲀⲘ ⲘⲘⲰⲦⲚ ⲚⲬⲒ Ⲁ
ⲢⲰⲦⲚ ⲚⲦⲘⲚⲦⲢⲢⲞ ⲚⲘⲠⲎⲨⲈ·
ⲦⲈⲈⲒ ⲈⲢⲈⲦⲚⲦⲘⲬⲒⲦⲤ ⲌⲒⲦⲚ ⲞⲨⲄⲚⲰ
ⲤⲒⲤ· ⲚⲦⲈⲦⲚⲀ<ϣ 6ⲒⲚⲦⲤ ⲈⲚ·

Apocryphon of James. CG I, 8.10-27.

NOTES
  [1] Or, "condition."

P5 / *The Ear of Grain*

For the kingdom of heaven is like an ear of grain which had grown up in a field. And when it had ripened it scattered its fruit and again filled the field with ears for another year. You also hasten to reap an ear of life for yourselves so that you may be filled with the kingdom.

ⲦⲘⲚⲦⲈⲢⲞ ⲄⲀⲢ
ⲚⲘⲠⲎⲨⲈ ⲈⲤⲈⲒⲚⲈ ⲚⲚⲞⲨⲌⲘⲤ Ⲉ
ⲀϤⲢⲰⲦ ⲌⲚⲚ ⲞⲨⲤⲰⲱⲈ· ⲀⲨⲰ ⲠⲈ
ⲈⲒ ⲚⲦⲀⲢⲈϤⲬⲈⲦⲈ· ⲀϤⲤⲒⲦⲈ ⲘⲠⲈϤ
ⲔⲀⲢⲠⲞⲤ ⲀⲨⲰ ⲀⲚ ⲀϤⲘⲞⲨⲌ ⲚⲦⲤⲰ
ⲱⲈ ⲚⲌⲚⲌⲘⲤ· ⲀⲔⲈⲢⲀⲘⲠⲈ· ⲚⲦⲰ
ⲦⲚ ⲌⲰⲦ· ⲦⲎⲚⲈ 6ⲈⲠⲎ· ⲀⲦⲢⲈⲦⲚⲰⲌⲤ
ⲚⲎⲦⲚ ⲚⲚⲞⲨⲌⲘⲤ· ⲚⲰⲚⲌ· ⲬⲈⲔⲀ
ⲤⲈ ⲈⲢⲈⲦⲚⲀⲘⲞⲨⲌ ⲀⲂⲀⲖ ⲌⲚ ⲦⲘⲚⲦ
ⲢⲢⲞ

Apocryphon of James. CG I, 12.22-31.

Parallels

    Mark 4:26-29.

NOTES
  See also *Thomas* 21c [W16].

P6 / *The Wise Fisherman*

And he said: Man is like a wise fisherman who threw his net into the sea; he pulled it up from the sea full of small fish. Among them the wise fisherman

48

found a large, good fish. He threw all the small fish back into the sea. He chose the large fish without difficulty. Whoever has ears to hear, let him hear.

ⲀⲨⲰ ⲠⲈ
ⲬⲀϤ ⲬⲈ ⲈⲠⲢⲰⲘⲈ ⲦⲚ̄ⲦⲰⲚ ⲀⲨⲞⲨⲰϨⲈ
Ⲣ̄ⲢⲘⲚ̄ϨⲎⲦ' ⲠⲀⲈⲒ Ⲛ̄ⲦⲀϨⲚⲞⲨⲬⲈ Ⲛ̄ⲦⲈϤⲀ
ⲂⲰ ⲈⲐⲀⲖⲖⲀⲤⲤⲀ ⲀϤⲤⲰⲔ Ⲙ̄ⲘⲞⲤ ⲈϨⲢⲀⲒ̄
ϨⲚ̄ ⲐⲀⲖⲖⲀⲤⲤⲀ ⲈⲤⲘⲈϨ Ⲛ̄ⲦⲂⲦ' Ⲛ̄ⲔⲞⲨⲈⲒ Ⲛ̄
ϨⲢⲀⲒ̄ Ⲛ̄ϨⲎⲦⲞⲨ ⲀϤϨⲈ ⲀⲨⲚⲞϬ Ⲛ̄ⲦⲂⲦ ⲈⲚⲀ
ⲚⲞⲨϤ' Ⲛ̄ϬⲒ ⲠⲞⲨⲰϨⲈ Ⲣ̄ⲢⲘⲚ̄ϨⲎⲦ' ⲀϤⲚⲞⲨ
ⲬⲈ Ⲛ̄ⲚⲔⲞⲨⲈⲒ ⲦⲎⲢⲞⲨ Ⲛ̄ⲦⲂⲦ' ⲈⲂⲞⲖ Ⲉ[ⲠⲈ]
ⲤⲎⲦ ⲈⲐⲀⲖⲖⲀⲤⲤⲀ ⲀϤⲤⲰⲦⲠ' Ⲙ̄ⲠⲚⲞϬ Ⲛ̄
ⲦⲂⲦ ⲬⲰⲢⲒⲤ ϨⲒⲤⲈ ⲠⲈⲦⲈ ⲞⲨⲚ̄ ⲘⲀⲀⲬⲈ Ⲙ̄ⲘⲞϤ
ⲈⲤⲰⲦⲘ̄ ⲘⲀⲢⲈϤ'ⲤⲰⲦⲘ̄

Gospel of Thomas 8. CG II, 33.28-34.3.

PARALLELS

For the present I do not comment on the parable in the gospel which says: The kingdom of heaven is like a man who threw a drag-net into the sea and from the great number of fish caught makes a selection of the better ones.

σιωπῶ τὰ νῦν τὴν ἐν τῷ εὐαγγελίῳ παραβολὴν λέγουσαν·
"ὁμοία ἐστὶν ἡ βασιλεία τῶν οὐρανῶν ἀνθρώπῳ σαγήνην
εἰς θάλασσαν βεβληκότι κἀκ τοῦ πλήθους τῶν ἑαλωκότων
ἰχθύων τὴν ἐκλογὴν τῶν ἀμεινόνων ποιουμένῳ."
Clement, *Strom.* 6.11.95. Stählin-Früchtel, *Clemens* 2³:479.

For there is the one pearl among the small pearls, and the good fish in the large catch of fish.

ἐν πολλοῖς γὰρ τοῖς μαργαρίταις τοῖς μικροῖς ὁ εἷς,
ἐν δὲ πολλῇ τῇ τῶν ἰχθύων ἄγρᾳ ὁ κάλλιχθυς
Clement, *Strom.* 1.1.16. Stählin-Früchtel, *Clemens* 2³:12.

A fisherman lifted up the net which he had cast shortly before. It happened to be full of various kinds of good fish. The little ones fled to the bottom and slipped out through the many holes of the net, but the big one was caught and spread out in the boat.

Ἁλιεὺς σαγήνην ἦν νεωστὶ Βεβλήκει ἀνεῖλετ'·
ὄφου δ'ἔτυχε ποικίλου πλήρης. τῶν δ' ἰχθύων
ὁ λεπτὸς εἰς βυθὸν φεύγων ὑπεξέδυνε δικτύου

πολυτρήτου, ὁ μέγας δ' ἀγρευθεὶς εἰς τὸ πλοῖον
ἠπλώθη.

> Aesop's Fable of the Fisherman and the Fish [Babrius 4]. Perry. *Babrius and Phaedrus*, 8.

Matt 13:47-50.

P7 / *The Sower*

Jesus said: Behold the sower went out, he filled his hand, he sowed. Some (seeds) fell on the road; the birds came (and) gathered them. Others fell on the rock and sent no root down to the earth and produced no ear.[1] And others fell among thorns; they choked the seed, and the worm ate them. And others fell on the good soil, and it brought forth good fruit. It produced sixty fold and one hundred and twenty fold.

ΠΕΧΕ ΙC ΧΕ ΕΙC 2Η
ΗΤΕ ΔϤΕΙ ΕΒΟΛ Ν6Ι ΠΕΤ'CΙΤΕ ΔϤΜΕ2 ΤΟΟΤϤ
ΔϤΝΟΥΧΕ Δ2ΟΕΙΝΕ ΜΕΝ 2Ε ΕΧΝ ΤΕ2ΙΗ'
ΔΥΕΙ Ν6Ι Ν2ΔΛΔΤΕ ΔΥΚΔΤϤΟΥ 2ΝΚΟΟΥΕ
ΔΥ2Ε ΕΧΝ ΤΠΕΤΡΔ ΔΥШ ΜΠΟΥΧΕ ΝΟΥΝΕ
ΕΠΕCΗΤ' ΕΠΚΔ2 ΔΥШ ΜΠΟΥΤΕΥΕ 2ΜC Ε2
ΡΔΪ ΕΤΠΕ ΔΥШ 2ΝΚΟΟΥΕ ΔΥ2Ε ΕΧΝ ΝШΟ
ΤΕ ΔΥШ6Τ' ΜΠΕ6ΡΟ6 ΔΥШ ΔΠϤΝΤ ΟΥΟΜΟΥ
ΔΥШ Δ2ΝΚΟΟΥΕ 2Ε ΕΧΝ ΠΚΔ2 ΕΤΝΔΝΟΥϤ'
ΔΥШ ΔϤϯ ΚΔΡΠΟC Ε2ΡΔΪ ΕΤΠΕ ΕΝΔΝΟΥϤ' ΔϤ
ΕΙ[2] ΝCΕ ΕCΟΤΕ ΔΥШ ШΕ ΧΟΥШΤ' ΕCΟΤΕ

> *Gospel of Thomas* 9. CG II, 34.3-13.

PARALLELS

> As my Lord said: The sower went out to sow the seed. And some fell onto the way, others into thorns, others upon rocky ground, and others on good ground.

> ὡς ὁ ἐμὸς κύριος εἶπεν· Ἐξῆλθεν ὁ σπείρων τοῦ σπεῖραι
> τὸν σπόρον· καὶ ὃ μὲν ἔπεσεν εἰς τὴν ὁδόν, ὃ δὲ εἰς τὰς
> ἀκάνθας, ὃ δὲ ἐπὶ τὰ πετρώδη, ὃ δὲ ἐπὶ τὴν γῆν τὴν καλήν.
> > Justin, *Dial.* 125.1. Goodspeed, *Die ältesten Apologeten*, 245.

> The sower went out and cast each of the seeds on the ground. Those which fall on the dry, barren ground perish. Then the

magnificence of the providence of the Lord raises them up from dissolution, and many develop from the one and bear fruit.

'Εξῆλθεν ὁ σπείρων καὶ ἔβαλεν εἰς τὴν γῆν ἕκαστον τῶν σπερμάτων, ἅτινα πεσόντα εἰς τὴν γῆν ξηρὰ καὶ γυμνὰ διαλύεται· εἶτ' ἐκ τῆς διαλύσεως ἡ μεγαλειότης τῆς προνοίας τοῦ δεσπότου ἀνίστησιν αὐτά, καὶ ἐκ τοῦ ἑνὸς πλείονα αὔξει καὶ ἐκφέρει καρπόν.

I Clement 24.5. Funk-Bihlmeyer, *Die Apostolischen Väter,* 49.

And he (Priscillian) demonstrates this point from a certain book called Memoria Apostolorum in which the Savior appears to be questioned by the disciples in secret and to show from the gospel parable which contains 'the sower went out to sow' that he was not a good sower, maintaining that had he been good, he would not have been negligent nor thrown seed by the wayside nor in rocky or uncultivated soil; thus wanting the sower to be understood as the one who scatters captive souls in different bodies as he wishes.

et hoc ipsum confirmans ex libro quodam qui inscribitur 'memoria apostolorum,' ubi saluator interrogari a discipulis uidetur secreto et ostendere de parabola euangelica quae habet exiit seminans seminare quia non fuerit seminator bonus, adserens quia si bonus fuisset, non fuisset neglegens uel secus uiam uel in petrosis uel in incultis iaceret semen, uolens intellegi hunc esse seminartem qui animas captas spargeret in corpora diuersa quae uellet.

Memoria Apostolorum, in Paulus Orosius, Communitorium de errore Priscillianistarum et Origenistarum. Schepss, *Priscillien Opera,* 154.

Mark 4:3-9, Matt 13:3-9, Luke 8:5-8. Mark 4:13-20, Matt 13:18-23, Luke 8:11-15.

NOTES

¹ The words, ૯2ₚⲀⲒ ૯ⲦⲚ૯, "up toward heaven," are omitted in the translation here and in line 12.

² ⲀϤ૯Ⲓ may represent ⲀϤϤⲒ, "it produced," as suggested in Guillaumont, *Thomas,* 6. This conjecture is accepted in the translation.

P8 / *The Weeds*

Jesus said: The kingdom of the Father is like a man who had [good] seed. His enemy came by night; he sowed a weed among the good seed. The man did

not permit them to pull the weed. He said to them: Lest you go to pull up
the weed and you pull up the wheat with it. For on the day of harvest the
weeds will be clearly visible; they will be pulled up and burned.

ПЄ

ХЄ ЇС ХЄ ТМNTЄРО МПЄІѠТ' ЄСТN̄Т̄Ѡ
ΛΥΡѠΜΕ ΕΥΝ̄ΤΑЧ М̄ΜΑΥ Ν̄ΝΟΥ6ΡΟ6
[ЄΝΑΝΟΥ]Ч' ΑΠΕЧХΑХΕ ΕΙ Ν̄ΤΟΥѠΗ'
ΑЧΟΙΤΕ Ν̄ΟΥΖΙΖΑΝΙ[Ο]Ν ΜΝ ΠΕ6ΡΟ[6 Є]
ΤΝΑΝΟΥЧ' Μ̄ΠΕΠΡѠΜΕ ΚΟΟΥ Ε2ѠΛΕ
Μ̄ΠΖΙΖΑΝΙΟΝ ΠΕХΑЧ ΝΑΥ ХΕ ΜΗΠѠΟ
Ν̄ΤΕΤΝ̄ΒѠΚ ХΕ ΕΝΑ2ѠΛΕ Μ̄ΠΖΙΖΑΝΙΟ
Ν̄ΤΕΤΝ̄2ѠΛΕ Μ̄ΠΟΟΥΟ ΝΜ̄ΜΑЧ' 2Μ̄ ΦΟ
ΟΥ ΓΑΡ Μ̄ΠѠ2Ο Ν̄ΖΙΖΑΝΙΟΝ ΝΑΟΥѠΝ2
ΕΒΟΛ' ΟΕ2ΟΛΟΥ Ν̄ΟΕΡΟΚ2ΟΥ

Gospel of Thomas 57. CG II, 42.32-43.7.

PARALLELS

    Matt 13:24-30.

P9 / *The Rich Fool*

Jesus said: There was a rich man who had many possessions. He said: I will
use my possessions that I may sow and harvest and plant and fill my store-
houses with fruit, so that I will not be in want of anything. Those were the
thoughts in his heart, and in that night he died. Whoever has ears, let him
hear.

ΠΕХΕ ЇС

ХΕ ΝΕΥΝ̄ ΟΥΡѠΜΕ Μ̄ΠΛΟΥΟΙΟΟ ΕΥΝ̄ΤΑЧ Μ̄
ΜΑΥ Ν̄2Α2 Ν̄ХΡΗΜΑ ΠΕХΑЧ ХΕ ϯΝΑΡ̄ХΡѠ Ν̄
ΝΑХΡΗΜΑ ХΕΚΑΑΟ ΕΕΙΝΑХΟ Ν̄ΤΑѠΟ2ᴵ
Ν̄ΤΑΤѠ6Ε Ν̄ΤΑΜΟΥ2 Ν̄ΝΑΕ2ѠΡ Ν̄ΚΑΡ
ΠΟΟ ѠΙΝΑ ХΕ ΝΙΡ̄ 6ΡѠ2 ΛΛΑΥ ΝΑΕΙ ΝΕ
ΝΕЧΜΕΕΥΕ ΕΡΟΟΥ 2Μ̄ ΠΕЧ2ΗΤ' ΑΥѠ 2Ν̄
ΤΟΥѠΗ ΕΤΜ̄ΜΑΥ ΑЧΜΟΥ ΠΕΤΕΥΜ̄ ΜΑХΕ
Μ̄ΜΟЧ' ΜΑΡΕЧ'ΟѠΤΜ̄

Gospel of Thomas 63. CG II, 44.2-10.

PARALLELS

    Luke 12:16-21.

NOTES

¹ 2 before C̄ cancelled in N̄TA̅Ш̅C2, "and harvest."

P10 / *The Banquet* _____

Jesus said: A man had guests, and when he had prepared the dinner he sent his servant to invite the guests. He went to the first; he said to him: My master invites you. He said to him: I have money for some merchants.¹ They will come to me in the evening. I will go and give them orders. I ask to be excused from the dinner. He went to another; he said to him: My master has invited you. He said to him: I have bought a house and am required for a day. I will not have time. He went to another; he said to him: My master invites you. He said to him: My friend will be married and I am to prepare the banquet. I will not be able to come. I ask to be excused from the dinner. He went to another; he said to him: My master invites you. He said to him: I have bought a village;² I go to collect the rent. I will not be able to come. I ask to be excused. The servant came back to his master (and) said: Those whom you have invited to the dinner have asked to be excused. The master said to his servant: Go out to the roads; bring those whom you find so that they may dine. Buyers and merchants [shall] not [enter] the places of my Father.

ПЕХЕ I̅C̅ ХЕ ОУР〇
МЕ ΝΕΥ̅Ν̅ΤΑЧ 2Ν〇ЩΜΜΟ ΑΥШ Ν̅ΤΑΡΕЧCΟΒ
ΤΕ Μ̅ΠΔΙΠΝΟΝ ΑЧΧΟΟΥ Μ̅ΠΕЧ2Μ2ΑΛ ЩI
ΝΑ ΕЧΝΑΤШ2Μ Ν̅Ν〇ЩΜΜΟΕΙ ΑЧΒШΚ' Μ̅
Π〇〇ΡΠ ΠΕΧΑЧ ΝΑЧ ХЕ ΠΑΧΟΕΙC ΤШ2Μ
Μ̅ΜΟΚ' ΠΕΧΑЧ ХЕ ΟΥ̅Ν̅ΤΑΕΙ 2Ν̅2ΟΜΤ'
Α2ΕΝΕΜΠΟΡΟC CΕΝ̅ΝΗΥ ЩΑΡΟΕΙ ΕΡΟΥ2Ε
†ΝΑΒШΚ' Ν̅ΤΑΟΥΕ2CΑ2ΝΕ ΝΑΥ †ΠΑΡΑΙ
ΤΕΙ Μ̅ΠΔΙΠΝΟΝ ΑЧΒШΚ' ЩΑ ΚΕΟΥΑ ΠΕ
ΧΑЧ ΝΑЧ ХЕ ΑΠΑΧΟΕΙC ΤШ2Μ̅ Μ̅ΜΟΚ'
ΠΕΧΑЧ ΝΑЧ ХЕ ΑΕΙΤΟΟΥ ΟΥΗΕΙ ΑΥШ CΕ
Ρ̅ΑΙΤΕΙ Μ̅ΜΟΕΙ Ν̅ΟΥ2ΗΜΕΡΑ †ΝΑC̅Ρ̅ЧΕ Α̅
ΑЧΕΙ ЩΑ ΚΕΟΥΑ ΠΕΧΑЧ ΝΑЧ ХΕ ΠΑΧΟ
ΕΙC ΤШ2Μ̅ Μ̅ΜΟΚ' ΠΕΧΑЧ ΝΑЧ ХΕ ΠΑЩΒΗΡ
ΝΑ̅Ρ̅ ЩΕΛΕΕΤ ΑΥШ ΑΝΟΚ' ΕΤΝΑ̅Ρ̅ΔΙΠΝΟΝ
†ΝΑЩ I ΑΝ †Ρ̅ΠΑΡΑΙΤΕΙ Μ̅ΠΔΙΠΝΟΝ' ΑЧ'
ΒШΚ' ЩΑ ΚΕΟΥΑ ΠΕΧΑЧ ΝΑЧ ХΕ ΠΑΧΟΕΙC
ΤШ2Μ̅ Μ̅ΜΟΚ' ΠΕΧΑЧ ΝΑЧ' ХΕ ΑΕΙΤΟΟΥ Ν̅
ΟΥΚШΜΗ ΕΕΙΒΗΚ' ΑΧΙ Ν̅〇ЩΜ2ΑΛ †ΝΑЩ I
ΑΝ †Ρ̅ΠΑΡΑΙΤΕΙ ΑЧΕΙ Ν̅ϬΙ Π2Μ2ΑΛ ΑЧΧΟ
ΟC ΑΠΕЧ ΧΟΕΙC ХΕ ΝΕΝΤΑΚ'ΤΑ2ΜΟΥ Α̅
ΠΔΙΠΝΟΝ ΑΥΠΑΡΑΙΤΕΙ ΠΕΧΕ ΠΧΟΕΙC Μ̅

ΠΕϤ2Μ2ΑΛ ϪΕ ΒⲰΚ' ΕΠⳞΑ ΝΒΟΛ ΑΝ2ΙΟ
ΟΥΕ ΝΕΤΚΝΑ2Ε ΕΡΟΟΥ ΕΝΙΟΥ ϪΕΚΑΑⳞ
ΕΥΝΑⲢ̄ΔΙΠΝΕΙ Ν̄ΡΕϤΤΟΟΥ ΜΝ̄ ΝΕϢΟ
[ΤΕ ΕΥΝΑΒⲰ]Κ ΑΝ' Ε2ΟΥΝ' ΕΝΤΟΠΟⳞ Μ̄ΠΑΪⲰΤ'

Gospel of Thomas 64. CG II, 44.10-35.

PARALLELS

Matt 22:2-10, Luke 14:16-24.

NOTES
¹ Or, "Some merchants owe me money."
² Or, "farm."

P11 / *The Wicked Tenants*

He said: A good man had a vineyard. He gave it to farmers so that they might cultivate it and he might receive its fruit from them. He sent his servant so that the farmers might give him the fruit of the vineyard. They seized his servant (and) beat him. A little more and they would have killed him. The servant came (and) told his master. His master said: Perhaps they did not recognize him.¹ He sent another servant; the farmers beat him also. Then the master sent his son. He said: Perhaps they will respect my son. Since the farmers knew that he was the heir of the vineyard, they seized him (and) killed him. Whoever has ears, let him hear.

ΠΕϪΑϤ ϪΕ ΟΥΡⲰΜΕ Ν̄ΧΡΗ[ⳞΤΟ]Ⳟ ΝΕΥΝ̄[ΤΑϤ]
Ν̄ΟΥΜΑ Ν̄ΕΛΟΟΛΕ ΑϤΤΑΑϤ Ν̄[2]Ν̄ΟΥΟΕΙΕ
ϢΙΝΑ ΕΥΝΑⲢ̄ 2ⲰΒ' ΕΡΟϤ' Ν̄ϤϪΙ Μ̄ΠΕϤΚΑΡ'
ΠΟⳞ Ν̄ΤΟΟΤΟΥ ΑϤϪΟΟΥ Μ̄ΠΕϤ2Μ2ΑΛ ϪΕ
ΚΑΑⳞ ΕΝΟΥΟΕΙΕ ΝΑϯ ΝΑϤ' Μ̄ΠΚΑΡΠΟⳞ Μ̄
ΠΜΑ Ν̄ΕΛΟΟΛΕ ΑΥΕΜΑ2ΤΕ Μ̄ΠΕϤ2Μ2ΑΛ
ΑΥ2ΙΟΥΕ ΕΡΟϤ' ΝΕΚΕΚΟΥΕΙ ΠΕ Ν̄ⳞΕΜΟΟΥΤϤ'
ΑΠ2Μ2ΑΛ ΒⲰΚ' ΑϤϪΟΟⳞ ΕΠΕϤϪΟΕΙⳞ ΠΕ
ϪΕ ΠΕϤϪΟΕΙⳞ ϪΕ ΜΕϢΑΚ' Μ̄ΠΕϤ'ⳞΟΥⲰ
ΝΟΥ¹ ΑϤϪΟΟΥ Ν̄ΚΕ2Μ2ΑΛ ΑΝΟΥΟΕΙΕ 2Ι
ΟΥΕ ΕΠΚΕΟΥΑ ΤΟΤΕ ΑΠϪΟΕΙⳞ ϪΟΟΥ Μ̄
ΠΕϤϢΗΡΕ ΠΕϪΑϤ' ϪΕ ΜΕϢΑΚ' ⳞΕΝΑϢΙΠΕ
2ΗΤϤ' Μ̄ΠΑϢΗΡΕ ΑΝ'ΟΥΟΕΙΕ ΕΤΜΜΑΥ ΕΠΕΙ
ⳞΕⳞΟΟΥΝ ϪΕ Ν̄ΤΟϤ ΠΕ ΠΕΚΛΗΡΟΝΟΜΟⳞ
Μ̄ΠΜΑ Ν̄ΕΛΟΟΛΕ ΑΥ6ΟΠϤ' ΑΥΜΟΟΥΤϤ'

ΠΕΤΕΥΝ ΜΑΑΧΕ ΜΜΟϤ' ΜΑΡΕϤ'ϹΩΤΝ

Gospel of Thomas 65. CG II, 45.1-16.

PARALLELS

Mark 12:1-8, Matt 21:33-39, Luke 20:9-15a.

NOTES

¹ Emending ΜΠΕϤϹΟΥΩΝΟΥ, "he did not recognize them," to ΜΠΟΥϹΟΥΩΝϤ, "they did not recognize him." See Guillaumont, *Thomas*, 38 and Leipoldt, *Das Evangelium nach Thomas*, 44.

P12 / *The Pearl Merchant* _____

Jesus said: The kingdom of the Father is like a merchant who had merchandise (and) found a pearl. This merchant was wise. He sold the merchandise; he bought the one pearl for himself. You, also, seek for his treasure[1] which does not perish, but which endures, where no moth enters to devour and no worm destroys.

ΠΕΧΕ ΙϹ ΧΕ
ΤΜΝΤΕΡΟ ΜΠΕΙΩΤ' ΕϹΤΝΤΩΝ ΑΥΡΩΜΕ
ΝΕϢΩΩΤ' ΕΥΝΤΑϤ' ΜΜΑΥ ΝΟΥΦΟΡΤΙ
ΟΝ ΕΑϤϨΕ ΑΥΜΑΡΓΑΡΙΤΗϹ ΠΕϢΩΤ'
ΕΤΜΜΑΥ ΟΥϹΑΒΕ ΠΕ ΑΥϮ ΠΕΦΟΡΤΙΟΝ
ΕΒΟΛ ΑϤΤΟΟΥ ΝΑϤ' ΜΠΙΜΑΡΓΑΡΙΤΗϹ
ΟΥΩΤ' ΝΤΩΤΝ ϨΩΤ' ΤΗΥΤΝ ϢΙΝΕ Ν
ϹΑ ΠΕϤϨΟ¹ ΕΜΑϤϢΧΝ ΕϤΜΗΝ' ΕΒΟΛ
ΠΜΑ ΕΜΑΡΕΧΟΟΛΕϹ Τ2ΝΟ ΕϨΟΥΝ'ΕΜΑΥ
ΕΟΥΩΜ' ΟΥΔΕ ΜΑΡΕϤϤΝΤ ΤΑΚΟ

Gospel of Thomas 76. CG II, 46.13-22.

PARALLELS

MATT 13:45-46, 6:19-20, LUKE 12:33.

NOTES
¹ The second Ε is added above the line in the manuscript. Guillaumont, *Thomas*, 42, and Leipoldt, *Das Evangelium nach Thomas*, 46, suggest ΠΕϨΟ, "the treasure," as a correction.

55

P13 / *The Leaven* _____

Jesus [said]: The kingdom of the Father is like [a] woman. She took a little leaven; [she hid] it in dough (and) made large loaves of it. Whoever has ears, let him hear.

[ΠΕΧΕ] ⲓ̅ⲥ̅ ⲭⲉ ⲧⲙ̅ⲛ
ⲧⲉⲣⲟ ⲙ̅ⲡⲉⲓⲱⲧ ⲉⲥⲧⲛ̅ⲧⲱ[ⲛ ⲉⲟⲩ]ⲥ2ⲓⲙⲉ
ⲁⲥⲭⲓ ⲛ̅ⲟⲩⲕⲟⲩⲉⲓ ⲛ̅ⲥⲁⲉⲓⲣ [ⲁⲥ2ⲟ]ⲡϥ′ 2ⲛ̅
ⲟⲩϣⲱⲧⲉ ⲁⲥⲁⲁϥ ⲛ̅2ⲛ̅ⲛⲟ[6] ⲛ̅ⲟⲉⲓⲕ′
ⲡⲉⲧⲉⲩⲙ̅ ⲙⲁⲁⲭⲉ ⲙ̅ⲙⲟϥ ⲙⲁ[ⲣⲉϥⲥ]ⲱⲧⲙ′

Gospel of Thomas 96. CG II, 49.2-6.

Parallels

Matt 13:33, Luke 13:20-21.

P14 / *The Woman with a Jar of Meal* _____

Jesus said: The kingdom of the [Father] is like a woman carrying a jar full of meal. As she was walking [on a] distant road, the handle of the jar broke. The meal flowed out behind her on the road. She did not know (it). She had noticed no problem. When she came into her house, she put the jar down and found it empty.

ⲡⲉⲭⲉ ⲓ̅ⲥ̅ ⲭⲉ ⲧⲙ̅ⲛ̅ⲧⲉⲣⲟ ⲙ̅ⲡ[ⲉⲓⲱⲧ ⲉⲥ]ⲧⲛ̅
ⲧⲱⲛ ⲁⲩⲥ2ⲓⲙⲉ ⲉⲥϥⲓ 2ⲁ ⲟⲩ6ⲁ[ⲙⲉⲉⲓ] ⲉϥ′
ⲙⲉ2 ⲛ̅ⲛⲟⲉⲓⲧ′ ⲉⲥⲙⲟⲟϣⲉ 2[ⲛ̅ ⲟⲩ]2ⲓⲏ′
ⲉⲥⲟⲩⲏⲟⲩ ⲁⲡⲙⲁⲁⲭⲉ ⲙ̅ⲡ6ⲁⲙ[ⲉⲉⲓ] ⲟⲩ
ϣ6ⲡ′ ⲁⲡⲛⲟⲉⲓⲧ· ϣⲟⲩⲟ ⲛ̅ⲥⲱⲥ [2]ⲓ ⲧⲉ2ⲓ
ⲏ ⲛⲉⲥⲥⲟⲟⲩⲛ ⲁⲛ ⲡⲉ ⲛⲉⲙ̅ⲡⲉⲥⲉⲓⲙⲉ
ⲉ2ⲓⲥⲉ ⲛ̅ⲧⲁⲣⲉⲥⲡⲱ2 ⲉ2ⲟⲩⲛ ⲉⲡⲉⲥⲏⲉⲓ
ⲁⲥⲕⲁ ⲡ6ⲁⲙⲉ ⲉⲓ ⲁⲡⲉⲥⲏⲧ ⲁⲥ2ⲉ ⲉⲣⲟϥ ⲉϥ′
ϣⲟⲩⲉⲓⲧ′

Gospel of Thomas 97. CG II, 49.7-15.

Notes
    [1] The reconstruction of the text follows those of Guillaumont, *Thomas*, 48, and Leipoldt, *Das Evangelium nach Thomas*, 50.

P15 / *The Assassin*

Jesus said: The kingdom of the Father is like a man who wished to kill a powerful man. He drew his sword in his house and thrust it into the wall, so that he might know that his hand would be strong. Then he killed the powerful man.

ⲠⲈϪⲈ Ⲓ̅Ⲥ̅ ⲦⲘⲚ̅ⲦⲈⲢⲞ Ⲙ̅ⲠⲈⲒⲰⲦ'
ⲈⲤⲦⲚ̅ⲦⲰⲚ ⲈⲨⲢⲰⲘⲈ ⲈϤⲞⲨⲰϢ ⲈⲘⲞⲨⲦ
ⲞⲨⲢⲰⲘⲈ Ⲙ̅ⲘⲈⲄⲒⲤⲦⲀⲚⲞⲤ ⲀϤϢⲰⲖⲘ' Ⲛ̅
ⲦⲤⲎϤⲈ ϨⲘ̅ ⲠⲈϤⲎⲈⲒ ⲀϤϪⲞⲦⲤ̅ Ⲛ̅ⲦϪⲞ ϪⲈ
ⲔⲀⲀⲤ ⲈϤⲚⲀⲈⲒⲘⲈ ϪⲈ ⲦⲈϤϬⲒϪ' ⲚⲀⲦⲰⲔ'
ⲈϨⲞⲨⲚ ⲦⲞⲦⲈ ⲀϤϨⲰⲦⲂ̅ Ⲙ̅ⲠⲘⲈⲄⲒⲤⲦⲀⲚⲞⲤ

Gospel of Thomas 98. CG II, 49.21-26.

P16 / *The Lost Sheep*

Jesus said: The kingdom is like a shepherd who had a hundred sheep. One of them, the largest, strayed. He left the ninety-nine (and) sought after the one until he found it. After he had exerted himself so, he said to the sheep: I love you more than the ninety-nine.

ⲠⲈϪⲈ Ⲓ̅Ⲥ̅ ϪⲈ ⲦⲘⲚ̅ⲦⲈⲢⲞ ⲈⲤⲦⲚ̅ⲦⲰ̅
ⲈⲨⲢⲰⲘⲈ Ⲛ̅ϢⲰⲤ ⲈⲨⲚ̅ⲦⲀϤ' Ⲙ̅ⲘⲀⲨ Ⲛ̅ϢⲈ Ⲛ̅
ⲈⲤⲞⲞⲨ ⲀⲞⲨⲀ Ⲛ̅ϨⲎⲦⲞⲨ ⲤⲰⲢⲘ' ⲈⲠⲚⲞϬ ⲠⲈ
ⲀϤⲔⲰ Ⲙ̅ⲠⲤⲦⲈⲮⲒⲦ ⲀϤϢⲒⲚⲈ Ⲛ̅ⲤⲀ ⲠⲒⲞⲨⲀ
ϢⲀⲚⲦⲈϤϨⲈ ⲈⲢⲞϤ' Ⲛ̅ⲦⲀⲢⲈϤϨⲒⲤⲈ ⲠⲈϪⲀϤ'
Ⲙ̅ⲠⲈⲤⲞⲞⲨ[1] ϪⲈ ϮⲞⲨⲞϢⲔ' ⲠⲀⲢⲀ ⲠⲤⲦⲈⲮⲒⲦ'

Gospel of Thomas 107. CG II, 50.22-27.

PARALLELS

Matt 18:12-13, Luke 15:3-6.

NOTES

[1] **Ⲙ̅ⲠⲈⲤⲞⲨⲞⲨ** has been corrected in the text to **Ⲙ̅ⲠⲈⲤⲞⲞⲨ**, "to the sheep," the first **Ⲩ** being struck over.

P17 / *The Hidden Treasure*

Jesus said: The kingdom is like a man who had in his field a [hidden] treasure of which he was unaware. And [after] he died he left it to his [son. The] son (also) did not know. He inherited the field and sold [it. And the one] who bought it came, and while he was plowing he [found] the treasure. He began to lend money at interest to whomever he wished.

ⲡⲉϫⲉ ⲓ̅ⲥ̅ ϫⲉ ⲧⲙⲛ̅ⲧⲉⲣⲟ ⲉⲥⲧⲛ̅ⲧⲱⲛ ⲉⲩⲣⲱ
ⲙⲉ ⲉⲩⲛ̅ⲧⲁϥ [ⲙⲙ]ⲁⲩ ϩⲛ̅ ⲧⲉϥ'ⲥⲱⲱϫⲉ ⲛ̅ⲛⲟⲩ
ⲉϩⲟ ⲉϥ2[ⲏⲡ ⲉϥ]ⲟ ⲛ̅ⲁⲧⲥⲟⲟⲩⲛ' ⲉⲣⲟϥ ⲁⲩ
ⲱ ⲙ̅[ⲛ̅ⲛⲥⲁ ⲧ]ⲣⲉϥⲙⲟⲩ ⲁϥⲕⲁⲁϥ ⲙ̅ⲡⲉϥ'
[ϣ]ⲏⲣⲉ ⲛⲉⲡ]ϣⲏⲣⲉ ⲥⲟⲟⲩⲛ ⲁⲛ' ⲁϥϥⲓ'
ⲧⲥⲱϣϫⲉ ⲉⲧⲙ̅ⲙⲁⲩ ⲁϥⲧⲁⲁ[ⲥ ⲉⲃⲟⲗ ⲁⲩⲱ ⲡⲉⲛ]
ⲧⲁϩⲧⲟⲟⲩⲥ ⲁϥⲉⲓ ⲉϥⲥⲕⲁⲓ ⲁ[ϥϩⲉ] ⲁⲡⲉϩⲟ ⲁϥ
ⲁⲣⲭⲉⲓ ⲛ̅ϯ ϩⲟⲙⲧ' ⲉⲧⲙⲏⲥⲉ ⲛ[ⲛⲉⲧ]ϥⲟⲩⲟϣⲟⲩ

Gospel of Thomas 109. CG II, 50.31-51.3.

PARALLELS

R. Simon the son of Yohai, giving a parable, says: To what can this be compared? To a man to whom there had fallen as an inheritance a residence in a far off country which he sold for a trifle. The buyer, however, went and discovered in it hidden treasures and stores of silver and of gold, of precious stones and pearls. The seller, seeing this, began to choke with grief.

    Mekilta de-Rabbi Ishmael, Beshallah 2. Trans. from Lauterbach, *Mekilta de-Rabbi Ishmael*, 1:198.

R. Simeon b. Yohai taught: [The Egyptians were] like a man who inherited a piece of ground used as a dunghill. Being an indolent man, he went and sold it for a trifling sum. The purchaser began working and digging it up, and he found a treasure there, out of which he built himself a fine palace, and he began going about in public followed by a retinue of servants—all out of the treasure he found in it. When the seller saw it he was ready to choke, and he exclaimed, "Alas, what have I thrown away."

    Song of Songs r. 4.12.1. Trans. from Simon, *Midrash Rabbah* 9:219-220.

A man's gift maketh room for him, and bringeth him before great men (Prov. 18.16). Once R. Eliezer and R. Joshua and R. Akiba went to the harbour-area of Antiochia, to make a collection for (the support of) scholars. There was a man there of the name of Abba Judan, who used to provide maintainence liberally (for the needy). He subsequently became impoverished, and when he saw the Rabbis there, his face turned the colour of saffron. When he came to his wife, she said to him: 'Why is your face sickly?' Said he to her: 'My Rabbis are here, and I do not know what to do.' His wife, who was even more saintly than he said: 'We have nothing left except yon field. Go, sell half thereof, and give them (the proceeds).' They prayed for him, saying: 'May the Allpresent make good your deficiency!' After some days he went to plough the half field he had retained; and as he was ploughing, his cow fell and its leg was broken. When he went down to lift it up, the Holy One, blessed be He, gave light to his eyes, and he found a treasure there. Said he: 'My cow's leg was broken, but it turned out to be for my benefit.' When our Rabbis came there again, they inquired after him, saying: 'How is Abba Judan doing?' They answered him: 'He is Abba Judan (known as the possessor) of servants, Abba Judan of goats, Abba Judan of camels, Abba Judan of oxen! Who can catch a glimpse of Abba Judan?' When the latter heard (of the Rabbis' presence), he went out to meet them. Said they: 'How is Abba Judan doing?' Said he to them: 'Your prayer has produced fruit, and fruit from the fruit.' Said they to him: 'As you live, even though others gave more than you did, we wrote you down at the head (of the list).' Then they took him and gave him a seat with themselves, and they applied to him this verse, 'A man's gift maketh room for him, and bringeth him before great men.'

> Leviticus r. 5.4. Trans. from Israelstam and Slotki, Midrash Rabbah 4:66-67.

But often we experience things, of which we beforehand have not even dreamed, such as the story of the farmer who, while digging his orchard to plant fruit trees, happened upon a treasure and enjoyed prosperity beyond his hopes.

πολλάκις δὲ ἐνετύχομεν τούτοις, ἃ μηδ᾽ ὄναρ πρότερον εἴδομεν ὥσπερ γεωπόνον φασί τινες ὑπὲρ τοῦ τι τῶν ἡμέρων δένδρων φυτεῦσαι σκάπτοντα χωρίον θησαυρῷ περιτυχεῖν ἀνελπίστῳ χρησάμενον εὐτυχίᾳ.

> Philo, The Unchangeableness of God 20.91. Colson and Whitaker, Philo Judaeus, 3:54,56.

A certain farmer about to come to the end of his life and wishing his sons to gain experience in farming, called them and said: My sons, I am already departing from life; search and you will find all the things which are buried in my vineyard. Therefore, after the death of the father, they dug up the entire ground of the vineyard, supposing a treasure to be buried there somewhere. They did not find a treasure, but the vineyard, having been well-cultivated, produced many times more fruit.

The fable points out that labor is treasure to humans.

Γεωργός τις, μέλλων καταλύειν τὸν βίον, καὶ βουλόμενος
τοὺς ἑαυτοῦ παῖδας πεῖραν λαβεῖν τῆς γεωργίας,
προσκαλεσάμενος αὐτοὺς ἔφη· παῖδες ἐμοί, ἐγὼ μὲν ἤδη
τοῦ βίου ὑπέξειμι, ὑμεῖς δ᾽, ἅπερ ἐν τῇ ἀμπέλῳ μοι
κέκρυπται, ζητήσαντες, εὑρήσετε πάντα. Οἱ μὲν οὖν
οἰηθέντες θησαυρὸν ἐκεῖ που κατορωρύχθαι, πᾶσαν τὴν
τῆς ἀμπέλου γῆν μετὰ τὴν ἀποβίωσιν τοῦ πατρὸς
κατέσκαψαν· καὶ θησαυρῷ μὲν οὐ περιέτυχον, ἡ δὲ
ἄμπελος, καλῶς σκαφεῖσα, πολλαπλασίονα τὸν καρπὸν
ἀνέδωκεν.
ʽΟ μῦθος δηλοῖ, ὅτι ὁ κάματος θησαυρός ἐστι τοῖς ἀνθρώποις.
Fables of Aesop 98a. Halm, *Fabulae Aesopicae Collectae*, 49.

A farmer, about to die and wishing to make his children ex-
perienced in farming, summoned them and said: "My children, a
treasure lies in one of my vineyards." After his death they took
plows and mattocks and dug up all his land. They found no
treasure, but the vineyard returned to them many times more
produce.
The story points out that labor is treasure to humans.

᾽Ανὴρ γεωργὸς μέλλων τελευτᾶν καὶ βουλόμενος
τοὺς αὐτοῦ παῖδας ἐμπείρους ποιῆσαι τῆς
γεωργίας, μετακαλεσάμενος αὐτοὺς ἔφη· τεκνία
μου, ἐν ἑνί μου τῶν ἀμπελώνων θησαυρὸς
ἀπόκειται. Οἱ δὲ μετὰ τὴν αὐτοῦ τελευτὴν ὕννας
τε καὶ δικέλλας λαβόντες πᾶσαν αὐτῶν τὴν γεωργίαν
ὤρυξαν, καὶ τὸν μὲν θησαυρὸν οὐχ εὗρον, ἡ δ᾽ ἄμπελος
πολλαπλασίονα τὴν φορὰν αὐτοῖς ἀντεδίδου.
ʽΟ λόγος δηλοῖ, ὅτι ὁ κάματος θησαυρός ἐστι
τοῖς ἀνθρώποις.
Fables of Aesop 98b. Ibid.

Matt 13:44.

PROPHETIC AND APOCALYPTIC SAYINGS

Pro1 / *The Fruitfulness of the Kingdom* _____

As the elders who had seen John, the disciple of the Lord, related that they heard from him how the Lord taught concerning these times and said: The days will come in which vines shall grow, each having ten thousand branches, and on each branch ten thousand twigs and on each twig ten thousand shoots and on each shoot ten thousand clusters and on each cluster ten thousand grapes and each grape will produce twenty five metretes[1] of wine when pressed. And when one of the saints takes a cluster another will cry: I am better, take me, bless the Lord through me. In the same way (He said) that a grain of wheat will produce five quarts of the finest pure flour. And the other fruit trees and seeds and grass will produce proportionately. And all the animals will feed on the produce of the earth and be at peace and harmony with each other and in complete subjection to humanity.

Καθὼς οἱ πρεσβύτεροι μέμνηνται οἱ Ἰωάννην τὸν μαθητὴν τοῦ Κυρίου ἑωρακότες ἀκηκοέναι παρ' αὐτοῦ πῶς περὶ τῶν χρονῶν τούτων ἐδίδασκεν ὁ Κύριος καὶ ἔλεγεν· "Ἐλεύσονται ἡμέραι ἐν αἷς ἀμπελῶνες ἀναφύσονται καθ' ἕνα ἕκαστον μύρια κλήματα ἔχοντες, καὶ ἐν ἑνὶ ἑκάστῳ κλήνατι μυρίους ὄζους, καὶ ἐν ἑνὶ ἑκάστῳ ὄζῳ μυρίας οἰναρίδας, καὶ ἐν μιᾷ ἑκάστῃ οἰναρίδι μυρίους βότρυας, καὶ ἐν ἑνὶ ἑκάστῳ βότρυϊ μυρίους ῥῶγας, καὶ εἷς ἕκαστος ῥὼξ ἐκθλιβεὶς δώσει εἴκοσι πέντε μετρητὰς οἴνου. Καὶ καταλαβόντος τινὸς τῶν ἁγίων βότρυα, ἄλλος ἐπιβοήσει βότρυς. Ἐγὼ βελτίων, ἐμὲ λαβέ, δι' ἐμοῦ τὸν Κύριον εὐλόγει. Ὡσαύτως καὶ τὸν κόκκον τοῦ σίτου μυρίους ἀναφύσειν στάχυας, καὶ ἓν ἕκαστον στάχυα μυρίους ἕξειν κόκκους, καὶ ἓν ἕκαστον κόκκον πέντε χοίνικας σεμιδάλεως δώσειν καθαρᾶς, καὶ τὴν λοιπὴν δὲ ὀπώραν καὶ τὰ σπέρματα καὶ τὸν κόρτον κατ' ἀναλογίαν τούτοις ἀκολούθως. Καὶ πάντα τὰ ζῷα, τοῖς βρώμασι τούτοις χρώμενα τοῖς ἀπὸ γῆς λαμβανομένοις, εἰρηναῖα ἀλλήλοις καὶ ὁμόλογα γενήσεσθαι, ὑποτεταγμένα τοῖς ἀνθρώποις μετὰ πάσης ὑποταγῆς."

> Papias, Fragments. Irenaeus, *Adv. haer.* 5.33.3. Rousseau, *Contre les hérésies* 5:415,417.

PARALLELS

The whole earth will be tilled in righteousness then, and trees will be planted in it, and it will be filled with blessing. And all the trees of the earth will rejoice. And they will plant vines, and the vine which they plant will produce wine in abundance, and each measure of seed will produce thousands. Each measure of olives will produce up to ten measures[2] (of oil).

τότε ἐργασθήσεται πᾶσα ἡ γῆ ἐν δικαιοσύνη καὶ φυτευθήσεται δένδρον ἐν αὐτῇ, καὶ πλησθήσεται εὐλογίας. καὶ πάντα τὰ δένδρα τῆς γῆς ἀγαλλιάσονται· φυτευθήσεται, καὶ ἔσονται φυτεύοντες ἀμπέλους, καὶ ἡ ἄμπελος ἣν ἂν φυτεύσωσιν, ποιήσουσιν προχοῦς οἴνου χιλιάδας καὶ σπόρου ποιήσει καθ' ἕκαστον μέτρον, ἐλαίας ποιήσει ἀνὰ βάτους δέκα.

I Enoch 10.18-19. Black, Apocalypsis Henochi Graece, 26.

The earth also shall yield its fruit ten thousandfold and on each (?) vine there shall be a thousand branches, and each branch shall produce a thousand clusters, and each cluster produce a thousand grapes, and each grape produce a cor of wine.

II Baruch 29:5. Trans. of the Syriac from Charles, Pseudepigrapha, 497–498.

From the root of each tree up to its heart there were ten thousand branches with tens of thousands of clusters, and there were ten thousand clusters on each branch, and there were ten thousand dates in each cluster. And it was the same with the grape vines. There were ten thousand branches on each vine, and each branch had on it [ten thousand] bunches, and there were ten thousand grapes in each bunch. And there were tens of thousands of tens of thousands of other trees there, and their fruit was in the same proportion.

ϪΙΝ ΤΝΟΥΝΕ ΝΤΟΥΕΪ ΤΟΥΕΙ ϢΑ 2ΡΑΪ Ε ΠΕϹ2ΗΤ'
ΟΥΝ ΟΥΤΒΑ Ν̄2ΩΠϢ· 2ΙΧ̄ΝΟΥΤΒΑ Ν̄ΛΩΟΥ: Ε ΟΥΝ ΟΥΤΒΑ
Ν̄ΛΩΟΥ 2Ι Π2ΩΠϢ Π2ΩΠϢ· Ε ΟΥΝ ΟΥΤΒΑ Ν̄ΒΝΝΕ
2Ι ΠΛϢΟΥ ΠΛϢΟΥ· ΑΥΩ ΤΒΩ Ν ΕΛΟΟΛΕ ΟΝ ΚΑΤΑ ΤΕΙ
2Ε· Ε ΟΥΝ ΟΥΤΒΑ Ν̄ϢΛ2̄ 2Ν̄ ΤΒΩ Ν ΕΛΟΟΛΕ· ΑΥΩ
Ν̄ϹΜΑ2 2Μ̄ ΠϢΕΛ2̄ ΠϢΛ2̄· Ε ΟΥΝ ΟΥΤΒΑ Ν̄ΒΑΒΙΛΕ
2Μ̄ ΠΕϹΜΑ2 ΠΕϹΜΑ2· Ν̄ΚΕ ϢΗΝ ΤΗΡΟΥ 2ΕΝΤΒΑ
Ν̄ΤΒΑ ΝΕ· ΑΥΩ ΝΕΥΚΑΡΠΟϹ ΚΑΤΑ ΤΕΙ 2Ε·

Apocalypse of Paul 22 (fol. 29a). Budge, Miscellaneous Coptic Texts, 562.

Amos 9:13, Isa 25:6, Ezek 34:25–27.

NOTES
[1] The metrete was equal to about nine gallons.
[2] The word is βάτος, which corresponds to the Hebrew measure bath, which contained about five and a half gallons.

Pro2 / *The Coming of the Son of God*

And our Lord answered and said to us, "Take heed that men deceive you not
and that ye do not become doubters and serve other gods. Many will come
in my name saying "I am the Christ." Believe them not and draw not near to
them. For the coming of the Son of God will not be manifest, but like the
lightning which shineth from the east to the west, so shall I come on the
clouds of heaven with a great host in my glory; with my cross going before
my face will I come in my glory, shining seven times as bright as the sun will
I come in my glory, with all my saints, my angels, when my Father will place
a crown upon my head, that I may judge the living and the dead and
recompense every man according to his work."

> *Apocalypse of Peter* 1. Trans. of the Ethiopic from Hennecke-
> Schneemelcher, *N.T. Apoc.* 2:668.

PARALLELS

> But he answered, saying to us: Truly I say to you, I will come as
> the sun that shines, shining seven times brighter than it in my
> brightness; with the wings of the clouds [carrying] me in splendor
> and the sign of the cross before me, I will come down upon the
> earth to judge the living and the dead.

ⲀϤⲞⲨ

Ⲱⲱ̅ⲂⲈ ⲆⲈ ⲈϤⲬⲞⲨ Ⲙ̅ⲘⲀⲤ ⲚⲈⲚ ⲬⲈ ⲀⲘⲎⲚ ⲄⲀⲢ ϯ
ⲬⲞⲨ Ⲙ̅ⲘⲀⲤ ⲚⲎⲦⲚⲈ ⲬⲈ ϯⲚⲎⲨ ⲄⲀⲢ Ⲛ̅ⲦⲌⲈ Ⲛ̅ⲠⲢⲒ ⲈⲦ
ⲠⲢⲒⲰⲞⲨ ⲀⲞⲨ ⲈⲈⲒⲈ ⲚⲞⲨⲀⲈⲒⲚⲈ ⲚⲤⲀϤ Ⲛ̅ⲔⲰⲂ ⲠⲀ
ⲢⲀⲢϤ ⲌⲚ̅ ⲠⲀⲈⲀⲨ ⲈⲚⲦⲚ̅Ⲍ Ⲛ̅ⲔⲖⲞⲞⲖⲈ ϤⲒ[ⲞⲨⳠ]ⲀⲠ¹ ⲌⲀⲢⲀⲒ̈
ⲌⲚ̅ ⲞⲨⲈⲀⲨ ⲈⲠ̅ⲤⲎⲘⲈⲒⲞⲚ [Ⲛ̅ⲠⳠ]ⲦⲀⲨⲢⲞⲤ ⲌⲒⲦⲀⲈⲒ
ⲀⲞⲨ ϯⲚⲎⲨ ⲀⲌⲢⲎⲒ̈ ⲀⲬⲚ̅ ⲠⲔⲀⲌ ⲦⲀϯⲌⲈⲠ ⲀⲚⲈⲦⲀⲚⲌ
Ⲙ̅Ⲛ ⲚⲈⲦⲘⲀⲨⲦ·

> *Epistula Apostolorum* 9 (Ethiopic 16). Schmidt, *Gespräche Jesu*, 6*.

> When the Messiah comes, he will come in the form of a dove with
> the crown of doves around him, coming on the clouds of heaven
> with the sign of the cross going before him. The entire world will
> see him like the sun which shines from east to west. So he will
> come with all his angels around him.

ⲠⲬ̅Ⲥ̅ ⲀϤⲱⲀⲈⲒ, ⲀϤⲚ̅ⲚⲎⲨ Ⲛ̅-
ⲦⲌⲈ ⲚⲞⲨ̅ⲤⲀⲘⲚ̅Ⲧ Ⲛ̅ϬⲢⲀⲀⲘⲠⲈ, Ⲉ-ⲠⲔ''
ⲖⲀⲘ Ⲛ̅ϬⲢⲀⲀⲘⲠⲈ ⲔⲰⲦⲈ ⲀⲢⲀϤ, ⲈϤ-
ⲘⲀⲀⲌⲈ ⲌⲒⲬⲚ̅-ⲚⲔⲎⲠⲈ Ⲛ̅ⲦⲠⲈ, Ⲉ-ⲠⲘⲈ''
ⲈⲒⲚⲈ Ⲙ̅ⲠⲤⲦⲀⲨⲢⲞⲤ ⲤⲰⲔ ⲌⲎⲦϤ, Ⲉ-Ⲡ''
ⲔⲞⲤⲘⲞⲤ ⲦⲎⲢϤ ⲚⲀⲚⲞ ⲀⲢⲀϤ Ⲛ̅ⲦⲌⲈ Ⲙ̅-

ⲡⲣⲓ ⲉⲧⲣ̄-ⲟⲩⲁⲓ̈ⲛⲉ ϫⲛ̄-ⲛ̄ⲥⲁ ⲙⲡⲣ̄ⲣⲓⲉ
ϣⲁⲛⲥⲁ ⲛ̄ⲍⲱⲧⲛ. ⲧⲉⲓ̈ ⲧⲉ ⲧ2ⲉ ⲉⲧ4ⲛ̄ⲁ''
ⲛ̄ⲏⲩ, ⲉ-ⲛⲉ4ⲁⲅⲅⲉⲗⲟⲥ ⲧⲏⲣⲟⲩ ⲕⲱ''
ⲧⲉ ⲁⲣⲁ4.

> *Apocalypse of Elijah* 31.19-32.9. Steindorff, *Die Apokalypse des Elias,* 86,88².

Matt 16:27, 24:4–5, 23–27, 30–31, 26:64, Mark 8:38, 13:5–6, 21–22, 26–27, 14:62, Luke 9:26, 21:8, 27, 17:23–24, Dan 7:13, 2 Thess 1:7, Rev 1:17, 14:14, 2:23, 1 Pet 4:5, 2 Tim 4:1.

NOTES

¹ Schmidt had initially restored this 2ⲓ[ⲟⲩⲥ]ⲁⲡ, "immediately," but following the discovery of the Ethiopic suggests 4ⲓ, "carrying," instead of 2ⲓ, and translates the passage, "with the wings of the clouds [carrying] me in splendor." See *Gespräche Jesu,* 57, n. 8.

² For the Sahidic text, see Pietersma and Comstock, *The Apocalypse of Elijah,* 42.

Pro3 / *The Punishment of the Wicked* _____

Then will men and women come to the place prepared for them. By their tongues with which they have blasphemed the way of righteousness will they be hung up. There is spread out for them unquenchable fire. . .

And behold again another place: this is a great pit filled, in which are those who have denied righteousness; and angels of punishment visit (them) and here do they kindle upon them the fire of their punishment. And again two women: they are hung up by their neck and by their hair and are cast into the pit. These are they who plaited their hair, not to create beauty, but to turn to fornication, and that they might ensnare the souls of men to destruction. And the men who lay with them in fornication are hung by their thighs in that burning place, and they say to one another, "We did not know that we would come into everlasting torture."

Ezrael, the angel of wrath, brings men and women with the half of their bodies burning and casts them into a place of darkness, the hell of men; and a spirit of wrath chastises them with all manner of chastisement, and a worm that never sleeps consumes their entrails. These are the persecutors and betrayers of my righteous ones. And near to those who live thus were other men and women who chew their tongues, and they are tormented with red-hot irons and have their eyes burned. These are the slanderers and those who doubt my righteousness.

Other men and women—whose deeds (were done) in deception—have
their lips cut off and fire enters into their mouths and into their entrails.
<These are those> who slew the martyrs by their lying.[1]

> *Apocalypse of Peter* 7.9. Trans. of the Ethiopic from Hennecke-
> Schneemelcher, *N.T. Apoc.* 2:672-676.

PARALLELS

The prophet Elias bears witness to a vision: The angel of the
Lord, he says, showed me a deep valley, which is called Gehenna,
burning with brimstone and pitch. In this place the souls of many
sinners dwell and are tormented in different ways. Some suffer
hanging from the genitals, others by the tongue, some by the eyes,
others head downwards. The women are tormented in their
breasts, and the young hang from their hands. Some virgins are
roasted on a gridiron, and other souls undergo an unceasing
torment. The multiplicity of the torments answers to the diversity
of the sins of each. The adulterers and the corrupters of such as
are under age are tormented in their genitals. Those who hang
from their tongues are the blasphemers and false witnesses. They
have their eyes burned who have stumbled through their glances
and who have looked at foul things with craving for them. Head
downwards there hang those who have detested the righteousness
of God, who have been evil-minded, quarrelsome towards their
fellows. Rightly then are they burned according to the punishment imposed on them. If some women are punished with torment in their breasts, then these are women who for sport have
surrendered their own bodies to men, and for this reason these
also hang from their hands.

Denique testatur propheta helias uidisse: Ostendit, inquid, mihi
angelus domini conuallem altam quae uocatur gehenna ardens-
que sculphore et bitumine. Et in illo loco sunt multae animae
peccatorum et taliter ibi cruciantur diuersis tormentis: paciuntur
aliqui pendentes natura[e], alii autem linguis, quidam uero oculis,
alii inuersi pendentes, et foemine mammillis suis cruciabuntur, et
iuuenes manibus pendentes, quaedam in craticula uirgines
uruntur et quaedam figuntur animae perpetuae poenae. Per ipsa
uero uaria suppicia ostenditur uniuscuiusque actus: naturalium
dolor utique adulteri sunt et pederasti; qui autem linguis suspen-
duntur blasphemi sunt, falsi etiam testes; qui oculis uero creman-
tur hii sunt qui in uidendo scandalizati sunt respicientes in con-
cupiscencia reatu gesta; qui uero inuersi pendebant hii sunt

odientes iusticiam dei, praui consilii, nec quisquam fratri consentit, merito ergo poenis sentenciae uruntur; nam quod foeminae mammillis torqueri iubentur istae sunt quae in ludibrio corpus suum tradiderunt masculis, ideoque et ipsi iuxta erunt in tormentis manibus pendentes p < ropt > er hanc rem.

> Ps. Titus Epistle [2]. de Bruyne, "Epistula Titi," 58. Trans. from N.T. Apoc. 2:158.

R. Joshua said. "Once upon a time I was walking on my way, and I found Elijah — may his memory be for blessing. He said to me 'Do you want me to make you stand near the gate of Gehenna?' and I said to him 'Yes.' Then he showed me men hanging by their hands and men hanging by their tongues and men hanging by their eyes and men hanging by their ears. And he showed me men who were made to eat fiery coals and men who were sitting and alive, while worms were eating them. And he showed me men who were made to eat fine sand: they were made to eat it against their will, and their teeth were broken by the sand. And the Holy One blessed be He says to them 'You ate things that you stole in this world, and they were sweet in your mouth; but now you do not have the strength to eat — to confirm what is said 'I have broken the teeth of the wicked.'" (Ps. 3:8)

> Chronicles of Jerahmeel 14.4. Trans. from Stone and Strugnell, The Books of Elijah, Parts 1-2, 16, 18.

There are five law courts (?) established in Gehenna, and Isaiah the son of Amoz saw them all. He entered the first court, and saw, and behold men carrying buckets of water on their shoulders, and they kept filling them and emptying them into a well, but the well never fills and the men never die. He (Isaiah) said to Him (God), "Reveal the mystery, O Revealer of Mysteries, explain to me the vision." And the Holy Spirit answered and said to him "These are the men who coveted what was not theirs while they were in the world, and transgressed against what is written in the Torah 'You shall not covet.' (Ex. 20:17) Now they are brought here and judged here." He entered the second court and he saw there men hanging by their tongues; and he said to him "O Revealer of Mysteries, explain the vision to me." The Holy Spirit answered him "These are the men who slandered their companions while they were in the world, and transgressed what is written in the Torah 'You shalt not go up and down as a slanderer among your people' (Lev. 19:16). And now they are brought here and judged here." He entered the third court, and saw men hanging by their testicles. He said to Him "O Revealer of Mysteries, explain to me the vision." The

Holy Spirit answered him and said to him "These are the men who were in the world and afflicted the daughters of Israel (?), who are compared to a calf—as it is said 'Ephraim was a trained heifer' (Hos. 10:11)—and walked after the daughters of the uncircumcised, who are compared to asses—as it is said 'whose flesh is that of asses' (Ezek. 23:20)—and now they are brought here and judged thus." He entered the fourth court, and saw there daughters of iniquity hanging by the nipples of their breasts; and he said to Him "O Revealer of Mysteries, explain to me the vision." The Holy Spirit answered him and said to him: "These are the women who uncovered their hair and rent their veil and sat in the open market place to suckle their children, in order to attract the gaze of men and to make them sin; therefore they are punished thus." He entered the fifth court, and found it full of smoke. There were all the governors, the chiefs, and Pharaoh the wicked presiding over them and watching over the gate of hell, and he says to them, "Why did you not learn from me when I was in Egypt?" Thus he sits there and watches at the gatehouse of hell.

> *Chronicles of Jerahmeel* 16.1-5. Trans. from Stone and Strugnell,
> *The Books of Elijah*, 20,22.

He showed me[2] another chasm, into which I looked and saw souls, some hanging by the tongue, others by the hair, others by the hands, others by the feet upside down, and they were blackened with smoke and brimstone. That man who was with me replied concerning them: These souls which hang by the tongue are slanderers and ones who speak false and disgraceful words and are not ashamed. Those who hang by the hair are the shameless, who are totally without modesty and who go about in the world bare-headed. Those who hang by the hands are the ones who robbed and stole the goods of others and never gave anything to the needy nor helped the afflicted, and did this because they wanted to take everything and had no concern for justice and the law. Those who hang upside down by the feet are the ones who casually and willingly ran on evil ways and lawless paths, not visiting the sick nor accompanying those who depart this life. And for this reason each soul receives the things done by it.

Ἄλλο μοι χάσμα ἔδειξεν, εἰς ὃ παρακύψασα εἶδον ψυχὰς
τὰς μὲν κρεμαμένας διὰ τῆς γλώττης, τὰς δὲ διὰ τῶν πλοκάμων,
τὰς δὲ διὰ τῶν χειρῶν, τὰς δὲ διὰ τῶν ποδῶν κατὰ κεφαλῆς,
καὶ καπνὸν καὶ θεῖον καπνιζομένας· περὶ ὧν ἀπεκρίνατό μοι
ὁ ἀνὴρ ἐκεῖνος ὁ σὺν ἐμοὶ ὤν· Αἱ μὲν ψυχαὶ αὗται αἱ
κρεμασθεῖσαι διὰ τῆς γλώσσης διάβολοί εἰσιν, καὶ ψευδεῖς
λόγους καὶ αἰσχροὺς φθεγγόμεναι, καὶ μὴ αἰδούμεναι. αἱ

δὲ διὰ τῶν τριχῶν κρεμάμεναι ἄχρωμοί εἰσιν αἱ μηδ' ὅλως
αἰδούμεναι καὶ γυμνοκέφαλοι ἐν τῷ κόσμῳ περιάγουσαι· αἱ
δὲ διὰ τῶν χειρῶν κρεμασθεῖσαι αὐταί εἰσιν αἱ τὰ ἀλλότρια
ἀφελόμεναι καὶ κλέψασαι, καὶ μετρίοις μὴ ἐπιδοῦσαι μηδέποτε
μηδέν, μηδὲ ἐπαρκήσασαι τοῖς τεθλιμμένοις, ἀλλὰ τοῦτο
ἐποίουν τὰ πάντα λαμβάνειν θέλουσαι, καὶ μηδὲ ὅλως τῆς
δίκης καὶ τῆς νομοθεσίας φροντίδα ποιησάμεναι· αἱ δὲ
διὰ τῶν ποδῶν διάστροφοι κρεμάμεναι αὐταί εἰσιν αἱ κούφως
μὲν καὶ προθύμως τρέχουσαι ὁδοῖς πονηραῖς καὶ πορείαις
ἀτάκτοις, νοσοῦντας μὴ ἐπισκεπτόμεναι καὶ τοὺς ἐξιόντας
τοῦ βίου μὴ προκομίζουσαι, καὶ διὰ τοῦτο μία καὶ ἑκάστη
ψυχὴ ἀπολαμβάνει τὰ πεπραγμένα αὐτῇ.

Acts of Thomas 56. Lipsius-Bonnet, AAA 2.2:172-173.

And again he showed me another pit, and I looked down into it
and saw dreadful things, to which are destined to come the souls
that do evil; and I saw there many tortures which are prepared
for men and women and youths and maidens. Those men who
leave their own wives, and have intercourse with the wives of their
fellows; and women, who go beyond intercourse with their own
husbands; and youths who do not keep their laws, but wantonly
indulge themselves with harlots in their lust, and for whom it is
not enough to transgress the law among harlots, but lie in wait for
virgins and wantonly indulge in sin; and maidens, who have not
kept their state of virginity, (but), because of their wanton lust,
have brought shame upon their parents; — (these) shall come to
this affliction and shall be recompensed, each according to his
works.

Syriac Acts of Thomas 56. Trans. of the Syriac from Klijn, Acts of
Thomas, 94-95.

And I[3] looked and I saw another hole below in the pit, and it had
the appearance of blood. And I asked and said: Sir, what is this
place? And he said to me: All (the) punishments flow together into
this pit. And I saw men and women submerged up to their lips
and I asked: Who are these, sir? And he said to me: These are
magicians who dispensed magical charms to men and women and
made it impossible for them to find peace until they died. And
again I saw men and women with very black faces in the pit of
fire; and sighing and weeping I asked: Who are these, sir? And he
said to me: These are fornicators and adulterers who although
they had their own wives committed adultery; and similarly the
women committed adultery in the same way, though they had their
own husbands. Therefore unceasingly they pay the penalty. . . .

And again I saw there men and women set with lacerated hands and feet (or with hands and feet cut off) and naked in a place of ice and snow, and worms consumed them. And when I saw it I wept and asked: Who are these, Sir? And he said to me: They are those who harmed orphans and widows and the poor, and did not hope in the Lord; therefore they pay their own particular penalty unceasingly.

And I looked and saw others hanging over a channel of water and their tongues were very dry and much fruit was placed within their sight and they were not allowed to take of it; and I asked: Who are these, sir? And he said to me: They are those who broke their fast before the appointed hour; therefore they pay these penalties unceasingly.

And I saw other men and women suspended by their eyebrows and hair, and a river of fire drew (?) them; and I said: Who are these sir? And he said to me: They are those who did not give themselves to their own husbands and wives but to adulterers, and therefore they pay their own particular penalty unceasingly.

Et inspexi et uidi alium senem deorsum in fouea, et erat aspectus eius sicut < s > anguis, et interrogaui et dixi: Domine, quis est hic locus? Et dixit mihi: In istam foueam influunt omnes pene. Et uidi uiros ac mulieres dimersos usque ad labia et interrogaui: Qui sunt isti, domine? Et dixit mihi: Hii sunt malefici qui prestiterunt uiris ac mulieribus maleficia magica et non inuenerunt requiescere eos usque dum morirentur.

Et iterum uidi uiros hac mulieres uultu nigro ualde in fouea ignis, et suspiraui < et > ploraui et interrogaui: Qui sunt hii, domine? Et dixit mihi: Hii sunt fornicatores et mouechi qui abent< es > proprias uxores mechati sunt; similiter et mulieres eodem more mechauerunt abentes proprios uiros; propterea indeficienter persoluunt penas. . . .

Et iterum aspexi illic uiros ac mulieres incisis manibus et pedibus constitutos ac nudos in locum glacie et niue, et uermes comedebant eos. Videns autem ego ploraui et interrogaui: Qui sunt isti, domine? Et dixit mihi: Hii sunt qui orfanos et uiduas et pauperes nocuerunt et non sperauerunt in dominum, propter quod indeficienter persoluunt proprias penas.

Et respexi et uidi alios pendentes super canela aque, et lingue eorum siccae satis, et multi fructus constituti in conspectu eorum, et non permittebantur sumere ex his, et interrogaui: Qui sunt hii, domine? Et dixit mihi: Hii sunt qui ante constituta ora soluunt ieiunium: propterea indeficientur persoluunt as penas.

Et uidi alios uiros ac mulieres suspensos a superciliis et capillis suis et igneum flumen traebat eos et dixi: Qui sunt hii, domine? Et dixit mihi: Hii sunt comitentes se non propriis uiris ac mulieribus sed mecis, et ideo indeficienter persoluunt proprias penas.

Apocalypse of Paul 38-39. James, Apocrypha Anecdota 1:31-32. Trans. from *N.T. Apoc.* 2:782-783.

And the all holy one said: And who are these wrapped in fire up to their breasts? And the commander-in-chief said: These are those who cast their wives away and defiled them in adultery and, therefore, they are thus punished here.

And in another place the all holy one saw a man hanging by the feet, and worms were devouring him. And she asked the commander-in-chief: Who is this and what is his sin? And the commander-in-chief said: This is the one who received interest for his gold and, therefore, he is thus punished here.

And the all holy one saw in another place an iron tree, and it had iron branches, and a multitude of men and women hung on it by their tongues. And when she saw them, the all holy one wept and asked the commander-in-chief saying: Who are these and what is their sin? And the commander-in-chief said: These are perjurers, blasphemers, slanderers, whoever separated brothers from brothers.

Καὶ εἶπεν ἡ παναγία· Καὶ τίνες εἰσιν οὗτοι ἕως τοῦ στήθους ἐγκειμένοι εἰς τὸ πῦρ; καὶ εἶπεν ὁ ἀρχιστρά-τηγος· Οὗτοί εἰσιν οἵτινες τοὺς συνδέκνους ἔριψαν καὶ εἰς πορνείαν ἐρύπωσαν, καὶ διὰ τοῦτο ὧδε οὕτως κολάζονται.

Καὶ εἶδεν ἡ παναγία εἰς ἕτερον τόπον ἄνθρωπον κρεμάμενον ὑπὸ πόδας, καὶ σκώληκες κατήσθιον αὐτόν· καὶ ἠρώτησεν τὸν ἀρχιστράτηγον· Τίς ἐστιν οὗτος, καὶ τί τὸ ἁμάρτημα αὐτοῦ; καὶ εἶπεν ὁ ἀρχιστράτηγος· Οὗτός ἐστιν ὁ τόκον λαμβάνων ἐκ τοῦ χρυσίου αὐτοῦ, καὶ διὰ τοῦτο ὧδε οὕτως κολάζεται.

Καὶ ἴδεν ἡ παναγία εἰς ἕτερον τόπον δένδρον σιδηροῦν, καὶ εἶχεν κλώνους σιδηροῦς, καὶ ἐκρεμνοῦντο ἐν αὐτῷ πλῆθος ἀνδρῶν καὶ γυναικῶν ἐκ τῶν γλωσσῶν. καὶ ἰδοῦσα αὐτοὺς ἡ παναγία ἐδάκρυσεν, καὶ ἠρώτησεν τὸν ἀρχιστράτηγον

λέγουσα· Τίνες εἰσιν οὗτοι, καὶ τί τὸ ἁμάρτημα αὐτῶν;
καὶ εἶπεν ὁ ἀρχιστράτηγος· Οὗτοί εἰσιν ἐπίορκοι, βλάσφημοι,
καταλαληταὶ, οἵτινες ἐχώρισαν ἀδελφοὺς ἀπὸ ἀδελφῶν.

> *Apocalypse of the Virgin Mary*, 6, 9, 14. James, *Apocrypha Anecdota*
> 1:118-120.

NOTES

[1] The three passages quoted are selected from the extensive descriptions of the
punishments of the wicked given in the Ethiopic as predictions of Jesus. For the
priority of the Ethiopic over the Akhmim fragment in Greek, in which these descriptions take the form of a vision of Peter, see the discussion in *N.T. Apoc.* 2:665-666, and
the literature referred to there.

[2] A young woman is speaking.

[3] Paul is speaking.

Pro4 / *Keeping the Commandments* _____

The Judaikon[1] has here as follows: If you are in my bosom and do not do the
will of my Father who is in heaven, I will cast you out of my bosom.

Τὸ Ἰουδαϊκὸν ἐνταῦθα οὕτως ἔχει· "ἐὰν ἦτε ἐν τῷ κόλπῳ μου καὶ
τὸ θέλημα τοῦ πατρός μου τοῦ ἐν οὐρανοῖς μὴ ποιῆτε, ἐκ τοῦ
κόλπου μου ἀπορρίψω ὑμᾶς."

> *Gospel of the Nazaraeans* [5], in Cod. N.T. 1424 (at Matt 7:5). Aland,
> *Synopsis*, 93.

PARALLELS

> For this reason, if you do these things, the Lord said: If you are
> with me, even gathered in my bosom, and do not keep my com-
> mandments, I shall cast you out and say to you: Go away from me,
> I do not know you (nor) where you are from, you workers of
> iniquity.
>
> διὰ τοῦτο, ταῦτα ὑμῶν πρασσόντων, εἶπεν ὁ κύριος· Ἐὰν ἦτε μετ'
> ἐμοῦ συνηγμένοι ἐν τῷ κόλπῳ μου καὶ μὴ ποιῆτε τὰς ἐντολάς μου,
> ἀποβαλῶ ὑμᾶς καὶ ἐρῶ ὑμῖν· Ὑπάγετε ἀπ' ἐμοῦ, οὐκ οἶδα ὑμᾶς,
> πόθεν ἐστέ, ἐργάται ἀνομίας.
>
> > *II Clement* 4.5. Funk-Bihlmeyer, *Die Apostolischen Väter*, 73.

> Matt 7:23, 25:12, Luke 13:27, Ps 6:8.

NOTES

[1] or, "The Jewish Gospel."

Pro5 / *Not All Will Be Saved* _____

For he says: Not everyone who says to me, Lord, Lord, will be saved, but the one who does righteousness.

λέγει γάρ· Οὐ πᾶς ὁ λέγων μοι· Κύριε κύριε, σωθήσεται, ἀλλ'
ὁ ποιῶν δικαιοσύνην.

> *II Clement* 4.2. Funk-Bihlmeyer, *Die Apostolischen Väter*, 72.

PARALLELS

> Matt 7:21, Luke 6:46.

Pro6 / *Divisions and Factions* _____

For he said: Many will come in my name, outwardly clothed in sheep skins, but inwardly they are ravenous wolves. And: There will be divisions and factions. And: Beware of false prophets, who will come to you, outwardly clothed in sheep skins, but inwardly they are ravenous wolves. And: Many false messiahs and false apostles will arise and deceive many of the faithful.

εἶπε γάρ· Πολλοὶ ἐλεύσονται ἐπὶ τῷ ὀνόματι μου, ἔξωθεν
ἐνδεδυμένοι δέρματα προβάτων, ἔσωθεν δέ εἰσι λύκοι
ἅρπαγες. καί· Ἔσονται σχίσματα καὶ αἱρέσεις. καί·
Προσέχετε ἀπὸ τῶν ψευδοπροφητῶν, οἵτινες ἐλεύσονται
πρὸς ὑμᾶς, ἔξωθεν ἐνδεδυμένοι δέρματα προβάτων, ἔσωθεν
δέ εἰσι λύκοι ἅρπαγες. καί· Ἀναστήσονται πολλοὶ
ψευδόχριστοι καὶ ψευδοαπόστολοι, καὶ πολλοὺς τῶν
πιστῶν πλανήσουσιν.

> Justin, *Dial.* 35.3. Goodspeed, *Die ältesten Apologeten*, 130.

PARALLELS

> as also our Lord and Saviour Jesus said: There shall be heresies and schisms: and again: Woe unto the world because of scandals. For it must needs be that scandals and schisms come: yet woe to the man by whom they come.
>> *Didascalia* 6.5. Trans. of the Syriac from Connolly, *Didascalia Apostolorum*, 197-198.

> There shall be divisions and factions among you.
>
> Ἔσονται ἐν ὑμῖν αἱρέσεις καὶ σχίσματα.
>> Didymus, *De Trinitate* 3.22. PG 39:920.

> Above all, it is appropriate we know that he and his representatives foretold that there would be many sects.

ante omnia scire nos conuenit et ipsum et legatos eius praedixisse
quod plurimae sectae haberent existere.

Lactantius, *Div. inst.* 4.30. Brandt, *Lactanti opera omnia* 1:394.

Matt 24:5, 7, 15, 1 Cor 11:18, 19, Gal 5:20, Matt 10:35, Luke 12:53,
Matt 24:11, Mark 13:22, 2 Cor 11:13.

Pro7 / *The Circumstances of Judgment*

Therefore our Lord Jesus Christ also said: In whatever circumstances I come
upon you, in them I will also judge you.

διὸ καὶ ὁ ἡμέτερος κύριος 'Ιησοῦς Χριστὸς εἶπεν· 'Εν οἷς
ἂν ὑμᾶς καταλάβω, ἐν τούτοις καὶ κρινῶ.

Justin, *Dial.* 47.5. Goodspeed, *Die ältesten Apologeten,* 146.

PARALLELS[1]

What the Lord said: As you are found, you will be taken up.

quid dixerit Dominus: Sicut inveniemini assumemini.
Liber Graduum 15.4. Kmosko, PatSy 1.3:343.

As you are found, he said, you will be taken up.

sicut, ait, inventi fueritis, assumemini.
Liber Graduum 3.3. Ibid., 51.

For, he says, in whatever circumstances I find you, in them I will
also judge you.

ἐφ' οἷς γὰρ ἂν εὕρω ὑμᾶς, φησίν, ἐπὶ τούτοις καὶ κρινῶ·
Clement, *Quis div. salv.* 40. Stählin-Früchtel, *Clemens,* 3²:186.

heeding God who said through the prophet: In whatever circumstance I find you, in it I will also judge you.

ἀκούσας τοῦ θεοῦ διὰ τοῦ προφήτου εἰπόντος, ὅτι "'Εν ᾧ εὕρω σε, ἐν
ἐκείνῳ καὶ κρινῶ σε."
Ps. Athanasius, *Quaestiones ad Antiochum* 36. PG 28:617.

Ah me, ah me. Where then was the word of Ezekiel that he should
say to them: In whatever circumstance I find you, in it I will also
judge you, says God.

Οἴ μοι, οἴ μοι, ποῦ ἦν τότε ἡ τοῦ 'Ιεζεκιὴλ φωνή, ἵνα

εἴπῃ πρὸς αὐτούς, ὅτι 'Εν ᾧ εὕρω σε, ἐν αὐτῷ καὶ κρινῶ σε, εἶπεν ὁ θεός.

Johannes Climacus, *Scala paradisi*, 7.16. PG 88:812.

In whatever state he finds each one, in it he will judge, as he declares by the prophetic word through Ezekiel.[2]

in quo quemque invenerit, in eo sit judicaturus, quod prophetica per Ezechielem voce testatur.

Evagrius, *Athanasius' Vita S. Antonii* 15. PL 73:136.

As I find you, he says, so I will judge you.

Οἷον γὰρ εὕρω σε, φησί, τοιοῦτόν σε κρινῶ.

Basil, Epistle 42, *Ad Chilonem*. PG 32:349-350.

Just as the Lord finds you when he calls you, so also he judges you.

qualem te inuenit Dominus cum uocat talem pariter et iudicat.

Cyprian, *De mortalitate* 17. Hartel, *Cypriani opera omnia* 1:308.

The Lord judges each one as he finds him.

Unumquemque judicat Deus sicut invenerit.

Jerome, Letter 122, *to Rusticus*, PL 22:1044.

Ezek 7:8, 18:30, 33:20.

NOTES

[1] Other parallels, mostly from later centuries, were collected by Resch. See *Agrapha²*, 322–324.

[2] The saying occurs in Evagrius' Latin translation, but not in the Greek of Athanasius.

Pro8 / *Passion and Resurrection Predicted* _____

And Christ, while he (John) was still sitting by the Jordan river, came and brought an end to his prophesying and baptizing and also himself preached, saying that the kingdom of heaven was near and that he must suffer many things from the scribes and Pharisees and be crucified and rise on the third day and appear again in Jerusalem and then eat and drink again with his disciples, and foretold in the time between his (first and second) advent, as I have said before, that priests[1] and false prophets would appear in his name.

καὶ Χριστὸς ἔτι αὐτοῦ καθεζομένου ἐπὶ τοῦ 'Ιορδάνου

ποταμοῦ ἐπελθὼν ἔπαυσέ τε αὐτὸν τοῦ προφητεύειν καὶ
βαπτίζειν, καὶ εὐηγγελίζετο, καὶ αὐτὸς λέγων ὅτι ἐγγύς
ἐστιν ἡ βασιλεία τῶν οὐρανῶν, καὶ ὅτι δεῖ αὐτὸν πολλὰ
παθεῖν ἀπὸ τῶν γραμματέων καὶ Φαρισαίων, καὶ σταυρωθῆναι
καὶ τῇ τρίτῃ ἡμέρᾳ ἀναστῆναι, καὶ πάλιν παραγενήσεσθαι
ἐν Ἰερουσαλὴμ καὶ τότε τοῖς μαθηταῖς αὐτοῦ συμπιεῖν
πάλιν καὶ συμφαγεῖν, καὶ ἐν τῷ μεταξὺ τῆς παρουσίας
αὐτοῦ χρόνῳ, ὡς προέφην, γενήσεσθαι ἱερεῖς[1] καὶ ψευδο-
προφήτας ἐπὶ τῷ ὀνόματι αὐτοῦ προεμήνυσε, . . .

> Justin, *Dial.* 51.2. Goodspeed, *Die ältesten Apologeten*, 150–151.

PARALLELS

And after the resurrection he ate and drank with them as a person
in the flesh; although, he was united in spirit with the Father.

μετὰ δὲ τὴν ἀνάστασιν συνέφαγεν αὐτοῖς καὶ συνέπιεν
ὡς σαρκικός, καίπερ πνευματικῶς ἡνωμένος τῷ πατρί.

> Ignatius, *Smyrnaeans* 3.3. Funk-Bihlmeyer, *Die Apostolischen Väter*, 106.

but after showing himself to them, that truly—not in
appearance—he was raised, he also ate and drank with them
throughout the whole forty days.

ἀλλὰ καὶ μετὰ τὸ ἐπιδεῖξαι ἑαυτὸν αὐτοῖς ὅτι ἀληθῶς
ἀλλ' οὐ τὸ δοκεῖν ἐγήγερται, καὶ συνέφαγεν αὐτοῖς καὶ
συνέπιεν ἄχρις ἡμερῶν ὅλων τεσσαράκοντα·

> Ps. Ignatius, *Smyrnaeans* 3. Lightfoot, *The Apostolic Fathers* 2.3:220.

To him who gave us himself as a pledge of the resurrection, who
was taken up into heaven by the power of his God and Father in
our sight, who ate and drank with him for forty days after he rose
from the dead, . . .

τῷ δόντι ἡμῖν ἀρραβῶνα τῆς ἀναστάσεως ἑαυτὸν καὶ εἰς
οὐρανοὺς ἀναληφθέντι διὰ τῆς δυνάμεως τοῦ θεοῦ καὶ πατρὸς
αὐτοῦ ἐπ' ὄψεσιν ἡμετέραις τοῖς συμφαγοῦσιν αὐτῷ καὶ συμπιοῦσιν
ἐπὶ ἡμέρας τεσσαράκοντα μετὰ τὸ ἀναστῆναι αὐτὸν ἐκ νεκρῶν.

> *Apostolic Constitutions* 6.30. Funk, *Didascalia et Constitutiones Apostolorum*, 383, 385.

Mark 8:31, 9:31, 10:33-34, Matt 16:21, 17:22–23, 20:18–20, Luke
9:22, 18:31–33, 24:7, Acts 10:41.

NOTES
[1] Goodspeed suggests the emendation αἱρέσεις, sects or factions.

Pro9 / Called and Elect

Faith is not one but diverse. Therefore the Savior says: May it be done according to your faith. Whence also it is said that the people of the "calling" will be deceived at the coming of the Antichrist, but this is impossible for the "elect." Therefore he says: And if possible, my elect. Again when he says: Go out from the house of my Father, he is speaking to the "called."[1]

Ἡ πίστις οὐ μία, ἀλλὰ διάφορος. ὁ γοῦν σωτήρ φησι·
"γενηθήτω σου κατὰ τὴν πίστιν·" ὅθεν εἴρηται τοὺς μὲν
τῆς κλήσεως ἀνθρώπους κατὰ τὴν παρουσίαν τοῦ
ἀντιχρίστου πλανηθήσεσθαι· ἀδύνατον δὲ τοὺς ἐκλεκτούς·
διό φησι· καὶ εἰ δύνατον τοὺς ἐκλεκτούς μου." πάλιν
ὅταν λέγῃ "ἐξέλθετε ἐκ τοῦ οἴκου τοῦ πατρός μου,"[1]
τοῖς κλητοῖς λέγει.

Clement, *Exc. ex Theod.* 9.2. Stählin-Früchtel, *Clemens* 3²:109.

PARALLELS

John 2:14–16, Mark 11:15–17, Matt 21:12–13, Luke 19:45–46.

NOTES
[1] Our concern is with this last saying, the first two sayings being close parallels to Matt 22:14 and 24:24. The saying is difficult to categorize because of the absence of a more specific context. It is best viewed as prophetic.

Pro10 / White-washed Tombs

This, he says, is what is said: You are white-washed tombs, filled inside, he says, with bones of the dead, because the man who lives is not in you.[1] And again he says: The dead will spring up from the graves, that is, from earthly bodies, regenerated as spiritual, not as fleshly persons. This, he says, is the resurrection which takes place through the gate of heaven, through which, he says, all those who do not enter remain dead.

τοῦτο, φησίν, ἐστὶ τὸ εἰρημένον· "τάφοι ἐστὲ
κεχονιαμένοι, γέμοντες," φησίν, "ἔσωθεν ὀστέων νεκρῶν,"
ὅτι οὐκ ἔστιν ἐν ὑμῖν ἄνθρωπος ὁ ζῶν· καὶ πάλιν,
φησίν, "ἐξαλοῦνται ἐκ τῶν μνημείων οἱ νεκροί,"
τουτέστιν ἐκ τῶν σωμάτων τῶν χοϊκῶν ἀναγεννηθέντες
πνευματικοί, οὐ σαρχικοί. αὕτη, φησίν, ἐστὶν ἡ
ἀνάστασις ἡ διὰ τῆς πύλης γινομένη τῶν οὐρανῶν,
δι᾽ ἧς οἱ μὴ εἰσελθόντες, φησί, πάντες μένουσι νεκροί.

Naassene Exegesis. Hippolytus, *Ref.* 5.8.23–24. Wendland, *Hippolytus* 3:93.

PARALLELS

Matt 23:27, John 5:28.

NOTES

¹ The extent of the first saying is difficult to determine with certainty. Wendland considered it to end with the words "bones of the dead." It is possible, however, that the clause, "because the man who lives is not in you," was viewed as part of the saying in Naassene circles.

Pro11 / *Crucifying the World* _____

Jesus, the living one, answered and said to his apostles: Blessed is the one who has crucified the world and has not permitted the world to crucify him.

ⲀⲓⲤ ⲠⲈⲦⲞⲚⲈ̣ ⲞⲨⲰⲰ̅Ⲃ ⲠⲈⲬ[Ⲁϥ]
ⲚⲚⲈϥⲀⲠⲞⲤⲦⲞⲖⲞⲤ ⲬⲈ-ⲚⲀⲓⲀⲦϥ
ⲘⲠⲈⲚⲦⲀϥⲀ[Ⲱ]Ⲧ]-ⲠⲔⲞⲤⲘⲞⲤ ⲀⲨⲰ
ⲘⲠⲈϥⲔⲀ-ⲠⲔⲞⲤⲘⲞⲤ ⲈⲀⲰⲦϥ

The First Book of Jeu 1. Schmidt-Macdermot, *The Books of Jeu*, 39–40.

PARALLELS

Gal 6:14.

Pro12 / *Weak and Strong* _____

For he said to us when he was preaching: The weak will be saved through the strong.

προέλεγε γὰρ ἡμῖν, ὅτε ἐδίδασκεν, ὅτι τὸ ἀσθενὲς διὰ
τοῦ ἰσχυροῦ σωθήσεται.

Apostolic Church Ordinances 26. Preuschen, *Antilegomena*, 27.

Pro13 / *Children of Cain* _____

Our redeemer said to them, "You are the children of Cain, and not the children of Abraham."

Aphrahat, *Demonstration* 16.8 (*De gentibus*). Trans. of the Syriac from Neusner, *Aphrahat and Judaism*, 67.

Parallels

Matt 3:9, Luke 3:8, John 8:33, 37, 39–44.

Pro14 / *Beatitudes and Woes*

And blessed are they that have hungered and thirsted,
for they will be filled there.
And woe to them that are full, for they shall hunger
and thirst there.
And blessed are they that have mourned and wept, for
they will laugh and be comforted there.
And woe to those who laugh now, for they shall mourn
and weep unceasingly there.
And blessed are those who have shown mercy, for they shall
be shown mercy there.
And woe to those who have not shown mercy, for they
will not be shown mercy.

καὶ μακάριοι οἱ πεινάσαντες καὶ διψήσαντες,
ὅτι ἐκεῖ χορτασθήσονται.
καὶ οὐαὶ οἱ ἐμπεπλησμένοι, ὅτι ἐκεῖ
πεινάσουσι καὶ διψήσουσι.
καὶ μακάριοι οἱ πενθήσαντες καὶ κλαύσαντες,
ὅτι ἐκεῖ γελάσουσι καὶ παρακληθήσονται.
καὶ οὐαὶ οἱ γελῶντες νῦν, ὅτι ἐκεῖ
πενθήσουσι καὶ κλαύσουσιν ἀπαύστως.
καὶ μακάριοι οἱ ἐλεήσαντες, ὅτι ἐκεῖ
ἐλεηθήσονται.
καὶ οὐαὶ τοῖς μὴ ἐλεήσασιν, ὅτι οὐκ
ἐλεηθήσονται.

> Ps. Ephrem, *Sermo compunctorius.* Assemanus, *Ephraem Syri, opera omnia* 1:30 E.

Parallels

Matt 5:4–7, Luke 6:21, 25.

Pro15 / *The Purification of the Kingdom*

Since he is Lord of the kingdom, he has resolved to purify it himself, the higher and lofty regions at the same time as the lower. That which He says:

He will purify the house of his kingdom of every cause of sin, concerns the earth and its creatures. For he will renew them and make his just ones dwell there.

> Ephrem, *Commentary on the Diatessaron* 18.7. Trans. based on Leloir's French rendering of the Armenian, *Commentaire de l'Évangile Concordant*, 319.

PARALLELS

Matt 13:41, 2 Pet 3:13.

Pro16 / *Predictions of the End* ─────────────

Just as the true prophet has said to us: First it is necessary that a false gospel come through some deceiver, and then, after the destruction of the holy place, that the true gospel be spread secretly in order to correct the heresies which are to come. And after these things, at the end, it is again necessary first for the antichrist to come and then for the true Christ, our Jesus, to re-appear, and after this, when eternal light will have arisen, all the things of darkness will disappear.

οὕτως δή, ὡς ὁ ἀληθὴς ἡμῖν προφήτης εἴρηκεν, πρῶτον
ψευδὲς δεῖ ἐλθεῖν εὐαγγέλιον ὑπὸ πλάνου τινὸς καὶ εἶθ'
οὕτως μετὰ καθαίρεσιν τοῦ ἁγίου τόπου εὐαγγέλιον ἀληθὲς
κρύφα διαπεμφθῆναι εἰς ἀπανόρθωσιν τῶν ἐσομένων αἱρέσεων·
καὶ μετὰ ταῦτα πρὸς τῷ τέλει πάλιν πρῶτον ἀντίχριστον
ἐλθεῖν δεῖ καὶ τότε τὸν ὄντως Χριστὸν ἡμῶν Ἰησοῦν
ἀναφανῆναι καὶ μετὰ τοῦτο αἰωνίου φωτὸς ἀνατείλαντος
πάντα τὰ τοῦ σκότους ἀφανῆ γενέσθαι.

> *Ps. Clementine Homilies* 2.17. Rehm-Irmscher, *Homilien*, 42.

PARALLELS

Mark 13:2, 6, 14, 22, 26, Matt 24:2, 5, 11, 14, 15, 23–25, 30, Luke 21:6, 8, 20, 27.

Pro17 / *The Good Things to Come* ─────────────

And Peter answered: The Prophet of truth said: It is necessary for good things to come, and blessed, he says, is the one through whom they come. Likewise it is necessary that evil things come, but woe to him through whom they come.

καὶ ὁ Πέτρος ἀπεκρίνατο ὅτι· Ὁ τῆς ἀληθείας προφήτης ἔφη·
"Τὰ ἀγαθὰ ἐλθεῖν δεῖ, μακάριος δὲ (φησίν) δι᾽ οὗ ἔρχεται·
ὁμοίως καὶ τὰ κακὰ ἀνάγκη ἐλθεῖν, οὐαὶ δὲ δι᾽ οὗ ἔρχεται."

Ps. Clementine Homilies 12.29. Rehm-Irmscher, Homilien, 189.

PARALLELS

And Peter answered me: Our Lord Jesus Christ, the Son of God,
said: It is necessary that good things come, and blessed, he says,
is he through whom they come. Likewise it is necessary that evil
things come, but woe to him through whom they come.

Καὶ ὁ Πέτρος μοι ἀπεκρίνατο· Ὁ Κύριος ἡμῶν Ἰησοῦς Χριστὸς
ὁ Υἱὸς τοῦ Θεοῦ ἔφη· Τὰ ἀγαθὰ ἐλθεῖν δεῖ. Μακάριος δὲ, φησὶ,
δι᾽ οὗ ἔρχεται. Ὁμοίως ἀνάγκη καὶ τὰ κακὰ ἐλθεῖν· οὐαὶ δὲ
δι᾽ οὗ ἔρχεται.

Clementine Epitome 96. PG 2:540.

This reflection has befallen me at this time concerning the shak-
ing that is to take place at this time, and the host that has
assembled itself for the sword. The times were disposed beforehand by God. The times of peace are fulfilled in the days of the
good and just; and the times of many evils are fulfilled in the days
of the evil and transgressors. For it is thus written: Good must
happen, and blessed is he through whom it shall come to pass;
and evil must happen, but woe to him through whom it shall
come to pass.

Aphrahat, Demonstration 5.1 (De bellis). Trans. of the Syriac from Gwynn,
NPNF, 2nd ser. 13:352.

The Good is destined to come; blessed is the one through whom
it comes. Evil also is about to take place; woe to the one because
of whom it comes.

ⲠⲀⲄⲀⲐⲞⲚ ⲤⲆⲚⲎⲨⲦ ⲀⲈⲒ ⲚⲈⲒⲈ̄Ⲧ̄ϥ ⲘⲠⲈⲦϥ̄ⲚⲎⲨ Ⲏ̄ⲒⲦⲞⲞ[Ⲧϥ] ⲠⲈ
Ⲧ̄ⲆⲀⲨ ⲀⲚ ⲆⲀⲚⲦ̄ Ⲇ̄ϢⲰⲠⲈ ⲞⲨⲀⲒ̄ ⲘⲠⲈⲦϥ̄ⲚⲎⲨ ⲚⲦⲈϥⲀ̄Ⲇ̄Ⲁ̄[Ⲓ6]Ⲉ

Manichaean Psalm-Book, Ps. 239.27–28. Allberry, A Manichaean Psalm-
Book, 39.

Matt 18:7, Luke 17:1.

Pro18 / *The Victory Prize*

The Lord said: After you have been wounded and flogged, if you prevail and
rise up from the contest and accept the prize of victory and go forth from

this age with the same victory prize, your failures will not be mentioned, but as you are found in victory, you will be taken up with garlands.[1]

dixit Dominus: Postquam percussistis et vapulastis, si viceritis et ascenderitis ex agone et bravium acceperitis et cum ipso bravio exieritis ex hoc saeculo: non memorabuntur defectus vestri, sed quemadmodum inventi fueritis in victoria, assumemini coronati.

> *Liber Graduum* 3.3. Kmosko, PatSy 1.3:51.

PARALLELS

1 Cor 9:24–27, James 1:12, Rev 2:10.

NOTES

[1] Concerning the last two clauses, see Justin, *Dial.* 47.5 and parallels [Pro6].

Pro19 / *Worthy of the Paraclete* _____

Therefore the Paraclete is coming, of whom the world is not worthy and whom no one is able to receive unless he become a stranger to the world, as the Lord said: The world is not worthy of the Paraclete, but the children of the age who are just are worthy of gifts of union (with Him).

Venit igitur Paraclitus, cuius mundus incapax est et quem nemo accipere potest, nisi peregrinus factus sit mundo, sicut dixit Dominus: Incapax est mundus Paracliti, sed doni commixtionis capaces sunt filii saeculi, qui iusti sunt.

> *Liber Graduum* 5.18. Kmosko, PatSy 1.3:131.

PARALLELS

John 14:16–17, 15:19.

Pro20 / *Self-knowledge Is Blessed* _____

A man called down to the world, saying: Blessed is he who will know his soul.

ⲀⲨⲢⲰⲘⲈ ⲘⲞⲨⲦⲈ ⲀⲠⲒⲦⲚ̄ ⲀⲠⲔⲞ
ⲤⲘⲞⲤ· ϪⲈ ⲚⲈⲒ̈ⲈⲦϥ̄ Ⲙ̄ⲠⲈⲦⲀⲢⲚⲞⲒ̈Ⲉ Ⲛ̄ⲦⲈϥⲮⲨⲬⲎ

> *Psalms of Thomas* 13.19–20. Text from Allberry, *Manichaean Psalm-Book*, 219.

Pro21 / A Thief in the Night

For neither did he unawares create a time which he did not have knowledge of, nor was he, on the other hand, ignorant of his own second coming, he who is in the Father and who has the Father in himself. It is clear that he has (this) knowledge, for if the Father who knows all things is in him, he himself, who beholds all things in the Father, also knows. For how could he not know, he who has light in himself, who leads all things into order and regulation, who is the creator of time, who set the boundary of creation and established the number of days of its (existence), and who said: The last day is coming as a thief in the night, and again: It will not be at night for the day to overtake you in darkness.

Οὐδὲ γὰρ ἔλαθεν δημιουργήσας χρόνον, ὃν οὐκ ἠπίστατο· οὐδ'
αὖ ἠγνόησεν τὴν ἑαυτοῦ δευτέραν παρουσίαν, ὁ ὢν ἐν τῷ Πατρὶ,
καὶ τὸν Πατέρα ἔχων ἐν ἑαυτῷ· δῆλον δ', ὅτι σὺν τῇ εἰδήσει·
εἰ γὰρ ἐν αὐτῷ ἐστιν ὁ Πατὴρ, ὁ πάντα εἰδώς, οἶδεν καὶ
αὐτός, ὁ πάντα θεωρῶν ἐν τῷ Πατρί. Πῶς γὰρ ἂν καὶ μὴ
βλέποι, ὁ τὸ φῶς ἔχων ἐν ἑαυτῷ, ὁ πάντα εἰς τάξιν καὶ
διακόσμησιν ἀγαγών, ὁ πάντα εἰδὼς πρὸ γενέσεως αὐτῶν, ὁ
δημιουργὸς τῶν χρόνων, ὁ καὶ ὅριον θέμενος τῇ κτίσει, καὶ
τὸ ποσὸν τῶν ἡμερῶν παγιώσας τῆς συστάσεως αὐτῆς, καὶ εἰπών·
"'Ὡς κλέπτης ἐν νυκτὶ ἔρχεται ἡ τελευταία ἡμέρα·" καὶ πάλιν·
"Οὐκ ἔσται ἐν νυκτί, ἵνα ἡ ἡμέρα ἐν σκοτίᾳ ὑμᾶς καταλάβῃ·"
Didymus, *De Trinitate* 3.22. PG 39:917.

PARALLELS

And the son knows when it is coming, for he brings in the day itself and he himself determines and guides and ends it. For he says: That day comes as a thief in the night, and he says: You are not in the night, that the day come upon you in darkness.

ὁ δὲ υἱὸς οἶδε πότε ἔρχεται· αὐτὸς γὰρ αὐτὴν φέρει τὴν ἡμέραν
καὶ αὐτὸς ὁρίζει καὶ ἄγει καὶ τελεῖ. λέγει γὰρ "ὡς κλέπτης
ἐν νυκτὶ ἔρχεται ἡ ἡμέρα ἐκείνη" καὶ φησιν "οὐκ ἔστε ἐν νυκτί,
ἵνα ἡ ἡμέρα ἐν σκότει ὑμᾶς καταλάβῃ."
Epiphanius, *Ancoratus* 21.2. Holl, *Epiphanius* 1:30.

For it shall be advanced to them that which was said by the Lord himself: Be prepared, let your loins be girded and your lamps in your hands, and be as good servants, expecting their own master, for as a thief (comes) in the night, so comes the day. And the holy apostle says: You are not children of darkness, but of the day, so that the day may not overcome you as a thief.

Προϋπαντήσεται γὰρ αὐτοῖς τὸ ὑπ' αὐτοῦ τοῦ κυρίου εἰρημένον ὅτι
"γίνεσθε ἕτοιμοι, <ἔστωσαν> αἱ ὀσφύες ὑμῶν περιεζωσμέναι καὶ αἱ
λαμπάδες ὑμῶν ἐν ταῖς χερσὶν ὑμῶν, καὶ ἔσεσθε ὡς καλοὶ δοῦλοι,
προσδοκῶντες τὸν ἴδιον δεσπότην. ὡς γὰρ λῃστὴς ἐν νυκτί, οὕτως
παραγίνεται ἡ ἡμέρα." καὶ ὁ ἅγιος ἀπόστολός φησιν "οὐκ ἐστὲ
σκότους τέκνα, ἀλλὰ ἡμέρας, ἵνα ἡ ἡμέρα ὑμᾶς μὴ ὡς κλέπτης
καταλάβῃ."
    Epiphanius, *Haer.* 69.44. Holl, *Epiphanius* 3:191–192.

1 Thess 5:2, 4, Matt 24:43, 44, Luke 12:35–40, 2 Pet 3:10, Rev 3:3,
16:15.

Pro22 / *Entering the Bridal Chamber* _____

Behold, my bridal chamber is prepared, but blessed is the one who is found
in it wearing his shining garment. For he is the one who receives the crown
upon his head. Behold, the supper is prepared, and blessed is the one who
is invited and is ready to go to him who has invited him. The harvest of the
field is great, and blessed is the good worker. Behold the lilies and all the
flowers, and the good farmer is the one who first receives a share of them.

ἰδοὺ ὁ νυμφών μου ἕτοιμός ἐστιν, ἀλλὰ μακάριός ἐστιν ὁ εὑρεθεὶς
ἐν αὐτῷ ἔχων τὸ ἔνδυμα λαμπρόν· αὐτὸς γάρ ἐστιν ὁ λαμβάνων τὸν στέφανον ἐπὶ τῆς κεφαλῆς αὐτοῦ. ἰδοὺ τὸ δεῖπνον
ἕτοιμον, καὶ μακάριος ὁ καλούμενος καὶ ἕτοιμος γενόμενος
ἐλθεῖν πρὸς τὸν κεκληκότα αὐτόν. πολύς ἐστιν ὁ θερισμὸς
τοῦ ἀγροῦ, μακάριος δέ ἐστιν ὁ ἐργάτης ὁ καλός. ἰδοὺ τὰ
κρίνα καὶ πάντα τὰ ἄνθη· ὁ δὲ καλὸς γεωργός ἐστιν ὁ πρῶ-
τος μεταλαμβάνων αὐτῶν.
    Acts of Philip 135. Lipsius-Bonnet, *AAA* 2.2:67.

PARALLELS

    Matt 6:28, 9:37–38, 22:2–14, Luke 10:2, 12:27, 14:16–24, John
4:35, James 1:12.

Pro23 / *Inheriting the Glory of Righteousness* _____

And they defended themselves saying: This age of lawlessness and faithless-
ness is under Satan, who does not permit the truth and power of God to
prevail over the unclean things of the spirits. Therefore, reveal your righteousness now. They said this to Christ. And Christ answered them: The limit
of the years of Satan's authority has been fulfilled, but other fearful things are
near. I was delivered to death for those who have sinned, in order that they

might return to the truth and sin no more and might inherit the spiritual and incorruptible glory of righteousness which is in heaven.

κάκεῖνοι ἀπελογοῦντο λέγοντες. ὅτι ὁ αἰὼν οὗτος τῆς
ἀνομίας καὶ τῆς ἀπιστίας ὑπὸ τὸν σατανᾶν ἐστιν, ὁ μὴ
ἐῶν τὰ ὑπὸ τῶν πνευμάτων ἀκάθαρτα τὴν ἀλήθειαν τοῦ θεοῦ
καταλαβέσθαι δύναμιν· διὰ τοῦτο ἀποκάλυφον σοῦ τὴν
δικαιοσύνην ἤδη, ἐκεῖνοι ἔλεγον τῷ Χριστῷ. καὶ ὁ Χριστὸς
ἐκείνοις προέλεγεν ὅτι πεπλήρωται ὁ ὅρος τῶν ἐτῶν τῆς
ἐξουσίας τοῦ σατανᾶ, ἀλλὰ ἐγγίζει ἄλλα δεινά· καὶ ὑπὲρ
ὧν ἐγὼ ἁμαρτήσαντων παρεδόθην εἰς θάνατον, ἵνα ὑποστρέφωσιν
εἰς τὴν ἀλήθειαν καὶ μηκέτι ἁμαρτήσωσιν ἵνα τὴν ἐν τῷ
οὐρανῷ πνευματικὴν καὶ ἄφθαρτον τῆς δικαιοσύνης δόξαν
κληρονομήσωσιν.

Freer ms. to Mark 16:14–15. Aland, *Synopsis*, 508.

Pro24 / *Tribulations*

And again he said to us: You must enter the kingdom of God through many tribulations.

καὶ πάλιν εἶπεν ἡμῖν· "ὅτι διὰ πολλῶν θλίψεων δεῖ ὑμᾶς
εἰσελθεῖν εἰς τὴν βασιλείαν τοῦ θεοῦ."

Prochorus, *Acts of John*. Zahn, *Acta Joannis*, 83.

PARALLELS

Thus he says: Those who wish to see me and take hold of my kingdom must receive me through affliction and suffering.[1]

οὕτω, φησίν, οἱ θέλοντές με ἰδεῖν καὶ ἅφασθαί μου τῆς
βασιλείας ὀφείλουσιν θλιβέντες καὶ παθόντες λαβεῖν με.

Barnabas 7.11b. Funk-Bihlmeyer, *Die Apostolischen Väter*, 19.

Therefore unless the living go through these difficult and deceptive experiences, they will not be able to receive those things which are reserved for them.

Si ergo non ingredientes ingressi fuerint qui uiuunt angusta et uana haec, non poterunt recipere quae sunt reposita.

4 Ezra 7:14. Bensly, *The Fourth Book of Ezra*, 26.

And therefore tribulation is necessary for those who are saved, in order that in this manner, having become broken and weakened

84

and scattered by suffering for the word of God and set on fire, they may be suited for the banquet of the king.

Et propterea tribulatio necessaria est his qui salvantur, ut quo-dammodo contriti, et attenuati, et conspersi per patientiam Verbo Dei, et igniti, apti sint ad convivium Regis.

> Irenaeus, *Adv. haer.* 5.28.3. Harvey, *Sancti Irenaei* 2:403.

It is necessary to travel through the rugged way itself, and to endure and be oppressed, and thus to enter into life.

δι᾽ αὐτῆς τῆς τραχείας ὁδοῦ διοδεῦσαι χρή καὶ
ὑπομεῖναι καὶ θλιβῆναι, καὶ οὕτως εἰσελθεῖν εἰς
τὴν ζωήν.

> Symeon, *Hom.* 27.20. Dörries, Klostermann, and Kroeger, *Geistliche Homilien*, 229.

Acts 14:21–22.

NOTES
[1] This is not to be taken as a saying of Jesus but as the author's inference from the context. In 7:5 it is even clearer that the author has given his conclusion as though it were a saying of Jesus. See Köster, *Synoptische Überlieferung*, 127–128.

Pro25 / *Signs of the Anti-Christ* _____

And these are the signs of him:
His head (is) as a fiery flame:
His right eye shot with blood,
His left (eye) blue-black,
and he hath two pupils.
His eyelashes are white;
and his lower lip is large;
but his right thigh slender;
his feet broad;
his great toe is bruised and flat.
This is the sickle of desolation.

> *Testament of the Lord* 1.11. Trans. of the Syriac from Cooper and Maclean, *The Testament of our Lord*[1], 57–58.

PARALLELS

And these are his signs:
his head is as a flame of fire,
his right eye is mixed with blood,
his left (eye) is dead.

85

The two pupils are white between the eyelids.
His lower lip is larger.
His feet are pressed flat.
This is the sickle of perdition.

> *Testament of the Lord in Galilee* 6. Trans. based on Wajnberg's German
> rendering of the Ethiopic in Schmidt, *Gespräche Jesu*, 61*–62*.

These are the signs of the Antichrist:
his head is as a flame of fire,
his eyes are like a cat's,
his right eye is mixed with blood,
but his left eye is bluish gray
and has two pupils.
His eyebrows are very white,
his lower lip is large,
his right thigh is thin,
his shin bones slender, his feet broad,
his big toe broken.
This one is the scythe of desolation,
and he will appear to many as Christ.

Hec sunt signa antichristi:
Caput eius sicut flamma ignis,
oculi eius fellini:
sed dexter sanguine mixtus erit,
sinister autem glaucus
et duos pupulos habens:
supercilia uero alba,
labium inferiorem maiorem,
dextrum femur eius macrum,
tibie tenues, pedes lati,
fractus erit maior digitus eius:
Iste est falx desolationis
et multis quasi christus adstabit.

> Codex Treverensis 36. James, *Apocrypha Anecdota* 1:153.

It is contained in apocryphal books that Elijah the prophet spoke
concerning the antichrist, in what manner he is then to appear.
His head is as a flame of fire,
his right eye is mixed with blood,
his left (eye) is gray and has two pupils,
his eyelids are white,
his lower lip is large,
his right thigh is thin,

his feet are broad,
and the big toe of his foot is crushed.

Ἐμφέρεται ἐν ἀποκρύφοις ὅτι Ἠλίας ὁ προφήτης εἶπε
περὶ τοῦ Ἀντιχρίστου· οἷος μέλλη τότε φαίνεσθαι· ἡ
κεφαλὴ αὐτοῦ φλὸξ πυρός· ὁ ὀφθαλμὸς αὐτοῦ ὁ δεξιὸς
κέχραται αἵματος· ὁ δὲ εὐώνυμος χαροπὸς ἔχων δύο κόρας·
τὰ δὲ βλέφ[αρα] αὐτοῦ λευκά, τὸ δὲ χεῖλος αὐτοῦ τὸ
κάτω μέγα· ὁ δεξιὸς αὐτοῦ μηρὸς λεπτός, καὶ οἱ πόδες
αὐτοῦ πλατεῖς, τέθλασται δὲ ὁ μέγας δάκτυλος τοῦ ποδὸς
αὐτοῦ.

> Ms. Parisinus Graecus 4, fol. 228ʳ. Stone and Strugnell, *The Books of Elijah*, 29.

I will tell you his marks so that you may recognize him:
He is a little thin,[2] young and lame,
he has a spot of white hair on his forehead,
he is bald,[3]
his eyebrows reach to his ears,
his hands have marks of leprosy.
He will change himself before those who look at him,
He will become a small child,
(then) he will become an old man.
He will change himself in each mark,
but the mark on his head will not be able to be changed.
By this you will know that he is the son of wickedness.

ⲈⲤ-ⲚⲈϤⲘⲈⲒ̈ⲚⲈ
ⲄⲀⲢ ⲦⲚⲀⲬⲞⲞⲨⲈ ⲀⲢⲰⲦⲚⲈ ⲬⲀⲦⲈ″
ⲦⲚⲀⲤⲞⲨⲰⲚϤ· ⲞⲨⲠⲈⲖⲎϬ[2] ⲚⲞⲨ2ⲎⲘ
ⲠⲈ ⲚⲤ̄ⲢⲠ̄-ϢⲒⲢⲈ ⲚϢ̄ⲀⲘ-ⲞⲨⲢⲎⲦⲈ, ⲈⲨⲚ̄-
ⲞⲨⲦⲀⲒ̈Ⲉ ⲚⲤⲔⲒⲘ 2ⲒⲦ2Ⲓ ⲚⲬⲰϤ, ⲚϢⲀ″
ⲦⲘⲈ2ⲀⲖ,[3] ⲚⲈϤⲚ2 Ⲛ̄ⲚⲎⲨ ϢⲀⲚⲈϤ-
ⲘⲈⲈⲬⲈ, ⲈⲨⲚ̄-ⲞⲨⲔⲞⲔ ⲚⲤ̄ⲰB2 2ⲒⲦ″
2Ⲓ ⲚⲚⲈϤϬⲒⲬ. ϤⲚⲀϢ̄ⲂⲦϤ ⲘⲠⲘ̄ⲦⲞ
ⲀⲂⲀⲖ ⲚⲚⲈⲦⳤⲀⲚⲦ ⲚⲤⲰϤ, ϤⲚⲀⲢ-ϢⲎ″
ⲢⲈ 2ⲎⲘ, ϤⲚⲀⲢ-2ⲀⲖⲖⲞ, ϤⲚⲀϢ̄ⲂⲦϤ 2Ⲙ̄-
ⲘⲈⲈⲒⲚⲈ ⲚⲒⲘ, ⲘⲘⲈⲈⲒⲚⲈ ⲚⲦⲀϤ
ⲚⲦϤⲀⲠⲈ ⲚⲞⲨ2-ϢⲒⲂⲈ. 2ⲘⲠⲈⲒ̈ ⲀⲦⲈ″
ⲦⲚⲀⲤⲞⲨⲰⲚϤ ⲬⲈ-ⲚⲦⲀϤ ⲠⲈ ⲠϢⲎ″
ⲢⲈ Ⲛ̄ⲦⲀⲚⲞⲘⲒⲀ

> *Apocalypse of Elijah* 33–34. Steindorff, *Die Apokalypse des Elias*, 90, 92.[4]

And they took me to the North,
and I saw there a man held by iron bars.

And I asked: Who is this? And he said to me: This is the one who said, I am the Son of God, who made the stones bread and the water wine. And the prophet said: Lord make known to me what his form is, and I will inform the race of men so that they may not believe him. And he said to me:
The shape of his face is like that of a wild beast,
his right eye is like the morning star,
and his other eye is motionless,
his mouth is a cubit wide,
his teeth are a span long,
his fingers are like sickles,
his feet are two spans long,
and on his face is inscribed "antichrist."
He has been exalted to heaven;
he will go down to Hades.
At one time he will become a little child,
at another an old man.

καὶ ἀπήγαγόν με ἐπὶ
βορρᾶν, καὶ ἴδον ἐκεῖ
ἄνθρωπον σιδηροῖς μοχλοῖς
κατεχόμενον. καὶ ἐπερώτησα·
τίς ἐστιν οὗτος; καὶ εἶπεν μοι·
οὗτός ἐστιν ὁ λέγων· ἐγώ εἰμι
ὁ υἱὸς τοῦ θεοῦ καὶ τοὺς λίθους
ἄρτους ποιήσας καὶ τὸ ὕδωρ οἶνον.
καὶ εἶπεν ὁ προφήτης· κύριε,
γνώρισόν μοι ποῖον σχῆμά ἐστιν,
κἀγὼ παραγγέλλω τὸ γένος τῶν
ἀνθρώπων, ἵνα μὴ πιστεύσωσιν
αὐτῷ. καὶ εἶπέν μοι· τὸ
εἶδος τοῦ προσώπου αὐτοῦ ὡσεὶ
ἀγροῦ· ὁ ὀφθαλμὸς αὐτοῦ ὁ
δεξιὸς ὡς ἀστὴρ τὸ πρωῒ ἀνατέλλων, καὶ ὁ ἕτερος ἀσάλευτος·
τὸ στόμα αὐτοῦ πῆχυς μία· οἱ
ὀδόντες αὐτοῦ σπιθαμιαῖοι·
οἱ δάκτυλοι αὐτοῦ ὡς
δρέπανα· τὸ ἴχνος τῶν ποδῶν
αὐτοῦ σπιθαμῶν δύο· καὶ εἰς
τὸ μέτωπον αὐτοῦ γραφὴ ἀντί-
χριστος. ἕως τοῦ οὐρανοῦ ὑψώθη,
ἕως τοῦ ᾅδου καταβήσει. ποτὲ

μὲν γενήσεται παιδίον, ποτὲ
γέρων.

   Apocalypse of Esdras. Tischendorf, *Apocalypses Apocryphae,* 28–29.

And again I said: Lord, reveal to me what he is like.
And I heard a voice saying to me:
the appearance of his face is gloomy,
the hairs of his head are sharp like darts,
his eyebrows are like a wild beast's,
his right eye is like the morning star,
while the other is like a lion's,
his mouth is a cubit wide,
his teeth are a span long,
his fingers are like sickles,
his feet are two spans long,
and on his forehead is inscribed "antichrist."
He will be exalted to heaven
and cast down to Hades,
making false shows of power.

καὶ πάλιν εἶπον· κύριε, ἀποκάλυψόν μοι
ποταμός ἐστιν. καὶ ἤκουσα φωνῆς
λεγούσης μοι· τὸ εἶδος τοῦ προσώπου
αὐτοῦ ζοφῶδες, αἱ τρίχες τῆς
κεφαλῆς αὐτοῦ ὀξεῖαι ὡς βέλη, οἱ
ὄφρυες αὐτοῦ ὡσεὶ ἀγροῦ, ὁ ὀφθαλμὸς
αὐτοῦ ὁ δεξιὸς ὡς ὁ ἀστὴρ ὁ πρωῒ
ἀνατέλλων, καὶ ὁ ἕτερος ὡς λέοντος,
τὸ στόμα αὐτοῦ ὡς πῆχυν μίαν, οἱ
ὀδόντες αὐτοῦ σπιθαμιαῖοι, οἱ
δάκτυλοι αὐτοῦ ὡς δρέπανα, τὸ
ἴχνος τῶν ποδῶν αὐτοῦ σπιθαμῶν δύο
καὶ εἰς τὸ μέτωπον αὐτοῦ γραφὴ
ἀντίχριστος· ἕως τοῦ οὐρανοῦ
ὑψωθήσεται καὶ ἕως τοῦ ἅδου κατα-
βήσεται, ποιῶν ψευδοφαντασίας.

   Apocryphal Apocalypse of John. Tischendorf, *Apocalypses Apocryphae,*
   74–75.

The hairs of his head are like sharp darts;
his teeth are a span long,
his fingers are like sickles,
his legs are like a cock's,
his feet are two spans long,
his eyebrows are full of all stench and wildness,

on his forehead is inscribed "antichrist."
He holds in his hand a cup of death,
and all who worship him drink from it.
One eye was like the morning star,
the other like that of a lion,
when he was captured by the archangel Michael and he took his
divine nature from him. And I was sent from the bosom of my
Father and I lowered his stained head and his eye was extin-
guished. . . . And I said: My Lord, what signs will he do? Listen,
righteous John. He will move mountains and hills and will beckon
with his stained hand, Come to me, all. And by feigned deeds and
deceit they will be gathered in the proper place. He will not raise
the dead, but he will pretend to do all other things as though he
were God.

αἱ τρίχες τῆς κεφαλῆς αὐτοῦ ὡς βέλη ἠκονημένα,
οἱ ὀδόντες αὐτοῦ σπιθαμήν· οἱ δάκτυλοι αὐτοῦ
ὡς δρέπανα, τὰ σκέλη αὐτοῦ ὅμοια ἀλέκτορι·
τὸ ἴχνος τῶν ποδῶν αὐτοῦ σπιθαμῶν δύο· οἱ
ὀφρύες αὐτοῦ <πλήρεις> πάσης δυσωδίας καὶ
ἀγριότητος· καὶ εἰς τὸ μέτωπον αὐτοῦ γραφή,
ἀντίχριστος· κρατῶν ἐν τῇ χειρὶ αὐτοῦ ποτήριον
θανάτου, καὶ ἐξ αὐτοῦ πίνουσιν πάντες οἱ
προσκυνοῦντες αὐτόν. ὁ μὲν ὀφθαλμὸς αὐτοῦ ὡς
ἀστὴρ τὸ πρωῒ ἀνατέλλων, καὶ ὁ ἕτερος ὥσπερ
λέοντος, ὅτε αἰχμαλωτεύθη ὑπὸ τοῦ ἀρχαγγέλου
Μιχαὴλ, καὶ ἦρεν ἐξ αὐτοῦ τὴν θεότηταν· καὶ
ἀπεστάλην ἐγὼ ἐκ τῶν κόλπων τοῦ πατρός μου,
καὶ συνέστειλα τὴν κεφαλὴν αὐτοῦ τοῦ μεμιαμένον,
καὶ ἐσβέσθη ὁ ὀφθαλμὸς αὐτοῦ. . . . καὶ εἶπον·
Κύριέ μου, καὶ τί σημεῖα ποιεῖ; Ἄκουσον,
δίκαιε Ἰωάννη· ὄρη καὶ βουνοὺς μετακινήσει
καὶ διανεύσει τῆς μεμιαμένης χειρὸς αὐτοῦ·
Δεῦτε πρός με πάντες. καὶ διὰ φαντάσματα καὶ
πλάνης συνάγονται ἐν τῷ ἰδίῳ τόπῳ. νεκροὺς οὐκ
ἐγείρει· τὰ δὲ πάντα ἄλλα ὡς θεὸς ὑποδεικνύει.

A Venice ms. of the *Apocryphal Apocalypse of John*. James, *Apocrypha
Anecdota* 1:156–157.

NOTES

[1] Most of the first eighteen chapters of book one are in the form of sayings of Jesus.

[2] The meaning of ΠΕΛΗϬ, translated "thin," is unknown.

[3] ϢΑΤΜΕ2ΗΛ is difficult. "Bald" or "bald place" is frequently suggested, most recently by Černy, *Coptic Etymological Dictionary*, 99.

[4] For the Sahidic text, see Pietersma and Comstock, *The Apocalypse of Elijah*, 44, 46.

5 For additional, partly kindred material, see Stone and Strugnell, *The Books of Elijah*, 28–29.

Pro26 / *Unclean Souls*

Seeing in advance how such criminal doings would multiply until the end, Christ the Saviour was grieved and he said: Woe, woe unto the souls that despise their own judgement! For I see men who delight their souls in vanity and abandon themselves to the unclean world. I see also how all that is for the benefit of the enemy! Therefore I can stand by them and say: O souls that apply yourselves to unchastity and have no fear before God!

Huius ergo sceleris actus cum uidisset saluator christus multiplicari ad finem dolitus est et dixit: Euge me, euge me contemptores suae sentencia animae, uideo enim quosdam refrigerantes animas suas in uanitatem et tradentes se ipsos seculo inmundo et plurimum esse ad inimicum, possum autem adsistere eis et dicere: O animae quae luxoriae uacatis et timor dei in uobis non est.

> *Ps. Titus Epistle* [3]. de Bruyne, "Epistula Titi," *RBén* 37:56–57. Trans. from *N. T. Apoc.* 2.156.

Pro27 / *On Excesses*

Therefore what pleasure of the body can there be in the future age, as the voice of the Lord says: What manner of virgin, what manner of woman! Such a mystery of the resurrection you have shown me, you who in the beginning of the world established empty feasts for yourselves and who have indulged yourselves in the excesses of the heathen and have done things similar to those things in which they take delight.

Quae igitur iucunditas eius corporis constare in futuro saeculo possit, cum domini uox dicat: O qualis uirgo, o qualis femina, talem mysterium resurreccionis ostendistis mihi qui constituistis uobis festas uanas in origine mundi, et iucundastis uos in luxoriis gencium et similia his qui iucundantur fecistis.

> *Ps. Titus Epistle* [4]. de Bruyne, "Epistula Titi," *RBén* 37:50.

Pro28 / *Inheriting Eternal Life*

As the Lord also said in the gospel: If anyone should leave all things for the sake of my name, he shall inherit eternal life at the second coming.

καθ᾽ ὡς καὶ ὁ κύριος ἐν τῷ εὐαγγελίῳ ἔφη Εἴ τις ἀφήσει πάντα

διὰ τὸ ὄνομά μου, ἐν τῇ δευτέρᾳ παρουσίᾳ ζωὴν αἰώνιον
κληρονομήσει.

> *Agathangelus* 65. de Lagarde, *Agathangelus*, 34.

PARALLELS

Mark 10:29–30, Matt 19:29, Luke 18:29–30.

Pro29 / *The Unclosed Eye*

For the Lord Christ said (to Peter): Truly your eye will never be closed in
eternity for the light of this world.

> *Vita Schnudi.* Trans. based on Jacob Iselin's German rendering of the
> Arabic, *Eine bisher unbekannte Version des ersten Teils der Apostellehre*,
> 26.

NOTES

The saying does not occur in the Coptic version.

Pro30 / *Not Tasting Death*

And he said: He who finds the interpretation of these words will not taste
death.

ⲀⲨⲰ ⲠⲈⲬⲀϤ ⲬⲈ ⲠⲈ
ⲦⲀⲌⲈ ⲈⲐⲈⲢⲘⲎⲚⲈⲒⲀ ⲚⲚⲈⲈⲒⲰⲀⲬⲈ ϤⲚⲀ
ⲬⲒ ϮⲠⲈ ⲀⲚ ⲘⲠⲘⲞⲨ·

> *Gospel of Thomas* 1. CG II, 32.12–14.

PARALLELS

And he said: [Whoever finds the interpretation] of these words,
will not taste [death].

καὶ εἶπεν [ὅστις ἂν τὴν ἑρμηνεί]
αν τῶν λόγων τούτ[ων εὑρίσκῃ, θανάτου]
οὐ μὴ γεύσηται

> Π. Οχυ. 654.3–5. Fitzmyer, *Essays*, 366.

Mark 9:1, Matt 16:18, Luke 9:27, John 8:52.

Pro31 / *The Kingdom Is Within and Outside*

Jesus said: If those who lead you say to you: "Behold, the kingdom is in heaven," then the birds of heaven will be before you. If they say to you: "It is in the sea," then the fish will be before you. But the kingdom is within you and outside of you. When you know yourselves, then you will be known, and you will know that you are sons of the living Father. But if you do not know yourselves, then you are in poverty, and you are poverty.

ⲡⲉϫⲉ ⲓ̅ⲥ̅ ϫⲉ ⲉⲩϣⲁ
ϫⲟⲟⲥ ⲛⲏⲧⲛ̅ ⲛ̅ϭⲓ ⲛⲉⲧ'ⲥⲱⲕ ϩⲏⲧ' ⲧⲏⲩⲧⲛ̅
ϫⲉ ⲉⲓⲥ ϩⲏⲏⲧⲉ ⲉⲧ'ⲙⲛ̅ⲧⲉⲣⲟ ϩⲛ̅ ⲧⲡⲉ ⲉ
ⲉⲓⲉ ⲛ̅ϩⲁⲗⲏⲧ' ⲛⲁⲣ̅ ϣⲟⲣⲡ' ⲉⲣⲱⲧⲛ̅ ⲛ̅ⲧⲉ
ⲧⲡⲉ ⲉⲩϣⲁⲛϫⲟⲟⲥ ⲛⲏⲧⲛ̅ ϫⲉ ⲥϩⲛ̅ ⲑⲁ
ⲗⲁⲥⲥⲁ ⲉⲉⲓⲉ ⲛ̅ⲧⲃⲧ' ⲛⲁⲣ̅ ϣⲟⲣ̅ⲡ' ⲉⲣⲱⲧⲛ̅
ⲁⲗⲗⲁ ⲧⲙⲛ̅ⲧⲉⲣⲟ ⲥⲙ̅ⲡⲉⲧⲛ̅ϩⲟⲩⲛ' ⲁⲩⲱ
ⲥⲙ̅ⲡⲉⲧⲛ̅ⲃⲁⲗ' ϩⲟⲧⲁⲛ ⲉⲧⲉⲧⲛ̅ϣⲁⲛ
ⲥⲟⲩⲱⲛ ⲧⲏⲩⲧⲛ̅ ⲧⲟⲧⲉ ⲥⲉⲛⲁⲥⲟⲩⲱ̅
ⲧⲏⲛⲉ ⲁⲩⲱ ⲧⲉⲧⲛⲁⲉⲓⲙⲉ ϫⲉ ⲛ̅ⲧⲱⲧⲛ̅ ⲡⲉ
ⲛ̅ϣⲏⲣⲉ ⲙ̅ⲡⲉⲓⲱⲧ' ⲉⲧⲟⲛϩ ⲉϣⲱⲡⲉ ⲇⲉ
ⲧⲉⲧⲛⲁⲥⲟⲩⲱⲛ ⲧⲏⲩⲧⲛ̅ ⲁⲛ ⲉⲉⲓⲉ ⲧⲉⲧⲛ̅
ϣⲟⲟⲡ' ϩⲛ̅ ⲟⲩⲙⲛ̅ⲧϩⲏⲕⲉ ⲁⲩⲱ ⲛ̅ⲧⲱⲧⲛ̅
ⲡⲉ ⲧⲙⲛ̅ⲧϩⲏⲕⲉ

Gospel of Thomas 3. CG II, 32.19–33.5.

PARALLELS

Jesus says: [If] those who lead you [say to you]: "Behold the kingdom is in heav[en,]" the birds of heav[en will be before you. And if they say th]at it is under the earth, the fish of the se[a will enter before] you. And the king[dom of God] is within you [and outside (of you). Whoever] knows [himself] will fin[d] it, [and when you] know yourselves, [you will know that] you are [sons] of the li[ving] Father. [But if you do not] know yourselves, [you are] in [poverty] and you are pov[erty.]

λέγει Ἰ[η(σοῦς)· ἐὰν]
οἱ ἕλκοντες ἡμᾶς [εἴπωσιν ὑμῖν· ἰδοὺ]
ἡ βασιλεία ἐν οὐρα[νῷ, ὑμᾶς φθήσεται]
τὰ πετεινὰ τοῦ οὐρ[ανοῦ· ἐὰν δ' εἴπωσιν ὅ]
τι ὑπὸ τὴν γῆν ἐστ[ιν, εἰσελεύσονται]
οἱ ἰχθύες τῆς θαλά[σσης φθάσαν]
τες ὑμᾶς καὶ ἡ βασ[ιλεία τοῦ θεοῦ]
ἐντὸς ὑμῶν [ἐ]στι [κἀκτός. ὃς ἂν ἑαυτὸν]
γνῷ, ταύτην εὑρή[σει καὶ ὅτε ὑμεῖς]

ἑαυτοὺς γνώσεσθαι, [εἰδήσετε ὅτι υἱοί]
ἐστε ὑμεῖς τοῦ πατρὸς τοῦ ζ[ῶντος· εἰ δὲ μὴ]
γνῶσ<εσ>θε ἑαυτούς, ἐν [τῇ πτωχείᾳ ἐστὲ]
καὶ ὑμεῖς ἐστε ἡ πτω[χεία]

P. Oxy. 654.9–21. Fitzmyer, *Essays*, 375.[1]

When the Blessed One had said these things, he greeted them all
saying: Peace be with you. Receive my peace. Beware that no one
deceive you, saying, "Look, here!" or "Look, there!" For the Son
of Man is within you.

ΝΤΑ
ΡΕϤϪΕ ΝΑΪ ΝϬΙ ΠΜΑΚΑΡΙΟC ΑϤΑC
ΠΑΖΕ ΜΜΟΟΥ ΤΗΡΟΥ ΕϤϪΩ ΜΜΟ'C'
ϪΕ ΟΥΕΙΡΗΝΗ ΝΗΤΝ ΤΑΕΙΡΗΝΗ
ϪΠΟC ΝΗΤΝ ΑΡΕΖ ΜΠΡΤΡΕΛΑΑΥ Ρ
ΠΛΑΝΑ ΜΜΩΤΝ ΕϤϪΩ ΜΜΟC ϪΕ
ΕΙC ΖΗΠΕ ΜΠΕΪCΑ Η ΕΙC ΖΗΠΕ Μ
ΠΕΕΙΜΑ ΝϢΗΡΕ ΓΑΡ ΜΠΡΩΜΕ ΕϤ
ϢΟΠ ΜΠΕΤΝΖΟΥΝ

Gospel of Mary 8.12–19. Wilson & MacRae in *Nag Hammadi Codices and
P. Berol. 8502*, 459.

Look, the kingdom of heaven is within us. Look, it is outside us.
If we believe in it we shall live in it forever.

ΤΜΝΤΡΡΟ ΝΜΠΗΥΕ ΕΙCΤΕ ΜΠΝ2[ΟΥ]Ν ΕΙCΤΕ ΜΠ[Ν]
Β[ΑΛ] ΕΝΝΑΖΤΕ ΑΡΑC ΝΑΩΝΖ' ΝΖΗΤC' ϢΑΝΙΑΝΗΖΕ

Manichaean Psalm-book 160.20–21. Allberry, *Manichaean Psalmbook*, 160.

Luke 17:20–21, Job 12:7–8.

NOTES
[1] In line 10 read ὑμᾶς, "you," for ἡμᾶς, "us." In line 18 correct γνώσεσθαι to γνώσεσθε,
"you know." The reconstruction of Hofius ("Thomasevangelium," 3), differs in
substance primarily in line 16 where he has καὶ ὅστις ἂν ἑαυτόν, "and whoever (knows)
himself." There is thus no reference to the kingdom's being "outside of you" following
Hofius' reconstruction.

Pro32 / *The Old Ask the Young*

Jesus said: The man old in his days will not hesitate to ask a little child seven
days old about the place of life, and he will live. For there are many first who
will be last, and they will become a single one.

ΠΕϪΕ ΙC ϤΝΑϪΝΑΥ ΑΝ

ⲚϬⲒ ⲠⲢⲰⲘⲈ Ⲛ̄Ϩⲗ̄ⲗⲞ Ϩ̄Ⲛ ⲚⲈϤϨⲞⲞⲨ ⲈϪⲚⲈ
ⲞⲨⲔⲞⲨⲈⲒ Ⲛ̄ϢⲎⲢⲈ ϢⲎⲘ ⲈϤϨ̄Ⲛ ⲤⲰϢϥ̄
Ⲛ̄ϨⲞⲞⲨ ⲈⲦⲂⲈ ⲠⲦⲞⲠⲞⲤ Ⲙ̄ⲠⲰⲚϨ ⲀⲨⲰ
ϤⲚⲀⲰⲚϨ ϪⲈ ⲞⲨⲚ̄ ϨⲀϨ Ⲛ̄ϢⲞⲢⲠ' ⲚⲀⲢ̄ ϨⲀ
Ⲉ ⲀⲨⲰ Ⲛ̄ⲤⲈϢⲰⲠⲈ ⲞⲨⲀ ⲞⲨⲰⲦ
Gospel of Thomas 4. CG II, 33.5–10.

PARALLELS

[Jesus says:] A ma[n old in (his) da]ys will not hesitate to ask a
ch[ild seven days old] about the place of [life and he will live.] For
many (who are) f[irst] will be [last and] the last first and they [will
have eternal life.]

> [λέγει ᾽Ι(ησοῦ)ς·]
> οὐκ ἀποκνήσει ἄνθ[ρωπος παλαιὸς ἡμε]
> ρῶν ἐπερωτῆσε πα[ιδίον ἑπτὰ ἡμε]
> ρῶν περὶ τοῦ τόπου τῆ[ς ζωῆς καὶ ζή]
> σετε ὅτι πολλοὶ ἔσονται π[ρῶτοι ἔσχατοι καὶ]
> οἱ ἔσχατοι πρῶτοι καὶ [ζωὴν αἰώνιον ἕξου]
> σιν

P. Oxy. 654.21–27. Fitzmyer, *Essays*, 379.[1]

Concerning which (nature) they have an explicit tradition in the
gospel inscribed according to Thomas, saying thus: he who seeks
me will find (me) in children from seven years old. For there in
the fourteenth age I, who am hidden, am made manifest.

περὶ ἧς διαρρήδην ἐν τῷ κατὰ Θωμᾶν ἐπιγραφομένῳ εὐαγγελίῳ
παραδιδόασι λέγοντες οὕτως· "ἐμὲ ὁ ζητῶν εὑρήσει ἐν παιδίοις ἀπὸ
ἐτῶν ἑπτά· ἐκεῖ γὰρ ἐν τῷ τεσσαρεσκαιδεκάτῳ αἰῶνι κρυβόμενος
φανεροῦμαι."
Hippolytus, *Ref.* 5.7.20. Wendland, *Hippolytus* 3:83.

The little children instruct the grey-haired old men. Those who
are six years old instruct those who are sixty years old.

ⲚⲒϨ̄ⲗ̄ⲗⲀⲒ̈ ⲚⲀⲚⲒⲤⲔⲒⲘ ⲚⲒⲔⲞⲨⲒ̈ Ⲛ̄ⲀⲗⲞⲨ ⲚⲈⲦϯ ⲤⲂⲰ ⲚⲈⲨ
ⲚⲀϯⲤⲞⲈ Ⲛ̄ⲢⲀⲘⲠⲈ ⲚⲈⲦϯⲤⲂⲰ Ⲛ̄ⲚⲀϯⲤⲈ Ⲛ̄ⲢⲀⲘⲠⲈ
Pss. of Heracleides 192.2–3. Allberry, *Manichaean Psalm-Book*, 192.

Matt 11:25, Luke 10:21, Mark 10:31, Matt 19:30, 20:16, Luke 13:30.

NOTES
[1] Except in line 22 where he has πλήρης, "full." In line 23 correct ἐπερωτῆσε to
ἐπερωτῆσαι, "to ask." In lines 24 and 25 correct ζήσετε to ζήσεται, "he will live." Hofius

95

("Thomasevangelium," 32) reconstructs the last clause καὶ [εἷς γενήσου]σιν, "and they will become one," to correspond more closely to the Coptic. This clause is the least certain of the logion.

Pro33 / *The Hidden Will Be Revealed*

Jesus said: Know what is before your face and what is hidden from you will be revealed to you. For there is nothing hidden which will not be made visible.[1]

ΠΕΧΕ ΙC
COΥШΝ ΠΕΤΜΠΜΤΟ ΜΠΕΚ2Ο ΕΒΟΛ'
ΑΥШ ΠΕΘΗΠ' ΕΡΟΚ' ϤΝΑϬШΛΠ' ΕΒΟΛ
ΝΑΚ' ΜΝ ΛΑΑΥ ΓΑΡ ΕϤ2ΗΠ' ΕϤΝΑΟΥШΝ2
ΕΒΟΛ ΑΝ

> *Gospel of Thomas* 5. CG II, 33, 10-14.

PARALLELS

> Jesus says: K[now what is be]fore your sight, and [what is hidden] from you will be revealed [to you. For there is nothing] hidden which will not [be made] visi[ble] and nothing buried which [will not be raised up.]"

> λέγει 'Ιη(σοῦ)ς· γ[νῶθι τὸ ὂν ἔμπροσ]
> θεν τῆς ὄψεως σοῦ, καὶ [τὸ κεκαλυμμένον]
> ἀπὸ σου ἀποκαλυφ<θ>ήσετ[αί σοι·   οὐ γάρ ἐσ]
> τιν κρυπτὸν ὃ οὐ φανε[ρὸν γενήσεται]
> καὶ θεθαμμένον[2] ὃ ο[ὐκ ἐγερθήσεται].
> P. Oxy. 654.27–31. Fitzmyer, *Essays*, 381.

> Jesus said: There is nothing buried which will not be raised up.

> λέγει 'Ιησοῦς· οὔκ ἐστιν τεθαμμένον ὃ οὐκ ἐγερθήσεται.
> On a grave wrapping from Behnesa. Fitzmyer, *Essays*, 383.

> But concerning this mystery which is hidden to the sects, the Savior gave an indication to his disciples, saying: Know what is before your face, and that which is hidden from you will be revealed to you.

> ΕΤΒΕ ΠΙΜΥCΤΗ
> [Ρ]ΙΟΝ ΡШ ΕΤ2ΗΠ ΑΝΔΟΓΜΑ ΑΠCHΡ ΝΟΥΧΕ ΝΟΥΧШΡΜΕ
> [Ν]ΝΕϤΜΑΘΗΤΗC ΧΕ ΜΜΕ ΑΠΕΤШΟΟΠ ΜΠΜΤΟ ΑΒΑΛ Μ
> [Π]ΕΤΝ2Ο ΑΥШ ΠΕΤ2ΗΠ ΓΑΡ ΑΡШΤΝΕ ΝΑϬШΛΠ ΝΗΤΝ ΑΒΑΛ
> Mani, *Kephalaia* 65. Schmidt, *Kephalaia*, 163.26–29.

Mark 4:22, Matt 10:26, Luke 8:17, 12:2.

NOTES
  [1] See also *Thomas* 6 and P. Oxy. 654.38–40 [A18].
  [2] In line 31, read τεθαμμένον, "buried."

Pro34 / *The Lion Will Become Man*

Jesus said: Blessed is the lion which the man will eat and the lion will become man; and cursed is the man whom the lion will eat and the lion will become man.[1]

PEXE IC OY
MAKAPIOC PE PMOYEI PAEI ETE
PPWME NAOYOMU AYW NTEPMOYEI
UWPE PPWME AYW UBHT' NGI PPW
ME PAEI ETE PMOYEI NAOYOMU AY
W PMOYEI NAUWPE PPWME

Gospel of Thomas 7. CG II, 33.23–28.

PARALLELS

These bodies which are visible eat similar creatures. Therefore, the bodies change. But that which changes will be destroyed and perish. From now on it has no hope of life, for that body is a beast. Therefore as the body of beasts perishes, so will these bodies perish also.

NEEICWMA NTOOY ETOY
ON2 EBOA' EYWM' EBOA 2N NCWNT ETNE MMOOY
ETBE PAI 6E NCWMA CEUBE PETUBE AE UNATE
KO NUWXN AYW MNTEU 2EAPIC NWN2 XM PINAY
XE PICWMA TAP' OYTBNH PE NNOE 6E NNTBNOOYE
EUAPEPOYCWMA TEKO TEEI TE OE NNEEIPAACMA
CENATAKO·

The Book of Thomas the Contender. CG II, 139.2–8.

NOTES
  [1] Several translators indicate that the last clause may be an error and suggest the reading, "and the man will become a lion."

Pro35 / *Dead, Alive*

Jesus said: This heaven will pass away and that which is above it will pass away;[1] and the dead are not alive and those who are alive will not die. In the days when you ate that which is dead you made it alive. When you come into the light, what will you do? On the day you were one, you became two. But when you become two, what will you do?

ΠΕϪΕ ΙC Ϫε ΤΕΕΙΠΕ ΝΑΡΠΑ
ΡΑΓΕ ΑΥΩ ΤΕΤΝΤΠΕ ΜΜΟC ΝΑΡΠΑΡΑΓΕ
ΑΥΩ ΝΕΤΜΟΟΥΤ CΕΟΝ2 ΑΝ ΑΥΩ ΝΕΤΟΝ2
CΕΝΑΜΟΥ ΑΝ Ν2ΟΟΥ ΝΕΤΕΤΝΟΥΩΜ'
ΜΠΕΤΜΟΟΥΤ' ΝΕΤΕΤΝΕΙΡΕ ΜΜΟϤ ΜΠΕ
ΤΟΝ2 2ΟΤΑΝ ΕΤΕΤΝ ϢΑΝ ϢΩΠΕ 2Μ ΠΟΥ
ΟΕΙΝ ΟΥ ΠΕΤΕΤΝΑΑϤ 2Μ ϤΟΟΥ ΕΤΕΤΝ
Ο ΝΟΥΑ ΑΤΕΤΝΕΙΡΕ ΜΠCΝΑΥ 2ΟΤΑΝ ΔΕ
ΕΤΕΤΝ ϢΑ ϢΩΠΕ ΝCΝΑΥ' ΟΥ ΠΕ ΕΤΕ
ΤΝΝΑΑϤ'

Gospel of Thomas 11. CG II, 34.16–25.

PARALLELS

They say indeed: If you ate dead things and made them living, what will you do if you eat living things?

λέγουσι γοῦν· "εἰ νεκρὰ ἐφάγετε καὶ ζῶντα ἐποιήσατε, τί, ἂν ζῶντα φάγητε, ποιήσετε;"

Hippolytus, *Ref.* 5.8.32. Wendland, *Hippolytus* 3:95.

Mark 13:31, Matt 24:35, Luke 16:17, 21:33, Matt 5:18, Isa 51.6.

NOTES

[1] See *Thomas* 111 [Pro 58].

Pro36 / *Divisions, Fire, Sword* _____

Jesus said: Perhaps men think that I have come to cast peace upon the world and they do not know that I have come to cast divisions upon the earth, fire, sword, war![1] For there will be five in a house: three will be against two and two against three, the father against the son and the son against the father. And they will stand as solitaries.

ΠΕϪΕ ΙC Ϫε ΤΑΧΑ
ΕΥΜΕΕΥΕ Ν6Ι ΡΡΩΜΕ Ϫε ΝΤΑΕΙΕΙ ΕΝΟΥ
Ϫε ΝΟΥΕΙΡΗΝΗ ΕϪΜ ΠΚΟCΜΟC ΑΥΩ
CΕCΟΟΥΝ ΑΝ Ϫε ΝΤΑΕΙΕΙ ΑΝΟΥϪΕ Ν2Ν
ΠΩΡϪ' ΕϪΝ ΠΚΑ2 ΟΥΚΩ2Τ ΟΥCΗϤΕ'
ΟΥΠΟΛΕΜΟC ΟΥΝ ϯΟΥ ΓΑΡ ΝΑϢΩ[ΠΕ]
2Ν ΟΥΗΕΙ ΟΥΝ ϢΟΜΤ ΝΑϢΩΠΕ ΕϪΝ

CNAY AYW CNAY EXN ϢOMT' ΠEIWT'
EXM ΠϢHPE AYW ΠϢHPE EXM ΠEIWT'
AYW CENAϢ2E EPATOY EYO MMONA
XOC

> *Gospel of Thomas* 16. CG II, 35.31–36.5.

PARALLELS

And at that time friends will make war on friends like enemies,
and the earth and those who inhabit it will be terrified.

Et erit in illo tempore debellabunt amica amicos ut inimici, et ex-
pauescet terra cum his qui inhabitant eam.

> 4 Ezra 6:24. Bensly, *The Fourth Book of Ezra*, 22.

Luke 12:49, 51–53, Matt 10:34–36.

NOTES

[1] See *Thomas* 10 [I47].

Pro37 / *Becoming Disciples* _____

Jesus said: Blessed is the one who was before he came into existence.[1] If you
become my disciples and hear my words, these stones will minister to you.
For there are five trees for you in paradise which are undisturbed in summer
(and) winter and whose leaves do not fall. The one who comes to know them
will not taste death.

ΠEXE IC XE OYMAKAPIOC
ΠE NTA2ϢWΠE 2ATE2H EMΠATEϤϢW
ΠE ETETNϢ)ANϢWΠE NAEI MMAΘH
THC NTETNCWTM ANAϢAXE NEEIW
NE NAPΔIAKONEI NHTN OYNTHTN
ΓAP' MMAY N†OY NϢHN 2M ΠAPA'
ΔICOC ECEKIM AN NϢWM' MΠPW
AYW MAPENOY6WBE 2E EBOΛ ΠET'
NACOYWNOY ϤNAXI †ΠE AN' MMOY

> *Gospel of Thomas* 19. CG II, 36.17–25.

PARALLELS

For there are [five] trees in paradise . . . in summer and winter.[2]

99

ⲦⲞⲨ] ⲄⲀⲢ ⲚⲰϨⲚ ⲚⲈⲦϨⲚⲠⲠⲀⲢⲀⲆⲒⲤ[ⲞⲤ] . . .
ⲖⲈ ϨⲚⲠⲰϢⲘ ⲀⲨⲰ ⲘⲚⲠⲢⲰ

> *Manichaean Psalmbook* 161.17–18. Text from Allberry, *Manichaean Psalmbook*, 161.

Jer 1:5, Ezek 47:12, Rev 2:7, 22:2, Gen 2:8, 9.

NOTES

[1] See *Gospel of Philip* 57 [Pro 59].

[2] The couplet above is part of a series of mentions of things numbered in fives. The reconstruction of the first part of line 17 is therefore justified. In line 18, read ⲘⲚⲦⲠⲢⲰ instead of ⲘⲚⲠⲢⲰ.

Pro38 / *The Watchful Householder*

Therefore I say (to you): If the master of the house knows that the thief is coming, he will be watching before he comes and will not let him break into his house of his kingdom to carry away his goods. But you, be on guard against the world. Gird up your loins with great strength lest robbers find a way to come to you, for they will find the advantage which you expect.[2]

ⲆⲒⲀ ⲦⲞⲨⲦⲞ ϮⲖⲰ ⲘⲘⲞⲤ ⳉⲈ ⲈϤ'
ϢⲀⲈⲒⲘⲈ ⲚϬⲒ ⲠⳉⲈⲈ[Ⲥ][1] ⲚⲎⲈⲒ ⳉⲈ ϤⲚⲎⲨ ⲚϬⲒ
ⲠⲢⲈϤⳉⲒⲞⲨⲈ ϤⲚⲀⲢⲞⲈⲒⲤ ⲈⲘⲠⲀⲦⲈϤ'ⲈⲒ ⲚϤⲦⲘ
ⲔⲀⲀϤ' ⲈϢⲞⳉⲦ' ⲈϨⲞⲨⲚ ⲈⲠⲈϤⲎⲈⲒ ⲚⲦⲈ ⲦⲈϤ'
ⲘⲚⲦⲈⲢⲞ ⲈⲦⲢⲈϤϤⲒ ⲚⲚⲈϤ'ⲤⲔⲈⲨⲞⲤ ⲚⲦⲰⲦⲚ
ⲆⲈ ⲢⲞⲈⲒⲤ ϨⲀⲦⲈϨⲎ ⲘⲠⲔⲞⲤⲘⲞⲤ ⲘⲞⲨⲢ' Ⲙ
ⲘⲰⲦⲚ ⲈⳉⲚ ⲚⲈⲦⲚϮⲠⲈ ϨⲚⲚ ⲞⲨⲚⲞϬ ⲚⲀⲨ
ⲚⲀⲘⲒⲤ ϢⲒⲚⲀ ⳉⲈ ⲚⲈⲚⲖⲎⲤⲦⲎⲤ ϨⲈ ⲈϨⲒⲎ ⲈⲈⲒ
ϢⲀⲢⲰⲦⲚ ⲈⲠⲈⲒ ⲦⲈⳉⲢⲈⲒⲀ ⲈⲦⲈⲦⲚϬϢϢⲦ'
ⲈⲂⲞⲖ ϨⲎⲦⲤ ⲤⲈⲚⲀϨⲈ ⲈⲢⲞⲤ·

> *Gospel of Thomas* 21b. CG II, 37.6–15.

PARALLELS

Matt 24:43–44, Luke 12:35–40.

NOTES

[1] A variant of ⲠⳉⲞⲈⲒⲤ, "the master". See Kasser, *Compléments au Dictionnaire Copte de Crum*, 109.

[2] The third person plural here could also be understood as representing the passive. Metzger's translation is, "For the thing which you await will be found" (Aland, *Synopsis*, 520). Lambdin renders the clause "for the difficulty which you expect will (surely) materialize" (in Robinson, *Nag Hammadi Library*, 120).

Pro39 / *The Uprooted Vine*

Jesus said: A vine has been planted apart from the Father, and since it has not become strong, it will be pulled up by its roots, and it will perish.

ΠΕϪΕ ῙC ΟΥΒΕ ΝΕλΟΟλΕ λΥ
ΤΟ6C Μ̄ΠΟλ ΝΒΟλ Μ̄ΠΕΙⲰΤ' λΥⲰ ΕCΤλ
ϪΡΗΥ λΝ CΕΝλΠΟΡ̄ΚC 2λ ΤΕCΝΟΥΝΕ Ν̄C
ΤλΚΟ

Gospel of Thomas 40. CG II, 40.13–16.

PARALLELS

> [Every] plant which my Father who is in heaven [has not] planted [will be] pulled up.
>
> ΤⲰ6Ε [ΝΙΜ ΕΜ]
> ΠΕ ΠλΕΙⲰΤ' ΕΤ2Ν̄ Μ̄ΠΗΥΕ ΤΟ69 [CΕΝλ]
> ΠΟΡΚ9'[1]
>
> *Gospel of Philip* 126. CG II, 85.29–31.

> Flee, therefore, from the wicked offshoots which produce deadly fruit, which if anyone eats he will die. For these are not the planting of the Father.
>
> Φεύγετε οὖν τὰς κακὰς παραφυάδας τὰς γεννώσας καρπὸν θανατη-φόρον, οὗ ἐὰν γεύσηταί τις, παρ' αὐτὰ ἀποθνήσκει. οὗτοι γὰρ οὐκ εἰσὶν φυτεία πατρός.
>
> Ignatius, *Trall.* 11.1. Funk-Bihlmeyer, *Die Apostolischen Väter,* 95.

> Keep away from evil plants which Jesus Christ does not cultivate, because they are not the planting of the Father.
>
> ᾿Απέχεσθε τῶν κακῶν βοτανῶν, ἅστινας οὐ γεωργεῖ ᾿Ιησοῦς Χριστός, διὰ τὸ μὴ εἶναι αὐτοὺς φυτείαν πατρός·
>
> Ignatius, *Phil.* 3.1a. Ibid., 102.

> Matt 15:13, 3:10, 7:19, Luke 3:9, Isa 5:1–7, Ezek 19:10–14.

NOTES
[1] The reconstruction follows that of Till (*Das Evangelium nach Philippos,* 68) and Ménard (*L'Évangile selon Philippe,* 114).

Pro40 / *Having and Not Having*

Jesus said: He who has in his hand, to him will be given, and he who does not have, from him will be taken even the little which he has.

ⲡⲉⲭⲉ ⲓ̅ⲥ̅ ⲭⲉ ⲡⲉⲧⲉⲩⲛ̅ⲧⲁϥ' ⲍ̅ⲛ ⲧⲉϥ'
ϭⲓⲭ ⲥⲉⲛⲁϯ ⲛⲁϥ' ⲁⲩⲱ ⲡⲉⲧⲉ ⲙⲛ̅ⲧⲁϥ ⲡⲕⲉ
ⲱ̣ⲏⲙ ⲉⲧⲟⲩⲛ̅ⲧⲁϥ' ⲥⲉⲛⲁϥⲓⲧϥ̅ ⲛ̅ⲧⲟⲟⲧϥ'

Gospel of Thomas 41. CG II, 40.16–18.

PARALLELS

Therefore I said: To every one who has it will be given, and he
will have even more. But (as for) the one who does not have—
namely, the man of the place, who is completely dead, who is
removed from the planting of the creation of begetting[1], whom,
if one of the immortal essence should appear, they think they
possess—it will be taken from him and be added to the one
who is.

ⲉⲧⲃⲉ
ⲡⲁⲓ̈ ⲁⲉⲓⲭⲟⲟⲥ ⲭⲉ ⲟⲩⲟⲛ ⲛⲓⲙ
ⲉⲧⲉⲟⲩⲛ̅ⲧⲁϥ ⲥⲉⲛⲁϯ ⲛⲁϥ ⲁⲩ
ⲱ ⲟⲩⲟⲛ ⲛⲁⲣ̅ⲍⲟⲩⲟ ⲉⲣⲟϥ· ⲡⲏ
ⲇⲉ ⲉⲧⲉⲙⲙⲛ̅ⲧⲁϥ ⲉⲧⲉ ⲡⲁⲓ̈ ⲡⲉ
ⲡⲓⲣⲱⲙⲉ ⲛ̅ⲧⲉⲡⲓⲧⲟⲡⲟⲥ ⲉϥ
ⲱⲟⲟⲡ ⲧⲏⲣϥ̅ ⲉϥⲙⲟⲟⲩ[ⲧ] ⲉϥ
ⲟⲩⲟⲧⲃ̅ ⲉⲃⲟⲗ ⲍ̅ⲙ ⲡⲓⲧⲱϭ[ⲉ] ⲛ̣̅
ⲧⲉⲡⲓⲥⲱⲛⲧ̅ ⲛ̅ⲧⲉⲡⲓⲭⲡ[ⲟ]
ⲉⲧⲉ ⲉⲱⲱⲡⲉ ⲉⲣⲱ̣ⲁⲛⲟⲩⲁ
ⲟⲩⲱⲛⲍ̅ ⲉⲃⲟⲗ ⲛ̅ⲧⲉϯⲟⲩⲥⲓⲁ
ⲛ̅ⲛⲁⲧⲙⲟⲩ· ⲱⲁⲩⲙⲉⲉⲩⲉ ⲭⲉ
ⲥⲉⲁⲙⲁⲍⲧⲉ ⲙ̅ⲙⲟϥ· ⲥⲉⲛⲁϥⲓ
ⲧϥ̅ ⲛ̅ⲧⲟⲟⲧϥ̅· ⲁⲩⲱ ⲥⲉⲛⲁⲟⲩ
ⲁⲍϥ̅ ⲉⲡⲏⲉⲧ'ⲱⲟⲟⲡ·

Apocalypse of Peter, CG VII, 83.26–84.6.

Therefore, Ezra, empty things are for the empty and full things
are for the full.

Propter hoc, Ezra, uacua uacuis et plena plenis.

4 Ezra 7:25. Bensly, The Fourth Book of Ezra, 27.

Mark 4:25, Matt 13:12, 25:29, Luke 8:18, 19:26.

NOTES
[1] Bullard renders the phrase "from the planting of the creation of what is begotten"
(in Robinson, Nag Hammadi Library, 345).

Pro41 / *Greater than John the Baptist* _____

Jesus said: From Adam to John the Baptist there is among those born of women none greater than John the Baptist, so that his eyes do not break.[1] But I have said that whoever among you shall become a little one will know the kingdom and he will be greater than John.

ΠΕϪΕ ĪC ϪΕ ϪΙΝʹ ΑΔΑΜ ϢΑ ΪѠ2Α
ΝΗC ΠΒΑΠΤΙCΤΗC 2Ν ΝϪΠΟ ΝΝ2ΙΟΜΕ
ΜΝ ΠΕΤϪΟCΕ ΑΪѠ2ΑΝΝΗC ΠΒΑΠΤΙ
CΤΗC ϢΙΝΑ ϪΕ ΝΟΥѠ6Π[1] Ν6Ι ΝΕϤΒΑΛ
ΑΕΙϪΟΟC ΔΕ ϪΕ ΠΕΤΝΑϢѠΠΕ 2Ν ΤΗΥ
ΤΝ ΕϤΟ ΝΚΟΥΕΙ ϤΝΑCΟΥѠΝ ΤΜΝΤΕ
ΡΟ ΑΥѠ ϤΝΑϪΙCΕ ΑΪѠ2ΑΝΝΗC

Gospel of Thomas 46. CG II, 41.6–12.

PARALLELS

Matt 11:11, 18:3, Luke 7:28.

NOTES

[1] The text is difficult at this point and may be corrupt. Guillaumont (*Thomas*, 26) suggests ΝΟΥΟΥѠ6Π as a correction. The translation would then be "so that his eyes will not be broken." Lambdin (in Robinson, *Nag Hammadi Library*, 123), offers an attractive alternative, ". . . there is no one so superior to John the Baptist that his eyes should not be lowered (before him)."

Pro42 / *Moving Mountains* _____

Jesus said: If two make peace with one another in this one house, they will say to the mountain, "Move," and it will move.[1]

ΠΕϪΕ ĪC ϪΕ ΕΡϢΑCΝΑΥ Ρ̄ ΕΙΡΗΝΗ ΜΝ
ΝΟΥΕΡΗΥ 2Μ ΠΕΙΗΕΙ ΟΥѠΤʹ CΕΝΑϪΟΟC
ΜΠΤΑΥ ϪΕ ΠѠѠΝΕ ΕΒΟΛ ΑΥѠ ϤΝΑΠѠ
ѠΝΕ

Gospel of Thomas 48. CG II, 41.24–27.

PARALLELS

for it is written in the Gospel: If two shall agree together, and shall ask concerning any thing whatsoever, it shall be given them. And if they shall say to a mountain that it be removed and fall into the sea, it shall so be done.

Didascalia 3.6. Trans. of the Syriac from Connolly, *Didascalia*, 134.

Mark 11:23, Matt 17:20, 18:19, 21:21, Luke 17:6, 1 Cor 13:2, Eph 2:15.

NOTES
  [1] See *Thomas* 106 [Pro 57].

Pro43 / *Blessed Are the Single Ones*

Jesus said: Blessed are the solitary ones and the elect, for you will find the Kingdom; for you (have come) from it, (and) you will go there again.

ΠΕΧΕ Ι̅C̅ ΧΕ ϨΕΝΜΑΚΑΡΙΟC ΝΕ Ν
ΜΟΝΑΧΟC ΑΥⲰ ΕΤCΟΤΠ′ ΧΕ ΤΕΤΝΑ
ϨΕ ΑΤΜΝ̅ΤΕΡΟ ΧΕ Ν̅ΤⲰΤΝ̅ ϨΝ̅ΕΒΟΛ
Ν̅ϨΗΤC̅ ΠΑΛΙΝ ΕΤΕΤΝΑΒⲰΚ′ ΕΜΑΥ
  Gospel of Thomas 49. CG II, 41.27–30.

PARALLELS

John 16:28.

Pro44 / *Blessed Are the Poor*

Jesus said: Blessed are the poor, for yours is the kingdom of heaven.

ΠΕΧΕ Ι̅C̅ ΧΕ ϨΝ̅ΜΑΚΑΡΙΟC ΝΕ Ν̅ϨΗ
ΚΕ ΧΕ ΤⲰΤΝ̅ ΤΕ ΤΜΝ̅ΤΕΡΟ ΝΜ̅ΠΗΥΕ′
  Gospel of Thomas 54. CG II, 42.23–24.

PARALLELS

Blessed are the poor and those who are persecuted for righteousness' sake, for theirs is the kingdom of God.

μακάριοι οἱ πτωχοὶ καὶ οἱ διωκόμενοι ἕνεκεν δικαιοσύνης,
ὅτι αὐτῶν ἐστὶν ἡ βασιλεία τοῦ θεοῦ.
  Polycarp, *Phil.* 2.3. Funk-Bihlmeyer, *Die Apostolischen Väter*, 115.

Matt 5:3, Luke 6:20b, James 2:5.

Pro45 / *Blessed Are Those Who Suffer*

Jesus said: Blessed is the man who has suffered;[1] he has found life.

ΠΕΧΕ ⲓ̅ⲥ̅
ⲬⲈ ⲞⲨⲘⲀⲔⲀⲢⲒⲞⲤ ⲠⲈ ⲠⲢⲰⲘⲈ ⲚⲦⲀ2̅2ⲒⲤⲈ
ⲀϤ2Ⲉ ⲀⲠⲰⲚ2

> *Gospel of Thomas* 58. CG II, 43.7–9.

PARALLELS

> Blessed are those who obey these commands. Though they suffer
> evil in this world for a short time, they will gather the immortal
> fruit of the resurrection.

> μακάριοι οἱ τούτοις ὑπακούοντες τοῖς προστάγμασιν·
> κἂν ὀλίγον χρόνον κακοπαθήσωσιν ἐν τῷ κόσμῳ τούτῳ,
> τὸν ἀθάνατον τῆς ἀναστάσεως καρπὸν τρυγήσουσιν.
> *II Clement* 19.3. Funk-Bihlmeyer, *Die Apostolischen Väter*, 80.

> *James 1:12, 1 Pet 3:14.*

NOTES
[1] or "labored."

Pro46 / *Two on a Bed* —————————————————————

Jesus said: Two will rest on a bed; one will die, one will live.

ΠΕΧΕ ⲓ̅ⲥ̅ ⲞⲨⲚ̅ ⲤⲚⲀⲨ ⲚⲀ̅Ⲙ̅
ⲦⲞⲚ′ Ⲙ̅ⲘⲀⲨ 2Ⲓ ⲞⲨ6ⲖⲞ6 ⲠⲞⲨⲀ ⲚⲀⲘⲞⲨ ⲠⲞⲨ
Ⲁ ⲚⲀⲰⲚ2

> *Gospel of Thomas* 61a. CG II, 43.21–25.

PARALLELS

> Luke 17:34–35, Matt 24:40–41.

Pro47 / *Blessed Are the Persecuted* ————————————

Jesus said: Blessed are you, when you are hated and persecuted. They will
find no place there, where you have been persecuted.[1]

ΠΕΧΕ ⲓ̅ⲥ̅ ⲬⲈ Ⲛ̅ⲦⲰⲦⲚ̅ 2̅Ⲙ̅ⲘⲀⲔⲀⲢⲒⲞⲤ 2ⲞⲦⲀ̅
ⲈⲨ(ⲱ)ⲀⲚⲘⲈⲤⲦⲈ ⲦⲎⲨⲦⲚ̅ Ⲛ̅ⲤⲈⲢ̅ⲆⲒⲰⲔⲈ Ⲙ̅
Ⲙ(Ⲱ)ⲦⲚ̅ ⲀⲨ(ⲱ) ⲤⲈⲚⲀ2Ⲉ ⲀⲚ ⲈⲦⲞⲠⲞⲤ 2Ⲙ̅ ⲠⲘⲀ
ⲈⲚⲦⲀⲨⲆⲒⲰⲔⲈ Ⲙ̅ⲘⲰⲦⲚ̅ 2ⲢⲀ̈Ⲓ Ⲛ̅2ⲎⲦϤ′

> *Gospel of Thomas* 68. CG II, 45.21–24.

PARALLELS

Jesus said: Blessed are those who have been persecuted in their heart. These are they who have truly known the Father. Blessed are the hungry, for the belly of him who desires will be filled.

ⲡⲉ
ϫⲉ ⲓⲥ ⳃⲙⲙⲁⲕⲁⲣⲓⲟⲥ ⲛⲉ ⲛⲁⲉⲓ ⲛⲧⲁⲩⲇⲓⲱⲕⲉ
ⲙⲙⲟⲟⲩ ⳃⲣⲁⲓ ⳃⲙ ⲡⲟⲩⳃⲏⲧ′ ⲛⲉⲧⲙⲙⲁⲩ′
ⲛⲉⲛⲧⲁⳃⲥⲟⲩⲱⲛ ⲡⲉⲓⲱⲧ′ ⳃⲛ ⲟⲩⲙⲉ ⳃⲙ
ⲙⲁⲕⲁⲣⲓⲟⲥ ⲛⲉⲧⳃⲕⲁⲉⲓⲧ′ ϣⲓⲛⲁ ⲉⲩⲛⲁ
ⲧⲥⲓⲟ ⲛⲑⲏ ⲙⲡⲉⲧⲟⲩⲱϣ

Gospel of Thomas 69. CG II, 45.24-29.

And I think it is the epitome of all virtue that the Lord teaches us that it is necessary on account of love for God in true knowledge to despise death. He says: Blessed are those who are persecuted for righteousness, for they will be called sons of God, or as some of those who transpose the Gospels say: Blessed are those who are persecuted for righteousness, for they will be perfect. And: Blessed are those who are persecuted on my account, for they will have a place where they will not be persecuted. And: Blessed are you when men hate you, when they exclude (you) and when they cast out your name as evil on account of the Son of Man.

Κεφάλαιον δ᾿, οἶμαι, πάσης ἀρετῆς κύριος παιδεύων ἡμᾶς τὸ δεῖν γνωστικώτερον δι᾿ ἀγάπην τὴν πρὸς τὸν θεὸν θανάτου καταφρονεῖν· "μακάριοι," φησίν, "οἱ δεδιωγμένοι ἕνεκεν δικαιοσύνης, ὅτι αὐτοὶ υἱοὶ θεοῦ κληθήσονται," ἤ ὥς τινες τῶν μετατιθέντων τὰ εὐαγγέλια· "μακάριοι," φησίν, "οἱ δεδιωγμένοι ὑπὲρ τῆς δικαιοσύνης, ὅτι αὐτοὶ ἔσονται τέλειοι. καὶ μακάριοι οἱ δεδιωγμένοι ἕνεκα ἐμοῦ, ὅτι ἕξουσι τόπον ὅπου οὐ διωχθήσονται." "καὶ μακάριοί ἐστε, ὅταν οἱ ἄνθρωποι μισήσωσιν ὑμᾶς, ὅταν ἀφορίσωσιν, ὅταν ἐκβάλωσι τὸ ὄνομα ὑμῶν ὡς πονηρὸν ἕνεκα τοῦ υἱοῦ τοῦ ἀνθρώπου·"

Clement, *Strom.* 4.6.41. Stählin-Früchtel, *Clemens* 2³:266.

What the Savior preached; he said: Blessed are those who are persecuted, for they shall rest in light. Blessed are those who hunger and thirst, for they shall be satisfied.

Mani, Unpublished Letter. Böhlig, "Christliche Wurzeln in Manichäismus," 57, n.5.

Blessed are you who know beforehand the stumbling blocks and who flee from alien things. Blessed are you who are reproached and not esteemed because of the love your[2] Lord has toward you. Blessed are you who weep and are afflicted by those who have no hope, for you will be freed from every bondage.

NΑΕΙΑΤ' ΤΗΝΕ
ΝΕΤΡ̄ϢΡ̄Π ΝΜΜΕ· ΑΝCΚΑΝΔΑΛΟΝ' ΑΥⲰ ΕΤΠⲰΤ'
2ΗΤϥ̄ Ν̄ΝΑΛΛΟΤΡΙΟΝ' ΝΑΕΙΑΤ' ΤΗΝΕ ΝΕΤΟΥΝΟϬ
ΝΕϬ Μ̄ΜΟΟΥ ΑΥⲰ ΕΥⲰΠ Μ̄ΜΟΟΥ ΑΝ' ΕΤΒΕ ΠΜΑΕΙΕ
ΕΤΕΥΝ̄ΤΑϥϥ' Ε2ΟΥΝ ΕΡΟΟΥ Ν̄ϬΙ ΠΟΥΧΟΕΙC ΝΑΕΙΑΤ'
ΤΗΝΕ ΝΕΤΡΙΜΕ· ΑΥⲰ ΕΤΟΥϷΘΛΙΒΕ Μ̄ΜΟΟΥ 2ΙΤΝ̄
ΝΕΤΕΜ[Ν̄ΤΕ]Υ 2ΕΛΠΙC ΧΕ CΕΝΑΒⲰΛ ΤΗΝΕ 2ΙΤΜ̄ ΜΠ̄
ΠΕ ΝΙΜ·

The Book of Thomas the Contender, CG II, 145:1–8.

Matt 5:6, 10–11, 10:22, Luke 6:21–22, 1 Pet 3:14, 4:14, Ps 107:9.

NOTES
[1] The meaning of this sentence is not fully clear. The translation renders ΤΟΠΟC as "place," but implies that this is not to be understood simply as a designation of location. Guillaumont (*Thomas*, 39) suggests the translation, "you will find a place, where you will not be persecuted." Ménard (*L'Évangile selon Thomas*, 68) is in agreement. A close parallel to this translation is found in Clement, *Strom.* 4.6.41. Metzger makes a simple emendation, "no place will be found where you have not been persecuted." (in Aland, *Synopsis*, 526). Lelyveld considers the passage to refer to persecution in a secret or unknown place (*Les Logia de la Vie dans l'Évangile selon Thomas*, 21). The translation would then be, "The place where you have been persecuted will not be found."
[2] The beatitude begins with the second person address but shifts to third person in the relative clause, "the love their Lord has toward them." The meaning may be best expressed in English using the second person throughout.

Pro48 / *What Is Within Will Save*

Jesus said: If you bring forth that which is within you, that which you have will save you. If you do not have it within you, that which you do not have within you will kill you.

ΠΕΧΕ ΙC̄ 2Ο
ΤΑΝ ΕΤΕΤΝ̄ϢΑΧΠΕ ΠΗ 2Ν̄ ΤΗΥΤΝ̄ ΠΑΪ
ΕΤΕΥΝ̄ΤΗΤΝ̄ϥ ϥΝΑΤΟΥΧΕ ΤΗΥΤΝ̄ ΕϢⲰ
ΠΕ ΜΝ̄ΤΗΤΝ̄ ΠΗ 2Ν̄ [ΤΗΥΤ]Ν̄ ΠΑΕΙ ΕΤΕ
ΜΝ̄ΤΗΤΝ̄ϥ 2Ν̄ ΤΗΝΕ ϥ[ΝΑΜ]ΟΥΤ' ΤΗΝΕ

Gospel of Thomas 70. CG II, 45.29–33.

PARALLELS

Mark 4:25, Matt 13:12, 25:29, Luke 8:18, 19:26.

Pro49 / *Many Are at the Door*

Jesus said: Many are standing at the door, but the solitary ones are they who will enter the bridal chamber.

ΠΕΧΕ ĪC ΟΥΝ ϪΑϪ ΑϨΕΡΑΤΟΥ
ϨΙΡΜ̄ ΠΡΟ ΑΛΛΑ Μ̄ΜΟΝΑΧΟC ΝΕΤΝΑΒΩΚ'
ΕϨΟΥΝ ΕΠΜΑ Ν̄ϢΕΛΕΕΤ'

Gospel of Thomas 75. CG II, 46.11–13.

PARALLELS

For behold the five wise virgins, sober and occupying themselves with the host of their nature, receiving the oil in the containers of their hearts, which is the gift of the spirit from above, are able to enter with the bridegroom into the heavenly bridechamber.

Ἰδοὺ γὰρ αἱ πέντε παρθένοι αἱ φρόνιμοι, νήψασαι καὶ
γοργευσάμεναι τὸ ξένον τῆς ἑαυτῶν φύσεως, λαβοῦσαι τὸ
ἔλαιον ἐν τοῖς ἀγγείοις τῆς καρδίας αὐτῶν, τουτέστι
τὴν ἄνωθεν χάριν τοῦ πνεύματος, ἠδυνήθησαν συνεισελθεῖν
τῷ νυμφίῳ εἰς τὸν ἐπουράνιον νυμφῶνα.

Symeon, *Hom.* 4.6. Dörries, Klostermann, and Kroeger, *Geistliche Homilien*, 31.

. . . who, because they did not bring with them the spiritual oil in the containers of their hearts, which is the working of the previously mentioned virtues through the spirit, are called fools and are excluded from the spiritual bridechamber of the kingdom.

αἵτινες διὰ τὸ μὴ ἐντεῦθεν ἐπικομίσασθαι ἐν τοῖς τῆς
καρδίας ἀγγείοις τὸ πνευματικὸν ἔλαιον, ὅπερ ἐστὶν
ἡ τῶν προειρημένων ἀρετῶν διὰ τοῦ πνεύματος ἐνέργεια,
μωραὶ ὀνομασθεῖσαι τοῦ πνευματικοῦ τῆς βασιλείας
νυμφῶνος ἀπεκλείσθησαν. . . .

Symeon, *Great Letter.* Jaeger, *Two Rediscovered Works*, 275.3–7.

wherefore also scripture called them foolish, their virtue having been quenched before the bridegroom came, and because of this he shut out the wretched ones from the heavenly bridechamber.

ὅθεν καὶ μωρὰς εἰκότως ὠνόμασεν ἡ γραφή, σβεσθείσης
αὐτῶν τῆς ἀρετῆς πρὶν ἐλθεῖν τὸν νυμφίον, καὶ διὰ τοῦτο
τοῦ ἄνω νυμφῶνος τὰς ἀθλίας ἀπέκλεισεν·

Gregory of Nyssa, *De instituto Christiano* 83.9–12. Jaeger, *Gregorii Nysseni opera ascetica*, 83.

Indeed this path of great commandments leads to the house of the Lord and enters into his bridechamber.

Haec quidem via praeceptorum magnorum ad domum Domini ducit et ad thalamum eius intrat;
Liber Graduum 19.36. Text from Kmosko, PatSy 1.3:514.

Matt 25:10.

Pro50 / *The Hidden Light*

Jesus said: The images are manifest to man, but the light in them is hidden in the image of the light of the Father. He will be revealed, but his image is hidden by his light.

ΠΕϪΕ ӀC̄
ϪΕ Ν2ΙΚΩΝ ⲤⲈⲞⲨⲞⲚ2 ⲈⲂⲞⲖ ⲘⲠⲢⲰ
ⲘⲈ ⲀⲨⲰ ⲠⲞⲨⲞⲈⲒⲚ ⲈⲦⲚ̄2ⲎⲦⲞⲨ Ϥ2ⲎⲠ'
2Ⲛ̄ ⲐⲒⲔⲰⲚ Ⲙ̄ⲠⲞⲨⲞⲈⲒⲚ Ⲙ̄ⲠⲈⲒⲰⲦ' ϤⲚⲀ
6ⲰⲖⲠ' ⲈⲂⲞⲖ ⲀⲨⲰ ⲦⲈϤ2ⲒⲔⲰⲚ 2ⲎⲠ'
ⲈⲂⲞⲖ 2ⲒⲦⲚ̄ ⲠⲈϤ'ⲞⲨⲞⲈⲒⲚ
Gospel of Thomas 83. CG II, 47.19–24.

Pro51 / *Adam's Unworthiness*

Jesus said: Adam came into being from a great power and a great wealth and he did not become worthy of you. For if he had been worthy, [he would] not [have tasted] death.

ΠΕϪΕ ӀC̄ ϪΕ
Ⲛ̄ⲦⲀⲀⲆⲀⲘ Ⲱ)ⲰⲠⲈ ⲈⲂⲞⲖ 2Ⲛ̄Ⲛ ⲞⲨⲚⲞ6
Ⲛ̄ⲆⲨⲚⲀⲘⲒⲤ ⲘⲚ̄ ⲞⲨⲚⲞ6 Ⲙ̄ⲘⲚ̄ⲦⲢⲘⲘⲀ
Ⲟ ⲀⲨⲰ Ⲙ̄ⲠⲈϤⲰ)ⲰⲠⲈ Ⲉ[ϤⲘⲠ]'Ⲱ)Ⲁ Ⲙ̄ⲘⲰ
ⲦⲚ̄ ⲚⲈⲨⲀ2ⲒⲞⲤ ⲄⲀⲢ ⲠⲈ [ⲚⲈϤⲚⲀϪⲒ ϯ]Π]Ⲉ]¹
ⲀⲚ Ⲙ̄ⲠⲘⲞⲨ
Gospel of Thomas 84. CG II, 47.29–34.

PARALLELS

The soul of Adam came into existence from a breath. Its partner is the spirit.

ⲦⲮⲨϪⲎ Ⲛ̄ⲀⲆⲀⲘ' Ⲛ̄
ⲦⲀⲤⲰ)ⲰⲠⲈ Ⲉ[Ⲃ]ⲞⲖ 2Ⲛ̄Ⲛ ⲞⲨⲚⲒϤⲈ ⲠⲈⲤ
2ⲰⲦⲢ̄ ⲠⲈ Π[ⲠⲚⲀ]
Gospel of Philip 80. CG II, 70.22–24.

Adam came into being from two virgins, from the spirit and from the virgin earth. Because of this Christ was begotten from a virgin, in order that he might set aright the fall which happened in the beginning.

ⲀⲆⲀⲘ' ϢⲰⲠⲈ ⲈⲂⲞⲖ ⲌⲚ ⲠⲀⲢⲐⲈⲚⲞⲤ
ⲤⲚⲦⲈ ⲈⲂⲞⲖ ⲌⲘ ⲠⲠⲚⲀ ⲀⲨⲰ ⲈⲂⲞⲖ'
ⲌⲘ ⲠⲔⲀⲌ ⲘⲠⲀⲢⲐⲈⲚⲞⲤ' ⲈⲦⲂⲈ ⲠⲀⲈⲒ
ⲀⲨⳀⲠⲈ ⲠⲈⳘⲤ ⲈⲂⲞⲖ ⲌⲚ ⲞⲨⲠⲀⲢⲐⲈⲚⲞⲤ
ⳘⲈⲔⲀⲀⳞ ⲠⲈⳞⲖⲞⲞⲦⲈ ⲚⲦⲀⲌϢⲰⲠⲈ
ⲌⲚ ⲦⲈⲌⲞⲨⲈⲒⲦⲈ ⲈⳚⲚ[ⲀⲤⲈⲌ]ⲰⲂ ⲈⲢⲀⲦⳚ

Gospel of Philip 83. CG II, 71.16–21.

Gen 2:7.

NOTES
[1] The reconstruction follows that of Guillaumont, *Thomas*, 44, 46.

Pro52 / *The Wretched Body*

Jesus said: Wretched is the body that depends on a body, and wretched is the soul that depends upon these two.

ⲠⲈⳚⲀⳚ ⲚⳞⲒ ⲒⳞ ⳘⲈ ⲞⲨⲦⲀⲖⲀⲒ
ⲠⲰⲢⲞⲚ' Ⲡ[Ⲉ] ⲠⲤⲰⲘⲀ ⲈⲦⲀϢⲈ ⲚⲞⲨⲤⲰⲘⲀ'
ⲀⲨⲰ ⲞⲨⲦ[Ⲁ]ⲖⲀⲒⲠⲰⲢⲞⳞ ⲦⲈ Ⲧ⳿ⲮⲨⳃⲎ ⲈⲦⲀϢⲈ
ⲚⲚⲀⲈⲒ ⲘⲠⳞⲚⲀⲨ

Gospel of Thomas 87. CG II, 48.4–7.

PARALLELS

Jesus said: Woe to the flesh which depends upon the soul; woe to the soul which depends upon the flesh.

ⲠⲈⳚⲈ ⲒⳞ ⳘⲈ ⲞⲨⲞⲈⲒ
ⲚⲦⲤⲀⲢⳃ' ⲦⲀⲈⲒ ⲈⲦⲞϢⲈ ⲚⲦ⳿ⲮⲨⳃⲎ ⲞⲨⲞⲈⲒ
ⲚⲦ⳿ⲮⲨⳃⲎ ⲦⲀⲈⲒ ⲈⲦⲞϢⲈ ⲚⲦⲤⲀⲢⳃ

Gospel of Thomas 112. CG II, 51.10–12.

Woe to the body whenever it has remained fixed in its own nature, because that becomes corrupt and dies. And woe to the soul if it remains fixed only in its own nature and does only its own works, not having fellowship with the divine spirit; for it dies, not having been counted worthy of the eternal life of divine nature.

οὐαι σώματι, ὁπόταν εἰς τὴν ἑαυτοῦ φύσιν ἑστήκεν, ὅτι
διαφθείρεται καὶ ἀποθνήσκει· καὶ οὐαι ψυχῇ, εἰ εἰς τὴν
ἑαυτῆς φύσιν μόνον ἕστηκε καὶ εἰς τὰ ἑαυτῆς ἔργα μόνον
πέποιθε, μὴ ἔχουσα θείου πνεύματος κοινωνίαν, ὅτι
ἀποθνήσκει ζωῆς αἰωνίου θεότητος μὴ καταξιωθεῖσα.

> Symeon, *Hom.* 1.11. Dörries, Klostermann, and Kroeger, *Geistliche Homilien*, 12.

Pro53 / Angels and Prophets Will Serve

Jesus said: The angels and the prophets (will) come to you, and they will give you what belongs to you. And you, also, give them what is in your hands, (and) say to yourselves: On what day will they come and take what is theirs.

ΠΕΧΕ ΙC ΧΕ ΝΑΓΓΕΛΟC
ΝΗΥ ϢΑΡⲰΤⲚ ΜⲚ ⲚⲠΡΟΦΗΤΗC ΑΥⲰ CΕ
ΝΑϮ ΝΗΤⲚ ⲚΝΕΤΕΥⲚΤΗΤⲚCΕ ΑΥⲰ'
ⲚΤⲰΤⲚ ⲈⲰΤ' ΤΗΥΤⲚ ΝΕΤⲚΤΟΤ' ΤΗΝΕ
ΤΑΑΥ ΝΑΥ ⲚΤΕΤⲚΧΟΟC ΝΗΤⲚ ΧΕ ΑϢ Ⲛ
ⲈΟΟΥ ΠΕΤΟΥⲚΝΗΥ ⲚCΕΧΙ ΠΕΤΕ ΠⲰΟΥ

> *Gospel of Thomas* 88. CG II, 48.7–12.

Pro54 / Knowing the Danger

Jesus said: Blessed is the man who knows in [which] part (of the night) the thieves will come,[1] so that he may get up, gather his [. . .][2] and gird up his loins before they come in.[3]

ΠΕΧΕ ΙC
ΧΕ ΟΥΜ[ΑΚΑ]ΡΙΟC ΠΕ ΠΡⲰΜΕ ΠΑΕΙ ΕΤCΟΟΥ
ΧΕ Ⲉ[Ν ΑϢ] ⲘΜΕΡΟC ΕΝΑΗCΤΗC ΝΗΥ ⲈΟΟΥ
ϢΙΝΑ [ΕϤΝ]ΑΤⲰΟΥΝ' Ⲛ϶CⲰΟΥ²⁴ ⲚΤΕϤ'
ΜⲚΤ[. .]² ΑΥⲰ Ⲛ϶ΜΟΥΡ ⲘΜΟϤ' ΕΧⲚ ΤΕϤ'
ϮΠΕ [ⲈΑ]ΤΕⲈΗ ΕΜ'ΠΑΤΟΥΕΙ ΕⲈΟΥΝ

> *Gospel of Thomas* 103. CG II, 50.5–10.

PARALLELS

Matt 24:43, Luke 12:39, 1 Thess 5:2, 2 Pet 3:10, Rev 3:3, 16:15.

NOTES

¹ See Didymus, *De Trinitate* 3.22 and parallels [Pro22].

² Most translators leave a gap here. Lambdin (in Robinson, *Nag Hammadi Library*, 129) renders the phrase "muster his domain."

³ See *Thomas* 21b [Pro39].
⁴ The manuscript has 2 marked through after Ⲱ in ⲚϤⲤⲰⲞⲨ2.

Pro55 / *When Two Become One* ───────────────

Jesus said: When you make the two one[1] you will become sons of man, and when you say, "Mountain, move," it will move.[2]

ⲠⲈⲬⲈ ⲒⲤ ⲬⲈ
2ⲞⲦⲀⲚ ⲈⲦⲈⲦⲚⲰϢⲀⲢ ⲠⲤⲚⲀⲨ ⲞⲨⲀ ⲦⲈⲦⲚⲀϢⲰ
ⲠⲈ ⲚϢⲎⲢⲈ ⲘⲠⲢⲰⲘⲈ ⲀⲨⲰ ⲈⲦⲈⲦⲚϢⲀⲚ'
ⲬⲞⲞⲤ ⲬⲈ ⲠⲦⲞⲞⲨ ⲠⲰⲰⲚⲈ ⲈⲂⲞⲖ' ϤⲚⲀ
ⲠⲰⲰⲚⲈ

Gospel of Thomas 106. CG II, 50.18–22.

PARALLELS

Mark 11:23, Matt 17:20, 21:21, Luke 17:6, 1 Cor 13:2, Eph 2:15.

NOTES
¹ See *Gospel of the Egyptians* [3] and parallels [A6].
² See *Thomas* 48 [Pro43].

Pro56 / *The Living Will Not Die* ───────────────

Jesus said: The heavens and the earth will be rolled up in your presence,[1] and he who lives from the Living One will not see death. Does not Jesus say: He who has found himself, of him the world is not worthy.

ⲠⲈⲬⲈ ⲒⲤ ⲬⲈ ⲘⲠⲎⲨⲈ ⲚⲀ6ⲰⲖ ⲀⲨⲰ ⲠⲔⲀ2
ⲘⲠⲈⲦⲚⲘⲦⲞ ⲈⲂⲞⲖ' ⲀⲨⲰ ⲠⲈⲦⲞⲚ2 ⲈⲂⲞⲖ 2Ⲛ
ⲠⲈⲦⲞⲚ2 ϤⲚⲀⲚⲀⲨ ⲀⲚ ⲈⲘⲞⲨ ⲞⲨⲬ² 2ⲞⲦⲒ ⲈⲒⲤ
ⲬⲰ ⲘⲘⲞⲤ ⲬⲈ ⲠⲈⲦⲀ2Ⲉ ⲈⲢⲞϤ' ⲞⲨⲀⲀϤ ⲠⲔⲞⲤ
ⲘⲞⲤ ⲘⲠϢⲀ ⲘⲘⲞϤ' ⲀⲚ

Gospel of Thomas 111. CG II, 51.6–10.

PARALLELS

Isa 34:4, Heb 1:12, Rev 6:14, Mark 13:31, Matt 24:35, Luke 21:33, John 8:51.

NOTES
¹ See *Thomas* 11 [Pro36].
² ⲞⲨⲬ is sufficiently clear in the Facsimile Edition, whereas Guillaumont (*Thomas*, 54), reads ⲞⲨⲖ. Several translators have utilized Guillaumont's conjecture

that ΟΥΑΕ ΕΖΟΤΕ ΖΟΤΙ has become ΟΥΑ ΟΤΙ by haplography. The translation results in ". . . will neither see death nor fear, for Jesus says . . ."

Pro57 / *Blessed Is He Who Is* _____

The Lord said: Blessed is he who is before he came into being,[1] for he who is has been and will be.

ПЄ
ϪЄ ПϪΟЄΙϹ ϪЄ ΟΥΜΑΚΑΡΙΟϹ ПЄ ПЄΤ′ϢΟ
ΟП ΖΑΤЄΖΗ ЄΜ′ПΑΤЄϤ′ϢϢΠЄ ПЄΤϢΟ
ΟП′ ΓΑΡ ΑϤϢϢΠЄ ΑΥϢ ϤΝΑϢϢΠЄ

Gospel of Philip 57. CG II, 64.9–12.

PARALLELS

> And again he (Jeremiah) says: Blessed is He who existed before He was made man.
>
> Irenaeus, *Proof of the Apostolic Preaching*, 43. Trans. of the Armenian from Smith, *Proof of the Apostolic Preaching*, 75.

> Whence it is said in Jeremiah: Before I formed you in the womb, I knew you. And again: Blessed is he who was before he was born.
>
> unde aput Hieremiam ita dicitur: priusquam to formarem in utero, noui te. item: beatus quo erat, antequam nasceretur;
>
> Lactantius, *Div. inst.* 4.8. Brandt, *Lactanti opera* 1:295.

Jer 1:5.

NOTES
[1] See *Thomas* 19a [Pro38].

Pro58 / *Entering the Kingdom Laughing* _____

The Lord said it well: Some entered the kingdom of heaven laughing and have come out.[1]

ΚΑΛϢϹ
ΑПϪΟЄΙϹ ϪΟΟ[Ϲ Ϫ]Є ΑΖΟЄΙΝЄ ΒϢΚ′ ЄΤΜΝ̄
ΤЄΡΟ Ν̄Μ̄ПΗΥ[Є Є]ΥϹϢΒЄ ΑΥϢ ΑΥЄΙ ЄΒΟΛ
[. . .]

Gospel of Philip 97. CG II, 74.24–26.

NOTES

[1] The lacunae in the lines following the quote make it impossible to be confident where the saying of Jesus ends. I follow Isenberg (in Robinson, *Nag Hammadi Library*, 144) and view it as being complete.

Pro59 / *The Axe at the Root*

Because of this the Logos[1] says: Already the axe is laid at the root of the trees.

> ЄТВЄ ПΛЄІ ПΛΟΓΟС ХѠ M̄
> МОС ХЄ НΔΗ ТΔϩЄІΝΗ СM̄МОΝΤ′ ΔΤΝΟΥ
> ΝЄ Ν̄ΝѠꙢΗΝ

      Gospel of Philip 123 [1]. CG II, 83.11–13.

PARALLELS

    Matt 3:10.

NOTES

[1] Most likely this is a reference to Jesus, although the parallel in Matt 3:10 is attributed to John the Baptist.

Pro60 / *The Truth Will Make You Free*

The Logos said: If you know the truth, the truth will make you free.

> ПЄХΔϥ′ Ν̄ϬІ
> ПΛΟΓΟС ХЄ ЄТЄТN̄ѠꙢΑΝСΟΥѠΝ ТΔΛΗ
> ѲЄІΔ ТΔΛΗѲЄІΔ ΝΔP̄ ΤΗΝЄ ΝЄΛЄΥѲЄΡΟС

    Gospel of Philip 123 [2]. CG II, 84.7–9.

PARALLELS

    The one who has knowledge of the truth is free.

> ПЄΤЄΥN̄ΤΔϥ′ M̄
> МΔΥ Ν̄ΤΓΝѠСІС Ν̄ΤМЄ ΟΥЄΛЄΥѲЄΡΟС

    Gospel of Philip 110, CG II, 77.15–16.

    John 8:32.

WISDOM SAYINGS

W1 / *Pearls before Swine*

Let no one eat or drink of your eucharist except those who have been baptized in the name of the Lord. For the Lord said concerning this: Do not give that which is holy to the dogs.

μηδεὶς δὲ φαγέτω μηδὲ πιέτω ἀπὸ τῆς εὐχαριστίας ὑμῶν, ἀλλ᾽ οἱ βαπτισθέντες εἰς ὄνομα κυρίου· καὶ γὰρ περὶ τούτου εἴρηκεν ὁ κύριος· Μὴ δῶτε τὸ ἅγιον τοῖς κυσί.

Didache 9.5. Funk-Bihlmeyer, *Die Apostolischen Väter,* 6.

PARALLELS

< Jesus said > : Do not give what is holy to dogs, lest they throw them on the dung-heap. Do not throw pearls to swine, lest they make it . . .¹

М̄ΠΡ̄† ΠЄΤΟΥΑΑΒ Ν̄ΝΟΥϨΟΟΡ' ϪЄΚΑС
ΝΟΥΝΟϪΟΥ ЄΤΚΟΠΡΙΑ Μ̄ΠΡ̄ΝΟΥϪЄ Ν̄Μ̄
ΜΑΡΓΑΡΙΤ[ΗС Ν]ΝЄϢΑΥ ϢΙΝΑ ϪЄ ΝΟΥΑΑϥ'
[. .]ΑΑ[. . . .]

Gospel of Thomas 93. CG II, 48.30–33.

This, he says, is what he (Jesus) means: Do not throw that which is holy to dogs nor pearls to swine, saying that the intercourse of woman with man is the work of swine and dogs.

τοῦτ᾽ ἔστιν ὃ λέγει, φησί· "μὴ βάλητε τὸ ἅγιον τοῖς κυσὶ μηδὲ τοὺς μαργαρίτας τοῖς χοίροις," χοίρων καὶ κυνῶν ἔργον λέγοντες εἶναι τὴν γυναικὸς πρὸς ἄνδρα ὁμιλίαν.

Naassene exegesis, Hippolytus, *Ref.* 5.8.33. Wendland, *Hippolytus* 3:95.

We, he says, are men, but all others are swine and dogs. Therefore, he said: Do not cast pearls before swine nor give that which is holy to dogs.

ἡμεῖς, φησίν, ἐσμὲν οἱ ἄνθρωποι, οἱ δὲ ἄλλοι πάντες ὕες καὶ κύνες. καὶ διὰ τοῦτο εἶπεν· μὴ βάλητε τοὺς μαργαρίτας ἔμπροσθεν τῶν χοίρων μηδὲ δῶτε τὸ ἅγιον τοῖς κυσίν.

Basilides, *Exegetica,* Epiphanius, *Haer.* 24.5.2. Holl, *Epiphanius* 1:262.

On this account the Lord said: Do not throw what is holy to dogs nor pearls to swine, lest they trample them with their feet and turn and break you away from your doctrines.

Hanc ob rem dixit Dominus: Nolite proiicere sanctum canibus, neque margaritas ante porcos, ne forte conculcent eas pedibus suis et conversi disrumpant vos a doctrina vestra.
Liber Graduum 30.11. Kmosko, PatSy 1.3:887.

Matt 7:6.

NOTES
[1] Lambdin has an attractive translation, "lest they grind it [to bits]" (in Robinson, *Nag Hammadi Library*, 128).

W2 / *Seek, Find, Rule*

The one who seeks will not cease until he finds,[1] and when he has found he will be amazed, and when he has been amazed he will reign, and when he has reigned he will rest.

"οὐ παύσεται ὁ ζητῶν, ἕως ἂν εὕρῃ· εὑρὼν δὲ θαμβηθήσεται,
θαμβηθεὶς δὲ βασιλεύσει, βασιλεύσας δὲ ἐπαναπαήσεται."
Gospel of the Hebrews [1a], Clement, *Strom.* 5.14.96. Stählin-Früchtel, *Clemens* 2³:389.

PARALLELS

As also it is written in the Gospel according to the Hebrews: The one who has been amazed will reign, and the one who has reigned will rest.

ἢ κἂν τῷ καθ' Ἑβραίους εὐαγγελίῳ "ὁ θαυμάσας βασιλεύσει"
γέγραπται "καὶ ὁ βασιλεύσας ἀναπαήσεται."
Gospel of the Hebrews [1b], Clement, *Strom.* 2.9.45. Ibid., 137.

Jesus said: Let him who seeks not cease seeking until he finds. And when he finds he will be troubled, and when he is troubled he will be astonished, and he will rule over the All.

ΠΕΧΕ ῙC ΜΝ̄ΤΡΕϤ'
ΛΟ Ν̄ϬΙ ΠΕΤ'ϢΙΝΕ ΕϤϢΙΝΕ ϢΑΝΤΕϤ'
ϬΙΝΕ ΑΥⲰ 2ΟΤΑΝ' ΕϤϢΑΝϬΙΝΕ ϤΝΑ
ϢΤΡ̄ΤΡ̄ ΑΥⲰ ΕϤϢΑΝ'ϢΤΟΡΤΡ̄ ϤΝΑ Ρ̄
²ϢΠΗΡΕ ΑΥⲰ ϤΝΑΡ̄
Ρ̄ΡΟ ΕΧΜ̄ ΠΤΗΡϤ
Gospel of Thomas 2. CG II, 32.14–19.

[Jesus says:] Let the one who seeks not cease [seeking until] he finds, and when he finds [he will be amazed, and] when he has been [am]azed he will reign, and [when he has reigned] he will [re]st.

[λέγει 'Iη(σοῦ)ς·]
μὴ παυσάσθω ὁ ζη[τῶν τοῦ ζητεῖν ἕως ἂν]
εὕρῃ, καὶ ὅταν εὕρῃ, [θαμβηθήσεται καὶ θαμ]
βηθεὶς βασιλεύσῃ³ κα[ὶ βασιλεύσας ἀναπα]
ήσεται.

P. Oxy. 654.5–9. Fitzmyer, *Essays*, 371.

When the disciples had said these things, the Savior continued and said to his disciples: When you go to cities or kingdoms or countries, first preach to them saying: seek always and do not cease until you find the mysteries of the light which will lead you into the kingdom of the light.

NAÏ
6E N̄TEPOYⲬOOY N̄6I M̄MAⲐHTHC A4OYⲰⲢ ON ETO-
OT4 N̄6I ΠCⲰTHP ΠEⲬA4 N̄NE4MAⲐHTHC· ⲬE ETETN̄-
ⲰANBⲰK' EⲢENΠOⲖIC H̄ ⲢENMN̄TEPO H̄ ⲢENⲬⲰPA· KH-
PYCCE NAY N̄ⲰOPΠ ETETN̄ⲬⲰ M̄MOC ⲬE ⲰINE N̄NAY
NIM· AYⲰ M̄ΠPKATETHY̅TN̅ EBOⲖ· ⲢEⲰC ⲰANTETN̄-
6INE NMMYCTHPION M̄ΠOYOEIN· NAÏ ETNAⲬITHY̅TN̅
EⲢOYN ETMN̄TEPO M̄ΠOYOEIN·

Pistis Sophia 111. Schmidt-MacDermot, *Pistis Sophis*, 280.

Jesus continued in the discourse and said to his disciples: When I have gone to the light, preach to all the world and say to them: do not cease seeking day or night and do not let yourselves relax until you find the mysteries of the kingdom of light, which will purify you and make you into pure light and lead you into the kingdom of light.

A4OYⲰⲢ ON ETOOT4 N̄6I IC ⲢM ΠⲰAⲬE ΠEⲬA4 N̄-
NE4MAⲐHTHC ⲬE EÏⲰANBⲰK EΠOYOEIN KHPYCCE M̄-
ΠKOCMOC THP4 AⲬIC EPOOY ⲬE M̄ΠPKATOTTHY̅TN̅⁴
EBOⲖ MΠEⲢOOY MN TEYⲰH ETETN̄ⲰINE AYⲰ M̄ΠP-
ANAKTA MMⲰTN̄ ⲢEⲰC ⲰANTETN̄6INE N̄MMYCTHPION
N̄TMN̄TEPO M̄ΠOYOEIN· NAÏ ETNACET4THNOY N̄CEP-
THY̅TN̅ N̄ⲢIⲖIKPINEC N̄OYOEIN· N̄CEⲬITHY̅TN̅ ETMN̄T-
EPO M̄ΠOYOÏN·

Pistis Sophia 102. Ibid., 256.

Because of this, therefore, preach to the whole race of mankind: Do not cease seeking day and night until you find the mysteries of purification.

ETBE ΠΑΪ 6E KHPΥCCE ΜΠΓΕ
NOC ΝΤΜΝΤΡΩΜΕ THPϥ XE ΜΠΡΚΑΤΕΤΗΥΤΝ ΕΒΟΛ
ΕΤΕΤΝϢΙΝΕ 2Μ ΠΕ2ΟΟΥ ΜΝ ΤΕΥϢΗ· 2ΕΩC ϢΑΝΤΕ-
ΤΝ2Ε ΕΜΜΥCTHPION ΝΡΕϥCΩΤϥ·

Pistis Sophia 100. Ibid., 250–251.

And say to them; Do not cease seeking day or night, and do not
let yourselves relax until you find the mysteries of purification,
which will purify you and make you pure light. And you will go
to the height and inherit the light of my kingdom.

ΑΥΩ
ΑXIC ΕΡΟΟΥ XE ΜΠΡΚΑΤΕΤΗΥΤΝ ΕΒΟΛ ΕΤΕΤΝϢΙΝΕ
2Μ ΠΕ2ΟΟΥ ΜΝΤΕΥϢΗ· ΑΥΩ ΜΠΡΑΝΑΚΤΕ⁵ ΜΜΩΤΝ
ϢΑΝΤΕΤΝ6ΙΝΕ ΝΜΜΥCTHPION ΝΡΕϥCΩΤϥ· ΝΑΪ ΕΤΝΑ-
CEΤϥTHNOΥ· NCEPTHΥΤΝ Ν2ΙΛΙΚΡΙΝΕC ΝΟΥΟΕΙΝ ΝΤΕ-
ΤΝΒΩΚ' ΕΠXΙCE ΝΤΕΤΝΚΛΗΡΟΝΟΜΙ ΜΠΟΥΟΕΙΝ ΝΤΑ-
ΜΝΤΕΡΟ·

Pistis Sophia 100. Ibid., 251–252.

And he who [knows, let] him seek and find and [rejoice].

ΑΥΩ ΠΕΤCO
[OΥΝ ΜΑΡ]ΕϥϢΙΝΕ Νϥ6ΙΝΕ Νϥ'PΑ
[Ϣ]Ε]

Dialogue of the Savior. CG III, 129.14–16.

And [the Savior] answered, saying: [Blessed is] the wise man who
[sought for the truth, and] when he found it, he rested upon it
forever and had no fear of those who wished to disturb him.

ΑϥΟΥΩϢΒ ΔΕ Ν6[Ι ΠCΩΡ] ΕϥXΩ
[ΜΜΟC XE ΝΑΕΙΑΤϥ' Μ]ΠCΑΒΕ ΝΡΩΜΕ ΝΤΑϥ'[Ϣ]Ι]
[ΝΕ ΝCΑ ΤΜΗΕ ΑΥΩ ΝΤ]ΑΡΕϥ6ΝΤC ΑϥΜΤΟΝ' Μ
ΜΟϥ' Ε2ΡΑΪ ΕXΩC ϢΑΕΝΕ2 ΑΥΩ ΜΠϥ2ΟΤΕ 2ΗΤΟΥ
ΝΝΕΤΟΥΩϢΕ ΑϢΤΡΤΩΡϥ'⁶

The Book of Thomas the Contender, CG II, 140.40–141.2.

And the apostle said: The treasury of the holy king is open. And
those who worthily receive the good things there rest, and resting
they reign.

Καὶ ὁ ἀπόστολος εἶπεν· Τὸ ταμιεῖον τοῦ ἁγίου βασιλέως

ἀναπέπταται, καὶ οἱ ἀξίως μεταλαμβάνοντες τῶν ἐκεῖ
ἀγαθῶν ἀναπαύονται καὶ ἀναπαυόμενοι βασιλεύουσιν.

Acts of Thomas 136. Lipsius-Bonnet, *AAA* 2.2:243.

And you have not ceased seeking until you found all the mysteries
of the kingdom of light, which purified you and made you very
purified light, and you have become purified light. Concerning
this I once said to you: Seek and you will find.

ΑΥⲰ ⲘⲠⲈⲦⲚⲔΑⲦⲞⲦⲦⲎΥⲦⲚ
ⲈⲂⲞⲖ ⲈⲦⲈⲦⲚⳜⲒⲚⲈ ⳞⲈⲰⲤ ⳜΑⲚⲦⲈⲦⲚ6ⲒⲚⲈ ⲚⲘⲘΥⲤⲦⲎⲢⲒⲞⲚ
ⲦⲎⲢⲞΥ ⲚⲦⲘⲚⲦⲈⲢⲞ ⲘⲠⲞΥⲞⲈⲒⲚ ⲚΑⲒ̈ ⲚⲦΑΥⲤⲰⲦ4 ⲘⲘⲰⲦⲚ
ΑΥⲢⲦⲎΥⲦⲚ ⲚⳞ2ⲒⲖⲒⲔⲢⲒⲚⲈⲤ ⲚⲞΥⲞⲈⲒⲚ Ⲉ4ⲤⲞⲦ4 ⲈⲘΑⳜⲞ
ΑΥⲰ ΑⲦⲈⲦⲚⳜⲰⲠⲈ ⲚⲞΥⲞⲈⲒⲚ Ⲉ4ⲤⲞⲦ4· ⲈⲦⲂⲈ ⲠΑⲒ̈ 6Ⲉ
ⲀⲒ̈ⳢⲞⲞⲤ ⲈⲢⲰⲦⲚ ⲘⲠⲞΥⲞⲈⲒⳜ ⳢⲈ ⳜⲒⲚⲈ ⲦΑⲢⲈⲦⲚ6ⲒⲚⲈ·

Pistis Sophia 100. Schmidt-MacDermot, *Pistis Sophia,* 249–250.

Matt 7:7–8, Luke 11:9–10.

NOTES

¹ See also Thomas 92 [I60] and Thomas 94 [W38].

² Space for eleven or twelve letters has been erased and left blank at the beginning
of line 18.

³ In line 8, correct βασιλεύσῃ to βασιλεύσει, "he will reign."

⁴ In line 3, correct ⲘⲠⲢⲔΑⲦⲞⲦⲦⲎΥⲦⲚ to ⲘⲠⲢⲔΑⲦⲞⲞⲦⲦⲎΥⲦⲚ, "do not
cease."

⁵ In line 3, correct ⲘⲠⲢΑⲚΑⲔⲦⲈ ⲘⲘⲰⲦⲚ to ⲘⲠⲢΑⲚΑⲔⲦΑ ⲘⲘⲰⲦⲚ, "do
not let yourselves relax."

⁶ The completion of the Coptic text is from Turner, *The Book of Thomas the Contender,* 18.

W3 / *Faithful in What Is Small*

For the Lord says in the Gospel: If you have not kept that which is small, who
will give you that which is great? For I tell you that he who is faithful in the
least is faithful also in much. He means, then, this: Keep the flesh pure, and
the seal spotless, in order that we may receive eternal life.

λέγει γὰρ ὁ κύριος ἐν τῷ εὐαγγελίῳ· Εἰ τὸ μικρὸν οὐκ ἐτηρή-
σατε, τὸ μέγα τίς ὑμῖν δώσει; λέγω γὰρ ὑμῖν, ὅτι ὁ πιστὸς
ἐν ἐλαχίστῳ καὶ ἐν πολλῷ πιστός ἐστιν. ἄρα οὖν τοῦτο λέγει·
τηρήσατε τὴν σάρκα ἁγνὴν καὶ τὴν σφραγῖδα ἄσπιλον, ἵνα τὴν
αἰώνιον ζωὴν ἀπολάβωμεν.

II Clement 8.4–6. Funk-Bihlmeyer, *Die Apostolischen Väter,* 75.

PARALLELS

And for this reason the Lord declared to those who were ungrateful towards him: If you have not been faithful in what is little, who will give you what is great?

Et ideo Dominus dicebat ingratis exsistentibus in eum: Si in modico fideles non fuistis, quod magnum est quis dabit vobis?.
> Irenaeus, *Adv. haer.* 2.34.3. Harvey, *Sancti Irenaei* 1:382–383.

If you have not been faithful in that which is little, who will give you that which is great?

Si in modico fideles non fuistis, quod majus est quis dabit vobis?
> Hilary, *Epistola seu libellus* 1. PL 10:733.

Luke 16:10–12, 19:17, Matt 25:21, 23.

W4 / *Mind and Treasure* _____

Seek the kingdom of heaven, and all these things will be added to you. For where the treasure is, there is the mind of man.

ζητεῖτε δὲ τὴν βασιλείαν τῶν οὐρανῶν, καὶ ταῦτα πάντα προστεθήσεται ὑμῖν. ὅπου γὰρ ὁ θησαυρός ἐστιν, ἐκεῖ καὶ ὁ νοῦς τοῦ ἀνθρώπου.
> Justin, *Apol.* 15.16. Goodspeed, *Die ältesten Apologeten*, 36.

PARALLELS

For where someone's mind is, it says, there also is his treasure.

ὅπου γὰρ ὁ νοῦς τινος, φησίν, ἐκεῖ καὶ ὁ θησαυρὸς αὐτοῦ.
> Clement, *Strom.* 7.12.77.6. Stählin-Früchtel, *Clemens* 3²:55.

For where the mind of a man is, there also is his treasure.

ὅπου γὰρ ὁ νοῦς τοῦ ἀνθρώπου, ἐκεῖ καὶ ὁ θησαυρὸς αὐτοῦ.
> Clement, *Quis div. salv.* 17.1. Ibid., 170.

He answered and said to me: Blessed are you, because you did not waver at the sight of me. For where the mind is, there is the treasure.[1]

ΑϤΟΥϢϢΒ ΠΕ
ΧΑϤ ΝΑΪ ΧΕ ΝΑΪΑΤΕ ΧΕ ΝΤΕΚΙΜ ΑΝ

ϾΡϾΝΑΥ ϾΡΟϾΙ ΠΜΑ ΓΑΡ ϾΤϾΡϾΠΝΟΥϹ
ΜΜΑΥ ϾϤΜΜΑΥ ΝϬΙ ΠϾ2Ο

Gospel of Mary 10:13–16. Wilson and MacRae, in Parrott, *Nag Hammadi Codices V, 2–5 and VI, P. Berol. 8502*, 462.

For it says: Where your mind is, there also is your treasure.

Λέγει γὰρ, "Ὅπου ὁ νοῦς σου, ἐκεῖ καὶ ὁ θησαυρός σου.
Symeon, *Hom.* 43.3. Dörries, Klostermann, and Kroeger, *Geistliche Homilien*, 286.

Concerning this I once said to you: Where your heart is, there will be your treasure.

        ϾΤΒϾ ΠΑΪ ϬϾ ΑΪΧΟΟϹ ϾΡШΤΝ ΜΠΙΟΥΟϾΙШ
ΧϾ ΠΜΑ ϾΤϤΜΜΑΥ ΝϬΙ ΠϾΤΝ2ΗΤ ϾϤΝΑШШΠϾ ΜΜΑΥ
ΝϬΙ ΠϾΤΝΑ2Ο

Pistis Sophia 90. Schmidt and MacDermot, *Pistis Sophis*, 408.

. . . according to your word which you proclaimed: Where your mind . . ?[2]

        ΚΑΤΑ ΠΚϹϾΧϾ ϾΤΑΚΤϾΟΥΑϤ ΧϾ ΠΜΑ
Μ[. . .] ΚΝΟΥϹ . . . Α ΜΠ . . . . ΠϾ

Manichaean Psalm-Book, Ps. 294.24–25. Allberry, *A Manichaean Psalm-Book*, 94.

As the Savior said: Where your heart is, your treasure will be.

        ΚΑΤΑ Τ2Ϯ ϾΤΑ ΠϹΗΡ ΧΟΟϹ ΧϾ [ΠΜΑ]
ϾΤϾΡϾ ΠϾΤΝ2ΗΤ ΜΜϾΥ ϾΡϾ ΠϾΤΝϾ2Ο ΝΑШ[ШΠϾ]

Mani, *Kephalaia* 89.3–4. Schmidt, *Kephalaia*, 223.

So that where his heart is his treasure will also be.

        ΧϾϹΑ
ΑϹ [ΠΜ]Α ϾΤϾΡϾ ΠϾϤ2ΗΤ ΜΜϾΥ ϾΡϾ ΠϾϤϾ2Ο ΑΝ ΝΑШШ
ΠϾ [ΜΜ]ϾΥ

Mani, *Kephalaia* 91.8–10. Ibid., 234.

Where your thought is, there is your goodness.

ὅπου σου τὸ φρονοῦν, ἐκεῖ σου τὸ ἀγαθόν.
Sentences of Sextus 316. Chadwick, *Sentences*, 48.

Where your thought is, there is your goodness.

        ΠΜΑ Ϲ
ΤϤШΟΟΠ ΜΜϾΥ ΝϬΙ ΠϾΚΜϾ

ⲉⲩ ⲉϥϣⲟⲟⲡ ⲙ̄ⲙⲉⲩ ⲛ̄ϭⲓ ⲡⲉⲕ
[ⲁ]ⲅⲁⲑⲟⲛ·

Sentences of Sextus 316. CG XII, 27.17–20.

As your custom is, so your life will be.

οἷον ἂν ᾖ σου τὸ ἦθος, τοιοῦτος ἔσται σου καὶ ὁ βίος.

Sentences of Sextus 326a. Chadwick, *Sentences,* 48.

As your heart is, so your life will be.

ⲛ̄ⲑⲉ ⲉⲧϥ̄ϣⲟⲟⲡ ⲙ̄ⲙⲟ[ⲥ ⲛ]
ϭⲓ ⲡⲉⲕϩⲏⲧ ϥⲛⲁϣⲱⲡⲉ ⲙ̄ⲙ[ⲟⲥ]
ⲛ̄ϭⲓ ⲡⲉⲕⲃⲓⲟⲥ

Sentences of Sextus 326a. CG XII, 28.20–22.

Matt 6:21, Luke 12:34.

NOTES

[1] Till (*Die gnostischen Schriften,* 69) translated the last Coptic word "your countenance" and considered "the treasure" less likely.

[2] Though the lacunae cannot be restored with confidence, the saying is likely a version of the one under consideration. The word "treasure" occurs in the line immediately before the words quoted.

W5 / Alike and Different

And we said to him: O master, do we have together with them one hope of the inheritance? He answered and said to us: Are the fingers of the hand alike or the ears of corn in the field? Or do the fruitbearing trees give the same fruit? Do they not bring forth fruit according to their nature?

Epistula Apostolorum 32. Trans. of the Ethiopic from *N. T. Apoc.* 1:213 (The Coptic has a lacuna from 31–38.).

PARALLELS

Matt 7:16–18, 12:33, Luke 6:43–44.

W6 / *Seek Great Things*

One part of the kingly office is divine—that which is according to God and his holy Son, by whom are supplied the good things from the earth, external things and perfect happiness. For, he says, seek the great things and the small will be added to you.

τοῦ δὲ βασιλικοῦ τὸ μὲν θεῖον μέρος ἐστίν, οἷον τὸ κατὰ
τὸν θεὸν καὶ τὸν ἅγιον υἱὸν αὐτοῦ, παρ᾽ ὧν τά τε ἀπὸ γῆς
ἀγαθὰ καὶ τὰ ἐκτὸς καὶ ἡ τελεία εὐδαιμονία χορηγεῖται·
"αἰτεῖσθε γάρ," φησί, "τὰ μεγάλα, καὶ τὰ μικρὰ ὑμῖν προστεθήσεται."

> Clement, *Strom.* 1.24.158.2. Stählin-Früchtel, *Clemens* 2³:99–100.

PARALLELS

Forbidding to bring to God such a request, the Savior said: Ask for great things and little things will be added to you; ask for heavenly things and earthly things will be added to you.

ἣν (ref. to αἴτησις) ἀπαγορεύων ὁ Σωτὴρ προσφέρειν τῷ Πατρὶ
φησιν· "Αἰτεῖτε τὰ μεγάλα, καὶ τὰ μικρὰ ὑμῖν προστεθήσεται·
αἰτεῖτε τὰ ἐπουράνια, καὶ τὰ ἐπίγεια προστεθήσεται ὑμῖν."

> Origen, *Selecta in Ps.* 4.4. PG 12:1141.

That man who has been tested would say, Attend to my petition, sending up fitting requests to God in prayer, not entreating God for small and ordinary, nor for mortal and human requests. Therefore the Savior also taught this, saying: Ask for the great things and the little things will be added to you.

Τὸ δέ, Πρόσχες τῇ δεήσει μου, εἴποι ἂν ἐκεῖνος ὁ βεβασανισ-
μένος καὶ πρεπούσας Θεῷ ἐν τῇ προσευχῇ ἀναπέμπων δεήσεις,
ὁ μὴ ἐπὶ μικροῖς καὶ τοῖς τυχοῦσιν αἰτήμασι, μηδ᾽ ἐπὶ θνητοῖς
καὶ ἀνθρωπίνοις παρακαλῶν τὸν Θεόν. Τοῦτο γοῦν καὶ ὁ Σωτὴρ
ἐδίδασκε λέγων· Αἰτεῖτε τὰ μεγάλα, καὶ τὰ μικρὰ προστεθήσεται
ὑμῖν.

> Eusebius, *In. Ps.* 16.2. PG 23:160.

Finally, it is written: Ask for the great things and the small will be added to you. Ask for heavenly things and earthly things will be added (to you).

Denique scriptum est: Petite magna, et parva adjicientur vobis. Petite coelestia, et terrena adjicientur.

> Ambrose, *Epist.* 1.36.3, *Ad Horantianus.* PL 16:1082.

And again, for your Father knows that you need all these things. But seek first the kingdom of heaven and righteousness, for these are great things, and the things which are small and concern this life will be added to you.

καὶ πάλιν· "οἶδεν γὰρ ὁ πατὴρ ὑμῶν ὅτι χρῄζετε τούτων
ἀπάντων· ζητεῖτε δὲ πρῶτον τὴν βασιλείαν τῶν οὐρανῶν καὶ
τὴν δικαιοσύνην, ταῦτα γὰρ μεγάλα, τὰ δὲ μικρὰ" καὶ περὶ
τὸν βίον, ταῦτα "προστεθήσεται ὑμῖν."
> Clement, *Strom.* 4.34.6. Stählin-Früchtel, *Clemens* 2³:263.

Such is an example of what one ought (to pray for): Ask for great
things, and small things will be added to you. And ask for heavenly
things, and earthly things will be added to you.

οἷον ὡς ἐπὶ παραδείγματος τὸ μὲν ὃ δεῖ· "αἰτεῖτε τὰ μεγάλα, καὶ τὰ μικρὰ
ὑμῖν προστεθήσεται," καὶ "αἰτεῖτε τὰ ἐπουράνια,
καὶ τὰ ἐπίγεια ὑμῖν προστεθήσεται."
> Origen, *On Prayer* 2.2. Koetschau, *Origenes* 2:299.

Let us consider the words: Ask for great things, and small things
will be added to you. And ask for heavenly things, and earthly
things will be added to you.

κατανοήσωμεν τὸ "αἰτεῖτε τὰ μεγάλα, καὶ τὰ μικρὰ ὑμῖν προσ-
τεθήσεται· καὶ αἰτεῖτε τὰ ἐπουράνια, καὶ τὰ ἐπίγεια ὑμῖν
προστεθήσεται."
> Origen, *On Prayer* 14.1. Ibid., 330.

For he has learned from Jesus to seek for nothing small, that is,
sensible objects, but to ask only for what is great and truly divine.

ἔμαθε γὰρ ἀπὸ τοῦ Ἰησοῦ μηδὲν μικρόν, τουτέστιν αἰσθητόν,
ζητεῖν ἀλλὰ μόνα τὰ μεγάλα καὶ ἀληθῶς θεῖα.
> Origen, *Contra Celsum* 7.44. Ibid., 196.

Therefore, everyone who asks God for things which are earthly
and small disobeys him who commanded (us) to ask things which
are heavenly and great from the knowing God, who does not grant
that which is earthly and small.

πᾶς τοιγαροῦν ὁ "τὰ ἐπίγεια" καὶ "μικρὰ" αἰτῶν ἀπὸ τοῦ
θεοῦ παρακούει τοῦ ἐντειλαμένου "ἐπουράνια" καὶ "μεγάλα"
αἰτεῖν ἀπὸ τοῦ μηδὲν ἐπίγειον μηδὲ μικρὸν χαρίζεσθαι
ἐπισταμένου θεοῦ.
> Origen, *On Prayer* 16.2. Ibid., 336.

But it is fitting for believers not to take up food and not to go to
the bath before saying a prayer. For the refreshment and nourishment of the spirit are to be held before those of the flesh, and
heavenly things before earthly things.

Sed et cibum non prius sumere et lauacrum non prius adire quam
interposita oratione fideles decet. Priora enim habenda sunt
spiritus refrigeria et pabula quam carnis, quia priora caelestia
quam terrena.

Tertullian, *De oratione* 25.6. Diercks, *Tertulliani opera* 1:273.

Matt 6:33.

W7 / *Skillful Money-changers*

Keeping the commandment of Jesus which says: Be skillful money-changers,[1]
and the teaching of Paul who says: Test everything; hold fast what is good;
abstain from every form of evil.

τηρούντων τὴν ἐντολὴν Ἰησοῦ λέγουσαν· "Γίνεσθε δόκιμοι
τραπεζῖται," καὶ τὴν Παύλου διδαχὴν φάσκοντος· "Πάντα δοκιμάζετε, τὸ καλὸν κατέχετε, ἀπὸ παντὸς "εἴδους πονηροῦ ἀπέχεσθε;"

Origen, *Commentary on John* 19.7.2. Preuschen, *Origenes' Johannes-
kommentar,* 307.

PARALLELS

With good reason our Teacher said: Be skillful money-changers.[2]

εὐλόγως ὁ διδάσκαλος ἡμῶν ἔλεγεν· Γίνεσθε τραπεζῖται δόκιμοι.

Ps. Clem. Hom. 2.51. Rehm-Irmscher, *Homilien,* 55.

Above all, both Christ and his Apostle exhort us to be skillful
money-changers, so that we might test all things, holding fast
what is good.

Ἄλλως τε παρεγγυῶσιν ἡμῖν ὅ τε Χριστὸς καὶ ὁ τούτου Ἀπόστολος, γίνεσθαι τραπεζῖται δόκιμοι, ὥστε τὰ πάντα δοκιμάζειν, τὸ καλὸν κατέχοντας.

Socrates, *Ecclesiastical History* 3.16. PG 67:421.

Let him know that I willingly hear this statement of the Apostle:
Test all things; keep what is good, and the words of the Savior who
said: Be skillful money-changers.

sciate me illud Apostoli libenter audire: Omnia probate, quod
bonum est, tenete, et Salvatoris verba dicentis: Estote probati
nummularii.

Jerome, Letter 119, *Ad Minervium et Alexandrum.* PL 22:979.

And quickly I think of that which the Savior said: Be skillful money-changers.

καὶ τάχα οἶμαι περὶ τούτου τὸν Σωτῆρα εἰρηκέναι τό·
Γίνεσθε δόκιμοι τραπεζῖται.

        Vita St. Syncleticae 100. PG 28:1549.

The Savior answered and said to Mary: I once said to you, Become like the wise money-changers, take what is good, throw away what is bad.

ⲀϤⲞⲨⲰϢⲂ ⲚϬⲒ ⲠⲤⲰⲦⲎⲢ
ⲠⲈⲬⲀϤ ⲘⲘⲀⲢⲒⲀ ⲬⲈ ⲀⲒ̈ⲬⲞⲞⲤ ⲈⲢⲰⲦⲚ ⲘⲠⲒⲞⲨⲞⲈⲒⲰ ⲬⲈ
ϢⲰⲠⲈ ⲚⲐⲈ ⲚⲚⲒⲤⲀⲂⲈ ⲚⲦⲢⲀⲠⲈⲌⲈⲒⲦⲎⲤ ⲬⲈ ⲠⲈⲦⲚⲀⲚⲞⲨϤ
ⲬⲒⲦϤ ⲠⲈⲐⲞⲞⲨ ⲚⲞⲬϤ ⲈⲂⲞⲖ·

        Pistis Sophia 134. Schmidt-MacDermot, *Pistis Sophia*, 348.

The God of the universe, confirming the words of the servants, said in the gospels: Be skillful money-changers, separating the spurious from the genuine.

Ὁ δὲ τῶν ὅλων Θεὸς τῶν οἰκετῶν ἐπισφραγίζων τὰ ῥήματα
ἐν Εὐαγγελίοις φησί, Γίνεσθε τραπεζῖται δόκιμοι,
διακρίνοντες ἐκ τοῦ τὸ κίβδηλον.

        Caesarius, *Dial.* 3, *Interrog.* 140. PG 38:1060.

We ought then carefully to notice this threefold order, and with a wise discretion to analyze the thoughts which arise in our hearts, tracking out their origin and cause and author in the first instance, that we may be able to consider how we ought to yield ourselves to them in accordance with the desert of those who suggest them, so that we may, as the Lord's command bids us, become good money-changers, . . .

Hanc igitur tripertitam rationem oportet nos iugiter obseruare et uniuersas cogitationes quae emergunt in corde nostro sagaci discretione discutere, origines earum et causas auctoresque primitus indagantes, ut quales nos eis praebere debeamus ex illorum merito qui eas suggerunt considerare possimus, ut efficiamur secundum praeceptum domini probabiles trapezitae.

        Cassian, *Conlationes* 1.20. Petschenig, *Iohannis Cassiani Conlationes*, 29.
        Trans. from Gibson, NPNF, 2nd ser. 11:304.

We want then to learn how it ought to be gained, or how we can tell whether it is genuine and from God, or whether it is spurious and from the devil: so that (to use the figure of that gospel parable which you discussed on a former occasion, in which we are bidden to become good money-changers) we may be able to see the figure of the true king stamped on the coin and to detect what is not stamped on coin that is current, . . .

quomodo ergo adquiri debeat cupimus edoceri, aut quemadmodum utrum uera et ex deo, an falsa et diabolica sit possit agnosci, ut secundum illam euangelicam quam superiore tractatu disseruisti parabolam, qua iubemur fieri probabiles trapezitae, nomismati inpressam ueri regis imaginem peruidentes deprehendere ualeamus quod non sit in moneta legitima figuratum, . . .

> Cassian, *Conlationes* 2.9. Petschenig, *Iohannis Cassiani Conlationes*, 48. Trans. from Gibson, NPNF, 2nd ser. 11:311.

For thus he (Apelles) says: It says in the gospel, become skillful money-changers.

οὕτως γάρ, φησίν, ἔφη ἐν τῷ εὐαγγελίῳ,
γίνεσθε δόκιμοι τραπεζῖται

> Apelles, in Epiphanius *Haer.* 44.2.6. Holl, *Epiphanius* 2:192.

Therefore the Scripture, desiring to make us such dialecticians, rightly exhorts us: Be skillful money-changers, rejecting some things but retaining what is good.

εἰκότως ἄρα καὶ ἡ γραφὴ τοιούτους τινὰς ἡμᾶς διαλεκτικοὺς
οὕτως ἐθέλουσα γενέσθαι παραινεῖ· "γίνεσθε δὲ δόκιμοι
τραπεζῖται," τὰ μὲν ἀποδοκιμάζοντες, τὸ δὲ καλὸν κατέχοντες.

> Clement, *Strom.*, 1.28. Stählin-Früchtel, *Clemens* 2³:109.

The one who is called by scripture skillful money-changer also knows to test all things, to keep what is good, but to avoid every kind of evil.

ὁ κατὰ τὴν γραφὴν ὀνομαζόμενος δόκιμος τραπεζίτης καὶ
εἰδὼς "πάντα δοκιμάζειν καὶ τὸ μὲν καλὸν κατέχειν,
ἀπέχεσθαι δὲ παντὸς εἴδους πονηροῦ."

> Origen, *Commentary on Matthew* 17.31. Klostermann, *Origenes* 10:673–74.

In the same way the blessed Paul also said: Be wise money-changers, test all things, keep what is good, avoid every kind of evil.

Τοιοῦτόν τι καὶ ὁ μακάριος Παῦλός φησι· "Γίνεσθε
φρόνιμοι τραπεζῖται, πάντα δοκιμάζετε, τὸ καλὸν
κατέχετε, ἀπὸ παντὸς εἴδους πονηροῦ ἀπέχεσθε."

> Cyril of Alexandria, *Commentary on Isaiah* 1.2. PG 70:101.

I accept the view, since I agree with the apostolic voice which
said to the more powerful: Be skillful money-changers.

ἀπεδεξάμην τὸ ὅραμα, ὡς ἀποστολικῇ φωνῇ συντρέχον τῇ
λεγούσῃ πρὸς τοὺς δυνατωτέρους γίνεσθε δόκιμοι
τραπεζῖται.

> Dionysius of Rome, Eusebius, *Eccl. hist.* 7.7.3. Schwartz, *Eusebius*
> 2.2:644.

Let the one who begins to judge, like a good money-changer,
separate and distinguish the nature of the facts, lest the genuine
be mixed and confused with the spurious.

καὶ ὁ δικάζειν εἰσιὼν καθάπερ ἀργυραμοιβὸς ἀγαθὸς διαιρείτω
καὶ διακρινέτω τὰς φύσεις τῶν πραγμάτων, ἵνα μὴ φύρηται
συγχεόμενα τοῖς παρασήμοις τὰ δόκιμα.

> Philo, *De spec. leg.* 4.77. Colson, *Philo* 8:54.

1 Thess. 5:21, 22.

NOTES

[1] There are about 70 citations or allusions to this saying or its imagery. It is
unnecessary to cite all of these, and the reader is referred to Resch, *Aprapha*[2] for a
full listing of the passages. Here we cite the most important passages in which the
saying was attributed to Jesus as well as its earliest parallels.

[2] See also *Hom.* 3.50 and 18.20 for the same saying attributed to Jesus.

W8 / *Wisdom's Children*

The children of wisdom are also recorded in the gospel: And wisdom sends
forth her children.

τὰ δὲ τέκνα τῆς σοφίας καὶ ἐν τῷ εὐαγγελίῳ ἀναγέγραπται·
"καὶ ἀποστέλλει ἡ σοφία τὰ τέκνα αὐτῆς."

> Origen, *Homilies on Jeremiah* 14.5. Klostermann, *Origenes* 3:110.

PARALLELS

I sent my servants the prophets to you, whom you have taken and
killed and torn their bodies apart, whose blood I will require, says
the Lord.

Ego misi pueros meos prophetas ad uos, quos acceptos inter-fecistis et laniastis corpora illorum: quorum sanguinem exquiram, dicit dominus.

4 Ezra 1.32. Bensley, *The Fourth Book of Ezra*, 3.

Luke 7:35, 11:49, Matt 11:19, Prov 9:3, Jer 7:25, 25:4, 26:5, 35:15, 44:4.

W9 / *Near and Far*

And pray for your enemies. For he who is not [against you] is for you. [He who] is far away [today] will be [near you] tomorrow.[1]

       κ]αὶ π[ρ]οσεύχεσθε ὑπὲρ
[τῶν ἐχθ]ρῶν ὑμῶν· ὁ γὰρ μὴ ὢν
[κατὰ ὑμ]ῶν ὑπὲρ ὑμῶν ἐστιν.
[ὁ σήμερον ὢ]ν μακρὰν αὔριον
[ἐγγὺς ὑμῶν γ]ενήσεται.

       Oxyrhynchus Papyrus 1224, 2^r. Grenfell and Hunt, *The Oxyrhynchus Papyri* 10:9.

PARALLELS

    Mark 9:40, Matt 12:30, Luke 9:50, 11:23.

NOTES

[1] The second and third sayings are our concern here. The several occurrences of 'pray for your enemies' are treated in C5.

W10 / *The Rope and the Needle*

It is easier for a rope[1] to go through the eye of a needle than for a rich man to enter the kingdom of God.

εὐκοπώτερόν ἐστιν κάμιλον διὰ τῆς τρυμαλιᾶς τῆς ῥαφίδος
διελθεῖν ἢ πλούσιον εἰς τὴν βασιλείαν τοῦ θεοῦ εἰσελθεῖν.

      Manuscript variants to Mark 10:25, Matt 19:24, Luke 18:25. Aland, *Synopsis*, 341.

PARALLELS

Verily I say to you: It is easier for a holy one to fall into unholiness and for a man of light to fall into darkness than for you to reign or not reign.

ⲤⲈ ⲘⲘⲀⲚ ϮⲬⲞⲨ ⲘⲘⲀⲤ ⲚⲎⲦⲚ̄
ⲬⲈ ⲤⲘⲀⲦⲚ̄ ⲀⲦⲢⲈⲞⲨⲠⲈⲦⲞⲨⲀ
ⲀⲂ ⲈⲒ ⲀⲠⲒⲦⲚ̄ ⲀⲨⲬⲰ2Ⲙ̄ ⲀⲨⲱ Ⲛ̄
ⲦⲈⲞⲨⲢⲠ̄ⲘⲚ̄ⲞⲨⲀⲈⲒⲚ ⲈⲒ ⲀⲠⲒⲦⲚ̄
ⲀⲠⲔⲈⲔⲈⲒ Ⲛ̄2ⲞⲨⲞ ⲀⲢⲰⲦⲚ̄ ⲀⲢ̄ Ⲣ̄
ⲢⲞ Ⲏ̄ ⲀⲦⲘⲈⲒⲢⲈ·

Apocryphon of James, CG I, 10.1–6.

Mark 10:25, Matt 19:24, Luke 18:25.

NOTES
[1] Methodius of Olympus is the earliest witness to this reading. See *On Leprosy* 16.7 in Bonwetsch, *Methodius von Olympus*, 472.

W11 / Illness and the Physician

But where the illness is, there the physician runs. I go to the stone-throwers, because instead of stone-throwers they will become interpreters (of God's plan).[1]

Ephrem, *Commentary on the Diatessaron* 17.1. Trans. based on the Latin rendering of the Syriac in Leloir, *Saint Ephrem: Commentaire de L'Évangile Concordant*, 193.

PARALLELS

Mark 2:17, Matt 9:12, Luke 5:31.

NOTES
[1] Leloir's note indicates the Syriac words rendered stone-thrower and interpreter constitute a word play.

W12 / Opportunity for Satan

And Peter said: It is impossible for me to deny the assertion of my teacher. Therefore, I also admit that the evil one exists, because the teacher, who spoke the truth in all things, has frequently said that he exists. For instance, then, he acknowledges that he conversed with him and tempted him for forty days. And I know that he has said elsewhere: If Satan casts out Satan, he is divided against himself. How then can his kingdom stand? And he pointed out that he saw the evil one falling from heaven like lightning. And elsewhere he said: He who sowed the bad seed is the devil. And again: Give no opportunity to the evil one.[1]

καὶ ὁ Πέτρος· Ἀδύνατόν ἐστίν μοι φωνὴν τοῦ ἐμοῦ
ἀρνήσασθαι διδασκάλου, διὸ καὶ ὁμολογῶ εἶναι τὸν πονηρόν,
ὅτι πολλάκις αὐτὸν ὑπάρχειν ὁ πάντα ἀληθεύσας εἴρηκεν διδάσκαλος. αὐτίκα γοῦν ὁμολογεῖ ἐπὶ τεσσαράκοντα ἡμέρας
διαλεχθέντα πεπειρακέναι αὐτόν. καὶ ἄλλῃ που οἶδα αὐτὸν
εἰρηκότα· Εἰ ὁ σατανᾶς τὸν σατανᾶν ἐκβάλλει, ἐφ' ἑαυτὸν
ἐμερίσθη· πῶς οὖν αὐτοῦ στήκῃ ἡ βασιλεία; καὶ ὅτι ἑώρακεν
τὸν πονηρὸν ὡς ἀστραπὴν πεσόντα ἐκ τοῦ οὐρανοῦ ἐδήλωσεν.
καὶ ἄλλοθι ἔφη· Ὁ δὲ τὸ κακὸν σπέρμα σπείρας ἐστὶν ὁ
διάβολος. καὶ πάλιν· μὴ δότε πρόφασιν τῷ πονηρῷ.

Ps. Clementine Homilies, 19.2.4. Rehm-Irmscher, *Homilien*, 253.

PARALLELS

Do not become a place for the devil, for you have already destroyed him.

**ⲘⲠⲢϢⲰⲠⲈ ⲈⲢⲈⲦⲚ ⲞⲈⲒ ⲚⲦⲞ
ⲠⲞⲤ ⲘⲠⲆⲒⲀⲂⲞⲖⲞⲤ ϪⲈ ⲀⲦⲈ
ⲦⲚⲞⲨⲰ ⲈⲢⲈⲦⲚⲞⲨⲰⲤϤ ⲘⲘⲀϤ**

Gospel of Truth. CG I, 33.19–21.

Eph 4:27, 1 Tim 5:14.

NOTES

[1] Our concern here is only with this last saying.

W13 / *He Who Dies Will Live*

I abandoned myself to death, trusting in the . . . divine word: he who dies will live, he who humbles himself will be exalted.

**[ⲀⲒⲦ]ⲈⲈⲦ ⲀⲠⲘⲞⲨ ⲈⲒ̈ⲔⲀϨⲦⲀⲒ̈Ⲧ' ⲀⲠⲤⲈϪⲈ Ⲙ . . . ⲚⲚⲞⲨ
. [Ⲧ]Ⲉ ϪⲈ ⲠⲈⲦⲀⲘⲞⲨ ϤⲀⲰⲚϨ ⲠⲈⲦⲀⲐⲂⲒⲀϤ [ⲤⲈⲚ]ⲀϪⲈⲤⲦ[Ϥ]**

Manichaean Psalm-Book, Ps. 273.10–11. Allberrry, *Manichaean Psalm-Book*, 93.

PARALLELS

he who humbles himself will be received, he who [exalts himself] will be [humbled, he who] dies will live, he who labors will have rest.

[ΠΕΤΑΘ]ΒΙΑϤ ⲤⲞⲨⲀ·ⲬⲒⲦϤ ΠΕ[ⲦⲀⲬⲈⲤⲦϤ Ⲥ]ⲈⲚⲀ[Θ]Ⲃ[ⲒⲀϤ]
[ΠΕⲦ·ⲰⲀϤ]ⲘⲞⲨ ·ⲰⲀϤⲰⲚⲌ ΠΕ·ⲰⲀϤ2ⲒⲤⲈ ·ⲰⲀϤⲘ̄ⲦⲀⲚ

Manichaean Psalm-Book 159.15–16. Ibid., 159.

Mark 8:35, Matt 10:39, 16:25, Luke 17:33, Matt 23:12, Luke 14:11, 18:14.

W14 / *Two Types of Shame*

Such is also the meaning of the gospel: there is a shame[1] which leads to death and there is a shame which leads to life.

Tale quid et illud Evangelii sonat: Est confusio quae ducit ad mortem, et est confusio quae ducit ad vitam.

> Jerome, *Commentary on Ezekiel,* to Ezek 16:52. PL 25: 162.

PARALLELS

For there is a shame which brings sin, and there is a shame which brings glory and favor.

Est enim confusio adducens peccatum, et est confusio adducens gloriam et gratiam.

> Sirach 4:25. *Biblia Sacra juxta Latinam Vulgatam Versionem* 12:165.

For there is a shame which brings sin, and there is a shame which is glory and favor.

ἔστιν γὰρ αἰσχύνη ἐπάγουσα ἁμαρτίαν, καὶ ἔστιν αἰσχύνη δόξα καὶ χάρις.

> Sirach 4:21. Rahlfs, *Septuaginta* 2:384.

There is a shame which brings sin, and there is a shame which is glory and favor.

ἔστιν αἰσχύνη ἐπάγουσα ἁμαρτίαν, καὶ ἔστιν αἰσχύνη δόξα καὶ χάρις.

> Prov 26:11b (LXX). Ibid., 2:230.

NOTES

[1] "Shame" is a possible though not a very common translation of "confusio." Confusio is used in the Vulgate of the close parrallel in Sirach 4:25 as the rendering of "αἰσχύνη," "shame," which occurs in the LXX of Sirach 4:21.

W15 / *The Hand on the Plow*

Then the Lord appeared to Philip and said: O Philip, have you not heard, 'do not render evil for evil?'[1] Why have you wrought such great obliteration? O Philip, who puts his hand to the plow and looks back—is his furrow straight? Or who gives his own lamp to another and himself sits in darkness? Or who abandons his own dwelling and dwells on a dunghill himself? And who gives his own garment away in winter and goes naked? Or what enemy takes pleasure in the joy of the one who hates him? And what soldier goes to war without full armor? And what servant who has performed his master's command will not be praised? And who, having run the race nobly, does not receive the prize? And who, having washed his garments, gladly soils them?

Τότε ὁ κύριος φανεὶς τῷ Φιλίππῳ εἶπεν· ῏Ω Φίλιππε,
οὐκ ἤκουσας Μὴ ἀποδώσῃς κακὸν ἀντὶ κακοῦ; Καὶ διὰ τί
τοσοῦτον ἔπληξας ἀφανισμῷ; ὦ Φίλιππε, τίς θέμενος
τὴν χεῖρα αὐτοῦ ἐπ' ἄροτρον καὶ βλέπων εἰς τὰ ὀπίσω
εὐθετός ἐστιν αὐτοῦ ἡ αὖλαξ; ἢ τίς παραχωρεῖ τὸν
ἑαυτοῦ λύχνον ἑτέρῳ καὶ αὐτὸς ἐν σκότει καθέζεται;
ἢ τίς καταλείπει τὸ ἑαυτοῦ οἰκητήριον καὶ αὐτὸς οἰκεῖ
ἐν κοπρίᾳ; τίς δὲ ἐάσας τὸ ἑαυτοῦ ἔνδυμα ἐν χειμῶνι
πορεύεται γυμνός; ἢ τίς χαρήσεται ἐχθρὸς ἐν τῇ χαρᾷ
τοῦ μισοῦντος αὐτόν; τίς δὲ στρατιώτης πορεύεται ἐπὶ
πόλεμον ἄνευ πανοπλίας; τίς δὲ δοῦλος πληρώσας τὸ τοῦ
κυρίου αὐτοῦ πρόσταγμα οὐκ ἐπαινεθήσεται; τίς δὲ ἐν
σταδίῳ γενναίως δραμὼν οὐ λαμβάνει τὸ βραβεῖον; τίς
δὲ πλύνας τὰ ἱμάτια αὐτοῦ ἡδέως αὐτὰ μολύνει;

Acts of Philip 135. Lipsius-Bonnet, *AAA* 2.2:66–67.

PARALLELS

I (Thomas) have put my hands to the yoked plow and have not looked back, so that the furrows might not be crooked.

τὰς χεῖράς μου ἐπέθηκα τῷ ἀρότρῳ τῷ ζευκτῷ καὶ εἰς τὰ
ὀπίσω οὐκ ἀπεστράφην, ἵνα οἱ αὖλακες μὴ σκαμβασθῶσιν.

Acts of Thomas 147. Ibid., 255.

As the furrows before the ploughman, who has laid his hand to the ploughshare and looks back, will not be considered straight, so also you, who have been called to this gift of service, be careful lest you be troubled by the affairs of this world and be hindered from that to which you have been called.

The Teaching of Addai, f28b. Trans. of the Syriac from Howard, *The Teaching of Addai*, 91.

Luke 9:62.

NOTES

[1] "Do not render evil for evil" is treated in C32.

W16 / *The Prudent Farmer*

Let there be among you a prudent man. When the grain ripened he came quickly with his sickle in his hand (and) reaped it. Whoever has ears to hear let him hear.

ΜΑΡΕϥϢϢΠΕ
2Ν ΤΕΤΝΜΗΤΕ Ν6Ι ΟΥΡϢΜΕ ΝΕΠΙСΤΗ
ΜϢΝ ΝΤΑΡΕΠΚΑΡΠΟС ΠϢ2 ΑϥΕΙ 2ΝΝ ΟΥ
6ΕΠΗ ΕΠΕϥΑС2 2Ν ΤΕϥ6ΙΧ Αϥ2ΑСϥ ΠΕ
ΤΕ ΟΥΝ ΜΑΑΧΕ ΜΜΟϥ ΕСϢΤΜ ΜΑΡΕϥСϢΤΜ

Gospel of Thomas 21c. CG II, 37.15–19.

PARALLELS

Mark 4:29, Rev 14:15–19, Joel 3:13a.

W17 / *Splinter and Beam*

Jesus said: You see the splinter in your brother's eye, but you do not see the beam in your own eye. When you take the beam out of your own eye, then you will see clearly to take the splinter out of your brother's eye.

ΠΕΧΕ ΙС ΧΕ ΠΧΗ
ΕΤ2Μ ΠΒΑΛ ΜΠΕΚ'СΟΝ ΚΝΑΥ ΕΡΟϥ ΠСΟΕΙ
ΔΕ ΕΤ2Μ ΠΕΚΒΑΛ ΚΝΑΥ ΑΝ ΕΡΟϥ 2ΟΤΑΝ
ΕΚϢΑΝΝΟΥΧΕ ΜΠСΟΕΙ ΕΒΟΛ 2Μ ΠΕΚ'
ΒΑΛ' ΤΟΤΕ ΚΝΑΝΑΥ ΕΒΟΛ ΕΝΟΥΧΕ ΜΠΧΗ
ΕΒΟΛ 2Μ ΠΒΑΛ ΜΠΕΚСΟΝ

Gospel of Thomas 26. CG II, 38.12–17.

PARALLELS

and then you will see clearly to take out the splinter which is in your brother's eye.[1]

καὶ τότε διαβλέψεις
ἐκβαλεῖν τὸ κάρφος
τὸ ἐν τῷ ὀφθαλμῷ
τοῦ ἀδελφοῦ σου.
> P. Oxy. 1.1–4. Fitzmyer, *Essays*, 389.

It was taught in a Baraitha: R. Tarfon said, I wonder whether there is any one in this generation who accepts reproof, for if one says to him; Remove the mote from between your eyes, he would answer: Remove the beam from between your eyes!
> *b. 'Arakin* 16b. Epstein, *The Babylonian Talmud* 5.1:94.

Matt 7:3–4, Luke 6:41–42.

NOTES
[1] The first part of the saying is not preserved.

W18 / *Wealth amidst Poverty*

Jesus said: If the flesh came into being because of the spirit, it is a marvel. But if the spirit (came into being) because of the body, it is a marvel of marvels. But I marvel at this, how this great wealth has made its home in this poverty.

ΠΕΧΕ ΙC ΕϢΧΕ ΝΤΑΤCΑΡΣ'
ϢϢΠΕ ΕΤΒΕ ΠΝΑ ΟΥϢΠΗΡΕ ΤΕ ΕϢ
ΧΕ ΠΝΑ ΔΕ ΕΤΒΕ ΠCϢΜΑ ΟΥϢΠΗΡΕ
ΝϢΠΗΡΕ ΠΕ· ΑΛΛΑ ΑΝΟΚ' †Ρ ϢΠΗΡΕ
ΜΠΑΕΙ ΧΕ ΠϢ[C] ΑΤ[ΕΕ]ΙΝΟϬ ΜΜΝΤΡΜΜΑ
Ο ΑCΟΥϢ2 2Ν ΤΕΕΙΜΝΤ2ΗΚΕ
> *Gospel of Thomas* 29. CG II, 38.31–39.2.

PARALLELS

2 Cor 8:9.

W19 / *Prophet and Physician*

Jesus said: No prophet is accepted in his own village; no physician heals those who know him.

ΠΕΧΕ ΙC ΜΝ ΠΡΟΦΗ
ΤΗC ϢΗΠ 2Μ ΠΕϤϮΜΕ ΜΑΡΕCΟΘΕΙΝ ΡΘΕ
ΡΑΠΕΥΕ ΝΝΕΤ'COOΥΝ ΜΜΟϤ'

Gospel of Thomas 31. CG II, 39.5–7.

PARALLELS

Jesus said: A prophet is not acceptable in his own country, nor does a physician heal those who know him.

λέγει 'Ι(ησοῦ)ς οὐ
κ ἔστιν δεκτὸς προ
φήτης ἐν τῷ π(ατ)ρίδι αὐ
τ[ο]ῦ οὐδὲ ἰατρὸς ποιεῖ
θεραπείας εἰς τοὺς
γεινώσκοντας¹ αὐτό(ν)

P. Oxy. 1.30–35. Fitzmyer, *Essays*, 401.

Mark 6:4–5, Matt 13:57–58, Luke 4:23–24, John 4:44.

NOTES
¹ In line 35, correct γεινώσκοντας to γινώσκοντας, "know."

W20 / The City on the Mountain _____

Jesus said: A city that is built on a high mountain (and) fortified cannot fall, nor can it be hidden.

ΠΕΧΕ ΙC
ΧΕ ΟΥΠΟΛΙC ΕΥΚШΤ ΜΜΟC 2ΙΧΝ ΟΥΤΟ
ΟΥ ΕϤΧΟCΕ ΕCΤΑΧΡΗΥ ΜΝ 6ΟΜ ΝC2Ε
ΟΥΔΕ CΝΑϢ 2ШΠ'ΑΝ

Gospel of Thomas 32. CG II, 39.7–10.

PARALLELS

Jesus said: A city that is built on the top of a high mountain and firmly established can neither fall nor be hidden.

λέγει 'Ι(ησοῦ)ς· πόλις οἰκοδο
μημένη ἐπ' ἄκρον
[ὄ]ρους ὑψηλοῦς καὶ ἐσ

τηριγμένη οὔτε πε
[σ]εῖν δύνηται οὔτε χρυ
[β]ῆναι[1]

    P. Oxy. 1.36–41. Fitzmyer, *Essays*, 402.

Matt 5:14, 7:24–25, Luke 6:47–48.

NOTES

[1] In line 36, correct οἰκοδομημένη to ὠκοδομημένη, "built"; in line 18, correct ὑψηλούς to ὑψηλοῦ, "high."

W21 / *Lamps are for Lampstands* _____

Jesus said: What you will hear in your ear[1] proclaim on your roof-tops. For no one lights a lamp and puts it under a bushel, nor does he put it in a hidden place, but he puts it on a lampstand so that every one who goes in and comes out may see its light.

        ΠΕΧΕ Ī͞С ΠΕΤ'ΚΝΑ
СШΤ͞М ΕΡΟϤ 2Μ̄ ΠΕΚ'ΜΑΑΧΕ 2Μ̄ ΠΚΕΜΑ
ΑΧΕ[1] ΤΑϢΕΟΕΙϢ)' Μ̄ΜΟϤ 2ΙΧ͞Ν ΝΕΤΝ̄ΧΕ
ΝΕΠШΡ' ΜΑΡΕΛΑΑΥ' ΓΑΡ ΧΕΡΕ 2ΗΒС Ν̄Ϥ'
ΚΑΑϤ' 2Α ΜΑΑΧΕ ΟΥΔΕ ΜΑϤΚΑΑϤ· 2Μ̄ ΜΑ
ΕϤ2ΗΠ' ΑΛΛΑ ΕϢΑΡΕϤΚΑΑϤ' 2ΙΧ͞Ν ΤΛΥ
ΧΝΙΑ ΧΕΚΑΑС ΟΥΟΝ ΝΙΜ' ΕΤΒΗΚ' Ε2ΟΥΝ
ΑΥШ ΕΤΝ̄ΝΗΥ ΕΒΟΛ ΕΥΝΑΝΑΥ ΑΠΕϤΟΥ
ΟΕΙΝ.

    Gospel of Thomas 33. CG II, 39.10–18.

PARALLELS

> Jesus said: What you hear in your one ear proclaim on the rooftops.

        λέγει Ἰ(ησοῦ)ς· <ὃ> ἀκούεις
    [ε]ἰς τὸ ἓν ὠτίον σου, το[ῦ]
    [το κήρυξον ἐπὶ τῶν]
    [δωμάτων]

    P. Oxy. 1.41–44. Fitzmyer, *Essays*, 404.

Matt 10:27, Luke 12:3, Mark 4:21, Matt 5:15, Luke 8:16, 11:33.

NOTES

[1] The words 2Μ̄ ΠΕΜΑΑΧΕ, "in the other ear," are probably to be viewed as dittography and are omitted in the translation. The translation, "What you will hear in

your ear proclaim in the other ear on your rooftops," is a possibility, as is "What you will hear in your ear (and) in the other ear proclaim on your rooftops."

W22 / The Blind Leading the Blind _____

Jesus said: If a blind man leads a blind man, they both fall into a pit.

ΠΕΧΕ ĪC ΧΕ ΟΥΒⲖⲖΕ ΕϤϢⲀⲚⲤⲰⲔ′
2ΗΤϤ′ ⲚⲚΟΥΒⲖⲖΕ ϢⲀΥ2Ε ⲘΠΕⲤⲚⲀΥ·
ΕΠΕⲤΗΤ′ ΕΥ2ΙΕΙΤ′

Gospel of Thomas 34. CG II, 39.18–20.

PARALLELS

Matt 15:14, Luke 6:39.

W23 / Binding the Strong Man _____

Jesus said: It is impossible for anyone to enter the house of a strong man and take it by force, unless he (first) binds his hands; then he will plunder his house.

ΠΕΧΕ ĪC ⲘⲚ 6ΟⲘ′
ⲚΤΕΟΥⲀ ΒⲰⲔ′ Ε2ΟΥⲚ ΕΠΗΕΙ ⲘΠΧⲰ
ϢⲢΕ ⲚϤΧΙΤϤ′ ⲚΧⲚⲀ2 ΕΙⲘΗΤΙ ⲚϤⲘΟΥⲢ
ⲚⲚΕϤ6ΙΧ′ ΤΟΤΕ ϤⲚⲀΠⲰⲰⲚΕ ΕΒΟⲖ
ⲘΠΕϤΗΕΙ

Gospel of Thomas 35. CG II, 39.20–24.

PARALLELS

And the Savior exhorts us to bind it (the body) and to seize its possessions as those of a strong man who is making war against the heavenly soul.

καὶ "δῆσαι" παραινεῖ καὶ "ἁρπάσαι ὡς ἰσχυροῦ τὰ σκεύη," τοῦ ἀντιπολεμοῦντος τῇ οὐρανίῳ ψυχῇ, ὁ σωτήρ.

Clement, *Exc. ex Theod.* 52.1. Stählin-Früchtel, *Clemens* 3²:124.

Mark 3:27, Matt 12:29, Luke 11:21–22, Matt 24:43, Luke 12:39.

W24 / *Food and Clothing*

Jesus said: Do not be concerned from morning until evening and from evening until morning about what you will put on.

ΠЄΧЄ ĪC Μ͞Ν͞ϤΙ ΡΟΟΥϢ ΧΙ
2ΤΟΟΥЄ ϢΑ ΡΟΥ2Є ΑΥϢ ΧΙΝ 2ΙΡΟΥ2Є
ϢΑ 2ΤΟΟΥЄ ΧЄ ΟΥ ΠЄ ЄΤΝΑΤΑΑϤ 2ΙϢΤ΄
ΤΗΥΤ͞Ν

Gospel of Thomas 36. CG II, 39.24–27.

PARALLELS

[Jesus said: Do not be anxious] from morning until [evening, nor] from evening [until] morning either [for] your [food], what [you will] eat, [or] for [your] clo[thing], what you [will] put on. [You] are of much more value than [the lili]es which grow but do not s[pi]n nor have clothing. What do [you lack]? Who of you can add to his lifespan? He will give you your clothing.

[λέγει ’Ι(ησοῦ)ς· μή μεριμνᾶ]
[τε ἀπ]ὸ πρωὶ ἕ[ως ὀψὲ]
[μήτ]ε ἀφ’ ἑσπ[έρας]
[ἕως π]ρωὶ μήτε [τῇ]
[τροφῇ ὑ]μῶν τί φά
[γητε μήτε] τῇ στ[ο]
[λῇ ὑμῶν] τί ἐνδύ
[ση]σθε. [πολ]λῷ χρεί[σ]
[σον]ές ἐ[στε] τῶν [κρί]
νων ἅτι[να α]ὐξά
νει οὐδὲ ν[ήθ]ει μ[ηδ]
ἐν ἔχοντ[α ἔ]νδ[υ]
μα. τί ἐν[δεῖτε] καὶ
ὑμεῖς; τίς ἂν προσθ<εί>η
ἐπὶ τὴν εἱλικίαν
ὑμῶν; αὐτὸ[ς δ]ώσει
ὑμεῖν τὸ ἔνδυμα ὑ
μῶν.[1]

P. Oxy. 655. i.1–17. Fitzmyer, *Essays*, 406.

Matt 6:25–34, Luke 12:22–31.

NOTES
[1] In line 14, correct εἱλικίαν to ἡλικίαν, "lifespan"; in line 16, correct to ὑμεῖν to ὑμῖν, "(to) you."

W25 / Grapes from Thorn Trees _____

Jesus said: Grapes are not gathered from thorn-trees, nor are figs picked from
thistles, for they do not produce fruit. A good man brings forth good from his
treasure; a wicked man brings forth evil things from his evil treasure, which
is in his heart, and speaks evil things. For out of the abundance of the heart
he brings forth evil things.

ПЕХЄ ІС МАУХЄЛЄ ЄЛОО
ЛЄ ЄВОЛ 2Н ϢОНТЄ ОУТЄ МАУКШТϤ'
КNТЄ ЄВОЛ 2Н СР̄6АМОУЛ' МАУϯ КАРПОС
[ГАР ОУАГ]АѲОС Р̄РШМЄ ϢАϤЄІНЄ N̄
ОУАГАѲОН ЄВОЛ 2[М] ПЄϤЄ2О ОУКА[КОС]
Р̄РШМЄ ϢАϤЄІНЄ N̄2N̄ПОНΗΡΟΝ ЄВОЛ
2М̄ ПЄϤЄ2О ЄѲООУ ЄТ2N̄ ПЄϤ2ΗΤ' ΑΥ
Ш N̄ϤХШ N̄2N̄ПОНΗΡΟΝ ЄВОЛ ГАР 2М̄
ФОУО М̄ФΗΤ' ϢАϤ'ЄІНЄ ЄВОЛ N̄2N̄ПО
ΝΗΡΟΝ

Gospel of Thomas 45. CG II, 40.31–41.6.

PARALLELS

> One does not gather grapes from thorns, nor figs from thistles, for
> a good tree produces good fruit and a bad tree produces bad fruit.
> A good tree cannot yield bad fruit, and a bad tree cannot yield
> good fruit. A good man brings forth and speaks good things from
> the good treasures which are in his heart, and an evil man brings
> forth and speaks evil things from the abundance of his heart, for
> the lips speak from the abundance of the heart.
>
> > Aphrahat, *Demon.* 14.48 [Bert, 14.29] *Exhortatoria.* Trans. based on the
> > German in Bert, *Aphrahat's Homilien*, 256–257.

> Remember what our Savior says: The good tree produces good
> fruit, and the bad tree produces bad fruit. The bad tree cannot
> produce good fruit, and the good tree cannot produce bad fruit,
> for the tree is known by its fruit. So the good man produces and
> speaks good things from the good treasures which are in his heart,
> and the evil man produces and speaks evil things from the evil
> treasures which are in his heart. For the lips speak from the
> abundance of the heart.
>
> > Aphrahat, *Demon.* 9.11 [Bert, 9.8] *De humilitate.* Trans. based on the Ger-
> > man in Bert, *Aphrahat's Homilien*, 154–155.

> For they do not gather figs from thorns or from thorn trees, if they
> are wise, nor grapes from thorns.

OYTE ΓΑΡ ΜΑΥΚΕΤϥ ΚN
TE ЄBOΛ 2N 2ЄNCOYPЄ· H ЄBOΛ
2N 2ЄNϢONTE· ЄϢϢΠЄ ЄY
ϢΑΝP̄CΑBЄ· OYΔЄ ЄΛΟΟΛЄ
ЄBOΛ 2N COYPЄ

Apocalypse of Peter, CG VII, 76.4–8.

And Jesus said: 'Who can make wine from thorns (or) wheat from thistles?'

Dialogue between Christ and the Devil 5. Trans. of the Slavonic[1] from Casey and Thomson, "A Dialogue between Christ and the Devil," 57.

Its fruit makes known the cultivation of a tree; so also the word of a man (makes known the cultivation) of the thought of his heart.

γεώργιον ξύλου ἐκφαίνει ὁ καρπὸς αὐτοῦ, οὕτως λόγος
ἐνθυμήματος καρδίας ἀνθρώπου.

Sirach 27.6. Rahlfs, *Septuaginta* 2:423.

Luke 6:44–45, Matt 7:16, 12:33–35, James 3:12.

NOTES
[1] The saying does not occur in the Greek versions.

W26 / *Serving Two Masters*

Jesus said: It is impossible for a man to mount two horses (or) stretch two bows. And it is impossible for a servant to serve two masters; otherwise, he will honor the one and insult the other.

ΠЄΧЄ IC̄
ΧЄ· MN 6OM N̄TЄOYPϢMЄ TЄΛΟ Α2TO
CNΑY N̄ϥΧϢΛΚ' M̄ΠITЄ CN̄TЄ ΑYϢ MN̄
6OM' N̄TЄOY2M2ΑΛ ϢMϢЄ ΧOЄIC CNΑY
H ϥΝΑP̄TIMΑ M̄ΠOYΑ· ΑYϢ ΠΚЄOYΑ ϥΝΑ
P̄2YBPIZЄ M̄MOϥ'

Gospel of Thomas 47a. CG II, 41.12–17.

PARALLELS

For he (Nicolaus) did not wish, I suppose, as the Savior commanded, to serve two masters, pleasure and God.

141

οὐ γάρ, οἶμαι, ἐβούλετο κατὰ τὴν τοῦ σωτῆρος ἐντολὴν "δυσὶ
κυρίοις δουλεύειν", ἡδονῇ καὶ θεῷ.

Clement, *Strom.* 3.26.2. Stählin-Früchtel, *Clemens* 2³:208.

For, although, he permitted (them) to come together again
because of Satan and incontinence, he indicated that the one who
complies serves two masters, God if there is agreement, but if
there is not agreement, incontinence, fornication, and the devil.

πάλιν γὰρ ἐπὶ ταὐτὸ συγχωρήσας γενέσθαι διὰ τὸν σατανᾶν
καὶ τὴν ἀκρασίαν, τὸν πεισθησόμενον "δυσὶ κυρίοις μέλλειν
δουλεύειν" ἀπεφήνατο, διὰ μὲν συμφωνίας θεῷ, διὰ δὲ τῆς
ἀσυμφωνίας ἀκρασίᾳ καὶ πορνείᾳ καὶ διαβόλῳ.

Clement, *Strom.* 3.81.2. (quoted from Tatian's *On Perfection according to
the Savior*). Ibid., 232.

Matt 6:24, Luke 16:13.

W27 / *Old and New Don't Fit* _____

No man drinks old wine and immediately desires to drink new wine. And new
wine is not put into old wineskins, lest they burst; nor is old wine put into
a new wineskin, lest it spoil it. An old patch is not sewn on a new garment,
because a tear will result.

  ⲘⲀⲢⲈⲢⲰⲘⲈ ⲤⲈ Ⲣ̄ⲠⲀⲤ
ⲀⲨⲰ Ⲛ̄ⲦⲈⲨⲚⲞⲨ Ⲛ̄Ϥ'ⲈⲠⲒⲐⲨⲘⲈⲒ ⲀⲤⲰ ⲎⲢⲠ'
Ⲃ̄ⲂⲢⲢⲈ ⲀⲨⲰ ⲘⲀⲨⲚⲞⲨⲬ' ⲎⲢⲠ· Ⲃ̄Ⲃ̄ⲢⲦⲈ ⲈⲀⲤ
ⲔⲞⲤ Ⲛ̄ⲀⲤ ⲬⲈⲔⲀⲀⲤ Ⲛ̄ⲚⲞⲨⲠⲰϨ ⲀⲨⲰ ⲘⲀⲨ
ⲚⲈⲬ ⲎⲢⲠ· Ⲛ̄ⲀⲤ ⲈⲀⲤⲔⲞⲤ Ⲃ̄ⲂⲢⲢⲈ ϢⲒⲚⲀ ⲬⲈ
ⲚⲈϤⲦⲈⲔⲀϤ' ⲘⲀⲨⲬⲀ̄Ϭ ⲦⲞⲈⲒⲤ Ⲛ̄ⲀⲤ ⲀϢⲦⲎ̄
Ⲛ̄ϢⲀⲈⲒ ⲈⲠⲈⲒ ⲞⲨⲚ ⲞⲨⲠⲰϨ ⲚⲀϢⲰⲠⲈ

  Gospel of Thomas 47b. CG II, 41.17–23.

PARALLELS

  Mark 2:21–22, Matt 9:16–17, Luke 5:36–38.

W28 / *The World Is a Corpse* _____

Jesus said: Whoever has known the world has found a corpse, and whoever has found a corpse, the world is not worthy of him.

ΠΕ
ΧΕ ⲒⲤ ΧΕ ⲠΕΤⲀⲆⲤⲞⲨⲰⲚ ⲠⲔⲞⲤⲘⲞⲤ ⲀϤ'
ⲆⲈ ⲈⲨⲠⲦⲰⲘⲀ ⲀⲨⲰ ⲠⲈⲚⲦⲀⲆⲆⲈ ⲈⲀⲠⲦⲰ
ⲘⲀ¹ ⲠⲔⲞⲤⲘⲞⲤ ⲘⲠϢⲀ ⲘⲘⲞϤ ⲀⲚ

Gospel of Thomas 56. CG II, 42.29–32.

PARALLELS

Jesus said: He who has known the world has found the body, and he who has found the body, the world is not worthy of him.

ⲠⲈΧⲈ ⲒⲤ ΧⲈ ⲠⲈⲚⲦⲀⲆⲤⲞⲨⲰⲚ
ⲠⲔⲞⲤⲘⲞⲤ ⲀϤⲆⲈ ⲈⲠⲤⲰⲘⲀ ⲠⲈⲚⲦⲀⲆⲆⲈ
ⲆⲈ ⲈⲠⲤⲰⲘⲀ ⲠⲔⲞⲤⲘⲞⲤ ⲘⲠϢⲀ ⲘⲘⲞϤ'
ⲀⲚ'

Gospel of Thomas 80. CG II, 47.12–15.

Does not Jesus say: Whoever has found himself, of him the world is not worthy.

ⲞⲨΧ² ⲆⲞⲦⲒ ⲈⲒⲤ
ΧⲰ ⲘⲘⲞⲤ ΧⲈ ⲠⲈⲦⲀⲆⲈ ⲈⲢⲞϤ' ⲞⲨⲀⲀϤ ⲠⲔⲞⲤ
ⲘⲞⲤ ⲘⲠϢⲀ ⲘⲘⲞϤ' ⲀⲚ

Gospel of Thomas 111b. CG II, 51.8–10.

I have handled the world; I have known it, that there is not a bit[3] of life in it.

ⲀⲒϬⲀⲘϬⲘ ⲠⲔⲞⲤⲘⲞⲤ
ⲀⲒⲤⲚⲞⲨⲰⲚⲈϤ· ΧⲈ ⲘⲚ ⲞⲨⲤⲀⲀⲀⲠⲒⲚ ⲚⲰⲚⳞ ⲚⳞⲎⲦϤ

Psalms of Thomas 17.24–25. Allberry, *Manichaean Psalm-Book*, 223.

NOTES

¹ Correct ⲈⲀⲠⲦⲰⲘⲀ to ⲈⲨⲠⲦⲰⲘⲀ, "a corpse."

² ⲞⲨΧ, "not" is sufficiently clear in the Facsimile Edition, whereas Guillaumont (*Thomas*, 54) reads ⲞⲨⲀ, "nor." Several translators have utilized Guillaumont's conjecture that ⲞⲨⲆⲈ ⲈⲆⲞⲦⲈ ⲆⲞⲦⲒ, "nor fear for," has become ⲞⲨⲀ ⲆⲞⲦⲒ by haplography. The translation of the end of 111a and the beginning of 111b would then become, ". . . he who lives from the Living One will neither see death nor fear, for Jesus says. . ." For Thomas 111a, see Pro58.

³ Literally, "a little finger."

W29 / *Left and Right Hands* _____

Do not let your left (hand) know what your right (hand) will do.

$\overline{\text{ПЕ[Т]Є}}$ ТЄКОΥΝΑΜ ΝΑΑϥ
Ṃ̇ΝΤΡΕΤΕΚ2ΒΟΥΡ· ЄΙΜЄ ХЄ ЄСР ΟΥ

> *Gospel of Thomas* 62b. CG II, 44.1–2.

PARALLEL

Matt 6:3.

W30 / *The Rejected Stone* _____

Jesus said: Show me that stone which the builders rejected. It is the cornerstone.

$\qquad\qquad\qquad\qquad\overline{\text{ПЄ}}$
ХЄ $\overline{\text{ΙС}}$ ХЄ ΜΑΤСЄΒΟΕΙ ЄΠШΝЄ ΠΑΕΙ $\overline{\text{ΝΤΑΥ}}$
СΤΟϥ' ЄΒΟΛ' $\overline{\text{Ν}}$6Ι ΝЄΤ'ΚШΤ' $\overline{\text{ΝΤΟϥ}}$ ΠЄ ΠШШ
ΝЄ $\overline{\text{ΝΚШ2}}$

> *Gospel of Thomas* 66. CG II, 45.16–19.

PARALLELS

The phrase "of the rock," he says, refers to Adam. This, he says is Adam, the cornerstone which has become the head of the corner. For in the head is the impressed brain, the substance from which the entire family is fashioned. Which Adam, he says, I place as the foundations of Zion.

πέτρης, φησί, τοῦ 'Αδάμαντος λέγει. οὗτος, φησίν, ἐστὶν
ὁ ἀδάμας "ὁ λίθος ὁ ἀκρογωνιαῖος εἰς κεφαλὴν γεγενημένος
γωνίας"—ἐν κεφαλῇ γὰρ εἶναι τὸν χαρακτηριστικὸν ἐγκέφαλον,
τὴν οὐσίαν, "ἐξ οὗ πᾶσα πατριὰ χαρακτηρίζεται"—, "ὄν,"
φησίν, "ἐντάσσω ἀδάμαντα εἰς τὰ θεμέλια Σιών·"

> Hippolytus, *Ref.* 5.7.35. Wendland, *Hippolytus* 3:87.

Mark 12:10–11, Matt 21:42, Luke 20:17, Ps 118:22, Isa 28:16, 1 Pet 2:4–8.

W31 / *On Self-knowledge*

Jesus said: He who knows the All but fails (to know) himself fails everywhere.[1]

ΠΕϪΕ ⲒⲤ ϪΕ ΠΕΤⲤΟΟΥΝ ⲘΠΤΗΡϤ'
ΕϤⲠ ⲞΡⲰ2 ΟΥⲀⲀϤ Ⲣ ⲞΡⲰ2 ⲘΠΜⲀ ΤΗΡϤ'

Gospel of Thomas 67. CG II, 45.19–20.

PARALLELS

Mark 8:36, Matt 16:26, Luke 9:25.

NOTES

[1] Lambdin's translation (in Robinson, *Nag Hammadi Library,* 126) is quite different. Jesus said, "Whoever believes that the All itself is deficient is (himself) completely deficient."

W32 / *Laborers for the Harvest*

Jesus said: The harvest is bountiful, but the laborers are few. Beseech the Lord to send laborers out to the harvest.

ΠΕϪΕ ⲒⲤ ϪΕ ΠⲰ2Ⲥ
ΜΕΝ ΝⲀϢⲰϤ' ⲚΕΡΓⲀΤΗⲤ ⲆΕ ⲤΟΒⲔ' ⲤΟΠⲤ
ⲆΕ ⲘΠϪΟΕⲒⲤ ϢΙΝⲀ ΕϤΝⲀΝΕϪ' ΕΡΓⲀΤΗⲤ
ΕΒΟⲖ' ΕΠⲰ2Ⲥ

Gospel of Thomas 73. CG II, 46.6–9.

PARALLELS

Matt 9:37–38, Luke 10:2.

W33 / *Many at the Cistern*

He said: Lord, there are many around the cistern, but there is no one[1] in the cistern.

ΠΕϪⲀϤ ϪΕ ΠϪΟΕⲒⲤ ΟΥⲚ
2Ⲁ2 ⲘΠⲰΤΕ ⲚΤϪⲰΤΕ [2] ⲘⲚ ⲖⲀⲀΥ ⲆΕ 2Ⲛ
ΤϢⲰΝΕ·[2]

Gospel of Thomas 74. CG II, 46.9–11.

PARALLELS

How is it that there are many around the well but no one (goes) into it.[3]

πῶς πολλοὶ περὶ τὸ φρέαρ, καὶ οὐδεὶς εἰς τὸ φρέαρ;

Origen, *Contra Celsum* 8.15.16. Koetschau, *Origenes* 2:233.

NOTES

[1] Or, "nothing."

[2] In line 11, correct ⲦⲰⲰⲚⲈ to ⲦⲰⲰⲦⲈ, "cistern" (see Guillaumont, *Thomas*, 40). Guillaumont also corrects ⲦⲬⲰⲦⲈ to ⲦⲰⲰⲦⲈ in line 10. Kasser, however, views ⲬⲰⲦⲈ as a dialect form of ⲰⲰⲦⲈ with the same meaning (*Complements au Dictionnaire de Crum*, 89).

[3] The saying is quoted from Celsus who attributes it to a "Heavenly Dialogue."

W34 / A Reed Shaken by the Wind

Jesus said: Why have you come out into the field? To see a reed shaken by the wind? And to see a man clothed in fine garments? Look, your kings[1] and great men are those who are clothed in fine garments, and they will not be able to know the truth.

ⲠⲈⲬⲈ ⲓ̅ⲥ̅ ⲬⲈ ⲈⲦⲂⲈ ⲞⲨ
ⲀⲦⲈⲦⲚ̅ⲈⲒ ⲈⲂⲞⲖ ⲈⲦⲤⲰⲱ̅ϢⲈ ⲈⲚⲀⲨ ⲈⲨⲔⲀϢ
ⲈϤⲔⲒⲘ Ⲉ[ⲂⲞⲖ] ϨⲒⲦⲘ̅ ⲠⲦⲎⲨ ⲀⲨⲰ ⲈⲚⲀⲨ
ⲈⲨⲢ[ⲰⲘⲈ ⲈϨ]Ⲛ̅Ϣ̅ⲦⲎⲚ ⲈⲨ6ⲎⲚ ϨⲒⲰⲰⲂ·
[ⲈⲒⲤ ⲚⲈⲦⲚ]Ⲣ̅Ⲣ̅ⲰⲞⲨ ⲘⲚ̅ ⲚⲈⲦⲘ̅ⲘⲈⲄⲒ
ⲤⲦⲀⲚⲞⲤ ⲚⲀⲈⲒ ⲈⲚ[Ϣ]ⲦⲎ]Ⲛ Ⲉ[Ⲧ]
6ⲎⲚ ϨⲒⲰⲞⲨ ⲀⲨⲰ ⲤⲈ[ⲚⲀ]Ϣ ⲤⲞⲨ̅Ⲛ
ⲦⲘⲈ ⲀⲚ

Gospel of Thomas 78. CG II, 46.28–47.3.

PARALLELS

And when she came in, Judas said to her: What have you come to see? A strange, poor, despicable man, having neither wealth nor possessions?

εἰσελθούσης δὲ αὐτῆς εἶπεν αὐτῇ 'Ιούδας· Τί ἐλήλυθας ἰδεῖν; ξένον ἄνθρωπον καὶ πένητα καὶ εὐκαταφρόνητον καὶ πτωχόν, μήτε πλοῦτον ἔχοντα μήτε κτῆσιν;

Acts of Thomas 136. Lipsius-Bonnet, *AAA* 2.2:242.

Matt 11:7–8, Luke 7:24–25, John 18:38.

NOTES

[1] I follow the reconstruction of Guillaumont, (*Thomas*, 42), in 46.32, as have most translators. Lambdin (in Robinson, *Nag Hammadi Library*, 127) offers an alternate translation, "And to see a man clothed in fine garments like your kings and great men? Upon them are the fine garments, . . ."

W35 / *Seeing Living Images* ─────────────

Jesus said: When you see your likeness, you rejoice. But when you see your images which came into being before you, which neither die nor are manifested, how much will you bear.

ПЄХЄ ĪC N̄2O
ОУ ЄТЄТN̄NAУ ЄПЄТN̄ЄINЄ Ϣ∆РЄТN̄
Р∆ϢЄ 2ОТ∆N ∆Є ЄТЄТN̄Ϣ∆NN∆У·
∆NЄТN̄2IКⲰN' N̄Т∆2Ϣⲱ̄ПЄ 2I ТЄТNЄ
2H ОУТЄ М∆УМОУ ОУТЄ М∆УОУⲰN2
ЄВОⲖ ТЄТN∆ϤI 2∆ ОУHР'

Gospel of Thomas 84. CG II, 47.25–29.

PARALLELS

He established chambers of life; he set up living images in them; he set up living images in them which never perish.

∆ϤCMN 2N̄Т∆МI
О]N N̄ⲰN2̄· ∆ϤCЄ2О 2N̄2IКⲰN ЄУ∆N2̄ [N̄2Р]HÏ N̄2H
ТОУ· ∆ϤCЄ2О 2N̄2IКⲰN2̄ ЄУ∆N2̄ N̄2HТОУ ЄМ∆У
ОУⲰCϤ ∆NH2Є ∆ТМЄТ'

Ps. of Thomas 1.14–17. Allberry, *Manichaean Psalmbook*, 203.

W36 / *Foxes Have Holes* ─────────────

Jesus said: [Foxes have their holes] and birds have their nests, but the son of man has no place to lay his head and rest.

ПЄХЄ ĪC ХЄ [NВ∆ϢОР ОУ]
[NТ∆]У N[ЄУВHВ] ∆УⲰ N̄2∆Ⲗ∆ТЄ ОУNТ∆У
ММ∆У М̄[ПЄ]УМ∆2 ПϢHРЄ ∆Є М̄ПРⲰМЄ

147

M̄NTA϶ʹ N̄N[OY]MA ϶PIK϶ N̄T϶϶ʹAΠ϶ N̄϶ʹ
M̄TON M̄[MO϶]¹
> *Gospel of Thomas* 86. CG II, 47.34–48.4.

PARALLELS

Matt 8:20, Luke 9:58.

NOTES
¹ The reconstruction of the text follows that of Guillaumont, *Thomas*, 46.

W37 / *Seek, Knock* ──────────────────

Jesus [said]: He who seeks will find,¹ [and he who knocks], it will be opened
to him.

[Π϶X϶] I̅C Π϶T(Ϣ)IN϶ ϶NA6IN϶
[AYϢ Π϶TTϢ2M ϶]2OYN C϶NAOYϢN NA϶ʹ²
> *Gospel of Thomas* 94. CG II, 48.33–34.

PARALLELS

Matt 7:7–8, Luke 11:9–10.

NOTES
¹ See *Gospel of the Hebrews* [1] and parallels [W1] and also *Thomas* 92 [160].
² The reconstruction of the text follows that of Guillaumont, *Thomas*, 48.

W38 / *The Dog in the Manger* ──────────────

Jesus said: Woe to them, the Pharasees! For they are like a dog lying in the
manger of oxen, for he neither eats nor permits the oxen to eat.

Π϶X϶ I̅C [X϶ O]YO϶I NAY M̄ΦAPICAIOC X϶
϶Y϶IN϶[϶ N]OYOY2OP ϶϶N̄KOTKʹ 2IXN̄ ΠOY
ON϶϶ʹ N̄[2϶N]϶2OOY X϶ OYT϶ ϶OYϢM AN
OYT϶ ϶K[Ϣ A]N N̄N϶2OOY ϶OYϢM
> *Gospel of Thomas* 102. CG II, 50.2–5.

PARALLELS

They thought it to be sufficient enjoyment not only not to enjoy
(riches) themselves, but also to share the enjoyment with no one,
just as the dog in the manger which neither ate the barley nor
allowed the hungry horse to eat.

ἱκανὴν ἀπόλαυσιν οἰμένους οὐ τὸ αὐτοὺς ἀπολαύειν ἔχειν,
ἀλλὰ τὸ μηδενὶ μεταδιδόναι τῆς ἀπολαύσεως, καθάπερ τὴν
ἐν τῇ φάτνῃ κύνα μήτε αὐτὴν ἐσθίουσαν τῶν κριθῶν μήτε
τῷ ἵππῳ πεινῶντι ἐπιτρέπουσαν.

> Lucian, *Timon* 14. Harmon, *Lucian* 2:340, 342.

Therefore you could lend the books to someone who wants them,
since you cannot use them yourself. However, you never lent a
book to anyone, but you act like the dog lying in the manger who
neither eats the barley herself nor allows the horse to eat, which
can.

καὶ σὺ τοίνυν ἄλλῳ μὲν δεηθέντι χρήσειας ἂν τὰ βιβλία,
χρήσασθαι δὲ αὐτὸς οὐκ ἂν δύναιο. καίτοι οὐδὲ ἔχρησάς
τινι βιβλίον πώποτε, ἀλλὰ τὸ τῆς κυνὸς ποιεῖς τῆς ἐν τῇ
φάτνῃ κατακειμένης, ἣ οὔτε αὐτὴ τῶν κριθῶν ἐσθίει οὔτε
τῷ ἵππῳ δυναμένῳ φαγεῖν ἐπιτρέπει.

> Lucian, *Adv. indoctum* 30. Ibid., 3:210.

A dog, lying in the manger, neither ate of the barley herself nor
allowed the horse to eat who could.[1]

Κύων τις, ἐν φάτνῃ κατακειμένη, οὔτε αὐτὴ τῶν κριθῶν ἤσθιεν,
οὔτε τῷ ἵππῳ δυναμένῳ φαγεῖν ἐπέτρεπεν.

> *Aesop's Fables* 228. Halm, *Fabulae Aesopicae Collectae*, 111.

Matt 23:13, Luke 11:52.[2]

NOTES

[1] For an expanded version of this, see Perry, *Babrius and Phaedrus*, 597.
[2] See also *Thomas* 39 [C37].

W39 / *Knowing Father and Mother* _____

Jesus said: He who knows the father and the mother will be called the son of a harlot.

ΠЄϪЄ ΙC ϪЄ ΠЄ
ΤΝΑCΟΥШΝ ΠЄΙШΤ′ ΜΝ ΤΜΑΑΥ CЄΝΑΜΟΥ
ΤЄ ЄΡΟϤ′ ϪЄ ΠШ)ΗΡЄ ΜΠΟΡΝΗ

Gospel of Thomas 105. CG II, 50.16–18.

PARALLELS

> He says that she was thrust out by her husband, a carpenter by trade, having been convicted of adultery. Then he says, after she had been driven out by her husband and while wandering about disgracefully, she secretly gave birth to Jesus.
>
> Φησὶ δ᾽ αὐτὴν καὶ ὑπὸ τοῦ γήμαντος, τέκτονος τὴν τέχνην
> ὄντος, ἐξεῶσθαι ἐλεγχθεῖσαν ὡς μεμοιχευμένην. Εἶτα
> λέγει ὡς ἐκβληθεῖσα ὑπὸ τοῦ ἀνδρὸς καὶ πλανωμένη ἀτίμως
> σκότιον ἐγέννησε τὸν Ἰησοῦν·
>
>   Origen, *Contra Celsum* 1.28. Borret, *Origène Contre Celse* 1:150, 152.

but they wrote thus: They called him a son of adultery, and one who leads astray, and other reproachful things, of which the apostles are silent, because of their filthiness.

sed scripserunt sic: Appellabant eum filium moechiae et seductorem et alia, ait, improperia, quae ob foeditatem eorum reticuerunt Apostoli.

    Liber Graduum 22.11. Kmosko, PatSy 1.3:659.

I-SAYINGS

I1 / Not a Bodiless Demon _____

For I know and believe that he was also in the flesh after the resurrection. And when he came to those around Peter, he said to them: Take hold and handle me and see that I am not a bodiless demon.[1] And immediately they touched him and believed, being joined to his flesh and spirit.

Ἐγὼ γὰρ καὶ μετὰ τὴν ἀνάστασιν ἐν σαρκὶ
αὐτὸν οἶδα καὶ πιστεύω ὄντα. καὶ ὅτε
πρὸς τοὺς περὶ Πέτρον ἦλθεν, ἔφη αὐτοῖς·
Λάβετε, ψηλαφήσατέ με καὶ ἴδετε, ὅτι
οὐκ εἰμὶ δαιμόνιον ἀσώματον. καὶ εὐθὺς
αὐτοῦ ἥψαντο καὶ ἐπίστευσαν, κραθέντες
τῇ σαρκὶ αὐτοῦ καὶ τῷ πνεύματι.

> Ignatius, *Smyrnaeans* 3.1-2. Funk-Bihlmeyer, *Die Apostolischen Väter*, 106.

PARALLELS[2]

> . . . from that little book called the Doctrine of Peter, where the Savior seems to say to the disciples: I am not a bodiless demon.

> . . . ex illo libello, qui Petri Doctrina appellatur, ubi salvator videtur ad discipulos dicere: "Non sum daemonium incorporeum," . . .

> Origen, *De princ.* 1, preface 8. Koetschau, *Origenes Werke* 5:14-15.

Luke 24:36–43, John 20:19–28.

NOTES

[1] See *Epistula Apostolorum* 11 and parallels [I12].
[2] Eusebius quotes this passage of Ignatius in *Eccl. hist.* 3.36.11. See Mommsen, *Eusebius Werke* 2.1:278. Jerome quotes the passage in *De viris inlustribus* 16, but attributes it to Ignatius' *Letter to Polycarp* and says Ignatius quoted it from the *Gospel of the Hebrews*. Jerome probably took the material from Eusebius, not from Ignatius directly. See Vielhauer in *N.T. Apoc.* 1:129. Jerome refers to the tradition, but with no reference to Ignatius, in his *Commentary on Isaiah* 18 (preface).

I2 / The Role of the Twelve ─────────────────

I chose you twelve, having determined you worthy to be my disciples (whom the Lord wished)[1] and faithful apostles. And I sent you into the world to proclaim to all men that they may know that there is one God and to reveal what things are to happen through faith in me (Christ), so that those who hear and believe may be saved and those who do not believe may testify that they have heard and not have an excuse to say: We have not heard.

"ἐξελεξάμην ὑμᾶς δώδεκα, μαθητὰς κρίνας ἀξίους ἐμοῦ, οὓς ὁ κύριος
ἠθέλησεν, καὶ ἀποστόλους πιστοὺς ἡγησάμενος εἶναι, πέμπων ἐπὶ
τὸν κόσμον εὐαγγελίσασθαι τοὺς κατὰ τὴν οἰκουμένην ἀνθρώπους,
γινώσκειν ὅτι εἷς θεός ἐστιν, διὰ τῆς τοῦ Χριστοῦ πίστεως ἐμῆς
δηλοῦντας τὰ μέλλοντα, ὅπως οἱ ἀκούσαντες καὶ πιστεύσαντες
σωθῶσιν, οἱ δὲ μὴ πιστεύσαντες ἀκούσαντες μαρτυρήσωσιν, οὐκ
ἔχοντες ἀπολογίαν εἰπεῖν· 'οὐκ ἠκούσαμεν.'"

Kerygma Petrou, Clement, *Strom.* 6.6.48. Stählin-Früchtel, *Clements*
2³:456.

PARALLELS

Therefore Peter reports that the Lord said to the apostles: If anyone in Israel wishes to repent and through my name believe in God, his sins will be forgiven. And after twelve years go out into the world, so that no one might say: We have not heard.

διὰ τοῦτό φησιν ὁ Πέτρος εἰρηκέναι τὸν κύριον τοῖς ἀποστόλοις·
"ἐὰν μὲν οὖν τις θελήσῃ τοῦ Ἰσραὴλ μετανοήσας διὰ
τοῦ ὀνόματός μου πιστεύειν ἐπὶ τὸν θεόν, ἀφεθήσονται αὐτῷ
αἱ ἁμαρτίαι. μετὰ ⟨δὲ⟩ δώδεκα ἔτη ἐξέλθετε εἰς τὸν κόσμον,
μή τις εἴπῃ· 'οὐκ ἠκούσαμεν.'"

Kerygma Petrou, Clement, *Strom.* 6.5.43. Ibid., 453.

He (Apollonius) speaks, moreover, about a tradition that the Savior commanded his apostles not to depart from Jerusalem for twelve years.

ἔτι δὲ ὡς ἐκ παραδόσεως τὸν σωτῆρά φησιν προστεταχέναι
τοῖς αὐτοῦ ἀποστόλοις ἐπὶ δώδεκα ἔτεσιν μὴ χωρισθῆναι
τῆς Ἱερουσαλήμ.

Eusebius, *Eccl. hist.* 5.18.14. Mommsen, *Eusebius* 2.1:478.

Matt 28:19–20, Mark 16:16, Luke 24:46–49.

NOTES
[1] This is probably a comment by Clement.

I3 / *The Most Worthy*

He (Christ) himself taught the reason for the separations of souls that take place in houses, as we have found somewhere in the Gospel that is spread abroad among the Jews in the Hebrew tongue, in which it is said: I choose for myself the most worthy; the most worthy are those whom my Father in heaven has given me.

> *Gospel of the Nazaraeans* [6], Eusebius, *Theophania* 4.12. Trans. of the Syriac from Hennecke-Schneemelcher, *N.T. Apoc.* 1:150.

PARALLELS

Matt 11:27, Luke 10:22, John 6:37, 39, 17:2, 6, 9.

I4 / *Jesus' Mother, the Holy Spirit*

If anyone accepts the Gospel according to the Hebrews, there the savior himself says: Then my mother, the Holy Spirit, took me by one of my hairs and carried me up to the great mount Tabor.

Ἐὰν δὲ προσιῆταί τις τὸ καθ' Ἑβραίους εὐαγγέλιον, ἔνθα αὐτὸς ὁ σωτήρ φησιν· "Ἄρτι ἔλαβέ με ἡ μήτηρ μου, τὸ ἅγιον πνεῦμα, "ἐν μιᾷ τῶν τριχῶν μου καὶ ἀπήνεγκέ με εἰς τὸ ὄρος τὸ μέγα Θαβώρ."

> *Gospel of the Hebrews* [2a]. Origen, *Commentary on John* 2.12. Preuschen, *Origenes* 4:67.

PARALLELS

And if any one accepts the saying: Then my mother, the Holy Spirit, took me and carried me up to the great mount Tabor.

εἰ δέ τις παραδέχεται τὸ "ἄρτι ἔλαβέ με ἡ μήτηρ μου τὸ ἅγιον πνεῦμα, καὶ ἀνήνεγκέ με εἰς τὸ ὄρος τὸ μέγα τὸ Θαβώρ."
> *Gospel of the Hebrews* [2b], Origen, *Homily on Jeremiah* 15.4. Klostermann, *Origenes* 3:128.

And should he believe the gospel, designated According to the Hebrews, which we have recently translated, in which it is said on the part of the Savior: Then my mother, the Holy Spirit, took me by one of my hairs, . . .

credideritque euangelio, quod secundum Hebraeos editum nuper transtulimus, in quo ex persona Saluatoris dicitur: Modo

tulit me mater mea, sanctus Spiritus in uno capillorum meorum, . . .
> Gospel of the Hebrews [2c], Jerome, *In Michaeam* 2 (to 7:6). Adriaen, *Hieronymi opera* 1.6:513.

but also in the gospel written in Hebrew which the Nazaraeans read, the Lord says: Then my mother, the Holy Spirit, took me.

Sed et in euangelio quod iuxta Hebraeos scriptum Nazaraei lectitant, Dominus loquitur: Modo me tulit mater mea, Spiritus sanctus.
> Gospel of the Hebrews [2d], Jerome, *In Esaiam* 11 (to 40:9). Ibid., 1.2:459.

and also in the gospel of the Hebrews, which the Nazaraeans read, the Savior is presented as saying: Then my mother, the Holy Spirit, took me; . . .

in euangelio quoque quod Hebraeorum lectitant Nazaraei, Saluator inducitur loquens, Modo me arripuit mater mea, Spiritus sanctus; . . .
> Gospel of the Hebrews [2e], Jerome, *In Hiezechielem* 4 (to 16:13). Gearia, *Hieronymi opera* 1.4:178.

Then the angel of the Lord took him by the top of his head and lifted him by his hair and put him down in Babylon over the den, with the rushing sound of the wind.

καὶ ἐπελάβετο ὁ ἄγγελος κυρίου τῆς κορυφῆς αὐτοῦ καὶ
βαστάσας τῆς κόμης τῆς κεφαλῆς αὐτοῦ ἔθηκεν αὐτὸν εἰς βαβυλῶνα
ἐπάνω τοῦ λάκκου ἐν τῷ ῥοίζῳ τοῦ πνεύματος αὐτοῦ.
> Bel and the Dragon 36. Rahlfs, *Septuaginta* 2:941.

Ezek 8:3.

I5 / *Cease Sacrificing*

They do not say that he is begotten from God the Father, but that he was created as one of the archangels, yet is far greater than they and that he is Lord over the angels and over all things made by the Omnipotent, and that he came and instructed, as the (book) they call the gospel[1] contains: I have come to abolish sacrifices, and if you do not cease sacrificing, the wrath (of God) will not cease from (being upon) you.

οὐ φάσκουσι δὲ ἐκ θεοῦ πατρὸς αὐτὸν γεγεννῆσθαι,
ἀλλὰ κεκρίσθαι ὡς ἕνα τῶν ἀρχαγγέλων, καὶ ἔτι
περρισσοτέρως, αὐτὸν δὲ κυριεύειν καὶ ἀγγέλων καὶ

πάντων ⟨τῶν⟩ ὑπὸ τοῦ παντοκράτορος πεποιημένων,
καὶ ἐλθόντα καὶ ὑφηγησάμενον, ὡς τὸ παρ' αὐτοῖς
εὐαγγέλιον καλούμενον περίεχει, ὅτι "ἦλθον
καταλῦσαι τὰς θυσίας, καὶ ἐὰν μὴ παύσησθε τοῦ
θύειν, οὐ παύσεται ἀφ' ὑμῶν ἡ ὀργή."

Gospel of the Ebionites [2], Epiphanius, Haer. 30.16.4–5. Holl, Epiphanius
1:354.

PARALLELS

But when the time began to approach that what was lacking in
Moses' institutions should be completed as we have said, and the
prophet whom he had foretold should appear, who would warn
them first by the mercy of God to cease sacrificing, lest they might
perhaps think that at the cessation of sacrifices there would be no
remission of sins for them, he instituted baptism by water among
them.[2]

Ut autem tempus adesse coepit, quo id quod deesse Moysei insti-
tutis diximus impleretur et propheta quem praecinerat appareret,
qui eos primo per misericordiam dei moneret cessare a sacrificiis,
et ne forte putarent cessantibus hostiis remissionem sibi non fieri
peccatorum, baptisma eis per aquam statuit, . . .

Ps. Clem. Recog. 1.39.[2] Rehm, Rekognitionen, 31.

And to those who have the preconception that God wishes
sacrifices, he said: God desires mercy and not sacrifice, knowledge of himself and not burnt offerings.

τοῖς δὲ προλαβοῦσιν ὅτι θυσιῶν ὀρέγεται ὁ θεός, ἔφη· "'Ο
θεὸς ἔλεος θέλει καὶ οὐ θυσίας, ἐπίγνωσιν αὐτοῦ καὶ οὐχ
ὁλοκαυτώματα."

Ps. Clem. Hom. 3.56. Rehm-Irmscher, Homilien, 77.

Hos 6:6, 1 Sam 15:22, Ps 40:6 (LXX 39:7), Matt 9:13, 12:7, Heb
10:5–6, 8.

NOTES

[1] Holl suggests that κατὰ Ματθαῖον belongs after εὐαγγέλιον. The translation would
then be, "the gospel they call 'according to Matthew.'"

[2] See also Recog. 1.54.1, 1.55.3, 1.63.3–64.1.

16 / Choosing the Apostles

In their gospel, called according to Matthew, which is not complete but corrupt and mutilated (they call it the Hebrew Gospel), it is reported: A certain man named Jesus appeared who chose us, and he was about thirty years old. When he came to Capernaum, he entered the house of Simon whose surname is Peter and opened his mouth and said: As I walked by Lake Tiberias, I chose John and James, sons of Zebedee, and Simon and Andrew and Thaddeus and Simon the Zealot and Judas Iscariot, and I called you Matthew, while you were sitting at the tax office, and you followed me. I wish you, therefore, to be twelve apostles as a testimony to Israel.

ἐν τῷ γοῦν παρ' αὐτοῖς εὐαγγελίῳ κατὰ Ματθαῖον
ὀνομαζομένῳ, οὐχ ὅλῳ δὲ πληρεστάτῳ ἀλλὰ
νενοθευμένῳ καὶ ἠκρωτηριασμένῳ, ('Εβραϊκὸν
δὲ τοῦτο καλοῦσιν) ἐμφέρεται ὅτι "ἐγένετό τις
ἀνὴρ ὀνόματι 'Ιησοῦς, καὶ αὐτὸς ὡς ἐτῶν
τριάκοντα, ὃς ἐξελέξατο ἡμᾶς. καὶ ἐλθὼν εἰς
Καφαρναοὺμ εἰσῆλθεν εἰς τὴν οἰκίαν Σίμωνος
τοῦ ἐπικληθέντος Πέτρου καὶ ἀνοίξας τὸ στόμα
αὐτοῦ εἶπεν· παρερχόμενος παρὰ τὴν λίμνην
Τιβεριάδος ἐξελεξάμην 'Ιωάννην καὶ 'Ιάκωβον,
υἱοὺς Ζεβεδαίου, καὶ Σίμωνα καὶ 'Ανδρέαν καὶ
Θαδδαῖον καὶ Σίμωνα τὸν ζηλωτὴν καὶ 'Ιούδαν
τὸν 'Ισκαριώτην, καὶ σὲ τὸν Ματθαῖον
καθεζόμενον ἐπὶ τοῦ τελωνίου ἐκάλεσα καὶ
ἠκολούθησάς μοι. ὑμᾶς οὖν βούλομαι εἶναι
δεκαδύο ἀποστόλους εἰς μαρτύριον τοῦ 'Ισραήλ.

> *Gospel of the Ebionites* [3]. Epiphanius, *Haer.* 30.13.2–3. Holl, *Epiphanius* 1:349–50.

PARALLELS

> Luke 3:23, Mark 1:16–20, Matt 4:18–22, Luke 5:8–11, Mark 3:14–19, Matt 10:2–4, Luke 6:13–16, Mark 2:14, Matt 9:9, Luke 5:27–28.

I7 / Jesus the Vegetarian

But they abandon the true sequence (of the words) and pervert what is said, as is plain to all from the attached readings, and have the disciples say: Where do you want us to prepare the passover for you? and have him then answer: Do I indeed desire to eat meat with you at this passover?

αὐτοὶ δὲ ἀφανίσαντες ἀφ᾽ ἑαυτῶν τὴν τῆς ἀληθείας ἀκολουθίαν
ἤλλαξαν τὸ ῥητὸν, ὅπερ ἐστὶ πᾶσι φανερὸν ἐκ τῶν συνεζευγμένων
λέξεων, καὶ ἐποίησαν τοὺς μαθητὰς μὲν λέγοντας "ποῦ θέλεις
ἑτοιμάσωμέν σοι τὸ Πάσχα φαγεῖν," καὶ αὐτὸν δῆθεν λέγοντα
"μὴ ἐπιθυμίᾳ ἐπεθύμησα κρέας τοῦτο τὸ Πάσχα φαγεῖν μεθ᾽
ὑμῶν."

> Gospel of the Ebionites [4]. Epiphanius, Haer. 30.22.4. Holl, Epiphanius
> 1:363.

PARALLELS

Mark 14:12–16, Matt 26:17–19, Luke 22:7–16.

18 / *The Works of the Female*

Those who oppose God's creation by means of continence, which has an
appealing name, also quote the words spoken to Salome which we mentioned
earlier. They are contained, I think, in the Gospel according to the Egyptians.
For they say: The Savior himself said, I have come to destroy the works of
the female, by "female" meaning desire, and by "works" birth and decay.[1]

Οἱ δὲ ἀντιτασσόμενοι τῇ κτίσει τοῦ θεοῦ διὰ τῆς
εὐφήμου ἐγκρατείας κἀκεῖνα λέγουσι τὰ πρὸς
Σαλώμην εἰρημένα, ὧν πρότερον ἐμνήσθημεν·
φέρεται δέ, οἶμαι, ἐν τῷ κατ᾽ Αἰγυπτίους εὐαγγελίῳ.
φασὶ γάρ, ὅτι αὐτὸς εἶπεν ὁ σωτήρ· "ἦλθον
καταλῦσαι τὰ ἔργα τῆς θηλείας," θηλείας μὲν τῆς
ἐπιθυμίας, ἔργα δὲ γένεσιν καὶ φθοράν.

> Gospel of the Egyptians [4], Clement, Strom. 3.9.63. Stählin-Früchtel,
> Clemens 2³:225.

PARALLELS

Judas said: You have said this [to us] from the mind of truth. When
we pray, how should we pray? The Lord said: Pray in the place
where there is no woman. Matthew said: He tells us, Pray in the
place where there is no woman, meaning, Destroy the works of
womanhood, not because there is another [way of giving birth]
but because they will cease [giving birth].[2]

ⲡⲉϫⲉ ⲓ̈ⲟⲩⲇⲁⲥ ϫⲉ ⲛ̄ⲧⲁ[ⲕ]
ϫⲱ ⲙ̄ⲡⲁⲓ̈ ⲛ[ⲉ]ⲛ ⲉⲃⲟⲗ ϩ̄ⲙ ⲡⲛⲟⲩⲥ ⲛ̄
ⲧⲙⲏⲉ ϩⲟⲧ[ⲁ]ⲛ ⲉⲛϣⲁϣⲗⲏⲗ ⲉⲛⲁ
ϣⲗⲏⲗ ⲛ̄ⲁϣ ⲛ̄ϩⲉ· ⲡⲉϫⲉ ⲡϫⲟⲉⲓⲥ [ϫⲉ]

ϢⲀⲎⲀ ⲌⲘ̄ ⲠⲘⲀ ⲈⲦⲈ ⲘⲚ̄ ⲤⲌⲒⲘⲈ Ⲙ̄[ⲘⲀⲨ]
ⲠⲈⳊⲈ ⲘⲀⲐⲐⲀⲒⲞⲤ ⳊⲈ ⲈϤⳊⲰ Ⲙ̄[ⲘⲞⲤ]
ⲚⲀⲚ ⳊⲈ ϢⲀⲎⲀ ⲌⲘ̄ ⲠⲘⲀ Ⲉ[ⲦⲈ ⲘⲚ̄ ⲤⲌⲒ]
ⲘⲈ Ⲙ̄ⲘⲀⲨ ⳊⲈ ⲈⲢⲒⲔⲀⲦⲀⲀⲨⲈ Ⲛ̄[ⲚⲈ]
ⲌⲂⲎⲞⲨⲈ Ⲛ̄ⲦⲘⲚⲦⲤⲌⲒⲘⲈ ⳊⲈ ⲤⲈ[ⳊⲠⲞ]²
ⲀⲚ ⲠⲈ ⲀⲖⲖⲀ ⳊⲈ ⲤⲈⲚⲀⲞⲨⲰ Ⲛ̄ⲤⲈ[ⳊⲠⲞ]

Dialogue of the Savior, CG III, 144.12–21.

NOTES

¹ See also the *Gospel of the Egyptians* [1] in Clement, *Strom.* 3.6.45, 3.9.64, and *Exc. ex Theod.* 67 [A4].

² The restoration of the end of lines 20 and 21 follows that of Emmel, *Nag Hammadi Codex III, 5*, 88.

19 / *Jesus' Triumph in Hades*

And I became useless to those who knew me [not].
Because I shall hide myself from those who possessed me not.
And I will be with those
Who love me.
All my persecutors have died,
And they who trusted me sought me, because I am living.
Then I arose and am with them,
And will speak by their mouths.
For they have rejected those who persecute them;
And I threw over them the yoke of my love.
Like the arm of the bridegroom over the bride,
So is my yoke over those who know me.
And as the bridal feast is spread out by the bridal pair's home,
So is my love by those who believe in me.
I was not rejected although I was considered to be so,
And I did not perish although they thought it of me.
Sheol saw me and was shattered,
And Death ejected me and many with me.
I have been vinegar and bitterness to it,
And I went down with it as far as its depth.
Then the feet and the head it released,
Because it was not able to endure my face.
And I made a congregation of living among his dead;
And I spoke with them by living lips;
In order that my word may not be unprofitable.
And those who had died ran towards me;
And they cried out and said, Son of God, have pity on us.

And deal with us according to Thy kindness,
And bring us out from the bonds of darkness.
And open for us the door
By which we may come out to Thee.
For we perceive that our death does not touch Thee.
May we also be saved with Thee,
Because Thou art our Saviour.
Then I heard their voice,
And placed their faith in my heart.
And I placed my name upon their head,
Because they are free and they are mine.

> *Odes of Solomon* 42.3–20. Trans. of the Syriac from Charlesworth, *The Odes of Solomon*, 145–146.

I10 / *Hearing Jesus and the Father* _____

For he who hears me and does the things I say hears the one who sent me.

ὃς γὰρ ἀκούει μου καὶ ποιεῖ ἃ λέγω ἀκούει τοῦ ἀποστείλαντός με.

> Justin, *Apol.* 1.16.10. Goodspeed, *Die ältesten Apologeten*, 37.

PARALLELS

He who hears me hears the one who sent me.

Ὁ ἐμοῦ ἀκούων ἀκούει τοῦ ἀποστείλαντός με.

> Justin, *Apol.* 1.63.5. Ibid., 72.

He who hears you hears me, and he who rejects you rejects me, and he who rejects me rejects him who sent me, and he who hears me hears him who sent me.[1]

Ὁ ἀκούων ὑμῶν ἐμοῦ ἀκούει, καὶ ὁ ἀθετῶν ὑμᾶς ἐμὲ ἀθετεῖ·
ὁ δὲ ἐμὲ ἀθετῶν ἀθετεῖ τὸν ἀποστείλαντά με, καὶ ὁ ἐμοῦ
ἀκούων ἀκούει τοῦ ἀποστείλαντός με.

> Luke 10:16 in mss. Θ, Φ, it, sy^s,c. Aland, *Synopsis*, 260.

Luke 10:16, Matt 10:40, John 13:20, 5:23, 12:44–45, Gal. 4:14.

NOTES
[1] Codex D contains the last clause but not the third.

I11 / *Words from the Cross* _____

And the Lord cried out, saying: My power, O power, you have forsaken me.
And after he said this, he was taken up.

Καὶ ὁ Κύριος ἀνεβόησε λέγων· "Ἡ δύναμίς μου, ἡ δύναμις,
κατέλειφάς με." καὶ εἰπὼν ἀνελήφθη.

> *Gospel of Peter* 5.19. Mara, *Évangile de Pierre*, 48.

PARALLELS

> Mark 15:34, Matt 27:46, Luke 23:46, John 19:30.

I12 / *Feet on the Ground* _____

Then he said to us: Why do you still doubt and do not believe. I am the one
who spoke to you concerning my flesh, my death, and my resurrection. So
that you may know that it is I, put your finger, Peter, in the nail prints of my
hands, and Thomas, put your finger in the lance-wounds of my side, and
Andrew, look at my feet and see if they do not touch the ground, for it is
written in the prophet: The foot of a phantom or demon[1] does not touch the
ground.

TOTE ΠΑΧΕϤ Ν[ΕΝ]
ΧΕ ΕΤΒΕ Ο ΤΕΤΝΡΔΙϹΤΑΖΕ ΕΤΙ ΤΕΤΝΕ ΝΑΤΝΑ
ϨΤΕ ΑΝΑΚ ΠΕ ΠΕΪ ΕΤΑϨΧΟΟϹ ΝΗΤΝΕ ΕΤΒΕ ΤΑ
ϹΑΡϨ ΜΝ ΠΑΜΟΥ ΜΝ ΠΑΤΩΝΕ ΧΕΚΑΑϹ ΑΤΕ
ΤΝΑΜΜΕ ΧΕ ΑΝΑΚ ΠΕ· ΠΕΤΡΕ ΤΩΚΕ ΝΝΕΚ
†ΒΕ ΑΝΕΙϤΤ ΝΝΑϬΙΧ ΑΟΥ ΝΤΑΚ ϨΟΥΟΥΚ ΘΩ
ΜΑϹ ΤΩΚΕ ΝΝΕΚ†ΒΕ ΑΝϹϨΝΛΟΓΧΗ ΝΠΑ
ϹΠΙΡ ΝΤΑΚ ΔΕ ΑΝΔΡΕΑϹ ΜΟΥϨ‹Τ› ΑΝΑΟΥΡΗΤΕ
ΚΝΟ ΧΕ ϹΕΤΩΜΕ ΕΝ ΑΠΚΑϨ ϤϹΗϨ ΓΑΡ ϨΝ ΠΠΡΟ
ΦΗΤΗϹ ΧΕ ΟΥΦΑΝΤΑϹΙΑ ΝΔΑΙΜΩΝ ΜΑ[ΡΕ]
ΡΕΤϤ ΤΟΥΜΕ ϨΙΧΝ ΠΚΑϨ

> *Epistula Apostolorum* 11. Schmidt, *Gespräche Jesu*, 3*.

PARALLELS

> I am not a shade such as belongs to the dead. A shade does not
> make a footprint.

> Non ego sum umbra, mortuorum qualis habetur: Vestigium
> umbra non facit.

> Commodian, *Apol.* 5.564–65. Martin, *Commodianus*, 93.

And I wished many times, as I walked with him, to see if his foot-print appeared on the ground, for I saw him raising himself from the earth. And I never saw it.

ἐβουλόμην δὲ πολλάκις σὺν αὐτῷ βαδίζων ἴχνος αὐτοῦ ἐπὶ τῆς γῆς ἰδεῖν εἰ φαίνεται· ἑώρων γὰρ αὐτὸν ἀπὸ τῆς γῆς ἑαυτὸν ἐπαίροντα· καὶ οὐδέποτε εἶδον.

> Acts of John 93.9. Lipsius-Bonnet, AAA 2.1:197.

John 20:20, 25, 27, Mark 16:14, Luke 24:36–39.

NOTES
¹ See Ignatius, *Smyrnaeans* 3.1–2 and parallels [I1].

I13 / *Hope of the Hopeless*

I am the hope of the hopeless, the helper of those who have no helper, the treasure of those in need, the physician of the sick, the resurrection of the dead.

> *Epistula Apostolorum* 21. Trans. of the Ethiopic from Hennecke-Schneemelcher, *N.T. Apoc.* 1:206.

PARALLELS

Luke 4:18, 7:22, John 11:25–26, Isa 61:1–3.

I14 / *I Am You, You Are I*

And he spoke to me and said: I am you and you are I, and wherever you are I am there, and I am sown in all things. And wherever you wish, you gather me, but when you gather me you gather yourself.

καὶ ἐλάλησε πρός με καὶ εἶπεν· ἐγὼ σὺ καὶ
σὺ ἐγώ, καὶ ὅπου ἐὰν ᾖς, ἐγὼ ἐκεῖ εἰμι,
καὶ ἐν ἅπασίν εἰμι ἐσπαρμένος. καὶ ὅθεν
ἐὰν θέλῃς, συλλέγεις με, ἐμὲ δὲ συλλέγων
ἑαυτὸν συλλέγεις.

> *Gospel of Eve*, Epiphanius, *Haer.* 26.3.1. Holl, *Epiphanius* 1:278.

PARALLELS

And truly I say to you: That man is I, and I am that man.¹

ⲁⲩⲱ ϩⲁⲙⲏⲛ ϯϫⲱ ⲙ̄ⲙⲟⲥ ⲛⲏⲧⲛ̄ ϫⲉ ⲡⲣⲱⲙⲉ
ⲉⲧⲙ̄ⲙⲁⲩ ⲡⲉ ⲁⲛⲟⲕ ⲁⲩⲱ ⲁⲛⲟⲕ ⲡⲉ ⲡⲣⲱⲙⲉ ⲉⲧⲙ̄ⲙⲁⲩ·
Pistis Sophia 96. Schmidt-MacDermot, *Pistis Sophia*, 231.

NOTES

¹ In the same chapter a similar statement occurs twice, "I am they and they are I" (ibid.).

I15 / *Not Understood*

Indeed I heard that he also said: Those with me have not understood me.

audiui enim et hoc eum dixisse: "Qui mecum sunt, non me intellexerunt."
Acts of Peter 10. Lipsius-Bonnet, *AAA* 1:58.

PARALLELS

Mark 8:17, Luke 18:34.

I16 / *Desiring to Hear*

But also in the saying, Many times I desired to hear one of these words and I had no one to speak (it) to me,¹ they say that through this "one" He who is the true God is shown, whom they had not known.

Sed et in eo quod dixerit: saepius concupivi audire unum ex sermonibus istis, et non habui qui diceret mihi, manifestantis dicunt esse per hoc unum, eum qui sit vere Deus, quem non cognoverint.
Irenaeus, *Adv. haer.* 1.20.2 (Harvey, 1.13.2). Harvey, *Sancti Irenaei* 1:179.

PARALLELS

But also in the saying, Many times I desired to hear one of these words and I had no one to speak (it), they say that by the "one" is shown the one true God whom they had not known.

ἀλλὰ καὶ ἐν τῷ εἰρηκέναι, "πολλάκις ἐπεθύμησα ἀκοῦσαι
ἕνα τῶν λόγων τούτων, καὶ οὐκ ἔσχον τὸν ἐροῦντα,"
ἐμφαίνοντός φασιν εἶναι διὰ τοῦ "ἕνα" τὸν ἀληθῶς ἕνα θεόν, ὃν
οὐκ ἐγνώκεισαν.
Epiphanius, *Haer.* 34.18. Holl, *Epiphanius* 2:34.

Matt 13:17, Luke 10:24.

NOTES

¹ See *Thomas* 38 [I53] and *Thomas* 92 [I60].

² Epiphanius has taken his material from Irenaeus. Several commentators have conjectured that originally the saying was in the third person plural, "Many times they wished. . . ." The change to first person would have happened simply by dropping the ν of ἐπεθύμησαν. The saying would then no longer be a self-reference by Jesus but a closer parallel to Matt 13:17 and Luke 10:24. See Resch, *Agrapha*², 179, Fitzmyer, *Essays*, 412, and Rousseau, *Irénée de Lyon Contre les Hérésies*, 291. The context in Irenaeus would seem to indicate those with whom he is disputing understood it as a saying of Jesus in the first person.

I17 / *My Love I Give*

And about to be offered up and giving himself as a ransom, he left us a new covenant: My love I give to you.

καὶ μέλλων σπένδεσθαι καὶ λύτρον ἑαυτὸν
ἐπιδιδοὺς καινὴν ἡμῖν διαθήκην
καταλιμπάνει· "ἀγάπην ὑμῖν δίδωμι τὴν
ἐμήν."

Clement, *Quis div. sal.* 37.4. Stählin-Früchtel, *Clemens* 3²:184.

PARALLELS

John 13:34, 14:27.

I18 / *Guarding the Mystery*

It is for only a few to understand these things. For it is not in the way of envy that he says the Lord announced in some gospel: My mystery is for me, and for the sons of my house; making the election safe and free from care, so that the things belonging to what it has chosen and taken may be beyond jealousy.

ἐπεὶ ὀλίγων ἐστὶ ταῦτα χωρῆσαι. "οὐ γὰρ
φθονῶν," φησί, "παρήγγειλεν ὁ κύριος" ἔν
τινι εὐαγγελίῳ· "μυστήριον ἐμὸν ἐμοὶ
καὶ τοῖς υἱοῖς τοῦ οἴκου μου," ἐν τῷ
ἀσφαλεῖ καὶ ἀμερίμνῳ τὴν ἐκλογὴν
ποιούμενος, ἵνα τὰ οἰκεῖα ὧν εἵλετο
λαβοῦσα ἀνωτέρα ζήλου γένηται·

Clement, *Strom.* 5.10. Stählin-Früchtel, *Clemens* 2³:368.

PARALLELS

And Peter said: We remember that our Lord and Teacher

commanded us and said: Keep the mysteries for me and the sons of my house. Therefore he also explained the mysteries of the kingdom of heaven privately to his disciples.

καὶ ὁ Πέτρος· Μεμνήμεθα τοῦ κυρίου ἡμῶν καὶ διδασκάλου ὡς ἐντελλόμενος εἶπεν ἡμῖν· "Τὰ μυστήρια ἐμοὶ καὶ τοῖς υἱοῖς τοῦ οἴκου μου φυλάξετε·" διὸ καὶ "τοῖς αὐτοῦ μαθηταῖς κατ᾽ ἰδίαν ἐπέλυε" τῆς τῶν οὐρανῶν βασιλείας τὰ μυστήρια.

Ps. Clem. Hom. 19.20. Rehm-Irmscher, Homilien, 263.

And therefore (it says) elsewhere: My mystery is for me and for those who are mine.

Διὸ καὶ ἀλλαχοῦ, "Τὸ μυστήριόν μου ἐμοὶ καὶ τοῖς ἐμοῖς.

St. John Chrysostom, In Epist. I ad Cor. Hom. 7. Johannis Chrysostomi 2:70.

And, my mysteries are for me and for those who are mine.[1]

Καὶ, τὰ μυστήριά μου ἐμοὶ, καὶ τοῖς ἐμοῖς.

Theodoret, In Psal. 65.16. PG 80:1369.

For my mysteries are given to those who are mine, with whom I shall rejoice and be glad with my Father.

Testament of the Lord 1.18. Cooper and Maclean, The Testament of Our Lord, 61.

The mystery is for me and for those who are mine.

τὸ μυστήριον ἐμοὶ καὶ τοῖς ἐμοῖς.

John of Damascus, De sacra parallelis 9.1. PG 96.9.

My mystery is for me and for those who are mine.

τὸ μυστήριόν μου ἐμοὶ καὶ τοῖς ἐμοῖς.

LXX (var.) to Isa 24:16.[2]

Mark 4:11, Matt 13:11, Luke 8:10.

NOTES
    [1] The same words occur in In Psal. 67.14. PG 80:1384.
    [2] See Zahn GNK 2:738, where the manuscript evidence is cited more fully than in Rahlfs's edition of the LXX, and where the relations of these readings to the translations by Symmachus and Theodotion and to the rescension of the LXX by Lucian are discussed.

I19 / *The True Gate* _____

Therefore, it says, Jesus said: I am the true gate.

διὰ τοῦτο, φησί, λέγει ὁ ᾽Ιησοῦς· "ἐγώ εἰμι ἡ πύλη ἡ ἀληθινή."

Naassene Exegesis. Hippolytus, *Ref.* 5.8.20. Wendland, *Hippolytus* 3:93.

PARALLELS

Therefore, being the true prophet, he said: I am the gate of life;
the one who enters through me enters into life.

διὰ τοῦτο αὐτὸς ἀληθὴς ὢν προφήτης ἔλεγεν·
"᾽Εγώ εἰμι ἡ πύλη τῆς ζωῆς· ὁ δι᾽ ἐμοῦ
εἰσερχόμενος εἰσέρχεται εἰς τὴν ζωήν."

Ps. Clem. Hom. 3.52. Rehm-Irmscher, *Homilien*, 76.

John 10:7, 9, Matt 7:13–14.

I20 / *Words of the Pre-existent Jesus* _____

But Jesus said: Look, Father,
(the work) of your breath wanders about on earth,
sought after by evil forces.
It seeks to flee from the bitter chaos
but does not know how to pass through.
Therefore, send me, Father.
Having the seals I will descend.
I will travel through all the aeons,
I will open all mysteries,
I will show the forms of the gods.
And summoning knowledge, I will deliver
the hidden things of the holy way.

εἶπεν δ᾽ ᾽Ιησοῦς· ἐσόρα πάτερ·
ζήτημα κακῶν ‹τόδ᾽› ἐπὶ χθόνα
ἀπὸ σῆς πνοϊῆς ἐπιπλάζεται.
ζητεῖ δὲ φευγεῖν τὸ πικρὸν χάος,
καὶ οὐκ οἶδεν ‹ὅ›πως διελεύσεται.
τούτου με χάριν πέμφον, πάτερ·
σφραγῖδας ἔχων καταβήσομαι
αἰῶνας ὅλους διοδεύσω
μυστήρια πάντα δ᾽ ἀνοίξω,
μορφὰς δὲ Θεῶν ἐπιδείξω·

[καὶ] τὰ κεκρυμμένα τῆς ἁγίας ὁδοῦ,
γνῶσιν καλέσας, παραδώσω.

> *Naassene Hymn.* Hippolytus, *Ref.* 5.10.2. Wendland, *Hippolytus* 3:103–104.

NOTES

The passage is distinctive, and perhaps unique, in that it is attributed to the pre-existent Jesus.

121 / Weak, Hungry, Thirsty

And Jesus indeed says: Because of the weak I was weak, and because of the hungry I hungered, and because of the thirsty I thirsted.

καὶ Ἰησοῦς γοῦν φησι διὰ τοὺς ἀσθενοῦντας ἠσθενοῦν
καὶ διὰ τοὺς πεινῶντας ἐπείνων καὶ διὰ τοὺς διψῶντας
ἐδίψων.

> Origen, *Commentary on Matthew* 13.2. Klostermann, *Origenes* 10:183.

PARALLELS

Matt 8:17, 25:35–45, John 19:28, 1 Cor 9:22, 2 Cor 4:3–4.

122 / As in a Mirror

for we also who believe in him see Christ in ourselves as in a mirror, as he himself instructs and admonishes us in the epistle of John his disciple to the people: thus you see me in yourselves, as one of you sees himself in water or in a mirror.

nam et nos qui illi credimus Christum in nobis tamquam in speculo uidemus ipso nos instruente et monente in epistula Iohannis discipuli sui ad populum: ita me in uobis uidete, quomodo quis uestrum se uidet in aquam aut in speculum, . . .

> Ps. Cyprian, *De montibus sina et sion* 13. Hartel, *Cyprianus* 3:117.

PARALLELS

For he is the beginningless First-Father who sees himself within himself as in a mirror.

ΠΕΤΜ̄
ΜΑⲨ [Γ]ΑΡ Π[ΑΝΑΡⲬ]ΟⳞ ΜΠΡΟ
ΠΑΤⲰ[Ρ] ΕϤΝΑⲨ ΕΡΟϤ Μ̄ΜΙΝ

ⲘⲘⲞϤ Ⲛ̄ⲢⲀⲒ̈ Ⲛ̄ϨⲎⲦϤ· Ⲛ̄ⲐⲈ Ⲛ̄ⲞⲨ
ⲈⲒⲀⲗ

Eugnostos the Blessed, CG III, 75.1–5.

For he is the beginningless First-Father who sees himself within
himself (as) in a mirror.

ⲠⲈⲦⲘ̄
ⲘⲀⲨ [ⲄⲀⲢ Ⲡ]ⲀⲚⲀⲢⲬⲞⲤ Ⲛ̄ⲠⲢⲞⲠⲀ
ⲦⲰ[Ⲣ ⲈϤ]ⲚⲀⲨ ⲈⲢⲞϤ Ⲙ̄ⲘⲒⲚ Ⲙ̄ⲘⲞϤ
Ⲛ̄ϨⲢ[ⲀⲒ̈] Ⲛ̄ϨⲎⲦϤ ϨⲚ̄ ⲞⲨⲈⲒⲀⲗ

The Sophia of Jesus Christ, CG III, 98.25–99.3.

1 Cor 13.2, James 1:23.

I23 / *I Am the Day*

And again he (Marcellus) continues and has the Savior say, I am the day, on
this occasion saying: For as there was previously darkness because of the
ignorance of the worship of God, and as the day was about to appear (for he
says: I am the day), he specified naturally the morning star.

προϊὼν δ' αὖθις ὁ αὐτὸς εἰσάγει τὸν σωτῆρα λέγοντα
"ἐγώ εἰμι ἡ ἡμέρα," ὧδέ πη φάσκων σκότους γὰρ ὄντος
πρότερον διὰ τὴν τῆς θεοσεβείας ἄγνοιαν, τῆς δὲ
ἡμέρας φαίνεσθαι μελλούσης ("ἐγὼ" γάρ "εἰμι" φησὶν
"ἡ ἡμέρα") εἰκότως τὸν ἀστέρα ἑωσφόρον ὀνομάζει.

Fragment of Marcellus, Eusebius, *Against Marcellus* 1.2. Klostermann,
Eusebius 4:12.

PARALLELS

John 8:12, 9:5, 12:46.

I24 / *Believing Without Seeing*

Blessed are you, because you have believed in me without having seen me.
For it is written concerning me that those who have seen me will not believe
in me and that those who have not seen me will believe and live.

Μακάριος εἶ πιστεύσας ἐν ἐμοί, μὴ ἑορακώς με. γέγραπται γὰρ

περὶ ἐμοῦ τοὺς ἑορακότας με μὴ πιστεύσειν ἐν ἐμοί, καὶ ἵνα οἱ
μὴ ἑορακότες με αὐτοὶ πιστεύσωσι καὶ ζήσονται.

> Eusebius, *Eccl. hist.* 1.13, *Letter of Jesus to Abgar.* Schwartz, *Eusebius* 2.1:88.

PARALLELS

Blessed are you who though not having seen me have believed in me. For it is written concerning me that those who see me will not believe in me, but those who do not see me will believe in me.

> *The Teaching of Addai,* f3b. Trans. of the Syriac from Howard, *The Teaching of Addai,* 9.

But it is written concerning me: Blessed are those who have seen me and have believed; thrice blessed are those who have not seen me and believed.

γέγραπται δὲ περὶ ἐμοῦ Μακάριοι οἱ ἰδόντες με καὶ πιστεύσαντες·
τρισμακάριοι δὲ οἱ μὴ ἑωρακότες με καὶ πιστεύσαντες.

> *Epistle of Abgar.* Lipsius-Bonnet, *AAA* 1:281.

He [answered and said] to us: More blessed are those who have not seen me and (still) have believed, for such will be called [children] of the kingdom [and they] will be perfect [in] the Perfect One. And I will be life [to them] in the kingdom of my Father.

ⲀϤⲞⲨ[ⲰϢ]ⲂⲈ ⲠⲀϪⲈϤ]
ⲚⲈⲚ ϪⲈ ⲊⲚ̄ⲘⲀⲔⲀⲢⲒⲞⲤ Ⲛ̄ⲦⲀϤ Ⲛ̄ⲊⲞ[ⲨⲞ ⲄⲀⲢ Ⲛ̄]
ⲄⲒ ⲚⲈⲦⲈ ⲘⲠⲞⲨⲚⲞ ⲀⲨⲢ̄ⲠⲒⲤⲦⲈⲨⲈ ϪⲈ [ⲚⲈⲈⲒ]
Ⲛ̄Ⲧ̇ⲘⲒⲚⲈ ⲤⲈⲚⲀⲘⲞⲨ[Ⲧ]Ⲉ ⲀⲢⲀⲨ ϪⲈ Ⲛ̄Ⲱ[ⲎⲢⲈ Ⲛ̄]
ⲦⲘⲚ̄Ⲧⲣ̄ⲢⲞ Ⲁ[ⲞⲨ ⲤⲈ]ⲚⲀⲊⲰⲠⲈ Ⲛ̄ⲦⲈⲖⲈⲒ[ⲞⲤ Ⲛ̄ⲦⲊⲈ Ⲛ̄?]¹
ⲠⲦⲈⲖⲈⲒⲞⲤ Ⲁ[ⲞⲨ] Ⲧ̇ⲚⲀⲊⲰⲠⲈ ⲚⲞⲨⲰⲚ[Ⲉ Ⲛ̄ⲔⲞⲞⲊ?]²
ⲊⲚ̄ ⲦⲘⲚ̄Ⲧⲣ̄ⲢⲞ Ⲛ̄ⲠⲀⲈⲒⲰⲦ·

> *Epistula Apostolorum* 25.1–7 (Ethiopic 29). Schmidt, *Gespräche Jesu,* 15.

Blessed will they be who have known me. Woe to those who have heard and have not believed. Blessed will they be who have not seen but [have believed].

ⲘⲘⲀⲔⲀⲢⲒⲞⲤ Ⲛ̄ⲄⲒ ⲚⲈⲚⲦⲀⲊ
ⲤⲞⲨⲰⲚ̄Ⲧ· ⲞⲨⲀⲈⲒ Ⲛ̄ⲚⲈⲈⲒ Ⲛ̄ⲦⲀⲊ
ⲤⲰⲦⲘ̄ ⲀⲨⲰ Ⲙ̄ⲠⲞⲨⲢ̄ⲠⲒⲤⲦⲈⲨⲈ· ⲤⲈ
ⲚⲀϢⲰⲠⲈ· ⲘⲘⲀⲔⲀⲢⲒⲞⲤ Ⲛ̄ⲄⲒ ⲚⲈ
ⲦⲈ Ⲙ̄ⲠⲞⲨⲚⲈⲨ Ⲁ[ⲖⲖ]Ⲁ [ⲀⲨⲚⲀⲊⲦⲈ]

> *Apocryphon of James,* CG I, 12.38–13.1.

I will give your house to a people who will come, who will believe though they have not heard me. Those to whom I have shown no signs will do what I have commanded.

Tradam domus uestras populo uenienti, qui me non audientes credunt; quibus signa non ostendi, facient quae praecepi.

> 4 Ezra 1:35. Bensly, *The Fourth Book of Ezra*, 3.

John 20:29, Isa 6:9, 52:15, Mark 4:11–12, Matt 13:14–17, Luke 8:9–10, John 12:39–40, Acts 28:25–27.

NOTES

[1] Schmidt indicates that the text is corrupt here and also in the corresponding passage in Ethiopic (*Gespräche Jesu*, 93) and suggests the translation "in."

[2] The Coptic text was printed before the discovery of the Ethiopic. The latter caused Schmidt to modify his restoration of the Coptic in several places. ⲚⲞⲨⲰⲚ[Ⲋ ⲚⲈⲨ], "life to them," was his revised restoration at this point (see *Gespräche Jesu*, 93, n. 6).

I25 / No One to Whom to Speak

Remember what I said between you and me on the Mount of Olives: I have something to say; I have no one to whom to say it.

[Ⲁ]ⲢⲓⲡⲘⲈⲨⲈ ⲘⲠⲈⲦⲀⲓ̈ⲭ̄ⲟⲟ⳽ ⲞⲨⲦⲰⲓ̈ ⲚⲈⲘⲈⲔ Ⲋⲛ̄ⲠⲦⲀⲨ
ⲚⲚⲭⲀⲓ̈Ⲧ ⲭⲈ ⲞⲨⲚ̄ⲦⲎⲓ̈ ⲠⲈ†ⲚⲀⲭⲟⲟ⳽. Ⲙⲛ̄ⲦⲎⲓ̈ ⲠⲈ†
ⲚⲀⲭⲟⲟ⳽ ⲀⲢⲀ⳽

> *Pss. Heracleides* 187.27–29, Allberry, *Manichaean Psalm-Book*, 187.

PARALLELS

John, there must be one person to hear these things from me, for I need one who is ready to hear.

Ἰωάννη, ἕνα δεῖ παρ' ἐμοῦ ταῦτα ἀκοῦσαι· ἑνὸς γὰρ χρῄζω τοῦ μέλλοντος ἀκούειν.

> *Acts of John* 98. Lipsius-Bonnet *AAA* 2.1:200.

John 16:4–5.

I26 / Near as Clothing

He is not far from us, my brothers, as he said in his preaching: I am near you, like the clothing of your body.

ϤΟΥΗΥ ⲘⲘⲀⲚ ⲚⲈⲚ ⲚⲀⲤⲚⲎⲨ ⲚⲐⲈ Ⲛ̄ⲦⲀϤⲬⲞⲞⲤ Ⲉ[ϤⲦ]Ⲁⲱ̣Ⲉ
Ⲁⲓ̈ⲱ ⲬⲈ ϯ2ⲎⲚ ⲀⲢⲱⲦⲚ̄ ⲚⲐⲈ Ⲛ̄ⲐⲂⲤⲱ ⲘⲠⲈⲦⲚ̄ⲤⲱⲘⲀ

Manichaean Psalm-Book, Ps. 239.23–24. Allberry, *Manichaean Psalm-Book,* 39.

PARALLELS

And it is promised through the prophets saying: I will be nearer to them than the tunic to their skin. For it says: I am a God near at hand and not a God far away, says the Lord.

καὶ ἐπαγγέλλεται διὰ τῶν προφητῶν λέγων· "ἐγγιῶ αὐτοῖς ἢ
ὁ χιτὼν τοῦ χρωτὸς αὐτῶν." "θεὸς" γάρ φησιν "ἐγγίζων ἐγώ
εἰμι, καὶ οὐχὶ θεὸς πόρρωθεν, λέγει κύριος."

Origen, *Hom. on Jeremiah* 18.9. Klostermann, *Origenes* 3:163.

He says therefore by Ezekiel, directing his discourse to the elders, and delivering to them a saving example of his reasonable thought: And the lame I will bind up, and the sick I will heal, and that which has wandered I will turn back; and I will feed them on my holy mountain. Such are the promises of the good Shepherd. Feed us, the children, as sheep. Yes, Master, fill us with righteousness, your pasture; yes, Instructor, shepherd us on your holy mountain, the Church, which is lifted up, which is above the clouds, which touches heaven. And, he says, I will be their Shepherd, and I will be near to them, as the tunic to their skin.[1] He wishes to save my flesh by clothing it with the robe of immortality, and He has anointed my body. They shall call me, He says, and I will say, I am here. You heard sooner than I expected, Master. And if they cross over, they shall not slip, says the Lord. For we who are crossing over to immortality shall not fall into corruption, for He will sustain us. For He has spoken and expressed His will.

φησὶν γοῦν διὰ Ἰεζεκιὴλ πρὸς τοὺς πρεσβυτέρους ἀποταθεὶς καί
τινα αὐτοῖς σωτήριον παρατιθέμενος εὐλόγου φροντίδος ὑπο-
γραμμόν· "καὶ τὸ χωλὸν καταδήσω καὶ τὸ ὀχλούμενον ἰάσομαι
καὶ τὸ πλανώμενον ἐπιστρέφω καὶ βοσκήσω αὐτοὺς ἐγὼ εἰς τὸ ὄρος τὸ
ἅγιόν μου." ταῦτ' ἐστὶν ἀγαθοῦ ποιμένος ἐπαγγέλματα·
βόσκησον ἡμᾶς τοὺς νηπίους ὡς πρόβατα. ναί, δέσποτα, τῆς
σῆς πλήρωσον νομῆς, τῆς δικαιοσύνης· ναί, παιδαγωγέ, ποίμανον
ἡμᾶς εἰς τὸ ἅγιόν σου ὄρος, πρὸς τὴν ἐκκλησίαν, τὴν
ὑψωμένην, τὴν ὑπερνεφῆ, τὴν ἁπτομένην οὐρανῶν. "καὶ ἔσομαι,"
φησίν, "αὐτῶν ποιμὴν καὶ ἔσομαι ἐγγὺς αὐτῶν" ὡς ὁ χιτὼν τοῦ

χρωτὸς αὐτῶν· σῶσαι βούλεταί μου τὴν σάρκα, περιβαλὼν τὸν
χιτῶνα τῆς ἀφθαρσίας, καὶ τὸν χρῶτά μου κέχρικεν. "καλέσουσί
με," φησί, "καὶ ἐρῶ ἰδοὺ πάρειμι." θᾶττον ὑπήκουσας
ἢ προσεδόκησα, δέσποτα· "καὶ ἐὰν διαβαίνωσιν, οὐκ ὀλισθήσουσι,
λέγει κύριος." οὐ γὰρ πεσούμεθα εἰς φθορὰν οἱ διαβαίνοντες
εἰς ἀφθαρσίαν, ὅτι ἀνθέξεται ἡμῶν αὐτός· ἔφη γὰρ
αὐτὸς καὶ ἠθέλησεν αὐτός.
Clement, Paed, 1.9.84. Stählin-Früchtel, Clemens 1:139.

The lame I will bind up, and the sick I will heal, and that which
has wandered I will turn back. And I will feed them, and I will
give them rest upon my holy mountain. And I will be their
Shepherd, and I will be near to them as the tunic to their skin.
And they shall call upon me and I will say, Behold I am here. If
they cross over, they will not slip, says the Lord. . . .

[το χωλο]ν κατεδησω και το ενο[χλουμε
[νον ια]σομαι και το πλανομε[νον επι
[στρεφω κ]αι βοσκησω αυτου[ς εγω και ανα
[παυσω ε]πι το ορος το αγιον [μου και ε
[σομαι αυ]τοις πυμην κ[αι εσομαι εγγυς
[αυτων ως ο χ]ιτων του χρ[ωτος αυτων και
[επικαλεσ]ονται με [και ερω ιδου παρει
[μι εαν διαβαι]νωσιν ο[υκ ολισθησου
[σιν λεγει κς] εχο²
Pseudo-Ezekiel. Bonner, The Homily on the Passion, 186.

Jer 13:11 (LXX), Ezek 23:14–16.

NOTES
¹ Stählin does not consider the possibility that Clement is quoting from a document rather than giving a free rendering of several biblical passages; hence, he does
not include the Greek for "as the tunic to their skin" as part of the quotation.
² In line 1, correct κατεδησω to καταδησω, "I will bind up." In line 2, correct το
πλανομενον, to το πλανωμενον, "that which has wandered." In line 5, correct πυμην to
ποιμην, "shepherd."

I27 / Chosen before Creation _____

But he (the Lord) had gone away; he had made himself invisible again for his
fast of forty days. And the souls of the grieved longed to hear a report of him,
for they were his chosen vessels according to that which he said: I chose you
before the earth was made.
Ephrem, Commentary on the Diatessaron 4.18. Trans. based on the Latin

rendering of the Armenian[1] from Leloir, *Saint Ephrem, Commentaire de l'Évangile Concordant,* 42.

PARALLELS

Matt 25:34, Eph 1:4, 2 Thes 2:13, Rev 13:8, 17:8.

NOTES
   [1] The Syriac of Ephraim's commentary has a lacuna from 1.27 to 9.14.

I28 / *Jesus Tested*

And that he was troubled agrees with that which he said: How long shall I be with you and bear with you? And in another place: That generation is repugnant to me. They put me to the test ten times, but these (have tested me) twenty times, ten and ten.

> Ephrem, *Commentary on the Diatessaron* 17.6. Trans. based on the Latin rendering of the Syriac from Leloir, *Saint Ephrem Commentaire, Texte Syriaque,* 197.

PARALLELS

Mark 9:19, Matt 17:17, Luke 9:41, Ps 95:9–10, Num 14:22.

I29 / *Christ as Example*

I came not to judge the world but to teach them in humility and to save them and to become an example to my disciples so that they might do as I.

Non veni, ut iudicem mundum, sed ut cum humilitate doceam eos et salvos faciam eos et exemplo fiam discipulis meis, ut ita faciant sicut ego.
> *Liber Graduum* 2.2. Kmosko, PatSy 1.3:30.

PARALLELS

John 3:17, 9:39.

I30 / *Perfection Restored*

And the Lord promised them: I will give you the perfection, which I will accomplish when I come. When I send the Paraclete I will make you perfect, you who wait for me and strive for the perfection of the angels above, from which Adam your father fell. I will take you and your father Adam up to the heights from which you have fallen.

Et Dominus promisit eis: Perfectionem, quam ego venturus fecero, dabo vobis: quando Paraclitum misero, etiam vos perficiam; quia expectastis me et perfectionem sectati estis Angelorum supernorum, de qua excidit Adam, pater vester: assumam vos patremque vestrum Adam ad celsitudinem, de qua excidistis.

> *Liber Graduum* 9.12. Ibid., 230.

PARALLELS

John 14:3, 15:26, 16:7.

I31 / *Coming to Make Perfect*

The Lord said to his elect: I promised through the prophets that I would come and make them perfect.

dixit Dominus electis suis: Promisi prophetis me venturum eosque perfecturum esse.

> *Liber Graduum* 9.13. Ibid., 231.

I32 / *To Destroy the Law*

The Judaizers wrote this: I came not to destroy the law but to fulfill it. But Christ did not speak in this way, for he said: I came not to fulfill the law but to destroy it.

Τοῦτο οἱ Ἰουδαϊσταὶ ἔγραψαν, τὸ οὐκ ἦλθον
καταλῦσαι τὸν νόμον ἀλλὰ πληρῶσαι· οὐκ
οὕτως δὲ εἶπεν ὁ Χριστός, λέγει γάρ· οὐκ
ἦλθον πληρῶσαι τὸν νόμον ἀλλὰ καταλῦσαι.

> *Dial. of Adamantius* 2.5. Sande Bakhuysen, *Der Dialogue des Adamantius*, 88.

PARALLELS

For they change the word of the Lord which says, I have come not to destroy the law or the prophets, and render it: Do you think that I have come to fulfill the law or the prophets? I have come to destroy, but not to fulfill.

Ἀμείψαντες γὰρ τὴν τοῦ Κυρίου φωνήν, "Οὐκ ἦλθον, λέγοντος,

καταλῦσαι τὸν νόμον ἢ τοὺς προφήτας," ἐποίησαν· Δοκεῖτε, ὅτι
ἦλθον πληρῶσαι τὸν νόμον ἢ τοὺς προφήτας; Ἦλθον καταλῦσαι,
ἀλλ' οὐ πληρῶσαι.

> Epistles of Isidore 1.371. PG 78: 393.

I, the Gospel,[1] came not to take away from the Torah of Moses, and
not (var. but) to add to the Torah of Moses.

> b. Shabbath 116b. Trans. from Jeremias, Unknown Sayings[2], 24–25, n. 3.

In short, the Messiah came to revive the Torah and to put it into
practice, saying: I have come to act according to the Torah and the
orders of the prophets before me; I have not come to abolish, but
to complete. It is easier in the eyes of God for heaven to fall upon
the earth than to abolish anything from the law of Moses. If any
man therefore sets aside anything of this, he will be called small
in the kingdom of heaven.

> 'Abd Al-Jabbar, Book on the Signs of Muhammad's Prophecy 70a. Trans.
> of the Arabic from Stern, JTS 19:133.

Matt 5:17, Rom 3:31, 10:4.

NOTES

[1] The English translation of the Talmud does not translate awon gillajon, which
Jeremias and others render as "the Gospel." See Freedman, The Babylonian Talmud,
Seder Mo'ed, Shabbath, 2:571.

133 / Proclaim My Death

In the same way he also mixed the cup of wine and water, and blessed it and
gave it to them, saying: All of you drink of this, for this is my blood which
is poured out for many for the remission of sins; do this in remembrance of
me. For as often as you eat this bread and drink this cup, you proclaim my
death until I come.

"ὡσαύτως καὶ τὸ ποτήριον" κεράσας ἐξ οἴνου
καὶ ὕδατος καὶ ἁγιάσας ἐπέδωκεν αὐτοῖς
λέγων· "Πίετε ἐξ αὐτοῦ πάντες, τοῦτό
ἐστι τὸ αἷμά μου τὸ περὶ πολλῶν
ἐκχυνόμενον εἰς ἄφεσιν ἁμαρτιῶν· τοῦτο
ποιεῖτε εἰς τὴν ἐμὴν ἀνάμνησιν ὁσάκις γὰρ
ἐὰν ἐσθίητε τὸν ἄρτον τοῦτον καὶ πίνητε
τὸ ποτήριον τοῦτο, τὸν θάνατον τὸν ἐμὸν
καταγγέλλετε, ἄχρις ἂν ἔλθω."

> Apostolic Constitutions 8.12.37. Funk, Didascalia et Constitutiones
> Apostolorum, 508.

For as often as you eat this bread and drink this cup you proclaim my death and confess my resurrection and ascension, until I come.

ὁσάκις γὰρ ἐὰν ἐσθίητε τὸν ἄρτον τοῦτον, πίνητε δὲ καὶ τὸ ποτήριον τοῦτο, τὸν ἐμὸν θάνατον καταγγέλλετε καὶ τὴν ἐμὴν ἀνάστασιν καὶ ἀνάληψιν ὁμολογεῖτε ἄχρις οὗ ἐὰν ἔλθω.

The Liturgy of St. Mark. Brightman, *Liturgies Eastern and Western* 1:133.

For as often as you eat this bread and drink this cup you proclaim my death (and) confess my resurrection.[1]

ὁσάκις γὰρ ἂν ἐσθίητε τὸν ἄρτον τοῦτον καὶ τὸ ποτήριον τοῦτο πίνητε τὸν ἐμὸν θάνατον καταγγέλλετε, τὴν ἐμὴν ἀνάστασιν ὁμολογεῖτε.

The Liturgy of St. Basil. Ibid., 328.

For as often as ye shall eat of this bread and drink of this cup ye do show my death, ye do confess my resurrection, ye do make my memorial until I come.

Liturgy of the Coptic Jacobites. Trans. from ibid., 177.

For as often as you eat this bread and drink this cup you proclaim the death of the son of man and confess his resurrection until he comes.

ὁσάκις γὰρ ἂν ἐσθίητε τὸν ἄρτον τοῦτον καὶ τὸ ποτήριον τοῦτο πίνητε, τὸν θάνατον τοῦ υἱοῦ τοῦ ἀνθρώπου καταγγέλλετε καὶ τὴν ἀνάστασιν αὐτοῦ ὁμολογεῖτε ἄχρις οὗ ἔλθῃ.

The Liturgy of St. James. Ibid., 52.

Mark 14:22, Matt 26:26–29, Luke 22:15–20, 1 Cor 11:23–26.

NOTES
[1] The modern text of this liturgy is essentially the same at this point (ibid., 405).

134 / *The Prophet Moses Foretold* _____

Still further he said: I am he concerning whom Moses prophesied, saying: the Lord our God will raise up a prophet for you from your brothers, just as he did me. Hear him in all things, and whoever does not hear that prophet will die.

ἔτι μὴν ἔλεγεν· "Ἐγώ εἰμι περὶ οὗ Μωυσῆς προεφήτευσεν εἰπών·
Προφήτην ἐγερεῖ ὑμῖν κύριος ὁ θεὸς ἡμῶν ἐκ τῶν ἀδελφῶν ὑμῶν
ὥσπερ καὶ ἐμέ· αὐτοῦ ἀκούετε κατὰ πάντα. ὃς ἂν δὲ μὴ ἀκούσῃ
τοῦ προφήτου ἐκείνου, ἀποθανεῖται."

Ps. Clementine Homilies 3.53. Rehm-Irmscher, Homilien, 76.

PARALLELS

Deut 18:15, 18–19, Acts 3:22–23.

I35 / *Death and Resurrection Prophesied*

And the governor commanded the Jews to leave the praetorium, and he
called Jesus and said to him: What shall I do with you? Jesus said to Pilate:
As it was given to you. Pilate responded: How was it given? Jesus said: Moses
and the prophets proclaimed beforehand concerning my death and
resurrection.

Ἐκέλευσε δὲ ὁ ἡγεμὼν ἐξελθεῖν τοὺς Ἰουδαίους ἔξω τοῦ
πραιτωρίου, καὶ προσκαλεσάμενος τὸν Ἰησοῦν λέγει αὐτῷ·
τί ποιήσω σοι; λέγει ὁ Ἰησοῦς τῷ Πιλάτῳ· ὡς ἐδόθη σοι.
λέγει ὁ Πιλᾶτος· πῶς ἐδόθη; λέγει ὁ Ἰησοῦς·
Μωυσῆς καὶ οἱ προφῆται προεκήρυξαν περὶ τοῦ θανάτου
μου καὶ τῆς ἀναστάσεως.

Acts of Pilate 4.3. Tischendorf, Evangelia Apocrypha, 232–33.

PARALLELS

. . . after his resurrection from the dead and after (they) had been
persuaded by him that even before he suffered he said to them
that it was necessary for him to suffer these things and that they
had been proclaimed beforehand by the prophets. . . .

μετὰ τὸ ἀναστῆναι αὐτὸν ἐκ νεκρῶν καὶ πεισθῆναι ὑπ'
αὐτοῦ ὅτι καὶ πρὸ τοῦ παθεῖν ἔλεγεν αὐτοῖς ὅτι ταῦτα
αὐτὸν δεῖ παθεῖν καὶ ἀπὸ τῶν προφητῶν ὅτι προεκεκήρυκτο
ταῦτα, . . .

Justin, Dial. 106. Goodspeed, Die ältesten Apologeten, 222.

Luke 24:44–46.

I36 / *The Great Inheritance* _____

Finally the Lord said to them: Why do you marvel at the signs? I give you a great inheritance, which the whole world does not have.

λοιπὸν ὁ κύριος ἔλεγεν αὐτοῖς· "τί θαυμάζετε τὰ σημεῖα, κληρονομίαν
μεγάλην δίδωμι ὑμῖν, ἣν οὐκ ἔχει ὅλος ὁ κόσμος."

> Symeon, *Hom.* 12.17. Dörries, Klostermann, and Kroeger, *Geistliche Homilien,* 119.

I37 / *I Am Here* _____

For our Lord Jesus Christ himself expressly announced in the gospel and said in harmony with the prophet: He who speaks in the prophets, behold I am here. And again: My Father is working still, and I am working.

αὐτὸς γὰρ ὁ κύριος ἡμῶν Ἰησοῦς Χριστὸς
διαρρήδην ἐκφωνεῖ ἐν τῷ εὐαγγελίῳ καὶ
λέγει συνῳδὰ τῷ προφήτῃ ὅτι "ὁ λαλῶν
ἐν τοῖς προφήταις, ἰδοὺ πάρειμι" καὶ
πάλιν "ὁ πατήρ μου ἕως ἄρτι
ἐργάζεται, κἀγὼ ἐργάζομαι."

> Epiphanius, *Haer.* 23.5.5. Text from Holl, *Epiphanius* 1: 253.

PARALLELS

He who came to his own then is not a stranger but is master of all. And therefore he says: He who speaks in the prophets, behold I am here.

ὁ γοῦν εἰς τὰ ἴδια ἐλθὼν οὐκ ἀλλότριός ἐστιν,
ἀλλὰ δεσπότης πάντων καὶ διὰ τοῦτο λέγει
"ὁ λαλῶν ἐν τοῖς προφήταις, ἰδοὺ πάρειμι."

> Epiphanius, *Haer.* 66.42. Ibid., 3:79.

Therefore how did the prophets proclaim beforehand the matters leading to Christ, unless it was one and the same power which spoke in the law, in the prophets, and in the gospels? Therefore he says: He who speaks in the prophets, behold I am here, and the rest.

πόθεν οὖν οἱ προφῆται τὰ εἰς Χριστὸν τετυπωμένα
προανεφώνησαν, εἰ μὴ μία ἦν καὶ ἡ αὐτὴ δύναμις
ἡ λαλήσασα ἐν νόμῳ καὶ ἐν προφήταις καὶ εὐαγγελίοις;

καθάπερ λέγει "ὁ λαλῶν ἐν τοῖς προφήταις ἰδοὺ πάρειμι"
καὶ τὰ ἐξῆς.

Epiphanius, *Haer.* 41.3. Ibid., 2:93.

And if the prophets do not lie but speak the truth according to
the word of the Savior, He who speaks in the prophets, behold I
am here, this matter needs thoughtful interpretation.

εἰ δὲ οὐ ψεύδονται οἱ προφῆται, ἀλλ᾿ ἀληθεύουσι, κατὰ τὸν τοῦ
σωτῆρος λόγον ὅτι "ὁ λαλῶν ἐν προφήταις, ἰδοὺ πάρειμι,"
νοήσεώς ἐστι τὸ πρᾶγμα καὶ ἀλληγορίας χρεία.

Epiphanius, *Ancoratus* 53. Ibid., 1:62.

John 5:17, Isa 52:6.

I38 / *Begotten from the Father*

For they utter falsely what is stated in the Gospel when they interpret, The
Father who sent me is greater than I. In the first place he says, The Father
who sent me and not, He who created me. For all the divine writings point
out his true birth with reference to the Father. He says: You begot me, Father,
and I came forth from the Father and have come here, and I am in the Father
and the Father in me.

λέγουσι γὰρ τὸ ῥητὸν τοῦ εὐαγγελίου κακῶς
ἑρμηνεύοντες ὅτι "ὁ ἀποστείλας με πατὴρ
μείζων μού ἐστι." καὶ πρῶτον μὲν "ὁ
ἀποστείλας με πατήρ" φάσκει, καὶ οὐχ "ὁ
κτίσας με." πᾶσαι γὰρ αἱ θεῖαι γραφαὶ
τὴν αὐτοῦ πρὸς πατέρα γνησιότητα
σημαίνουσιν. "ἐγέννησάς με" φησὶ
"πάτερ," καὶ "ἐγὼ ἐκ τοῦ πατρὸς ἐξῆλθον
καὶ ἥκω," καὶ "ἐγὼ ἐν τῷ πατρὶ καὶ ὁ
πατὴρ ἐν ἐμοί."

Epiphanius, *Haer.* 69.53.1-2. Holl, *Epiphanius* 3:199–200.

PARALLELS

And a voice from heaven said: You are my beloved son; I am well
pleased with you. And again: Today I have begotten you.

καὶ φωνὴ ἐκ τοῦ οὐρανοῦ λέγουσα· σύ μου εἶ ὁ υἱὸς ὁ ἀγαπητός,
ἐν σοί ηὐδόκησα, καὶ πάλιν· ἐγὼ σήμερον γεγέννηκά σε.

Gospel of the Ebionites [5], Epiphanius, *Haer.* 30.13. Ibid., 1:350.

You are my son; today I have begotten you.[1]

υἱός μου εἶ σύ, ἐγὼ σήμερον γεγέννηκά σε.

Luke 3:22 in mss. D, it. Aland, *Synopsis,* 27.

John 8:42, 14:10–11, 28, 16:27–28, Ps 2:7.

NOTES
[1] This reading is also attested by Justin, Clement of Alexandria, Origen, Methodius, Hilary, and Augustine.

I39 / *If Anyone Should Open*

And again, in another place: I knock and if anyone should open to me, we will come in to him, I and my Father, and make our home with him.

καὶ πάλιν ἐν ἄλλῳ τόπῳ· "ἐγὼ κρούω καὶ ἐάν τίς μοι
ἀνοίξῃ, εἰσελευσόμεθα πρὸς αὐτόν. ἐγὼ καὶ ὁ πατήρ μου,
καὶ μονὴν ποιήσομεν παρ' αὐτῷ."

Epiphanius, *Haer.* 69.63. Holl, *Epiphanius* 3:213.

PARALLELS

And again he said, explaining his consubstantiality with the Father to his disciples, saying: If anyone opens to me, I will come, and my Father (and I) will make our home with him.

καὶ πάλιν φησί, δεικνύων τοῖς αὐτοῦ μαθηταῖς περὶ τῆς
πρὸς τὸν πατέρα αὐτοῦ ὁμοουσιότητος, λέγων· "ἐάν τις
ἀνοίξῃ μοι, εἰσελθὼν ἐγὼ καὶ ὁ πατήρ μου μονὴν παρ'
αὐτῷ ποιήσομεν."

Epiphanius, *Haer.* 69.54. Ibid., 3:201.

If anyone opens to me, I will come in, and the Father, and we will make our home with him.

"ἐάν τις ἐμοὶ ἀνοίξῃ, εἰσέλθω ἐγὼ καὶ ὁ πατὴρ καὶ μονὴν
παρ' αὐτῷ ποιησόμεθα·

Epiphanius, *Ancoratus* 69.5. Ibid., 1:85.

John 14:23, Rev 3:20.

140 / *Not to Destroy But to Save* ⎯⎯⎯⎯⎯⎯⎯⎯

And he said: You do not know to what spirit you belong,[1] for the Son of Man did not come to destroy men's lives but to save them.

καὶ εἶπεν· οὐκ οἴδατε οἴου πνεύματός ἐστε ὑμεῖς, ὁ γὰρ
υἱὸς τοῦ ἀνθρώπου οὐκ ἦλθεν ψυχὰς ἀνθρώπων ἀπολέσαι ἀλλὰ
σῶσαι.

> Luke 9:55b, 56a in MSS. K Θ λ Φ al lat sy[c,p] bo[pt] Marcion. Aland, *Synopsis*, 255.

NOTES
[1] Codex D has the first clause of the saying.

141 / *Not Like Jesus* ⎯⎯⎯⎯⎯⎯⎯⎯⎯⎯

But Jesus cried out and said: He who is not like unto Me is not like unto Him that sent Me. And he who believeth in Me, believeth not in Me, but in Him that sent Me.

> Sinaitic Syriac to Jn 12:44. Trans. from Lewis, *The Old Syriac Gospels*, App. IV, X.

PARALLELS

Luke 10:16, Matt 10:40, John 12:44.

142 / *Growing in Service* ⎯⎯⎯⎯⎯⎯⎯⎯⎯

For I have not come in your midst as one who sits at the table but as one who serves, and you have grown in my service as one who serves.

Ἐγὼ γὰρ ἐν μέσῳ ὑμῶν ἦλθον οὐχ ὡς ἀνακείμενος, ἀλλ᾽
ὡς ὁ διακονῶν, καὶ ὑμεῖς ηὐξήθητε ἐν τῇ διακονίᾳ μου
ὡς ὁ διακονῶν.

> Codex D to Luke 22:27, 28. Aland, *Synopsis*, 440–441.

143 / *Loving the Father* ⎯⎯⎯⎯⎯⎯⎯⎯⎯

As the Lord himself testified somewhere, saying: He who loves the Father also loves the son begotten from him.

ὡς καὶ αὐτός που διεμαρτύρατο λέγων ὁ κύριος· "ὁ ἀγαπῶν

τὸν πατέρα ἀγαπᾷ καὶ τὸν υἱὸν τὸν ἐξ αὐτοῦ γεγεννημένον."
> Theodoret, *Church History* 1.4.45. Parmentier, *Theodoret Kirchengeschichte*, 20.

PARALLELS

1 John 5:1, John 5:23, 8:42, 12:44–45, 13:20, Matt 10:40, Luke 10:16.

144 / *The Living Water*

He says the Lord Jesus Christ is the baptism and there is no other, for it is written: I am the living water.

ἔλεγε τὸν κύριον Ἰησοῦν Χριστὸν ὑπάρχειν
τὸ βάπτισμα, καὶ οὐκ ἄλλο, διότι
γέγραπται· ἐγώ εἰμι τὸ ὕδωρ τὸ ζῶν.
> Peter of Sicily, *History of the Manichaeans* 29. Gieseler, *Manichaeorum*, 37.

PARALLELS

John 4:10, 7:37, 38, Rev 21:6, 22:17.

145 / *The Accomplishments of Christ*

The Lord . . . arose from the dead and uttered this cry:
Who is the one who contends against me?
Let him stand against me.
I freed the condemned;
I made the dead alive;
I raise the buried.
Who is the one who contradicts me?
I am the one, says the Christ,
I am the one who defeated death
and triumphed over the enemy
and trod upon Hades
and bound the strong one
and brought man to the heights of heaven.
I am the one, says the Christ.
Therefore, come, all families of men who are defiled
and receive forgiveness of sins.
For I am your forgiveness;

I am the Passover of salvation;
I am the lamb that was slain for you.
I am your ransom,
I am your life,
I am your light,
I am your salvation,
I am your resurrection,
I am your king.
I will raise you up with my right hand;
I lead you up to the heights of heaven;
There I will show you the eternal Father.

Κύριος . . . ἀνέστη ἐκ νεκρῶν καὶ ταύτην ἐβόησεν τὴν φωνήν·
Τίς ὁ κρινόμενος πρὸς ἐμέ; ἀντιστήτω μοι.
ἐγὼ τὸν κατάδικον ἀπέλυσα·
ἐγὼ τὸν νεκρὸν ἐζωογόνησα·
ἐγὼ τὸν τεθαμμένον ἀνίστημι·
τίς, ὁ ἀντιλέγων μοι;
ἐγώ, φησὶν ὁ Χριστός,
ἐγὼ ὁ καταλύσας τὸν θάνατον
καὶ θριαμβεύσας τὸν ἐχθρὸν
καὶ καταπατήσας τὸν ἅδην
καὶ δήσας τὸν ἰσχυρὸν
καὶ ἀφαρπάσας τὸν ἄνθρωπον εἰς τὰ ὑψηλὰ τῶν οὐρανῶν·
ἐγώ, φησιν ὁ Χριστός.
τοίνυν δεῦτε πᾶσαι αἱ πατριαὶ τῶν ἀνθρώπων
αἱ ἐν ἁμαρτίαις πεφυραμέναι
καὶ λάβετε ἄφεσιν ἁμαρτημάτων.
ἐγὼ γάρ εἰμι ὑμῶν ἡ ἄφεσις,
ἐγὼ τὸ πάσχα τῆς σωτηρίας,
ἐγὼ ὁ ἀμνὸς ὁ ὑπὲρ ὑμῶν σφαγείς·
ἐγὼ τὸ λύτρον ὑμῶν,
ἐγὼ ἡ ζωὴ ὑμῶν,
ἐγὼ τὸ φῶς ὑμῶν,
ἐγὼ ἡ σωτηρία ὑμῶν,
ἐγὼ ἡ ἀνάστασις ὑμῶν,
ἐγὼ ὁ βασιλεὺς ὑμῶν.
ἐγὼ ὑμᾶς ἀναστήσω διὰ τῆς ἐμῆς δεξιᾶς·
ἐγὼ ὑμᾶς ἀνάγω εἰς τὰ ὑψηλὰ τῶν οὐρανῶν·
ἐκεῖ ὑμῖν δείξω τὸν ἀπ᾽ αἰνώνων πατέρα.

Melito, *Homily on the Passion* 100–103. Hall, *Melito On Pascha*, 56, 58.

NOTES

The "sayings" in Melito's Homily are not "extracanonical sayings of Jesus" in the usual sense of the term. The passage is included because of its striking use of "I am" style.

I46 / *The World on Fire*

Jesus said: I have cast fire upon the world,[1] and look, I am guarding it until it is ablaze.

ΠⲈⲬⲈ ⲓ̄ⲥ̄ ⲬⲈ ⲀⲈⲒⲚⲞⲨⲬⲈ ⲚⲞⲨⲔⲰ̄Ⲧ′ ⲈⲬⲚ̄
ⲠⲔⲞⲤⲘⲞⲤ ⲀⲨⲰ ⲈⲒⲤ 2ⲎⲎⲦⲈ ⳁⲀⲢⲈ2 ⲈⲢⲞϥ′
ⲱⲀⲚⲦⲈϥⲬⲈⲢⲞ

> *Gospel of Thomas* 10. CG II, 34.14–16.

PARALLELS

Luke 12:49, 51, Matt 10:34.

NOTES
[1] See *Thomas* 16a [I47].

I47 / *Not Peace But a Sword*

Jesus said: Perhaps men think that I have come to cast peace upon the world, and they do not know that I have come to cast divisions upon the earth, fire,[1] sword, war.

ΠⲈⲬⲈ ⲓ̄ⲥ̄ ⲬⲈ ⲦⲀⲬⲀ
ⲈⲨⲘⲈⲈⲨⲈ Ⲛ̄ϬⲒ Ⲣ̄ⲢⲰⲘⲈ ⲬⲈ Ⲛ̄ⲦⲀⲈⲒⲈⲒ ⲈⲚⲞⲨ
ⲬⲈ Ⲛ̄ⲞⲨⲈⲒⲢⲎⲚⲎ ⲈⲬⲘ̄ ⲠⲔⲞⲤⲘⲞⲤ ⲀⲨⲰ
ⲤⲈⲤⲞⲞⲨⲚ ⲀⲚ ⲬⲈ Ⲛ̄ⲦⲀⲈⲒⲈⲒ ⲀⲚⲞⲨⲬⲈ Ⲛ̄2Ⲛ̄
ⲠⲰⲢⲬ′ ⲈⲬⲚ̄ ⲠⲔⲀ2 ⲞⲨⲔⲰ2Ⲧ ⲞⲨⲤⲎϥⲈ′
ⲞⲨⲠⲞⲖⲈⲘⲞⲤ

> *Gospel of Thomas* 16a. CG II, 35.31–36.

PARALLELS

I came not to bring peace but division of minds and a sword.

οὐχ ἦλθον βαλεῖν εἰρήνην ἀλλὰ διαμερισμὸν τῶν διανοιῶν καὶ μάχαιραν.

> Curetonian Syriac of Matt 10:34b. Aland, *Synopsis*, 147.

Luke 12:49, 51, Matt 10:34.

NOTES

[1] See *Thomas* 10 [146].

148 / *What Eye Has Not Seen*

Jesus said: I will give you what eye has not seen and ear has not heard and hand has not touched and (what) has not entered the heart of man.

ⲡⲉϫⲉ ⲓ̅ⲥ̅ ϫⲉ ϯⲛⲁϯ ⲛⲏⲧⲛ̅ ⲙ̅ⲡⲉⲧⲉ
ⲙ̅ⲡⲉⲃⲁⲗ ⲛⲁⲩ ⲉⲣⲟϥ ⲁⲩⲱ ⲡⲉⲧⲉ ⲙ̅ⲡⲉⲙⲁ
ⲁϫⲉ ⲥⲟⲧⲙⲉϥ· ⲁⲩⲱ ⲡⲉⲧⲉ ⲙ̅ⲡⲉϭⲓϫ ϭⲙ̅
ϭⲱⲙϥ̅· ⲁⲩⲱ ⲙ̅ⲡⲉϥⲉⲓ ⲉϩⲣⲁ︤ⲓ︥ ϩⲓ ⲫⲏⲧ'
ⲣ̅ⲣⲱⲙⲉ

Gospel of Thomas 17. CG II, 36.5–9.

PARALLELS[1]

Therefore, you also brethren, having taken refuge with him and having learned that in him alone you exist, will obtain those things of which he says to you: which eye has not seen nor ear heard, nor did they enter the heart of man. We pray then for the things you have promised to give us, undefiled Jesus.

ἐπὶ τοῦτον οὖν καὶ ὑμεῖς, ἀδελφοί, καταφυγόντες καὶ ἐν αὐτῷ μόνῳ τὸ ὑπάρχειν ὑμᾶς μαθόντες, ἐκείνων τεύξεσθε, ὧν λέγει ὑμῖν ἃ οὔτε ὀφθαλμὸς εἶδεν, οὔτε οὖς ἤκουσεν, οὔτε ἐπὶ καρδίαν ἀνθρώπου οὐκ ἀνέβη. αἰτοῦμεν οὖν περὶ ὧν ἡμῖν ὑπέσχου δοῦναι, ἀμίαντε Ἰησοῦ·

Martyrdom of Peter 10.[2] Lipsius-Bonnet, *AAA* 1:98.

. . . that I may redeem you from death and annihilation, I will give you what you have not seen with the eye nor heard with the ears nor grasped with the hand.

Turfan Manichaean fragment, M 789. Trans. based on the German of Müller, "Handschriften-Reste in Estrangelo-Schrift aus Turfan 2," 68.

Matthew said: Lord, tell me how the dead die and how the living live. The Lord said: [You have] asked me about a saying [. . .] which eye has not seen [nor] have I heard about it except from you. But I tell you that when that which enlivens man is withdrawn he will be called dead, and when that which is alive leaves what is dead ‹he› will be called alive.

ⲡⲉϫⲁϥ ⲛ̅ϭⲓ ⲙⲁⲑⲑⲁⲓ
[ⲟⲥ] ϫⲉ ϫⲟⲟⲥ ⲉ{ⲉ}ⲣⲟⲉⲓ ⲡϫⲟⲉⲓⲥ ϫⲉ ⲛ̅

[ⲁⲱ] ⲛ̄ⲍⲉ ⲛⲉⲧⲙⲟⲟⲩⲧ ⲥⲉⲙⲟⲩ
[ⲁⲩ]ⲱ ⲛ̄ⲁⲱ ⲛ̄ⲍⲉ ⲛⲉⲧⲟⲛ̄ⲍ ⲥⲉⲱⲛ̄ⲍ
ⲡⲉⲭⲉ ⲡⲭⲟ[ⲉⲓⲥ ⲭⲉ ⲁⲕ]ⲱⲓⲛⲉ ⲙ̄ⲙⲟ
ⲉⲓ ⲉⲩⲱⲁⲭⲉ [. . . . . . .]ⲓ̈ ⲉⲧⲉ ⲙ̄ⲡⲉ
ⲃⲁⲗ ⲛⲁⲩ ⲉⲣⲟ[ϥ ⲟⲩ]ⲁ̣ⲉ̣ ⲙ̄ⲡⲓⲥⲟⲧⲙⲉϥ
ⲉⲓ ⲙ̄ⲏⲧⲉ ⲛ̄ⲧⲟⲟⲧⲕ ⲧ̄ⲭⲱ ⲇⲉ ⲙ̄ⲙⲟⲥ
ⲛⲏⲧⲛ ⲭⲉ ⲍⲟⲧⲁⲛ ⲉⲩⲱⲁⲛⲥⲱⲕ ⲙ̄
ⲡⲁⲓ̈ ⲉⲧⲕⲓⲙ ⲉⲡⲣⲱⲙⲉ ⲥⲉⲛⲁⲙⲟⲩ
ⲧⲉ ⲉⲣⲟϥ ⲭⲉ ⲡⲉⲧⲙⲟⲟⲩⲧ· ⲁⲩⲱ ⲍⲟⲧⲁⲛ
ⲉⲣⲱⲁⲛⲡⲉⲧⲟⲛ̄ⲍ ⲕⲱ ⲛ̄ⲡⲉⲧⲙⲟⲟⲩⲧ
ⲥⲉⲛⲁⲙⲟⲩⲧⲉ ⲉⲡⲉⲧⲟⲛ̄ⲍ³

Dialogue of the Savior, CG III, 139.20–140.9.

As then we also have taken refuge in Him, and have learnt that
it is in Him alone to give, let us beg from Him those things which
He said that He would give us, which eye hath not seen and ear
hath not heard, and [which] have not entered into the heart of
man, the things which God hath prepared for them that love Him,
as Moses and some of the saints have said.

Testament of the Lord 1.28. Trans. from Cooper and Maclean, *Testament of Our Lord,* 89.

And the righteous who have walked in the way of righteousness
will inherit the glory of God. And his power will be given to them,
which no eye has seen nor ear heard. And they will rejoice in my
kingdom (var. in the kingdom of heaven).

Testament of the Lord in Galilee 11. Trans. based on the German rendering of the Ethiopic in Schmidt, *Gespräche Jesu,* 66*.

Then our Lord Christ came to Jericho; he gathered his disciples
and said to them: You are the Lord's fellow-heirs. I have prepared
the kingdom of heaven for you before the ages, indeed, before the
creation of the heavens and the earth. Because you are all pure—
therefore I have chosen you, but one of you is a devil. The rest
of you shall inherit the kingdom of heaven, whose delights no ear
has heard described, which no eye has seen and which has not
appeared to any human heart. Truly I say to you, on the day of
resurrection twelve of you shall sit on twelve thrones and judge
the twelve tribes of Israel.

Apocryphal Gospel of John. Trans. based on the Swedish rendering of the
Arabic text by Lofgren, *Det Apokryfiska Johannesevangeliet,* 72–73.

1 Cor 2:9.

NOTES

¹ Other relevant parallels from various sources have recently been published by Stone and Strugnell in *The Books of Elijah*, 42–73.

² *Acts of Peter* 39 is very similar. See *AAA* 1:99.

³ I accept the suggestion of Emmel (*Nag Hammadi Codex III,5,* 80) that line 9 may be corrupt and may have originally been CENAMOYTE E ‹POϤ ϪE› ΠΕΤΟΝ2, "he will be called alive."

149 / *One From a Thousand* _____

Jesus said: I shall choose you, one out of a thousand and two out of ten thousand, and they shall stand as a single one.

ΠΕϪΕ ΙC ϪΕ †ΝΑCΕΤΠ ΤΗΝΕ ΟΥΑ ΕΒΟΛ
2Ν ϢΟ ΑΥϢ CΝΑΥ ΕΒΟΛ 2Ν ΤΒΑ ΑΥϢ
CΕΝΑϢ2Ε ΕΡΑΤΟΥ ΕΥΟ ΟΥΑ ΟΥϢΤ'

          Gospel of Thomas 23. CG II, 38.1–3.

PARALLELS

> The Savior answered and said to Mary: I say to you, they will find one in a thousand and two in ten thousand to complete the mystery of the first mystery.

>   ΑϤΟΥϢ2Μ ΝϬΙ ΠCϢ
> ΤΗΡ ΠΕϪΑϤ ΜΜΑΡΙΑ· ϪΕ †ϪϢ ΜΜΟC ΝΗΤΝ ϪΕ CΕΝΑ2Ε
> ΕΟΥΑ 2Ν ϢΟ· CΝΑΥ 2Ν ΟΥΤΒΑ· ΕΤΒΕ ΠϪϢΚ ΕΒΟΛ
> ΜΠΜΥCΤΗΡΙΟΝ ΜΠϢΟΡΠ ΜΜΥCΤΗΡΙΟΝ·
>   *Pistis Sophia* 134. Schmidt-MacDermot, *Pistis Sophia,* 350.

> However, the multitude cannot understand these things, but one out of a thousand and two out of ten thousand.

> Non autem multos scire posse haec, sed unum a mille, et duo a myriadibus.
>   Irenaues, *Adv. haer.* 1.24.6 (Harvey 1.19.3). Harvey, *Sancti Irenaei* 1:202.

> And he (Basilides) says that it is necessary not to reveal to anyone at all the things that concern the Father and His mystery and to keep (these things) in silence among themselves, but to reveal (them) to one in a thousand and to two in ten thousand, and he charged his disciples, saying: Know all things, but let no one (else) know.

> φάσκει δὲ ὅλως περὶ πατρὸς καὶ τοῦ ἑαυτοῦ μυστηρίου μηδενὶ
> ‹δεῖν› ἀποκαλύπτειν, ἀλλὰ σιγῇ ἔχειν ἐν ἑαυτοῖς, ἑνὶ δὲ

ἀπὸ χιλίων ἀποκαλύπτειν καὶ δυσὶν ἀπὸ μυρίων, καὶ ὑποτίθεται
τοῖς αὐτοῦ μαθηταῖς λέγων ὅτι "σὺ πάντας γίνωσκε, σὲ δὲ
μηδεὶς γινωσκέτω."

Epiphanius, *Haer.* 24.5.4. Holl, *Epiphanius* 1:262.

He chose one out of a thousand
And from two thousand he chose two.

Mandaean Prayers, 90. Trans. from Drower, *The Canonical Prayerbook of
the Mandaeans,* 93.

Matt 22:14, Eccl 7:28.

I50 / *All Are Drunken*

Jesus said: I stood in the midst of the world, and I appeared to them in (the)
flesh. I found all of them drunken; I found none of them thirsty. And my soul
was afflicted for the sons of men, for they are blind in their hearts and do not
see; for they came into the world empty, (and) they seek also to leave the
world empty. But now they are drunken. When they shake off their wine,
then they will repent.

ΠΕΧΕ
ΙC ΧΕ ΔΕΙѠ2Ε ΕΡΔΤ' 2Ν ΤΜΗΤΕ ΜΠΚΟC
ΜΟC ΔΥѠ ΔΕΙΟΥѠΝ2 ΕΒΟΛ ΝΔΥ 2Ν CΔΡΧ
ΔΕΙ2Ε ΕΡΟΟΥ ΤΗΡΟΥ ΕΥΤΔ2Ε ΜΠΙ2Ε ΕΛΛ
ΔΥ Ν2ΗΤΟΥ ΕϤΟΒΕ ΔΥѠ ΔΤΔΨΥΧΗ † ΤΚΔC
ΕΧΝ ΝϢΗΡΕ ΝΡΡѠΜΕ ΧΕ 2ΝΒΛΛΕΕΥ
Ε ΝΕ 2Μ ΠΟΥ2ΗΤ' ΔΥѠ CΕΝΔΥ ΕΒΟΛ ΔΝ
ΧΕ ΝΤΔΥΕΙ ΕΠΚΟCΜΟC ΕΥϢΟΥΕΙΤ' ΕΥ
ϢΙΝΕ ΟΝ ΕΤΡΟΥΕΙ ΕΒΟΛ 2Μ ΠΚΟCΜΟC
ΕΥϢΟΥΕΙΤ' ΠΛΗΝ ΤΕΝΟΥ CΕΤΟ2Ε 2Ο
ΤΔΝ ΕΥϢΔΝΝΕ2 ΠΟΥΗΡΠ' ΤΟΤΕ CΕΝΔP
ΜΕΤΔΝΟΕΙ

Gospel of Thomas 28. CG II, 38.20–31.

PARALLELS

> Jesus said: I stood in the midst of the world and I appeared to
> them in the flesh, and I found all drunk, and I found none among
> them to be thirsty. And my soul is distressed for the sons of men,
> for they are blind in their hearts and do not see. . . .
>
> λέγει 'Ι(ησοῦ)ς· ἔ[σ]την
> ἐν μέσῳ τοῦ κόσμου
> καὶ ἐν σαρκεὶ ὤφθην

αὐτοῖς καὶ εὗρον πάν
τας μεθύοντας καὶ
οὐδένα εὗρον δειψῶ(ν)
τα ἐν αὐτοῖς καὶ πο
νεῖ ἡ ψυχή μου ἐπὶ
τοῖς υἱοῖς τῶν ἀν(θρώπ)ων
ὅτι τυφλοί εἰσιν τῇ καρ
δίᾳ αὐτῶ[ν] καὶ [οὐ] βλέπ
[ουσιν]

P. Oxy. 1.11–21 (i). Fitzmyer, *Essays*, 394.

John 1:14, 1 Tim 3:16.

I5I / *Where There Are Three*

Jesus said: Where there are three gods, they are gods; where there are two
or one, I am with him.

ΠΕΧΕ Ι̅C̅
ΧΕ ΠΜΑ ΕΥΝ̅ ϢΟΜΤ Ν̅ΝΟΥΤΕ Μ̅ΜΑΥ ϨΝ̅
ΝΟΥΤΕ ΝΕ ΠΜΑ ΕΥΝ̅ CΝΑΥ Η ΟΥΑ ΑΝΟΚ'
Τ̅ϢΟΟΠ' ΝΜΜΑϤ'

Gospel of Thomas 30. CG II, 39.2–5.

PARALLELS

[Jesus said:] Where there are [three gods, they are] gods. And
[where] there is [one] alone [by himself,] I am with him.

[λέγ]ει [’Ι(ησοῦ)ς· ὅ]που ἐὰν ὦσιν
[γ' θε]ο[ί,] ε[ἰσὶ]ν θεοί· καὶ
[ὅ]π[ου] ε[ἷ]ς ἐστιν μόνος
[αὐ]τῷ, ἐγώ εἰμι μετ' αὐ
τ[οῦ].

P. Oxy. 1.23–27. Fitzmyer, *Essays*, 398.

And as Christ has taken care of his flock in all necessities, so he
has consoled it in the sadness of solitude when he said: Where
one is, there am I, lest all who are in solitude be sad. For he
himself is our joy and he is with us. And where two are I am,
because his grace overshadows us. And when we are three—as we
come together in the church—this is the perfected body, the
image of Christ.

Ephrem, *Commentary on the Diatessaron* 14.24. Trans. based on the Latin
rendering of the Syriac from Leloir, *Saint Ephrem, Commentaire*, 135.

For they declare that the Lord meant to say: with the greater number there is the creator God, the primal cause of existence, but with the one, the elect one, there is the Redeemer, the Son of another God, namely of the good God.

βούλεσθαι γὰρ λέγειν τὸν κύριον ἐξηγοῦνται μετὰ μὲν τῶν πλειόνων τὸν δημιουργὸν εἶναι τὸν γενεσιουργὸν θεόν, μετὰ δὲ τοῦ ἑνὸς τοῦ ἐκλεκτοῦ τὸν σωτῆρα, ἄλλου δηλονότι θεοῦ τοῦ ἀγαθοῦ υἱὸν πεφυκότα.

Clement, *Strom.* 3.10.68. Stählin-Früchtel, *Clemens* 2³:227.

In connection with this passage the sages said: Wherever ten persons assemble in a synagogue the Shekinah is with them, as it is said: "God standeth in the congregation of God" (Ps. 82:1). And how do we know that He is also with three people holding court? It says: "In the midst of the judges He judgeth" (ibid.). And how do we know that He is also with two? It is said: "Then they that feared the Lord spoke one with another," etc. (Mal. 3:16). And how do we know that He is even with one? It is said: "In every place where I cause My name to be mentioned I will come unto thee and bless thee."

Mekilta, Bahodesh 11. Trans. from Lauterbach, *Mekilta de-Rabbi Ishmael* 2:287.

But if two sit together and words of the Law [are spoken] between them, the Divine Presence rests between them, as it is written, "Then they that feared the Lord spoke one with another: and the Lord hearkened, and heard, and a book of remembrance was written before him, for them that feared the Lord, and that thought upon his name." Scripture speaks here of "two"; whence [do we learn] that if even one sits and occupies himself in the Law, the Holy One, blessed is he, appoints him a reward? Because it is written, "Let him sit alone and keep silence, because he hath laid it upon him."

Pirke Aboth 3.2. Trans. from Danby, *The Mishnah*, 450.

R. Halafta b. Dosa of Kefar Hanania said: If ten men sit together and occupy themselves in the Law, the Divine Presence rests among them, for it is written, "God standeth in the congregation of God." And whence [do we learn this] even of five? Because it is written, "And hath founded his group upon the earth." And whence even of three? Because it is written, "He judgeth among the judges." And whence even of two? Because it is written, "Then they that feared the Lord spoke one with another: and the Lord hearkened, and heard." And whence even of one? Because it is written, "In every place where I record my name I will come unto thee and I will bless thee."

Pirke Aboth 3.6. Ibid., 450–51.

And how do you know that if ten people pray together the Divine Presence is with them? For it is said: "God standeth in the congregation of God." And how do you know that if three are sitting as a court of judges the Divine Presence is with them? For it is said: "In the midst of the judges He judgeth." And how do you know that if two are sitting and studying the Torah together the Divine Presence is with them? For it is said: "Then they that feared the Lord spoke one with another; and the Lord hearkened and heard, and a book of remembrance was written before Him, for them that feared the Lord and that thought upon His name." (What does it mean: "And that thought upon His name"?—R. Ashi says: If a man thought to fulfill a commandment and he did not do it, because he was prevented by force of accident, then the Scripture credits it to him as if he had performed it.) And how do you know that even if one man sits and studies the Torah the Divine Presence is with him? For it is said: "In every place where I cause My name to be mentioned I will come unto thee and bless thee." Now, since [the Divine Presence is] even with one man, why is it necessary to mention two?—The words of two are written down in the book of remembrance, the words of one are not written down in the book of remembrance. Since this is the case with two, why mention three?—I might think [the dispensing of] justice is only for making peace, and the Divine Presence does not come [to participate]. Therefore he teaches us that justice also is Torah. Since it is the case with three, why mention ten?—To [a gathering of] ten the Divine Presence comes first, to three, it comes only after they sit down.

b. Berakoth 6a. Trans. from Simon, *Seder Zera'im* I, *Berakoth*, 24–25.

Matt 18:20.

152 / *Desiring to Hear*

Jesus said: Many times you have desired to hear these words which I spoke to you, and you have no one else from whom to hear them.[1] There will be days (when) you will seek me (and) not find me.

     ΠⲈⲬⲈ ⲓ̄ⲥ̄ ⲬⲈ ⲌⲀⲌ Ⲛ̄ⲤⲞⲠ ⲀⲦⲈⲦⲚ̄
Ⲣ̄ⲠⲒⲐⲨⲘⲈⲒ ⲈⲤⲰⲦⲘ̄ ⲀⲚⲈⲈⲒⲰⲀⲬⲈ ⲚⲀⲈⲒ

є†ⲭⲱ ⲙ̄ⲙⲟⲟⲩ ⲚⲎⲦⲚ̄ ⲀⲨⲰ ⲘⲚ̄ⲦⲎⲦⲚ̄
ⲔⲈⲞⲨⲀ ⲈⲤⲞⲦⲘⲞⲨ Ⲛ̄ⲦⲞⲞⲦ̄ϥ ⲞⲨⲚ̄ ⲂⲚ̄ⲂⲞ
ⲞⲨ ⲚⲀⲱⲰⲠⲈ Ⲛ̄ⲦⲈⲦⲚ̄ⲱ)ⲒⲚⲈ Ⲛ̄ⲤⲰⲈⲒ ⲦⲈ
ⲦⲚⲀⲂⲈ ⲀⲚ′ ⲈⲢⲞⲈⲒ·

Gospel of Thomas 38. CG II, 40.2–7.

PARALLELS

Jesus said: Many times you desired to hear the words which I say
to you, and you have no one to say them to you. (The) days will
come when you will seek me and not find me.

λέ[γει ᾿Ι(ησοῦ)ς· π]
ο[λλάκις ἐπεθυμήσα]²
τα[ι ἀκοῦσαι τοὺς λό]
γ[ους οὓς ὑμῖν λέγω]
κα[ὶ οὐκ ἔχετε τὸ]
ν [ἐροῦντα ὑμῖν]
κα[ὶ ἐλεύσονται]
ἡμ[έραι ὅτε ζητή]
σε[τέ με καὶ οὐχ εὑ]
[ρήσετέ με.

P. Oxy. 655.30–38 (i). Fitzmyer, *Essays*, 412.

Also, in Baruch:³ For the time will come and you will seek me,
both you and those who will come after you, to hear the word of
wisdom and understanding, and you will not find me.

Item in Baruch: Veniet enim tempus, et quaeretis me et uos et qui
post uos uenerint, audire uerbum sapientiae et intellectus, et non
inuenietis.

Cyprian, *Testimoniorum libris tres ad Quirinum* 3.29. Hartel, *Cypriani*
1:143.

Matt 13:17, Luke 10:24, 17:22, John 7:34, 36, 8:21, 13:1, Hos 5:6,
Prov 1:28.

NOTES

¹ See Irenaeus, *Adv. haer.* 1.20.2 and parallels [116] and *Thomas* 92 [160].
² In lines 31–2 read ἐπιθυμήσατε for ἐπιθυμήσαται.
³ No extant writing associated with Baruch contains this passage.

I53 / *Seeing the Living One*

Jesus said: Look upon the Living One while you live, lest you die and seek to see him and be unable to see.

ΠΕΧΕ ΙC ΧΕ 6ⲱⲱⲧ ⲚCⲀ ΠΕ
ⲦⲞⲚⲎ ⲎⲰC ⲈⲦⲈⲦⲚⲞⲚⲎ ⲎⲒⲚⲀ ΧΕ ⲚⲈⲦⲘⲘⲞⲨ
ⲀⲨⲱ ⲚⲦⲈⲦⲚⲱϢⲒⲚⲈ ⲈⲚⲀⲨ ⲈⲢⲞϤ ⲀⲨⲱ ⲦⲈⲦⲚⲀϢ
6Ⲙ6ⲞⲘ ⲀⲚ ⲈⲚⲀⲨ

Gospel of Thomas 59. CG II, 43.9–12.

Parallels

Luke 17:22, John 7:33–34, 36, 8:21, 13:33.

I54 / *Worthy of His Mysteries*

Jesus said: I tell my mysteries to those [who are worthy of my] mysteries.[1]

ΠΕΧΕ [Ι]C ΧΕ ⲈⲒ
Χⲱ ⲚⲚⲀⲘⲨCⲦⲎⲢⲒⲞⲚ ⲚⲚ[ⲈⲦⲘⲠⲱ]Ⲁ Ⲛ]
[ⲚⲀⲘ]ⲨCⲦⲎⲢⲒⲞⲚ

Gospel of Thomas 62a. CG II, 43.34–44.1.

Parallels

For they will tell this name to those who are worthy of it.

ⲠⲢⲀⲚ ⲄⲀⲢ' [ⲈⲦⲘⲘⲀⲨ C]ⲈⲚⲀΧⲞⲞϤ'
ⲀⲚⲈⲦⲘⲠⲱⲀ ⲘⲘⲞϤ[2]

Apocryphon of John, CG II, 7.29–30.

Notes
[1] See Clement, *Strom.* 5.10 and parallels [I18].
[2] Essentially the same occurs in the versions of the *Apocryphon* in Codices III & IV and also in Codex Berolinensis. For the latter, see Till, *Die Gnostischen Schriften,* 104. The lacuna in II, 7.29 is completed on the basis of the parallel in IV, 11.24–12.2.

I55 / *Destroy This House*

Jesus said: I shall destroy [this] house, and no one will be able to [re]build it.

ΠΕΧΕ ΙC ΧΕ ϮⲚⲀ ϢⲞⲢ[Ϣ]Ⲣ ⲘⲠⲈⲈⲒⲎⲈⲒ
ⲀⲨⲱ ⲘⲚ ⲀⲀⲀⲨ ⲚⲀϢ ⲔⲞⲦϤ [ⲀⲚ ⲚⲔⲈCⲞⲠ]

Gospel of Thomas 71. CG II, 45.34–35.

Mark 14:58, 15:29, Matt 26:61, 27:40, John 2:19, Acts 6:14.

156 / *Jesus, the All*

Jesus said: I am the light which is over them all. I am the All. The All came
forth from me, and the All has extended to me. Split a (piece of) wood; I am
there. Lift up the stone, and you will find me there.

```
                  ΠΕΧΕ
ΙC ΧΕ ⲀⲚⲞⲔ ⲠⲈ ⲠⲞⲨⲞⲈⲒⲚ ⲠⲀⲈⲒ ⲈⲦⲌⲒ
ΧⲰⲞⲨ ⲦⲎⲢⲞⲨ ⲀⲚⲞⲔ' ⲠⲈ ⲠⲦⲎⲢϤ' ⲚⲦⲀ
ⲠⲦⲎⲢϤ' ⲈⲒ ⲈⲂⲞⲖ ⲚⲌⲎⲦ' ⲀⲨⲰ ⲚⲦⲀⲠⲦⲎⲢϤ'
ⲠⲰⲌ ⲰⲀⲢⲞⲈⲒ ⲠⲰⲌ ⲚⲚⲞⲨⲰϢⲈ ⲀⲚⲞⲔ'
ϮⲘⲘⲀⲨ ϤⲒ ⲘⲠⲰⲚⲈ ⲈⲌⲢⲀⲒ ⲀⲨⲰ ⲦⲈⲦⲚⲀ
ⲌⲈ ⲈⲢⲞⲈⲒ ⲘⲘⲀⲨ
```
Gospel of Thomas 77. CG II, 46.22–28.

Lift up the stone and you will find me there; split the wood and
I am there.

ἔγει[ρ]ον τὸν λίθο(ν) κἀκεῖ εὑρήσεις με, σχίσον τὸ ξύλον,
κἀγὼ ἐκεῖ εἰμι.
P. Oxy. 1.27–30. Fitzmyer, *Essays*, 398.

You are the All, and the All is you. You are Being, and there is
nothing that is, except you alone.

σὺ τὸ πᾶν καὶ τὸ πᾶν ἐν σοί· καὶ τὸ ὄν σύ, καὶ οὐκ ἔστιν
ἄλλο ὃ ἔστιν εἰ μὴ μόνος σύ.
Martyrdom of Peter 10. Lipsius-Bonnet, *AAA* 1:98.

God is not in heaven but permeates all things, such as wood and
stone and living beings, even the least significant.

ὁ θεὸς οὐκ ἐν οὐρανῷ ἐστιν ἀλλὰ διὰ πάντων
πεφοίτηκεν, οἷον ξύλων καὶ λίθων καὶ ζῴων, ἄχρι
καὶ τῶν ἀτιμοτάτων.
Lucian, *Hermotimus* 81. Dindorf, *Luciani Samosatensis opera*, 241.

John 1:4–5, 9, 3:19, 8:12, 9:5, 12:46, Rom 11:36, 1 Cor 8:6, 11:12,
Eph 4:6, Col 1:16, Heb 2:10, John 1:3.

157 / Near the Fire

Jesus said: Whoever is near me is near the fire, and whoever is far from me is far from the kingdom.

ΠΕϪΕ ΙC ϪΕ ΠΕΤ2ΗΝ
ΕΡΟΕΙ ΕϤ2ΗΝ ΕΤCΑΤΕ ΑΥШ ΠΕΤΟΥΗΥ′
̄ΜΜΟΕΙ ϤΟΥΗΥ ̄ΝΤ̄Μ̄ΝΤΕΡΟ

Gospel of Thomas 82. CG II, 47.17–19.

PARALLELS

I have read somewhere that the Savior said—and I question whether someone has assumed the role of the Savior, or has recalled this from memory, or if it is true that this was said, that the Savior himself said: He who is near me is near the fire; he who is far from me is far from the kingdom.

Legi alicubi quasi Salvatore dicente—et quaero, sive quis personam figuravit Salvatoris sive in memoriam adduxit, an verum sit hoc quod dictum est—,ait autem ibi Salvator: "qui iuxta me est, iuxta ignem est; qui longe est a me, longe est a regno."

Origen, *Homilies on Jeremiah* 3.3. Baehrens, *Origenes* 8:312.

Therefore the Savior said, He who is near me is near the fire; he who is far from me is far from the kingdom.

Διό φησιν ὁ Σωτήρ· ὁ ἐγγύς μου, ἐγγὺς τοῦ πυρός· ὁ δὲ μακρὰν ἀπ᾽ ἐμοῦ, μακρὰν ἀπὸ τῆς βασιλείας.

Didymus, *In Ps.* 88.8. PG 39.1488.

This is what our Savior-Redeemer said, he says, He who joins me, joins with fire, and he who is far from me is far from life.

Ps. Ephrem, *Exposition of the Gospel* 83. Trans. of the Armenian from Egan, *St. Ephrem, An Exposition of the Gospel*, 62.

He who is near Zeus is near the lightning.

Ὁ ἐγγὺς Διὸς ἐγγὺς κεραυνοῦ.

Paroimiai of Aesop. Perry, *Aesopica* 1:290.

Far from Zeus and far from the lightning.

Πόρρω Διὸς τὲ καὶ κεραυνοῦ.

Diogenianus. Leutsch and Schneidewin, *Corpus Paroemiographorum Graecorum* 1:300.

158 / *The Easy Yoke*

Jesus said: Come to me, for my yoke is easy and my lordship is gentle, and you will find repose for yourselves.

ΠⲈⲬⲈ ⲒⲎⲤ
ⲬⲈ ⲀⲘⲎⲈⲒⲦⲚ ⲰⲀⲢⲞⲈⲒ' ⲬⲈ ⲞⲨⲬⲢⲎⲤⲦⲞⲤ
ⲠⲈ ⲠⲀⲚⲀ2Ⲃ' ⲀⲨⲰ ⲦⲀⲘⲚⲦⲬⲞⲈⲒⲤ ⲞⲨⲢⲘ
ⲢⲀⲰ ⲦⲈ ⲀⲨⲰ ⲦⲈⲦⲚⲀ2Ⲉ ⲀⲨⲀⲚⲀⲨⲠⲀⲤⲒⲤ¹ ⲚⲎ
ⲦⲚ

Gospel of Thomas 90. CG II, 48.16–20.

PARALLELS

Come near to me, you who lack learning, and dwell in the house of instruction. Why do you say you are lacking in these things, and why are your souls exceedingly thirsty? I opened my mouth and spoke: Buy for yourselves without money. Put your neck under the yoke, and let your souls receive instruction. It is to be found near by. See with your eyes that I have labored little yet have found for myself much rest.

ἐγγίσατε πρός με, ἀπαίδευτοι, καὶ αὐλίσθητε ἐν οἴκῳ παιδείας.
τί ὅτι ὑστερεῖσθαι λέγετε ἐν τούτοις καὶ αἱ ψυχαὶ ὑμῶν
διψῶσι σφόδρα; ἤνοιξα τὸ στόμα μου καὶ ἐλάλησα Κτήσασθε
ἑαυτοῖς ἄνευ ἀργυρίου. τὸν τράχηλον ὑμῶν ὑπόθετε ὑπὸ ζυγόν,
καὶ ἐπιδεξάσθω ἡ ψυχὴ ὑμῶν παιδείαν. ἐγγύς ἐστιν εὑρεῖν
αὐτήν. ἴδετε ἐν ὀφθαλμοῖς ὑμῶν ὅτι ὀλίγον ἐκοπίασα καὶ
εὗρον ἐμαυτῷ πολλὴν ἀνάπαυσιν.
    Sirach 51:32–27. Rahlfs, *Septuaginta* 2:470.

Matt 11:28–30.

NOTES
¹ read ⲀⲨⲀⲚⲀⲠⲀⲨⲤⲒⲤ in line 19.

159 / *Seek, Ask*

Jesus said: Seek and you will find. But those things you asked me about in those days, I did not tell you then. Now I desire to tell them, and you do not inquire after them.¹

ΠⲈⲬⲈ
ⲒⲤ ⲬⲈ ⲰⲒⲚⲈ ⲀⲨⲰ ⲦⲈⲦⲚⲀ6ⲒⲚⲈ ⲀⲖⲖⲀ ⲚⲈ
ⲦⲀⲦⲈⲦⲚⲬⲚⲞⲨⲈⲒ ⲈⲢⲞⲞⲨ ⲚⲚⲒ2ⲞⲞⲨ ⲈⲘⲠⲒ

ⲬⲞⲞⲨ ⲚⲎⲦⲚ̄ ⲘⲪⲞⲞⲨ ⲈⲦⲘ̄ⲘⲀⲨ ⲦⲈⲚⲞⲨ
ⲈⲌⲚⲀⲒ ⲈⲬⲞⲞⲨ ⲀⲨⲰ ⲦⲈⲦⲚ̄Ⲱ)ⲒⲚⲈ ⲀⲚ Ⲛ̄Ⲥ(Ⲱ
ⲞⲨ·

   Gospel of Thomas 92. CG II, 48. 25–30.

PARALLELS

   Matt 7:7–8, Luke 11:9–10, John 16:4–5, 23–24.

NOTES
   [1] See Irenaeus, *Adv. haer.* 1.20.2 and parallels [116] and *Thomas* 38 and parallels [152].

160 / *Drinking from Jesus' Mouth* _____

Jesus said: Whoever drinks from my mouth will become like me. I myself will become he, and the things that are hidden will be revealed to him.

ⲠⲈⲬⲈ Ⲓ̄Ⲥ̄ ⲬⲈ ⲠⲈⲦⲀⲤⲰ ⲈⲂⲞⲖ Ⲍ̄Ⲛ ⲦⲀⲦⲀⲠⲢⲞ
ϤⲚⲀⲰ)ⲰⲠⲈ Ⲛ̄ⲦⲀⲌⲈ ⲀⲚⲞⲔ Ⲍ(Ⲱ ϮⲚⲀⲰ)ⲰⲠⲈ
ⲈⲚⲦⲞϤ ⲠⲈ ⲀⲨⲰ ⲚⲈⲐⲎⲠ ⲚⲀⲞⲨⲰⲚⲌ ⲈⲢⲞϤ

   Gospel of Thomas 108. CG II, 50.28–30.

PARALLELS

   (Marcus is speaking) Adorn yourself as a bride expecting her bridegroom, in order that you may be what I am and I what you are.

   Εὐτρέπισον σεαυτὴν, ὡς νύμφη ἐκδεχομένη τὸν νυμφίον ἑαυτῆς,
   ἵνα ἔσῃ ὃ ἐγώ, καὶ ἐγὼ ὃ σύ.
       Irenaeus, *Adv. haer.* 1.13.3 (Harvey, 1.7.2). Harvey, *Sancti Irenaei* 1:118.

   John 4:10, 14, 7:37, Rev 21:6, 22:17.

161 / *Things Above and Below* _____

The Lord said: I have come that I might make [the things below] like the things [above and the things outside] like the things [within.[1] I came to unite] them in [that] place.

[ⲠⲬⲞ]ⲈⲒⲤ [ⲠⲈⲬ]ⲀϤ
ⲬⲈ ⲀⲈⲒ ⲈⲦⲢⲀⲈⲒ[ⲢⲈ Ⲛ̄ⲚⲀ ⲠⲤⲀ Ⲙ̄ⲠⲒⲦ]Ⲛ̄ Ⲛ

ⲐⲈ ⲚⲚⲀ ⲠⲤⲀ Ⲛ[ⲦⲠⲈ ⲀⲨⲰ ⲚⲚⲀⲠⲤⲀ Ⲛ]ⲂⲞⲀ
ⲚⲐⲈ ⲚⲚⲀ ⲠⲤ[Ⲁ Ⲛ2ⲞⲨⲚ ⲀⲈⲒ ⲈⲦⲢⲀ2ⲰⲦ]
ⲢⲞⲨ ⲘⲠⲘⲀ ⲈⲦⲘ[ⲘⲀⲨ][2]

    Gospel of Philip 69. CG II, 67.30–34.

NOTES

  [1] See *Gospel of the Egyptians* [3] and parallels [A6].
  [2] Completion of the text follows that of Ménard, *L'Évangile selon Philippe*, 78.

COMMUNITY RULES

C1 / *Be Merciful*

Especially remembering the words of the Lord Jesus which he spoke when he was teaching gentleness and long suffering. For thus he spoke:
Be merciful, that you may obtain mercy.
Forgive, that you may be forgiven.
As you do, so it will be done to you.
As you give, so it will be given to you.
As you judge, so you will be judged.
As you are kind, so kindness will be shown to you.
With the measure you use, it will be measured back to you.

μάλιστα μεμνημένοι τῶν λόγων τοῦ κυρίου Ἰησοῦ, οὓς
ἐλάλησεν διδάσκων ἐπιείκειαν καὶ μακροθυμίαν. οὕτως
γὰρ εἶπεν·
    Ἐλεᾶτε, ἵνα ἐλεηθῆτε·
    ἀφίετε, ἵνα ἀφεθῇ ὑμῖν·
ὡς ποιεῖτε, οὕτω ποιηθήσεται ὑμῖν·
    ὡς δίδοτε, οὕτως δοθήσεται ὑμῖν·
    ὡς κρίνετε, οὕτως κριθήσεσθε·
    ὡς χρηστεύεσθε, οὕτως χρηστευθήσεται ὑμῖν·
    ᾧ μέτρῳ μετρεῖτε, ἐν αὐτῷ μετρηθήσεται ὑμῖν.
        1 Clement 13.1-2. Funk-Bihlmeyer, *Die Apostolischen Väter*, 42.

PARALLELS

But remembering what the Lord said when he taught: Do not judge, lest you be judged; forgive and you will be forgiven; be merciful that you may obtain mercy; with the measure you use, it will be measured back to you; and blessed are the poor and those who are persecuted for righteousness sake, for theirs is the kingdom of God.

μνημονεύοντες δὲ ὧν εἶπεν ὁ κύριος διδάσκων· Μὴ κρίνετε,
ἵνα μὴ κριθῆτε· ἀφίετε, καὶ ἀφεθήσεται ὑμῖν· ἐλεᾶτε, ἵνα
ἐλεηθῆτε· ᾧ μέτρῳ μετρεῖτε, ἀντιμετρηθήσεται ὑμῖν· καὶ
ὅτι μακάριοι οἱ πτωχοὶ καὶ οἱ διωκόμενοι ἕνεκεν δικαιοσύνης,
ὅτι αὐτῶν ἐστιν ἡ βασιλεία τοῦ θεοῦ.
        Polycarp, *Phil.* 2.3. Ibid., 115.

Be merciful, says the Lord, that you may obtain mercy. Forgive
that you may be forgiven. As you do, so it will be done to you. As
you give, so it will be given to you. As you judge, so you will be
judged. As you are kind, so kindness will be shown to you. With
the measure you use, it will be measured to you.

"ἐλεᾶτε," φησὶν ὁ κύριος, "ἵνα ἐλεηθῆτε· ἀφίετε, ἵνα
ἀφεθῇ ὑμῖν· ὡς ποιεῖτε, οὕτως ποιηθήσεται ὑμῖν· ὡς
δίδοτε, οὕτως δοθήσεται ὑμῖν· ὡς κρίνετε, οὕτως κριθήσεσθε· ὡς
χρηστεύεσθε, οὕτως χρηστευθήσεται ὑμῖν·
ᾧ μέτρῳ μετρεῖτε, ἀντιμετρηθήσεται ὑμῖν."

> Clement, *Strom.* 2.18.91. Stählin-Früchtel, *Clemens* 2³:161–62.

Now the way of peace is our Saviour Himself, as He said: Forgive
ye the sins of them that sin, that to you also your sins may be
forgiven: give, and it shall be given unto you. . . . Judge not that
ye be not judged . . . as the Lord said: With the judgment that ye
judge ye shall be judged; and as ye condemn, ye shall be condemned. Wherefore remember and have ready by you this saying:
Forgive and it shall be forgiven you and condemn not, that ye may
not be condemned.

> *Didascalia* 2.21,36,42. Trans. of the Syriac from Connolly, *Didascalia*, 66,
> 101, 106.

The way of peace is our savior Jesus Christ, who also taught us
saying: Forgive and you will be forgiven; give and it will be given
to you. . . . Do not judge, and you will not be judged. . . .
For if you condemn others unjustly, you pronounce judgment
against yourselves, because the Lord said: with the judgment you
judge, you will be judged, and as you condemn, you will be
condemned.

ὁδὸς δὲ εἰρήνης ἐστὶν ὁ σωτὴρ ἡμῶν Ἰησοῦς ὁ Χριστός, ὃς
καὶ ἐδίδαξεν ἡμᾶς λέγων· "'Ἄφετε καὶ ἀφεθήσεται ὑμῖν·
δίδοτε, καὶ δοθήσεται ὑμῖν.'" . . . "Μὴ κρίνετε, καὶ οὐ μὴ
κριθήσεσθε." . . . ἐὰν γὰρ ἑτέρους ἀδίκως κατακρίνητε, καθ᾽
ἑαυτῶν ἀποφαίνεσθε, ὅτι λέγει κύριος· "'Ὧι κρίματι κρίνετε,
κριθήσεσθε, καὶ ὡς καταδικάζετε, καταδικασθήσεσθε.'"

> *Ap. Const.* 2.21,36,42. Funk, *Didascalia et Constitutiones Apostolorum*,
> 79, 123, 135.

For when they heeded the Lord, forgive and you will be forgiven,
then they considered the evildoers (to be) benefactors.

ὅτε γὰρ ἤκουον τοῦ κυρίου "ἄφετε καὶ ἀφεθήσεται ὑμῖν," τότε
τοὺς ἀδικοῦντας εὐεργέτας ἐλογίζοντο, . . .

> Symeon, *Hom.* 37.2. Dörries, Klostermann, and Kroeger, *Geistliche Homilien*, 265.

Forgive your neighbor the wrong he has done, and then, when you pray, your sins will be pardoned.

ἄφες ἀδίκημα τῷ πλησίον σου, καὶ τότε δεηθέντος σου
αἱ ἁμαρτίαι σου λυθήσονται.

> Sirach 28:2. Rahlfs, *Septuaginta* 2:424.

Let us be merciful to one another that we ourselves may receive mercy; let us forgive one another that we ourselves may be forgiven.

[MⲀ]ⲢⲚⲚⲀⲈ ⲚⲚⲚⲈⲢⲎⲨ ⲬⲈⲨⲀⲚⲀⲈ ⲚⲈⲚ 2ⲰⲰⲚ MⲀⲢⲚ̄Ⲕ[Ⲱ]
ⲀⲂⲀⲖ Ⲛ̄ⲚⲈⲢⲎⲨ ⲬⲈⲨⲀⲔⲰ ⲚⲈⲚ ⲀⲂⲀⲖ 2ⲰⲰⲚ

> *Manichaean Psalm-Book*, Ps. 239.3-4. Allberry, *Manichaean Psalm-Book*, 41.

Luke 6:31, 36-38, 11:4, Matt 5:7, 6:12, 14, 7:1-2, 18:32-35, Mark 4:24, 11:25, Col 3:13, James 2:13.

C2 / *Pray for Enemies*

Now this is the teaching of these words: Bless those who curse you, and pray for your enemies and fast for those who persecute you. For what credit is there, if you love those who love you? Do not even the Gentiles do the same? But love those who hate you, and you will have no enemy.

Τούτων δὲ τῶν λόγων ἡ διδαχή ἐστιν αὕτη· εὐλογεῖτε
τοὺς καταρωμένους ὑμῖν καὶ προσεύχεσθε ὑπὲρ τῶν ἐχθρῶν
ὑμῶν, νηστεύετε δὲ ὑπὲρ τῶν διωκόντων ὑμᾶς· ποία γὰρ
χάρις, ἐὰν ἀγαπᾶτε τοὺς ἀγαπῶντας ὑμᾶς; οὐχὶ καὶ τὰ
ἔθνη τοῦτο ποιοῦσιν; ὑμεῖς δὲ φιλεῖτε τοὺς μισοῦντας
ὑμᾶς, καὶ οὐχ ἕξετε ἐχθρόν.

> *Didache* 1.3. Funk-Bihlmeyer, *Die Apostolischen Väter*, 1.

PARALLELS

And concerning our love for all men he taught these things: If you love those who love you, what new thing do you do? for even the fornicators do this. But I say to you: Pray for your enemies, and love those who hate you, and bless those who curse you, and pray for those who abuse you.

περὶ δὲ τοῦ στέργειν ἅπαντας ταῦτα ἐδίδαξεν· Εἰ ἀγαπᾶτε τοὺς ἀγαπῶντας ὑμᾶς, τί καινὸν ποιεῖτε; καὶ γὰρ οἱ πόρνοι τοῦτο ποιοῦσιν. Ἐγὼ δὲ ὑμῖν λέγω· Εὔχεσθε ὑπὲρ τῶν ἐχθρῶν ὑμῶν καὶ ἀγαπᾶτε τοὺς μισοῦντας ὑμᾶς καὶ εὐλογεῖτε τοὺς καταρωμένους ὑμῖν καὶ εὔχεσθε ὑπὲρ τῶν ἐπηρεαζόντων ὑμᾶς.

Justin, *Apol.* 1.15.9. Goodspeed, *Die ältesten Apologeten*, 35-36.

while all of us pray for you and for all men in general, as our Christ and Lord taught us to do when he commanded us to pray for our enemies and love those who hate us and bless those who curse us.

πάντων ἡμῶν εὐχομένων ὑπὲρ ὑμῶν καὶ ὑπὲρ πάντων ἁπλῶς ἀνθρώπων, ὡς ὑπὸ τοῦ Χριστοῦ ἡμῶν καὶ κυρίου ποιεῖν ἐδιδάχθημεν, παραγγείλαντος ἡμῖν εὔχεσθαι καὶ ὑπὲρ τῶν ἐχθρῶν καὶ ἀγαπᾶν τοὺς μισοῦντας καὶ εὐλογεῖν τοὺς καταρωμένους.

Justin, *Dial.* 133.6. Ibid., 256.

And in addition to all these things we pray for you, in order that you may be granted mercy by Christ, for he taught us to pray even for our enemies, saying: Be kind and merciful as is your heavenly Father.

καὶ πρὸς τούτοις πᾶσιν εὐχόμεθα ὑπὲρ ὑμῶν, ἵνα ἐλεηθῆτε ὑπὸ τοῦ Χριστοῦ. οὗτος γὰρ ἐδίδαξεν ἡμᾶς καὶ ὑπὲρ τῶν ἐχθρῶν εὔχεσθαι, εἰπών· Γίνεσθε χρηστοὶ καὶ οἰκτίρμονες, ὡς καὶ ὁ πατὴρ ὑμῶν ὁ οὐράνιος.

Justin, *Dial.* 96.3. Ibid., 211.

For this cause also I have already said to you in the Gospel: Pray for your enemies, and: Blessed are they that mourn, over the destruction of them that believe not.

Didascalia 5.14. Trans. from Connolly, Didascalia, 184.

And pray for your enemies. For he who is not [against you] is for you. [He who] is far away [today] will be [near you] tomorrow.

χ]αὶ π[ρ]οσεύχεσθε ὑπὲρ
[τῶν ἐχθ]ρῶν ὑμῶν· ὁ γὰρ μὴ ὢν
[κατὰ ὑμ]ῶν ὑπὲρ ὑμῶν ἐστιν.

[ὁ σήμερον ὢ]ν μακρὰν αὔριον
[ἐγγὺς ὑμῶν γ]ενήσεται.
P. Oxy. 1224, 2ʳ. Grenfell and Hunt, *The Oxyrhynchus Papyri* 10:9.

Pray for all the saints. Pray also for kings, and powers, and princes, and for those who persecute and hate you, and for the enemies of the cross, so that your fruit may be manifest among all people, that you may be perfected in Him.

Pro omnibus sanctis orate. Orate etiam pro regibus et potestatibus et principibus atque pro persequentibus et odientibus vos et pro inimicis crucis, ut fructus vester manifestus sit in omnibus, ut sitis in illo perfecti.[1]
Polycarp, *Philippians* 12.3. Funk-Bihlmeyer, *Die Apostolischen Väter*, 119.

We who hated and murdered one another and, because of different customs, would not associate with people of different races, now after the coming of Christ live together with them, and pray for our enemies, and attempt to convince those who hate us unjustly to live according to the good counsels of Christ.

οἱ μισάλληλοι δὲ καὶ ἀλληλοφόνοι καὶ πρὸς τοὺς οὐχ
ὁμοφύλους διὰ τὰ ἔθη καὶ ἑστίας κοινὰς μὴ ποιούμενοι,
νῦν μετὰ τὴν ἐπιφάνειαν τοῦ Χριστοῦ ὁμοδίαιτοι γινόμενοι,
καὶ ὑπὲρ τῶν ἐχθρῶν εὐχόμενοι, καὶ τοὺς ἀδίκως μισοῦντας
πείθειν πειρώμενοι, ὅπως οἱ κατὰ τὰς τοῦ Χριστοῦ
καλὰς ὑποθημοσύνας βιώσαντες. . . .
Justin, *Apol.* 1.14.3. Goodspeed, *Die ältesten Apologeten*, 34.

Therefore, we pray for you and for all other people who are at enmity with us, in order that, having repented with us, you might not blaspheme Him. . . .

διὸ καὶ ὑπὲρ ὑμῶν καὶ ὑπὲρ τῶν ἄλλων ἁπάντων ἀνθρώπων
τῶν ἐχθραινόντων ἡμῖν εὐχόμεθα, ἵνα μεταγνόντες σὺν
ἡμῖν μὴ βλασφημῆτε τὸν. . . .
Justin, *Dial.* 35.8. Ibid., 131.

The righteous person attempts also to love his enemies and to bless those who revile him and even to pray for his enemies.

δίκαιος πειρᾶται καὶ ἐχθροὺς ἀγαπᾶν καὶ λοιδοροῦντας
εὐλογεῖν, ἔτι μὴν καὶ ὑπὲρ ἐχθρῶν εὔχεσθαι.
Ps. Clem. Hom. 13.32. Rehm-Irmscher, *Homilien*, 190.

Pray for your enemies, bless those who revile you, that you might become good like your Father in heaven.

ⲱⲗⲏⲗ ⲁ̄ⲭ̄ⲛ̄ⲛⲉⲕⲭⲁⲭⲉ ⲥⲙⲟⲩ ⲁⲛⲉ̈ⲓ ⲉⲧⲥⲁⲩⲱ̄ ⲁⲣⲁⲕ ⲭⲉ ⲉ
[ⲕⲁ]ⲱⲱⲡⲉ ⲛ̄ⲁⲅⲁⲑⲟⲥ ⲛ̄ⲧⲍⲉ ⲙ̄ⲡⲉⲕⲓⲱⲧ ⲉⲧ[ⲍ̄ⲛⲙⲡⲏⲩ]ⲉ

Manichaean Psalms, Ps. 239.33-34. Allberry, *Manichaean Psalm-Book*, 40.

And in the Gospel also it is written again: Bless them that curse you. And to them that do you evil, do not you evil; and do good to them that hate you, and be patient and endure, for the Scripture saith: Thou shalt not say: I will render to mine enemy evil, even as he hath done to me: but be patient, and the Lord will be thy helper, and will bring a recompense upon him that doeth thee evil. And again He saith in the Gospel: Love them that hate you, and pray for them that curse you, and ye shall have no enemy.

> *Didascalia* 1.2. Trans. from Connolly, *Didascalia*, 6.

In the same manner it is written in the gospel: Bless those who curse you. If you are wronged, do not retaliate but endure, because scripture says: Do not say I will repay my enemy for the wrongs he has done to me, but endure, so that the Lord may help you and bring vengeance on the one who wrongs you. For again he says in the gospel: Love your enemies, do good to those who hate you and pray for those who abuse and persecute you, and you will be sons of the Father who is in heaven, for he makes his sun shine on the evil and the good and causes rain to fall upon the just and unjust.

ὁμοίως καὶ ἐν τῷ Εὐαγγελίῳ γέγραπται· "Εὐλογεῖτε τοὺς
καταρωμένους ὑμᾶς." ἀδικούμενοι μὴ ἀνταδικήσητε, ἀλλ᾽
ὑπομείνατε, ὅτι λέγει ἡ γραφή· "Μὴ εἴπῃς· τίσομαι τὸν
ἐχθρόν μου ἅ με ἠδίκησεν, ἀλλ᾽ ὑπόμεινον, ἵνα σοι
βοηθήσῃ ὁ κύριος καὶ ἐκδικίαν ἐπαγάγῃ τῷ ἀδικοῦντί
σε." καὶ γὰρ πάλιν ἐν τῷ Εὐαγγελίῳ λέγει· "Ἀγαπᾶτε
τοὺς ἐχθροὺς ὑμῶν, καλῶς ποιεῖτε τοῖς μισοῦσιν ὑμᾶς,
καὶ προσεύχεσθε ὑπὲρ τῶν ἐπηρεαζόντων ὑμᾶς καὶ διωκόντων·
καὶ ἔσεσθε υἱοὶ τοῦ πατρὸς ὑμῶν τοῦ ἐν τοῖς οὐρανοῖς,
ὅτι τὸν ἥλιον αὐτοῦ ἀνατέλλει ἐπὶ πονηροὺς καὶ ἀγαθοὺς
καὶ βρέχει ἐπὶ δικαίους καὶ ἀδίκους."

> *Apostolic Constitutions* 1.2. Funk, *Didascalia et Constitutiones Apostolorum*, 7. 9.

Bless those who curse you, pray for those who abuse you, love your enemies. For what credit is it to you if you love those who love you, for even the Gentiles do this. But love those who hate you, and you will have no enemy.

"εὐλογεῖτε τοὺς καταρωμένους ὑμᾶς, προσεύχεσθε ὑπὲρ τῶν ἐπηρεαζόντων ὑμᾶς, ἀγαπᾶτε τοὺς ἐχθροὺς ὑμῶν. ποία γὰρ ὑμῖν χάρις, ἐὰν φιλῆτε τοὺς φιλοῦντας ὑμᾶς; καὶ γὰρ καὶ οἱ ἐθνικοὶ τοῦτο ποιοῦσιν. ὑμεῖς δὲ φιλεῖτε τοὺς μισοῦντας ὑμᾶς, καὶ ἐχθρὸν οὐχ ἕξετε."
Apostolic Constitutions 7.2. Ibid., 388.

Matt 5:44-47, Luke 6:27-28, 32-33, Rom 12:14.

NOTES
 ¹ This passage is not extant in Greek.

C3 / *Bread for Tomorrow*

In the gospel called According to the Hebrews¹ instead of "supersubstantiale pane," "bread necessary for existence," I found "mohar," which means "tomorrow's." Therefore, the meaning is: "Our bread for tomorrow," that is, for the future, "give us today."

In euangelio quod appellatur secundum Hebraeos pro supersubstantiali pane maar repperi, quod dicitur crastinum, ut sit sensus: Panem nostrum crastinum, id est futurum, da nobis hodie.
Gospel of the Nazaraeans [7], Jerome, *Comm. on Matt* 6:11. Hurst and Adriaen, *Hieronymi opera* 1.7:37.

PARALLELS

   Matt 6:11, Luke 11:3.

NOTES
 ¹ I follow Vielhauer in assigning this passage to the *Gospel of the Nazaraeans* rather than to the *Gospel of the Hebrews*. See his discussion in *N.T. Apoc.* 1:126-136, especially the discussion of the quotations in Jerome.

C4 / *Loving the Brother*

As we have read in the Hebrew Gospel, the Lord says to his disciples: And never be joyful except when you look upon your brother with love.

ut in Hebraico quoque Evangelio legimus, Dominum ad discipulos loquentem: Et numquam, inquit, laeti sitis, nisi cum fratrem vestrum videritis in charite.

> *Gospel of the Hebrews* [3], Jerome, *Comm. on Ephesians* 3.5 (to Eph 5.4). PL 26:520.

C5 / *The Brother's Spirit*

And in the Gospel of the Hebrews which the Nazaraeans are accustomed to read, regarded as among the most serious offenses is: the one who has grieved the spirit[1] of his brother.

et in evangelio quod iuxta Hebraeos Nazaraei legere consuerunt, inter maxima ponitur crimina: qui fratris sui spiritum constristauerit.

> *Gospel of the Hebrews* [4], Jerome, *Comm. on Ezek* 6 (to Ezek 18:7). Gearia, *Hieronymi Opera* 1.4:237.

NOTES
  [1] See also Ps. Cyprian, *De aleatoribus* 3 [C15].

C6 / *The Soul Ascending*

They quote a gospel, forged in the name of the holy apostle Philip: The Lord revealed to me what the soul must say in ascending to heaven and how it must answer each of the powers above. I have recognized myself and have gathered myself from all places, and I have not sown children to the Archon but have uprooted his roots and gathered the scattered members. And I know you, who you are, for I belong to those from above.[1] And thus it is released. But if the soul is found to have borne a son, it is kept below until it is able to regain its children and turn them back to itself.

προφέρουσι δὲ εἰς ὄνομα Φιλίππου τοῦ ἁγίου μαθητοῦ
εὐαγγέλιον πεπλασμένον, ὅτι, φησίν, "ἀπεκάλυψέν μοι ὁ
κύριος τί τὴν ψυχὴν δεῖ λέγειν ἐν τῷ ἀνιέναι εἰς τὸν
οὐρανὸν καὶ πῶς ἑκάστῃ τῶν ἄνω δυνάμεων ἀποκρίνεσθαι·
ὅτι ἐπέγνων ἐμαυτήν, φησί, καὶ συνέλεξα ἐμαυτὴν ἐκ
πανταχόθεν, καὶ οὐκ ἔσπειρα τέκνα τῷ ἄρχοντι, ἀλλὰ
ἐξερρίζωσα τὰς ῥίζας αὐτοῦ καὶ συνέλεξα τὰ μέλη τὰ
διεσκορπισμένα, καὶ οἶδά σε τίς εἶ. ἐγὼ γάρ, φησί,
τῶν ἄνωθέν εἰμι." καὶ οὕτως, φησίν, ἀπολύεται.
ἐὰν δέ, φησίν, εὑρεθῇ γεννήσασα υἱόν, κατέχεται κάτω

ἕως ἂν τὰ ἴδια τέκνα δυνηθῇ ἀναλαβεῖν καὶ ἀναστρέψαι
εἰς ἑαυτήν.

> Gospel of Philip, from Epiphanius, Haer. 26.13.2-3. Holl, Epiphanius
> 1:292-293.

PARALLELS

And (they say that) he comes to those around the Demiurge and
says to them: I am a precious vessel, more so than the female who
made you. If your mother is ignorant of her origin, I have come
to know myself and understand from where I am, and I call upon
the incorruptible Sophia, . . .

Venire quoque ad eos qui sunt circa Demiurgum, et dicere eis:
Vas ego sum pretiosum, magis quam foemina quae fecit vos. Si
mater vestra ignorat radicem suam, ego autem novi meipsum, et
scio unde sim, et invoco incorruptibilem Sophiam, . . .

> Irenaeus, Adv. haer. 1.21.5. Harvey, Sancti Irenaei 1:187.

If anyone, he says, attains this knowledge and gathers himself out
of the world, away from the monthly cycles and river of desire, he
no longer is kept there but goes beyond the previously mentioned
archons.

εἰ δέ τις, φησίν, ἐν τῇ γνώσει γένηται ταύτῃ καὶ
συλλέξῃ ἑαυτὸν ἐκ τοῦ κόσμου διὰ τῶν ἐμμηνίων καὶ διὰ
τῆς ῥύσεως τῆς ἐπιθυμίας, μηκέτι ἐνταῦθα κατέχεσθαι
αὐτόν, ἀλλὰ ὑπερβαίνειν τοὺς προειρημένους ἄρχοντας.

> Epiphanius, Haer. 26.10.9. Holl, Epiphanius 1:288.

. . . If you strive diligently to ascend into yourself, gathering from
your body all your members which (from the earlier unity which
had great strength) have been scattered and divided into a great
number.

εἰ μελετῴης εἰς σεαυτὴν ἀναβαίνειν συλλέγουσα ἀπὸ
τοῦ σώματος πάντα τὰ διασκεδασθέντα σου μέλη καὶ
εἰς πλῆθος κατακερματισθέντα ἀπὸ τῆς τέως ἐν μεγέθει
δυνάμεως ἰσχυούσης ἑνώσεως.

> Porphyry, To Marcella 10. Pötscher, Porphyrios Pros Markellan, 16.

Therefore, doesn't purification turn out to be what has been mentioned before in the discussion: the separating of the soul as much
as possible from the body and its becoming accustomed to collect
and gather itself together from every part of the body and to

dwell, as far as is possible, both now and in the future, by itself
alone, being released from the body as from bonds?

Κάθαρσις δὲ εἶναι ἆρα οὐ τοῦτο συμβαίνει, ὅπερ πάλαι
ἐν τῷ λόγῳ λέγεται, τὸ χωρίζειν ὅτι μάλιστα ἀπὸ τοῦ
σώματος τὴν ψυχὴν καὶ ἐθίσαι αὐτὴν καθ᾽ αὑτὴν πανταχόθεν ἐκ τοῦ σώματος συναγείρεσθαί τε καὶ ἀθροίζεσθαι,
καὶ οἰκεῖν κατὰ τὸ δυνατὸν καὶ ἐν τῷ νῦν παρόντι καὶ
ἐν τῷ ἔπειτα μόνην καθ᾽ αὑτήν, ἐκλυομένην ὥσπερ ἐκ
δεσμῶν ἐκ τοῦ σώματος;

> Plato, *Phaedo* 67c. Burnet, *Platonis opera* 1:67c.

NOTES

[1]Partly analogous instructions are contained in *Thomas* 50 and parallels [C40] and
the *First Apocalypse of James* CG V, 33.11-34.20 and parallels [C47].

C7 / Save Yourself

And sleep for Adam was the forgetting of the soul which the spiritual seed,
placed in the soul by the Savior, maintained so that it did not dissolve. The
spiritual seed was the outflowing of the "male" and the "angelic." Therefore
the Savior said: Save yourself, you and your soul.

ὕπνος δὲ ἦν Ἀδὰμ ἡ λήθη τῆς ψυχῆς, ἣ συνεῖχε μὴ
διαλυθῆναι τὸ σπέρμα τὸ πνευματικόν, ὅπερ ἐνέθηκεν
τῇ ψυχῇ ὁ Σωτήρ. τὸ σπέρμα ⟨δ᾽⟩ ἀπόρροια ἦν. τοῦ
ἄρρενος καὶ ἀγγελικοῦ. διὰ τοῦτο λέγει ὁ Σωτήρ·
"σῴζου σὺ καὶ ἡ ψυχή σου."

> Clement, *Exc. ex Theod.* 2.2. Stählin-Früchtel, *Clemens* 3².106.

PARALLELS

Gen 19:17, Luke 17:28-33.

C8 / Concerning Marriage

Again the Lord says: Let him who is married not send (his wife) away, and
let him who is not married not marry; let him who has confessed not to marry
according to a resolve for sexual abstinence remain unmarried.

Πάλιν ὁ κύριός φησιν· "ὁ γήμας μὴ ἐκβαλλέτω καὶ ὁ μὴ γαμήσας
μὴ γαμείτω," ὁ κατὰ πρόθεσιν εὐνουχίας ὁμολογήσας μὴ γῆμαι
ἄγαμος διαμενέτω.

> Clement, *Strom.* 3.15.97. Stählin-Früchtel, *Clemens* 2³:241.

PARALLELS

> Matt 5:31-32, 19:9, Mark 10:11-12, Luke 16:18, 1 Cor 7:10-11, 27, 37-38, Matt 19:10-12.

C9 / Fellow Heirs

For my brothers, the Lord said, and fellow heirs are those who do the will of my Father.[1] Therefore, do not call (anyone) your father upon the earth, for there are masters on earth, but in heaven is the Father, from whom every family both in heaven and on earth (derives).[2]

"ἀδελφοί μου γάρ," φησὶν ὁ κύριος, "καὶ συγκληρονόμοι
οἱ ποιοῦντες τὸ θέλημα τοῦ πατρός μου." "μὴ καλέσητε
οὖν ἑαυτοῖς πατέρα ἐπὶ τῆς γῆς·" δεσπόται γὰρ ἐπὶ τῆς
γῆς, ἐν δὲ οὐρανοῖς ὁ πατήρ, "ἐξ οὗ πᾶσα πατριὰ ἔν τε
οὐρανοῖς καὶ ἐπὶ τῆς γῆς."

> Clement, *Eclogae Proph.* 20. Stählin-Früchtel, *Clemens* 3²:142.

PARALLELS

> Mark 3:33-35, Matt 12:49-50, 23:9, Luke 8:21, Rom 8:17, Eph 3:15.

NOTES

[1] See *Thomas* 99 and parallels [A35].

[2] It is difficult to determine precisely where Clement considered the sayings of Jesus to end. That he sometimes used material from the Pauline corpus as sayings of Jesus is shown by *Strom.* 3.15.97 [see C8] and by his inclusion of "fellow heirs" in the first saying above.

C10 / Unable to Enter

This, he says, is what was said by the Savior: Unless you drink my blood and eat my flesh, you will not enter into the kingdom of heaven, but even if you drink the cup which I drink, he says, you are not able to enter the place where I am going.

τοῦτο φησίν, ἐστὶ τὸ εἰρημένον ὑπὸ τοῦ σωτῆρος·
"ἐὰν μὴ πίνητέ μου τὸ αἷμα καὶ φάγητέ μου τὴν
σάρκα, οὐ μὴ εἰσέλθητε εἰς τὴν βασιλείαν τῶν
οὐρανῶν· ἀλλὰ κἄν πίητε, φησί, τὸ ποτήριον ὃ

ἐγὼ πίνω, ὅπου ἐγὼ ὑπάγω, ἐκεῖ ὑμεῖς εἰσελθεῖν
οὐ δύνασθε."

Naassene Exegesis, Hippolytus, *Ref.* 5.8.11. Wendland, *Hippolytus* 3:91.

PARALLELS

John 6:53, 8:21, 13:33, 18:11, Mark 14:36, Matt 20:22, 26:39, Luke
22:42.

C11 / *Concerning Fasting*

In the night, therefore, when the first day of the week drew on, He appeared
to Mary Magdalene and to Mary the daughter of James; and in the morning
of the first day of the week He went into (the house of) Levi; and then He
appeared also to us ourselves. And He said to us, teaching us: "Are ye fasting
for Me on these days? Or have I any need that ye should afflict yourselves?
But it is for your brethren that ye have done this; and do ye the same in these
days when ye fast, and on the fourth of the week and on the Friday always,
as it is written in Zechariah: The fourth fast and the fifth fast, which is the
Friday. For it is not lawful for you to fast on the first of the week, because
it is My resurrection; wherefore the first of the week is not counted in the
number of the days of the Fast of the Passion, but they are counted from the
second day of the week, and are five days. Wherefore, the fourth fast, and the
fifth fast, and the seventh fast, and the tenth shall be to the house of Israel.
Fast then from the second day of the week, six days wholly, until the night
after the Sabbath; and it shall be reckoned to you as a week. But the tenth —
because the beginning of My name is Yod⎑—wherein was made the inception
of the fasts. But (fast) not after the custom of the former People, but according
to the new testament which I have appointed you; that you may be fasting
for them on the fourth day of the week, because on the fourth of the week
they began to destroy their souls, and apprehended Me. — For the night after
the third of the week belongs to the fourth of the week, as it is written: There
was evening and there was morning, one day. The evening therefore belongs
to the following day: for on the third of the week at even I ate my Pascha with
you, and in the night they apprehended Me. — But fast for them also on the
Friday, because thereon they crucified Me, in the midst of their festival of
unleavened bread, as it is said of old in David: In the midst of their festivals
they set their signs, and they knew not.

And be ye constant in fasting during these days always, and especially you
who are of the Gentiles. For because the People was not obedient, I delivered
them (the Gentiles) from blindness and from the error of idols and received
them: that through your fast and theirs who are of the Gentiles, and your

service during those days, when you pray and intercede for the error and destruction of the People, your prayer and intercession may be accepted before My Father who is in heaven, as though from one mouth of all the faithful on earth; and (that) all things which they did unto Me may be forgiven them.

Didascalia, 5.14. Trans. of the Syriac from Connolly, *Didascalia*, 183-184.

PARALLELS

Therefore he instructed us to fast these six days because of the transgression of the Jews, commanding us to mourn for them and to lament their destruction. For he himself mourned for them, because they did not know the time of their visitation. And he instructed us to fast on the fourth and sixth days, on the fourth because of his betrayal, and on the sixth because of his passion. And he instructed us to break the fast on the seventh day at the sound of the cock's crow, but to fast on the Sabbath itself. The reason for fasting on the Sabbath is not that it is the rest from creation; rather, we should fast on that one Sabbath, because on it the Creator was under the earth. For on their feast day itself they seized the Lord, so that this word might be fulfilled which says: They set their signs in the midst of their feasts, and they did not know.

παρήγγειλεν οὖν ἡμῖν αὐτὸς νηστεύειν τὰς ἓξ ἡμέρας ταύτας
διὰ τὴν τῶν Ἰουδαίων δυσσέβειαν καὶ παρανομίαν, πενθεῖν
αὐτοὺς καὶ ὀδύρεσθαι παρακελευσάμενος ἐπὶ τῇ ἀπωλείᾳ αὐτῶν
καὶ γὰρ καὶ αὐτὸς "αὐτοῖς ἐπεδάκρυσεν, ἀγνοήσασι τὸν καιρὸν
τῆς ἐπισκοπῆς αὐτῶν" τετράδα δὲ καὶ παρασκευὴν προσέταξεν
ἡμῖν νηστεύειν, τὴν μὲν διὰ τὴν προδοσίαν, τὴν δὲ διὰ τὸ
πάθος· ἀπονηστεῦσαι δὲ προσέταξεν τῇ ἑβδόμῃ ἡμέρᾳ ἀλέκτορος
φωνήσαντος, αὐτὸ δὲ νηστεῦσαι τὸ σάββατον, οὐχ ὅτι δεῖ τὸ
σάββατον νηστεύειν, κατάπαυσιν δημιουργίας ὑπάρχον, ἀλλ'
ὅτι ἐκεῖνο μόνον χρὴ νηστεύειν, τοῦ δημιουργοῦ ἐν αὐτῷ
ἔτι ὑπὸ γῆν ὄντος. ἐν αὐτῇ γὰρ αὐτῶν τῇ ἑορτῇ κατέσχον τὸν
κύριον, ὅπως πληρωθῇ ἐκεῖνο τὸ φάσκον λόγιον· ""Ἔθεντο τὰ
σημεῖα αὐτῶν ἐν μέσῳ τῆς ἑορτῆς αὐτῶν, καὶ οὐκ ἔγνωσαν."
δεῖ οὖν πενθεῖν ὑπὲρ αὐτῶν, ὅτι ἐλθόντος τοῦ κυρίου οὐκ
ἐπίστευσαν αὐτῷ, ἀλλ' ἀπεσείσαντο τὴν διδασκαλίαν αὐτοῦ,
ἀναξίους κρίναντες ἑαυτοὺς σωτηρίας.

Apostolic Constitutions 14.20-21. Funk, *Didascalia et Constitutiones Apostolorum*, 279, 281.

Do not let your fasts be with the hypocrites, for they fast on the second and fifth days. But you should fast on the fourth and sixth days.

Αἱ δὲ νηστεῖαι ὑμῶν μὴ ἔστωσαν μετὰ τῶν ὑποκριτῶν. νηστεύουσι
γὰρ δευτέρα σαββάτων καὶ πέμπτῃ· ὑμεῖς δὲ νηστεύσατε τετράδα
καὶ παρασκευήν.

> *Didache* 8.1. Funk-Bihlmeyer, *Die Apostolischen Väter*, 5.

Matt 6:16.

NOTES
[1] Yod in Hebrew and iota in Greek are the first letter in the name Jesus and are
also used for the number ten.

C12 / *Christ the Head of Man* _____

And they continued to ask her. And since she did not want to ignore the
apostles, she said: Let us stand in prayer. And the apostles stood behind Mary.
But she said to Peter: Peter, great leader and pillar, do you stand behind us?
Did not the Lord say that Christ is the head of man [but man the head of
woman]:[1] Now, therefore, stand in front of me to pray.

Οἱ δὲ μᾶλλον προσετίθουν τοῦ ἐρωτᾶν αὐτήν. Αὐτὴ
δὲ μὴ θέλουσα παρακοῦσαι τῶν ἀποστόλων εἶπεν·
στῶμεν ἐν προσευχῇ. Καὶ ἔστησαν οἱ ἀπόστολοι
ὄπισθεν Μαρίας. Αὐτὴ δὲ λέγει τῇ Πέτρῳ· Πέτρε
κορυφαῖε καὶ στύλη μέγιστε, ὄπισθεν ἡμῶν ἐστήκεις;
Οὐκ εἶπεν ὁ κύριος ὅτι κεφαλὴ ἀνδρὸς ὁ Χριστός
[sed mulieris vir];[1] Νῦν οὖν ἔνπροσθέν μου σταθέντος
εὔξασθε.

> *Questions of Bartholomew* 2.6-7. Wilmart and Tisserant, "Fragments
> Grecs et Latins de l'Évangile de Barthélemy," 322.

PARALLELS

1 Cor 11:3, Eph 1:22, 4:15, 5:23, Col 1:18, 2:19.

NOTES
[1] The words in brackets are not found in the Greek manuscripts but do occur in
the Latin P and in the Slavonic. The sense of the passage would seem to indicate they
should be included.

C13 / *Concerning Temptation* _____

and do not permit us to be let into temptation, but deliver us from evil.[1]

et ne patiaris nos induci in temptationem, sed libera nos a malo.
> Cyprian, *De dominica oratione* 7. Hartel, *Cypriani* 1:271.

PARALLELS

Furthermore, the Lord necessarily exhorts us to say in prayer: And do not permit us to be led into temptation. In this part it is shown that the adversary can do nothing against us unless God shall have previously permitted it, so that all our reverence and devotion and obedience may be directed toward God, since in temptations nothing is permitted to the evil one unless power is given by Him.

Illud quoque necessarie monet Dominus uet in oratione dicamus: et ne patiaris nos induci in temptationem. qua in parte ostenditur nihil contra nos aduersarium posse, nisi Deus ante permiserit, ut omnis timor noster et deuotio adque obseruatio ad Deum conuertatur, quando in temptationibus nihil malo liceat, nisi potestas inde tribuatur.
> Cyprian, *De dominica oratione* 25, Ibid., 285-286.

Who, moreover, prays and says: Do not permit us to be led into temptation.

Qui autem orat et ducit: Ne nos induci patiaris in temptationem, . . .
> Arnobius Junior, *Conflictus de Deo Trino et Uno* 2.3. PL 53:315.

The sixth petition is: And do not lead us into temptation. Several codices have "inducas," which I consider to be of equal validity, for each is a translation of the Greek which says, εἰσενέγχῃς, "lead." Many, however, in praying speak in this way: Do not permit us to be led into temptation, explaining clearly in what manner "lead" is meant.[2]

Sexta petitio est, Et ne nos inferas in tentationem. Nonnulli codices habent, inducas, quod tantumdem ualere arbitror: nam ex uno graeco quod dictum est, εἰσενέγχῃς. utrumque translatum est. Multi autem in precando ita dicunt: Ne nos patiaris induci in tentationem; exponentes uidelicet quomodo dictum sit, inducas.
> Augustine, *De sermone Domini* 2.9.30. Mutzenbecher, *Aurelii Augustini opera* 7.2.119.

And the blessed Cyprian has cited it in this way: Do not permit us to be led into temptation. In the Greek gospel, nevertheless, this is not found, but rather, Do not lead us into temptation.

et hoc sic posuit beatissimus Cyprianus: Ne patiaris nos induci in tentationem. In Evangelio tamen graeco nusquam inveni, nisi, Ne nos inferas in tentationem.

> Augustine, *De dono perseverantiae* 6. PL 45:1000.

Do not permit us to be led into temptation.

ne patiaris nos induci in temptatione.

> Codices Dublinensis and Rushworthianus of the Vulgate of Matt 6:13. Wordsworth and White, *Novum Testamentum Latine* 1:60.

Do not permit us to be led into temptation.

ne passus fueris induci nos in temptatione.

> Codex Bobiensis to Matt 6:13. Jülicher, Matzkow, and Aland, *Itala: Das Neue Testament in altlateinischen Überlieferung* 1:31.

For it is also regularly contained in the Lord's prayer when it is said: Do not forsake us in temptation which we cannot endure. The Apostle understands that we are forsaken to temptation, but he knows also that God knows the extent of our weakness, saying: God is faithful and does not permit us to be tempted more than we are able (to endure).

Quod et in dominicae orationis ordine continetur, cum dicitur, Non derelinquas nos in tentatione quam ferre non possimus. Scit Apostolus derelinqui nos ad tentandum: sed novit et mensuram informitatis nostrae Deum nosse, dicens: Fidelis est Deus, qui non permittat nos tentari super quam possumus.

> Hilary, *On the Psalms* 118.15. PL 9:510-511.

For this is clearly demonstrated in another chapter of the Gospel, for it is written in this way: And do not lead us into temptation which we cannot endure. Also the Apostle declared this very thing, having attested it, saying: But God is faithful and does not permit you to be tempted beyond your power but, with the temptation to transgress, provides that you are able to endure.

quod ipsum in alio libro Evangelii evidenter ostensum est: sic enim scriptum est: Et ne nos inferas in tentationem, quam suffere non possumus. Apostolus quoque, ut id ipsum ostenderet, ita testatus est, dicendo: Fidelis autem Deus, qui non patitur tentari super id quod potestis, sed facit cum tentatione etiam transgressum, ut possitis tolerare.

> Chromatius, *Tract. 14, In Evangelium S. Matthaei.* PL 20:362.

but daily in prayer, saying: Do not lead us into temptation which we cannot endure.

sed quotidie in oratione dicentes: Ne inducas nos in tentationem, quam ferre non possumus.

> Jerome, *Comm. in Ezech.* 14 (to Ez. 48:16). Gearia, *Hieronymi opera* 1.4:735.

And do not permit us to be led into temptation, but deliver us from evil. Notice what he says: And do not permit us to be led into temptation which we cannot endure. He does not say: Do not lead us into temptation, but like an athlete, he wishes that type of testing which human nature can bear and that each one be delivered from evil, that is, from the enemy, from sin.

Et ne patiaris induci nos in tentationem, sed libera nos a malo. Vide quid dicat: Et ne patiaris induci nos in tentationem, quam ferre non possumus. Non dicat: Non inducas in tentationem, sed quasi athleta talem vult tentationem, quam ferre possit humana conditio; et unusquisque a malo, hoc est, ab inimico, a peccato liberetur.

> Ps. Ambrose, *De sacramentis* 5.29. PL 16:454.

And do not permit us to be led into temptation which we cannot endure, but deliver us from evil. Notice what he says, which we are unable to endure. He does not say: Do not lead us into temptation, but like an athlete, he wishes that type of testing which human nature can bear and that each one be delivered from evil, that is, from the enemy and from sin.

Et ne patiario nos induci in tentationem quam ferre non possumus: sed libera nos a malo. Vide quid dicat, quam ferre non possumus. Non dicat, Non inducas nos in tentationem; sed quasi athleta talem vult tentationem, quam ferre possit humana conditio, et unusquisque ut a malo, hoc est, ab inimico, et a peccato liberetur.

> Ps. Augustine, *Serm.* 84. PL 39:1909.

And do not lead us into temptation which we cannot endure.[3]

καὶ μὴ εἰσενέγκῃς ἡμᾶς εἰς πειρασμόν, ὃν ὑπενεγκεῖν
οὐ δυνάμεθα·

> Ms. Rotulus Vaticanus of the *Liturgy of Alexandria.* Swainson, *Liturgies,* 6.

Indeed, Lord, do not lead us into temptation, but deliver us from evil. For your great compassion knows that we cannot endure because of our great weakness; but provide with the temptation also the means of escape, in order that we be able to endure.

Ναί, Κύριε, μὴ εἰσενέγκῃς ἡμᾶς εἰς πειρασμόν, ἀλλὰ
ῥῦσαι ἡμᾶς ἀπὸ τοῦ πονηροῦ. οἶδεν γὰρ ἡ πολλή σου
εὐσπλαγχνία, ὅτι οὐ δυνάμεθα ὑπενεγκεῖν διὰ τὴν
πολλὴν ἡμῶν ἀσθένειαν· ἀλλὰ ποίησον σὺν τῷ πειρασμῷ
καὶ τὴν ἔκβασιν, τοῦ δύνασθαι ἡμᾶς ὑπενεγκεῖν.

> Embolism of the *Liturgy of Alexandria*. Swainson, *Liturgies*, 62.

And do not lead us into temptation which we cannot endure, Lord, Lord of powers, who knows our weakness, but deliver us from the evil one and his works and all his threats and crafty devices, because of your holy name which is invoked upon our lowliness.

Καὶ μὴ εἰσενέγκῃς ἡμᾶς εἰς πειρασμόν, Κύριε, Κύριε
τῶν δυνάμεων, ὃν ὑπενεγκεῖν οὐ δυνάμεθα, ὁ εἰδὼς
τὴν ἀσθένειαν ἡμῶν, ἀλλὰ ῥῦσαι ἡμᾶς ἀπὸ τοῦ πονηροῦ,
καὶ ἐκ τῶν ἔργων αὐτοῦ, καὶ πάσης ἐπηρείας καὶ
μεθοδείας αὐτοῦ, διὰ τὸ ὄνομά σου τὸ ἅγιον, τὸ
ἐπικληθὲν ἐπὶ τὴν ἡμετέραν ταπείνωσιν·

> Embolism of the *Liturgy of St. James*, from Paris ms. 476. Swainson, *Liturgies*, 307, 309.

Lord our God, do not lead us into temptation, which because of our being forsaken we are unable to bear [but provide also with the temptation the means so that we might be able to endure] and deliver us from evil.

> Syriac *Liturgy of St. James*. Trans. based on the Latin in Swainson, *Liturgies*, 343.

Matt 6:13, Luke 11:4, 1 Cor 10:13, James 1:12-14.

NOTES

[1] The passage quoted above is part of Cyprian's quotation of the Lord's prayer.

[2] Augustine is distinguishing between two alternate Latin renderings of the same Greek word for "do not lead" and a different version of the petition, "do not permit us to be led. . . ." This latter version avoids the implication that it is God who leads into temptation.

[3] The passage quoted is not part of the Lord's Prayer itself.

C14 / *Do Not Grieve the Spirit* _____

The Lord admonishes and says: Do not grieve the Holy Spirit which is in you, and do not extinguish the light which shines in you.

monet dominus et dicit: nolite contristare spiritum sanctum qui in vobis est, et nolite extinguere lumen, quod in vobis effulsit.

> Ps. Cyprian, *De aleatoribus* 3. Harnack, *Der Pseudocyprianische Tractat de Aleatoribus*, 17.

PARALLELS

When the doubleminded undertakes some task and fails in it because of his doublemindedness, this grief enters into the man and grieves the Holy Spirit and drives it out. . . . Both conditions, therefore, grieve the Spirit; doublemindedness, because he did not achieve his purpose, and bad temper grieves the Spirit because he acted wickedly. Both, then, are grievous to the Holy Spirit, doublemindedness and bad temper. Therefore, put grief far away from you and do not oppress the Holy Spirit which dwells in you, lest it appeal to God against you and depart from you. For the Spirit of God which is given to this flesh endures neither grief nor distress.

ὅταν ὁ δίψυχος ἐπιβάληται πρᾶξίν τινα, καὶ ταύτης
ἀποτύχῃ διὰ τὴν διψυχίαν αὐτοῦ, ἡ λύπη αὕτη εἰσπορεύεται
εἰς τὸν ἄνθρωπον, καὶ λυπεῖ τὸ πνεῦμα τὸ ἅγιον καὶ
ἐκτρίβει αὐτό. . . . ἀμφότεραι οὖν αἱ πράξεις λυποῦσι τὸ
πνεῦμα· ἡ μὲν διψυχία, ὅτι οὐκ ἐπέτυχε τῆς πράξεως
αὐτῆς, ἡ δὲ ὀξυχολία λυπεῖ τὸ πνεῦμα, ὅτι ἔπραξε τὸ
πονηρόν. ἀμφότερα οὖν λυπηρά ἐστι τῷ πνεύματι τῷ
ἁγίῳ, ἡ διψυχία καὶ ἡ ὀξυχολία. ἆρον οὖν ἀπὸ σεαυτοῦ
τὴν λύπην καὶ μὴ θλῖβε τὸ πνεῦμα τὸ ἅγιον τὸ ἐν σοὶ
κατοικοῦν, μήποτε ἐντεύξηται κατὰ σοῦ τῷ θεῷ καὶ ἀποστῇ
ἀπὸ σοῦ. τὸ γὰρ πνεῦμα τοῦ θεοῦ τὸ δοθὲν εἰς τὴν σάρκα
ταύτην λύπην οὐχ ὑποφέρει οὐδὲ στενοχωρίαν.

> *Shepherd of Hermas, Mand.* 10.2. Whittaker, *Der Hirt des Hermas*, 38-39.

The grieving man always does wickedly. First, he does wickedly because he grieves the Holy Spirit which is given to man in gladness. Second, he does wickedly by not praying and confessing to the Lord, thereby also grieving the Holy Spirit.

ὁ δὲ λυπηρὸς ἀνὴρ πάντοτε πονηρεύεται· πρῶτον μὲν
πονηρεύεται, ὅτι λυπεῖ τὸ πνεῦμα τὸ ἅγιον τὸ δοθὲν

τῷ ἀνθρώπῳ ἱλαρόν· δεύτερον δὲ λυπῶν τὸ πνεῦμα τὸ
ἅγιον ἀνομίαν ἐργάζεται, μὴ ἐντυγχάνων μηδὲ ἐξομολο-
γούμενος τῷ κυρίῳ.

Hermas, Mand. 10:3. Ibid.

For you will know that he who grieves the shepherd and teacher
among those who are of God grieves the Spirit of God, whose seat
and place this one holds. And he who disregards this one's words
disregards Christ and is found to be a transgressor of the Law.

Ἔσεσθε γὰρ εἰδότες ὡς ὁ τὸν ποιμένα τε καὶ διδάσκαλον
ἐν τοῖς κατὰ θεὸν λυπῶν, τὸ τοῦ θεοῦ πνεῦμα λυπεῖ,
οὗ τὴν καθέδραν οὗτος καὶ τὸν τόπον ἐπέχει· καὶ ὁ
τοὺς αὐτοῦ λόγους ἀθετῶν, Χριστὸν ἀθετεῖ, καὶ παραβάτης
νόμου εὑρίσκεται.

Clementine Epitome 146. PG 2:577.

Eph 4:30, 1 Thes 5:19-20, Isa 63:10.

C15 / *Repentance*

Behold, the amnesty of the forgiveness of sins has come. Jesus is the one who
gives repentance to him who repents. He is established in our midst. He
beckons to us secretly (saying): Repent and I will forgive you your sins.

ЄІС ТАМΝΗϹΤΙΑ ΑϹЄΙ Ν̄ΤЄ ΠΚΑΝΑΒЄ ΑΒΑΛ Π[ЄΙ Π]Є
ῙΗ̄Ϲ ΠЄϢΑϤϯ ΤΜЄΤΑΝΟΙΑ Μ̄ΠЄΤΑϤΜЄΤΑΝΟΪ[Є]
ϤΤΗΚ ΑΡЄΤϤ̄ 2Ν̄ΤΝ̄ΜΗΤЄ ϤΧϢΡΜЄ ΑΡΑΝ 2Ν̄ΟΥ[ΠЄ]Τ
2ΗΠ ΧЄ ΑΡΙΜЄΤΑΝΟΪЄ ΤΑΚΑ ΝЄΤΝ̄ΝΑΒЄ ΝΗΤΝ̄ ΑΒΑΛ

Manichaean Psalm-Book, Ps. 239. 19-22. Allberry, *Manichaean Psalm-Book*, 39.

PARALLELS

Mark 1:15, Matt 4:17, 3:2, Mark 2:5.

C16 / *Possess Nothing*

For I heeded the good teacher, as he had said to his own disciples in the
divine gospels: Possess nothing upon the earth.

τοῦ γὰρ ἀγαθοῦ διδασκάλου ἤκουσα ἐν τοῖς θείοις εὐαγγελίοις
φήσαντος τοῖς ἑαυτοῦ μαθηταῖς· μηδὲν ἐπὶ γῆς κτήσασθε.

Ephrem, *Testamentum*. Assemanus, *Ephraem Syri, opera omnia* 2:232.

PARALLELS

> But when Addai saw them (elaborate garments send by Abgar for
> Addai to be buried in) he sent to him [saying]: "During my life I
> took nothing from you; I will not deny in myself the word of the
> Messiah who said to me: 'Take nothing from any man, and acquire
> nothing in this world.'"
>
> *Teaching of Addai*, f30a and b. Trans. of the Syriac from Howard, *The
> Teaching of Addai*, 97.

> As the Lord said: The one who possesses anything is not worthy
> of me.
>
> sicut dixit Dominus: Qui possidet quidquam, non est me dignus.
> *Liber Graduum* 3.6. Text from Kmosko, PatSy 1.3:55.

> There are some who say straightforwardly that marriage is for-
> nication and teach that it was permitted by the devil. They arro-
> gantly say that they are imitating the Lord who neither married
> nor possessed anything in the world, boasting that they under-
> stand the gospel better than others.
>
> Εἰσὶν θ' οἳ πορνείαν ἄντικρυς τὸν γάμον λέγουσι καὶ
> ὑπὸ τοῦ διαβόλου ταύτην παραδεδόσθαι δογματίζουσι,
> μιμεῖσθαι δ' αὐτοὺς οἱ μεγάλαυχοί φασι τὸν κύριον
> μήτε γήμαντα μήτε τι ἐν τῷ κόσμῳ κτησάμενον, μᾶλλον
> παρὰ τοὺς ἄλλους νενοηκέναι τὸ εὐαγγέλιον καυχώμενοι.
>
> Clement, *Strom.* 3.6.49. Stählin-Früchtel, *Clements*, 2³:218.

> Mark 10:21, Matt 19:21, Luke 18:22, Mark 6:8, Matt 10:9-10, Luke
> 9:3, 10:4, Matt 6:19-21, Luke 12:33-34.

C17 / Pray Unceasingly

As it is written, our Lord said: Pray and do not become weary.

Aphrahat, *Dem.* 4.16 [Bert, 4.9] *De oratione*. Trans. based on the German
in Bert, *Aphrahat's Homilien*, 66.

For the Lord admonished us: Be untiring in prayer.

Et quod Dominus praecipit nobis: Estote assidui in oratione.
Liber Graduum 29.8. Text from Kmosko, PatSy 1.3.831.

Luke 18:1.

C18 / *Eliminating Faults*

He says: Anyone who has cursed or become angry or has been found to have a fault in himself, and has not eliminated it will not achieve perfection.

Qui, inquit, maledixerit, aut iratus fuerit, aut invenietur in ipso defectus nec exterminaverit eum: ad perfectionem non perveniet.
Liber Graduum 2.4.1. Ibid., 31.

Matt 5:22, 29-30, 7:3-5, 18:8-9, Mark 9:43, 45, 47, Luke 6:41-42.

C19 / *Sinners and Harlots*

Everyone, he says, who does not walk in my footsteps and enter into the house of sinners and harlots and teach them, as I have shown him, will not be perfect.

Omnis, inquit, qui non incedit in vestigiis meis, et ingreditur in domos publicanorum et meretricum et docet eos, sicut ostendi ei, non erit perfectus.
Liber Graduum 2.6.2. Ibid., 38.

C20 / *Leaving One's Family*

And whoever does not leave his wife and his children and his kindred and all which he has on earth is not worthy of me.[1]

Et qui non relinquit uxorem et filios et cognationem suam et omnia, quae habet in terra, non est me dignus.
Liber Graduum 19.14. Ibid., 475.

PARALLELS

> As he said: If one has not left all which he has and all which he possesses on earth and his father, his mother, his brothers, his sisters, his children, his kindred, and become superior to marriage, he is not worthy of me.

> sicut dixit: Si quis non reliquerit omnia, quae habet et omnia, quae possidet in terra, et patrem suum et matrem suam et fratres suos et sorores suas et filios suos et cognationem suam et superior fiat matrimonio: non est me dignus.
> > *Liber Graduum* 30.25. Ibid., 919, 922.

> Matt 10:37, 19:21, 29, Luke 14:26; 18:29-30.

NOTES
[1] See also *Thomas* 55 and parallels [C41].

C21 / *Prayer for Sinners* ———————————————

He says: Pray patiently for them that they be saved. If they repent, he says, behold, they will be ashamed of their offenses and come to you and have life. If they do not truly repent but remain in their iniquity, be comforted in that, on the day of judgment when I will appear in my glory, you will be glorified with me in the presence of all creation, and they will be cast to the ground before me in the presence of all creatures, of the upper regions and of the lower regions. You, however, he said, do not rejoice at their ruin, but pray for them, that they might rise.

Vos, inquit, patienter orate pro eis, ut salventur. Si paenitentiam, inquit, egerint, ecce eos ipsos pudebit delictorum suorum et adibunt vos et vivent. Si vero paenitentiam non agant et in sua iniquitate perseverent, solemini vos de hoc, nam die illa iudicii, qua ego apparebo in gloria mea, vos conglorifica-bimini mecum coram tota creatura et ipsi prostrabuntur coram me et coram tota creatura superorum et inferorum. Vos autem, ait, nolite gandere de strage ipsorum, sed orate pro eis, ut surgant.
> *Liber Graduum* 20:13. Kmosko, PatSy 1.3:563.

PARALLELS

> Matt 5:44, Luke 6:27-28.

C22 / Separation from the World _____

Indeed, as the Lord said: Be humble and sanctified and separated from the world and from marriage, and love all people and follow me. Do not be of the world as I was not of it nor have I worked in it. But follow me and be perfect.

Dicente enim Domino: humiliamini et separamini et sanctificamini a saeculo et coniugio et diligite omnes homines et sequimini me; nolite esse ex mundo, sicut nec ego fui ex eo nec laboravi in eo, sed sequimini me et estote perfecti.
> *Liber Graduum* 25.4. Ibid., 739.

PARALLELS

> Matt 5:48, John 15:19.

C23 / Sundown and Wrath _____

The prophet of the God of creation, in order that he might destroy more in battle, caused the sun to stand still in order that it might not go down until he finished destroying those who were attacking the people. But the Lord, being good, says: Do not let the sun go down on your wrath.

Ὁ προφήτης τοῦ θεοῦ τῆς γενέσεως, ἵνα πολεμῶν
πλείονας ἀνέλῃ, ἔστησε τὸν ἥλιον τοῦ μὴ δῦσαι μεχρὶ
συντελέσῃ ἀναιρῶν τοὺς πολεμοῦντας πρὸς τὸν λαόν·
ὁ δὲ κύριος, ἀγαθὸς ὤν, λέγει· ὁ ἥλιος μὴ ἐπιδυέτω
ἐπὶ τῷ παροργισμῷ ὑμῶν.
> *Dialogue of Adamantius* 13. de Sande Bakhuyzen, *Der Dialog des Adamantius*, 28.

PARALLELS

> So therefore, "Do not let the sun go down on your wrath" appears both in the law and in the gospel.
>
> ὡδὶ πέφηνε τοίνυν καὶ ἐν νόμῳ καὶ ἐν εὐαγγελίῳ
> εἶναι τό· ὁ ἥλιος μὴ ἐπιδυέτω ἐπὶ τῷ παροργισμῷ ὑμῶν.
> *Dialogue of Adamantius* 13. Ibid., 30.

> For I am confident that you are well trained in the scriptures, and nothing is hid from you, but that has not been granted to me. Only, as it is said in these scriptures: Be angry and do not sin, and: Do not let the sun go down on your wrath. Blessed is the one who remembers (this), which I believe is so with you.

Confido enim vos bene exercitatos esse in sacris literis, et nihil vos latet; mihi autem non est concessum. Modo, ut his scripturis dictum est, irascimini et nolite peccare, et sol non occidat super iracundiam vestram. Beatus, qui meminerit; quod ego credo esse in vobis.

Polycarp, *Philippians*, 12.1, Funk-Bihlmeyer, *Die Apostolischen Väter*, 119.

For he indicated that it was necessary not only to erase the mark, but not to leave behind even a trace of anger, and that when it ceased boiling it was to be calm and all memory of injury wiped away. And scripture says: Do not let the sun go down on your anger.

οὐ γὰρ τὸν τῦφον ἀφανίζειν μόνον δεῖν ἠνίττετο, ἀλλὰ μηδὲ ὀργῆς ἴχνος ἀπολιπεῖν, ἐπὰν δὲ ἀναζέσασα παύσηται, καθίστασθαι αὐτὴν καὶ πᾶσαν ἀπαλείφειν μνησικακίαν. ἥλιος δὲ ὑμῖν τῇ ὀργῇ, φησὶν ἡ γραφή, μὴ ἐπιδυέτω.

Clement, *Strom.* 5.5.27. Stählin-Früchtel, *Clemens* 2³:343.

And admonish those who have the suit and quarrel one with another, and teach them in the first place that it is not right for any man to be angry, because the Lord has said: Every one that is angry with his brother is liable to the judgment; and secondly, that if it should happen through the agency of the Enemy that some anger arise, they ought at once, that very day, to be reconciled and appeased, and to be at peace with one another. For it is written: Let not the sun go down upon thine anger against thy brother; and in David also He saith: Be angry, and sin not; that is, be speedily reconciled, lest, if anger continue, malice arise and beget sin. He saith in Proverbs: The soul that keepeth malice shall die. And our Lord and Saviour also said: If thou offer thy gift upon the altar, and there remember that thy brother keepeth any malice against thee, leave thy gift before the altar, and go, first be reconciled with thy brother: and then come, offer thy gift.

Didascalia 2.53. Trans. of the Syriac from Connolly, *Didascalia*, 115-116.

Therefore become just judges, peacemakers, without anger. For the one who is angry with his brother without cause is liable to the judgment. But if it happens that, by someone's action, you are angry with anyone, do not let the sun go down on your anger. For David said: Be angry but do not sin. That is, become quickly reconciled, lest continuing anger become malice and produce sin. For the souls of those who bear malice are destined for death, Solomon said. But our Lord and Savior Jesus Christ said in the gospels: If you bring your gift to the altar and there remember

that your brother has something against you, leave your gift there
before the altar, and go first and become reconciled with your
brother, and them come and offer your gift.

Διὸ γίνεσθε δίκαιοι κριταί, εἰρηνοποιοί, ἀόργητοι·
"ὁ ὀργιζόμενος" γὰρ "τῷ ἀδελφῷ αὐτοῦ εἰκῆ ἔνοχος ἔσται
τῇ κρίσει." εἰ δὲ καὶ συμβῇ ἐξ ἐνεργείας τινὸς ὀργισ-
θῆωαι ὑμᾶς κατά τινος, "ὁ ἥλιος μὴ ἐπιδυέτω ἐπὶ τῇ ὀργῇ
ὑμῶν. ὀργίζεσθε" γὰρ, φησὶν ὁ Δαυίδ, "καὶ μὴ ἁμαρτάνετε,"
τοῦτ᾽ ἔστιν, ταχέως διαλλάσσεσθε, ὅπως μὴ ἡ ἐπίμονος
ὀργὴ μνησικακία γένηται καὶ ἁμαρτίαν ἀπεργάσηται·
"Ψυχαὶ" γὰρ "μνησικάκων εἰς θάνατον," φησὶν ὁ Σολομών.
λέγει δὲ καὶ ὁ κύριος ἡμῶν καὶ σωτὴρ Ἰησοῦς ὁ Χριστὸς
ἐν Εὐαγγελίοις· "Ἐὰν προσφέρῃς τὸ δῶρόν σου ἐπὶ τὸ
θυσιαστήριον καὶ ἐκεῖ μνησθῇς ὅτι ὁ ἀδελφός σου
ἔχει τι κατὰ σοῦ, ἄφες ἐκεῖ τὸ δῶρόν σου ἔμπροσθεν τοῦ
θυσιαστηρίου καὶ ὕπαγε πρῶτον διαλλάγηθι τῷ ἀδελφῷ
σου, καὶ τότε ἐλθὼν πρόσφερε τὸ δῶρόν σου."

Apostolic Constitutions 2.53.1-3. Funk, *Didascalia et Constitutiones
Apostolorum*, 151, 153.

The things which by nature are necessary for reverence of God
are clear—these things are assigned by nature—such as not for-
nicating, not committing adultery, not behaving licentiously, not
practicing bigamy, not robbing, not treating unjustly, not being
drunk, gluttonous, idolatrous, not killing, practicing sorcery,
cursing, slandering, swearing, to be vexed and quickly appeased,
to be angry yet not sin, for the sun not to go down upon wrath.
But nature which is created and given as a trust from God will
demonstrate that being joined together with good order in marriage (takes place in accordance with God) and the other things
which are such have in different ways the measure of being a trust
(from God).

τὰ δὲ φύσει εἰς θεοσέβειαν ἐπάναγκες φανερά ἐστιν, ἃ τῇ
φύσει ἐπιμεμέτρηται, οἷον τὸ μὴ πορνεύειν τὸ μὴ μοιχεύειν
τὸ μὴ ἀσελγαίνειν τὸ μὴ ἐν ταύτῳ δευτερογαμεῖν τὸ μὴ
ἁρπάζειν τὸ μὴ ἀδικεῖν τὸ μὴ μεθεύειν τὸ μὴ ἀδηφαγεῖν τὸ
μὴ εἰδωλολατρεῖν τὸ μὴ φονεύειν τὸ μὴ φαρμακεύειν τὸ μὴ
καταρᾶσθαι τὸ μὴ λοιδορεῖν τὸ μὴ ὀμνύναι, ἀγανακτεῖν τε
καὶ ταχὺ καταπραΰνεσθαι, ὀργίζεσθαι καὶ μὴ ἁμαρτάνειν, μὴ
ἐπιδύνειν ἥλιον ἐπὶ τῷ παροργισμῷ· τὸ δὲ γάμῳ συναφθῆναι
μετὰ εὐνομίας ἡ φύσις δηλώσει ἐκ θεοῦ κεχτισμένη καὶ

ἐπιτραπεῖσα καὶ τὰ ἄλλα ὅσα ἐστὶ τοιαῦτα θατέρως ἔχει τῆς
ἐπιτροπῆς τὸ μέτρον.
    Epiphanius, *Haer.* 61.1.10. Holl, *Epiphanius* 2:381-382.

For if His wrath were absolutely immortal, there would be no
room for satisfaction or grace after wrong doing, although He
himself commands men to be reconciled before the sun sets. But
the divine wrath continues forever against those who continue in
sin.

nam si prorsus inmortalis fuisset ira eius, non esset satisfactioni
aut gratiae post delictum locus, cum ipse homines reconciliari
iubeat ante solis occasum, sed ira diuina in aeternum manet
aduersus eos qui peccant in aeternum.
    Lactantius, *De ira Dei* 21. Brandt, *Lactanti* 2:122.

For you do not obey the Savior who said: Go, first be reconciled
with your brother, and so offer your gift. And elsewhere He says:
Do not let the sun go down on your wrath.

Οὐ γὰρ ὑπακούουσι τοῦ Σωτῆρος λέγοντος, ὡς Ὕπαγε, πρῶτον
διαλλάγηθι τῷ ἀδελφῷ σου· καὶ οὕτω πρόσαγε τὸ δῶρόν σου·
καὶ ἀλλαχοῦ· Μὴ ἐπιδυέτω, φησὶν, ὁ ἥλιος ἐπὶ παροργισμῷ
ὑμῶν.
    Vita St. Syncleticae, sec. 63. PG 28:1524-1525.

The entire duration of your life you disobey the lawgiver who says:
Do not let the sun go down upon your wrath.

πάντα τὸν τῆς ζωῆς σου χρόνον παρακούεις τοῦ νομοθέτου τοῦ
λέγοντος· Μὴ ἐπιδυέτω ὁ ἥλιος ἐπὶ τῷ παροργισμῷ ὑμῶν.
    Vita St. Syncleticae, sec. 64. Ibid.

Let peace and gentleness be kept among you in every way. But
if at any time an offense should occur between one and another,
do not let the sun go down upon you while you are in this state.
Be cautious about judging the neighbor, for this is pharisaic and
liable to the judgment.

Τὸ εἰρηνικόν τε καὶ ἥμερον ἀλλήλοις παντὶ τρόπῳ περιποιείσθω.
Εἰ δὲ καὶ συμβαίη ποτὲ ἀλλήλων μεταξὺ σκάνδαλον, μὴ ἐπιδυέτω
ὑμῖν ὁ ἥλιος οὕτως ἔχουσι. Τοῦ κρίνειν τὸν πλησίον
εὐλαβεῖσθε· φαρισαϊκὸν γὰρ τοῦτο, καὶ κρίσεως ἔνοχον.
    Clementine Epitome 146. PG 2:577.

And we do not make an end—even until death—to our enmity for
such people, although the masterly goodness ordained that the

sun should not go down on our wrath, and although the Father
shows his imitators to be good to all, even to those who hate us —
He who causes it to rain upon the just and unjust and makes his
sun rise equally upon each class.

καὶ οὐκ ἂν οὐδὲ μέχρι θανάτου τὴν πρὸς τοὺς τοιούτους ἔχθραν
διελυόμεθα, κἂν τὸν ἥλιον μὴ ἐπιδύειν ἐπὶ τῷ παροργισμῷ ἡμῶν
τῆς δεσποτικῆς νομοθετούσης ἀγαθότητος καὶ τοῦ πατρὸς μιμητὰς
ἀποφαίνοντος ἐν τῷ πᾶσι καὶ τοῖς μισοῦσι χρηστοὺς εἶναι, ὃς
βρέχει ἐπὶ δικαίους καὶ ἀδίκους καὶ ἀνατέλλει τὸν ἥλιον αὐτοῦ
ἐφ᾽ ἑκάτεραν ὁμοίως μερίδα.

Photius, *Commentaries of Jobius*, Bk. 9. Henry, *Photius Bibliotheque*
3:224.

... for each man to rebuke his fellow in truth and humility and
loving mercy towards mankind. He shall not address him in anger
or with grumbling or with a (stiff) neck (or a hard heart or) spirit
of wickedness and he shall not hate him (and conceal it in) his
heart, but on the same day he shall rebuke him and not heap
iniquity upon him.

1QS 5.24-6.1. Trans. from Leaney, *The Rule of Qumran*, 176.

to reprove each man his brother according to the commandment
and "not to bear rancour" from one day to the next.

Zadokite Documents 7.2b. Trans. from Rabin, *The Zadokite Documents*,
26.

You shall not kill with the sword, you shall also not kill with the
tongue, you shall not fornicate with your body, you shall not
fornicate in your thoughts, you shall not go in to the young to
defile them, you shall not envy, you shall not be angry until the
sun sets, you shall not be boastful in disposition, you shall not
rejoice at the fall of your neighbor, you shall not slander, your eye
shall not look at a woman with desire, and do not wish to listen
at all to slander.

ⲞⲈⲚⲚⲈⲔϨⲰⲦⲂ̄ ⲚⲦⲤⲎⲂⲈ:—ⲚⲚⲈⲔϨⲰⲦⲂ̄ ⲞⲚ.
ϨⲘ̄ⲠⲖⲀⲤ:—ⲚⲚⲈⲔⲠⲞⲢⲚⲈⲨⲈ̄. ϨⲘ̄ⲠⲈⲔⲤⲰⲘⲀ:—
ⲚⲚⲈⲔⲠⲞⲢⲚⲈⲨⲈ̄. ϨⲚ̄ⲚⲈⲔⲘⲈⲈⲨⲈ̄:—ⲚⲚⲈⲔⲠⲰⲦ
ⲈϨⲞⲨⲚ ⲈⲔⲞⲨⲓ̈ ⲈⲤⲞⲟⲩⲞⲨ:—ⲚⲚⲈⲔⲔⲰϨ.
ⲚⲚⲈⲔⲚⲞⲨϬⲤ. ϢⲀⲚⲦⲈⲠⲢⲎ. ϨⲰⲦⲠ̄.—ⲚⲚⲈⲔϢⲰⲠⲈ.
Ⲙ̄ⲘⲀⲓϢⲞⲨϢⲞⲨ. Ⲛ̄ϨⲈϮⲤ:—ⲚⲚⲈⲔⲢⲀϢⲈ. ⲈϪⲘ̄ⲠϨⲈ
Ⲙ̄ⲠⲈⲐⲒ̈ⲦⲞⲨⲰⲔ:—Ⲛ̄ⲚⲈⲔⲔⲀⲦⲀⲖⲀⲖⲈⲓ̈:—ⲚⲚⲈⲠⲈⲔⲂⲀⲖ

ïⲱⲣ2̄. ⲚⲞⲨⲤ2ⲓⲘⲈ. 2ⲚⲞⲨⲈⲠ̈ⲒⲐⲞⲨⲘⲓⲀ̄:–ⲀⲨⲰ
ⲘⲠⲈⲢⲞⲨⲰⲱ ⲈⲤⲰⲦⲘ̄ ⲈⲦⲔⲀⲦⲀⲀⲀⲒⲀ̄ 2ⲰⲀⲞⲤ:

Testament of Isaac 19ᵛ-20ʳ. Kuhn, "The Sahidic Text of the Testament of Isaac (M 577, 12ᵛ-25ᵛ)," 233.

Next, we should imitate the Pythagoreans who, not related by race but who share a common practice, if they were ever led by anger into abuse, joined right hands, embraced one another, and became reconciled before the sun went down.

εἶτα μιμεῖσθαι τοὺς Πυθαγορικούς, οἳ γένει μηθὲν
προσήκοντες ἀλλὰ κοινοῦ λόγου μετέχοντες, εἴ ποτε
προαχθεῖεν εἰς λοιδορίαν ὑπ' ὀργῆς, πρὶν ἢ τὸν
ἥλιον δῦναι τὰς δεξιὰς ἐμβαλόντες ἀλλήλοις καὶ
ἀσπασάμενοι διελύοντο.

Plutarch, *Moralia* 6.488. Helmbold, *Plutarch's Moralia* 6:302.

Eph 4:26.

C24 / *Come, Holy Spirit*

For in that gospel instead of your kingdom come, it says thus: your Holy Spirit come upon us and cleanse us.

Οὕτως γὰρ ἐν ἐκείνῳ Εὐαγγελίῳ φησὶν, ἀντὶ τοῦ Ἐλθέτω
ἡ βασιλεία σου, Ἐλθέτω, φησὶ, τὸ ἅγιον Πνεῦμά σου ἐφ'
ἡμᾶς καὶ καθαρισάτω ἡμᾶς.

Gregory of Nyssa, *De oratione dominica* 3. PG 44:1157.

PARALLELS

Here Matthew says "kingdom." Elsewhere another of the evangelists invokes the Holy Spirit saying: Your Holy Spirit come and cleanse us.

Ὁ γὰρ ἐνταῦθα Ματθαῖός φησι βασιλείαν, ἀλλαχοῦ τῶν
εὐαγγελιστῶν ἕτερος Πνεῦμα κέκληκεν ἅγιον, φάσκων,
Ἐλθέτω σου τὸ Πνεῦμα τὸ ἅγιον, καὶ καθαρισάτω ἡμᾶς.

Maximus Confessor, *Expositio orationes dominicae.* PG 90:884.

Let your Holy Spirit come upon us and cleanse us.

ἐλθέτω τὸ πνεῦμά σου τὸ ἅγιον ἐφ' ἡμᾶς καὶ καθαρισάτω
ἡμᾶς.

> Variant to Luke 11:2 in codex 700. Aland, *Synopsis*, 268.

Father. let your Holy Spirit come upon us and cleanse us.

πάτερ, (ἐλθάτω) τὸ ἅγιον πνεῦμα (σου ἐφ' ἡμᾶς καὶ καθαρισάτω ἡμᾶς)·

> Marcion's version of the gospel 11:2. Harnack, *Marcion* 189*.

Come, Holy Spirit, and cleanse their minds and heart, and seal
them in the name of the Father, Son, and Holy Spirit.

ἐλθὲ τὸ ἅγιον πνεῦμα καὶ καθάρισον τοὺς νεφροὺς αὐτῶν
καὶ τὴν καρδίαν, καὶ ἐπισφράγισον αὐτοὺς εἰς ὄνομα
πατρὸς καὶ υἱοῦ καὶ ἁγίου πνεύματος.

> *Acts of Thomas* 27. Lipsius-Bonnet, *AAA* 2.2:143.

Come, Spirit of holiness, and purify their reins and hearts. And
he baptized them in the name of the Father and of the Son and
of the Holy Spirit of holiness.

> Syriac *Acts of Thomas* 27. Trans. of the Syriac from Klijn, *Acts of Thomas*,
> 77.

Luke 11:2, Matt 6:10.

C25 / Receiving without Need

For truly blessed is he who is able to support himself and does not take up
the place of the orphan, the stranger, and the widow, since the Lord said that
the giver is more blessed than the receiver. For again it is said by him: Woe
to those who have and receive in hypocrisy, or who are able to support
themselves and wish to receive from others. For each shall render an account
to the Lord God on the day of judgment.[1]

Καὶ γὰρ ἀληθῶς μακάριός ἐστιν, ὃς ἂν δυνάμενος βοηθεῖν
ἑαυτῷ μὴ θλίβῃ τόπον ὀρφανοῦ ξένου τε καὶ χήρας, ἐπεὶ καὶ
ὁ κύριος "μακάριον εἶπεν εἶναι τὸν διδόντα ἤπερ τὸν λαμβάνοντα·"
καὶ γὰρ εἴρηται πάλιν ὑπ' αὐτοῦ· "Οὐαὶ τοῖς ἔχουσιν καὶ ἐν
ὑποκρίσει λαμβάνουσιν, ἢ δυναμένοις βοηθεῖν ἑαυτοῖς καὶ
λαμβάνειν παρ' ἑτέρων βουλομένοις· ἑκάτερος γὰρ ἀποδώσει
λόγον κυρίῳ τῷ θεῷ ἐν ἡμέρᾳ κρίσεως."

> *Apostolic Constitutions* 4.2-3. Funk, *Didascalia et Constitutiones
> Apostolorum*, 221.

PARALLELS

And truly blessed is every one that is able to help himself, and shall not straighten the place of the orphan and the widow and the stranger. For woe from God to them that have, and receive in falsehood, [or are able to help themselves and (yet) receive;][2] for every one of those who receive shall give an account to the Lord God in the day of judgment, how he received.

> *Didascalia* 4.3. Trans. from Connolly, *Didascalia*, 154.

Give to everyone who asks from you and do not ask for it in return, for the Father wishes that all should receive from his own gifts. Blessed is the one that gives according to the commandment, for he is innocent. Woe to the one who receives; for if anyone having need receives, he is innocent, but the one who does not have need will give an account concerning why he received and for what purpose.

παντὶ τῷ αἰτοῦντί σε δίδου καὶ μὴ ἀπαίτει· πᾶσι γὰρ
θέλει δίδοσθαι ὁ πατὴρ ἐκ τῶν ἰδίων χαρισμάτων.
μακάριος ὁ διδοὺς κατὰ τὴν ἐντολήν· ἀθῷος γάρ ἐστιν.
οὐαὶ τῷ λαμβάνοντι· εἰ μὲν γὰρ χρείαν ἔχων λαμβάνει
τις, ἀθῷος ἔσται· ὁ δὲ μὴ χρείαν ἔχων δώσει δίκην,
ἱνατί ἔλαβε καὶ εἰς τί.

> *Didache* 1.5. Funk-Bihlmeyer, *Die Apostolischen Väter*, 2.

Give to all, for God wishes all to receive his benefits. Those who receive will render an account to God concerning why they received and for what purpose. For those who receive in distress will not be punished, but those who receive in hypocrisy will pay the penalty.

πᾶσιν δίδου· πᾶσιν γὰρ ὁ θεὸς δίδοσθαι θέλει ἐκ τῶν
ἰδίων δωρημάτων. οἱ οὖν λαμβάνοντες ἀποδώσουσιν λόγον
τῷ θεῷ, διατί ἔλαβον καὶ εἰς τί· οἱ μὲν γὰρ λαμβάνοντες
θλιβόμενοι οὐ δικασθήσονται, οἱ δὲ ἐν ὑποκρίσει
λαμβάνοντες τίσουσιν δίκην.

> *Hermas, Mand.* 2.4-5. Whittaker, *Der Hirt des Hermas*, 24.

Acts 20:35.

NOTES

[1] The woe occurs in nearly identical form in the *Catena of Nicetas* (ca. 1080) where it is erroneously attributed to Clement of Alexandria. In actuality it is taken from the *Constitutions* (see Stählin-Früchtel, *Clemens* 3[2]:xvii).

[2] The words in brackets occur in the Latin but not in the Syriac.

C26 / *Commission to the Apostles* ———————————

For we testify all these things concerning him, and the prophets testify the others. We, who ate and drank with him, and were spectators of his wonders, his life, conduct, words, suffering, death, and resurrection from the dead, and who received the command from him to preach the gospel to all the world, to make disciples of all nations, and to baptize them into his death, by the authority of the God of the universe, who is his father, and by the testimony of the Spirit, who is the comforter—we teach you all these things which he commanded before he was taken into heaven, in our sight, to the one who sent him.

ταῦτα γὰρ ἅπαντα ἡμεῖς περὶ αὐτοῦ μαρτυροῦμεν, τὰ δὲ ἄλλα
οἱ προφῆται. ἡμεῖς οἱ συμφαγόντες αὐτῷ καὶ συμπιόντες,
καὶ θεαταὶ γενόμενοι τῶν αὐτοῦ τεραστίων καὶ τῆς ζωῆς καὶ
τῆς πολιτείας καὶ τῶν λόγων καὶ τῶν παθημάτων καὶ τοῦ θανάτου
καὶ τῆς ἐκ νεκρῶν αὐτοῦ ἀναστάσεως, καὶ συναναστραφέντες
αὐτῷ ἡμέρας τεσσαράκοντα μετὰ τὴν ἔγερσιν αὐτοῦ, καὶ λαβόντες
ἐντολὴν παρ' αὐτοῦ "κηρῦξαι τὸ εὐαγγέλιον εἰς ὅλον τὸν κόσμον,
καὶ μαθητεῦσαι πάντα τὰ ἔθνη καὶ βαπτίσαι εἰς τὸν αὐτοῦ
θάνατον" ἐπὶ αὐθεντίᾳ τοῦ θεοῦ τῶν ὅλων, ὅς ἐστιν αὐτοῦ
πατήρ, καὶ μαρτυρίᾳ πνεύματος, ὅς ἐστι παράκλητος· διδάσκομεν
ὑμᾶς ταῦτα πάντα, ἃ διαταξάμενος ἡμῖν ἀνελήμφθη ἐπ' ὄψει
ἡμῶν εἰς τὸν οὐρανὸν πρὸς τὸν ἀποστείλαντα αὐτόν.

> *Apostolic Constitutions* 5.7. Funk, *Didascalia et Constitutiones
> Apostolorum*, 263.

PARALLELS

Matt 28:19-20, Mark 16:15-16, Luke 24:27.

C27 / *The Tempter* ———————————

But to those who think that God tempts (as the scriptures say) he said: The evil one is the tempter, who also tempted him.

τοῖς δὲ οἰομένοις ὅτι ὁ θεὸς πειράζει (ὡς αἱ γραφαὶ
λέγουσιν) ἔφη· "Ὁ πονηρός ἐστιν ὁ πειράζων," ὁ καὶ
αὐτὸν πείρασας.

> *Ps. Clementine Homilies* 3.55. Rehm-Irmscher, *Homilien*, 77.

PARALLELS

Mark 1:12-13, Matt 4:1-11, Luke 4:1-13, Heb 2:18, 4:15.

C28 / *Born Again*

For the prophet has sworn to us in this way, saying: Truly I say to you, unless you are born again by living water in the name of the Father, Son, and Holy Spirit, you will not enter the kingdom of heaven.

οὕτως γὰρ ἡμῖν ὤμοσεν ὁ προφήτης εἰπών· "'Αμὴν ὑμῖν λέγω,
ἐὰν μὴ ἀναγεννηθῆτε ὕδατι ζῶντι, εἰς ὄνομα πατρός, υἱοῦ,
ἁγίου πνεύματος, οὐ μὴ εἰσέλθητε εἰς τὴν βασιλείαν τῶν
οὐρανῶν.

> Ps. *Clementine Homilies* 11.26. Rehm-Irmscher, *Homilien*, 167.

PARALLELS

For Christ also said: Unless you are born again, you will not enter into the kingdom of heaven.

καὶ γὰρ ὁ Χριστὸς εἶπεν· "Αν μὴ ἀναγεννηθῆτε, οὐ μὴ
εἰσέλθητε εἰς τὴν βασιλείαν τῶν οὐρανῶν.

> Justin, *Apol.* 1.61.4. Goodspeed, *Die ältesten Apologeten*, 70.

John 3:3,5, Matt 28:19.

C29 / *Faith and Hope*

But heeding what the Lord said: Attend to faith and hope through which devout and humane love is produced, which brings eternal life.

ἀλλ' ἀκούων τοῦ κυρίου λέγοντος ἐπιμελεῖσθε πίστεως
καὶ ἐλπίδος, δι' ὧν γεννᾶται ἡ φιλόθεος καὶ φιλάνθρωπος
ἀγάπη ἡ τὴν αἰώνιον ζωὴν παρέχουσα.

> Symeon, *Homily* 37.1. Dörries, Klostermann, and Kroeger, *Geistliche Homilien*, 265.

PARALLELS

Above all, I am constrained for this, to love you more than my own life, for great faith and love dwell among you in hope of his life.

καὶ πάντως ἀναγκάζομαι κἀγὼ εἰς τοῦτο, ἀγαπᾶν ὑμᾶς ὑπὲρ
τὴν ψυχήν μου, ὅτι μεγάλη πίστις καὶ ἀγάπη ἐγκατοικεῖ
ἐν ὑμῖν ἐπ' ἐλπίδι ζωῆς αὐτοῦ.

> *Barnabas* 1.4. Funk-Bihlmeyer, *Die Apostolischen Väter*, 10.

There are, therefore, three doctrines of the Lord: the hope of life, the beginning and the end of our faith; and righteousness, the beginning and end of judgment; and love, a witness of the joy and gladness of works of righteousness.

τρία οὖν δόγματά ἐστιν κυρίου· ζωῆς ἐλπὶς ἀρχὴ καὶ τέλος
πίστεως ἡμῶν, καὶ δικαιοσύνη κρίσεως ἀρχὴ καὶ τέλος, ἀγάπη
εὐφροσύνης καὶ ἀγαλλιάσεως ἔργων δικαιοσύνης μαρτυρία.
    Barnabas 1.6. Ibid., 10-11.

1 Cor 13:13, Gal 5:5-6, 1 Thes 5:8, Col 1:4-5.

C30 / *Profaning the Eucharist* ————————————

If anyone partakes of the body of the Lord and then rinses out (the mouth) he will be accursed, just as the Lord said.

Εἴ τις μεταλάβῃ τὸ σῶμα τοῦ κυρίου καὶ λούσεται
ἐπικατάρατος ἔσται, καθὼς εἶπεν ὁ κύριος.
    Canonical Rule of the Holy Apostles 3. Preuschen, *Antilegomena*, 28.

C31 / *Evil for Evil* ————————————

And the Savior said: O Philip, since you have abandoned and not fulfilled this commandment of mine not to return evil for evil, you will be kept back from eternity for forty days, not living in the place promised to you.

Εἶπεν δὲ ὁ σωτήρ· ῏Ω Φίλιππε, ἐπειδὴ κατέλιπες τὴν
ἐντολήν μου ταύτην μόνον μὴ τελειώσας τοῦ μὴ ἀποδοῦναι
κακὸν ἀντὶ κακοῦ, διὰ τοῦτο κατασχεθήσῃ ἐν τοῖς αἰῶσιν
ἐπὶ τεσσαράκοντα ἡμέρας μὴ γενόμενος ἐν τῷ τόπῳ τῆς
ἐπαγγελίας σου.
    Acts of Philip 137. Lipsius-Bonnet, *AAA* 2.2:69.

PARALLELS

    . . . not returning evil for evil or abuse for abuse or blow for blow
    or curse for curse.

    μὴ ἀποδιδόντες κακὸν ἀντὶ κακοῦ ἢ λοιδορίαν ἀντὶ
    λοιδορίας ἢ γρόνθον ἀντὶ γρόνθου ἢ κατάραν ἀντὶ κατάρας.
        Polycarp, *Philippians* 2.2. Funk-Bihlmeyer, *Die Apostolischen Väter*, 115.

    I will return to no man evil recompense but for good will I pursue

my fellow, for with God is judgment over all that lives and it is he
that shall pay to a man his recompense.

> 1QS 10.17-18. Trans. from Leaney, *The Rule of Qumran*, 234.

If ill-requital befall you, return them not either to neighbor or
enemy.

> *Slavonic Enoch* 50.2-4. Trans. from Charles, *Pseudepigrapha*, 460.

We are men who worship God and it is not for us to return evil
for evil.

> ἡμεῖς ἄνδρες ἐσμὲν θεοσεβεῖς, καὶ οὐ προσήκει ἡμῖν
> ἀποδοῦναι κακὸν ἀντὶ κακοῦ.
>
> *Joseph and Asenath* 23.9. Batiffol, *Studia Patristica*, 75.

I pray you, spare your brothers and do not return to them evil for
evil.

> Δέομαι ὑμῶν, φείσασθε τῶν ἀδελφῶν ὑμῶν, καὶ μὴ ἀποδώσητε
> αὐτοῖς κακὸν ἀντὶ κακοῦ.
>
> *Joseph and Asenath* 28.5. Ibid., 83.

In no way, brother, return evil for evil to your neighbor, for the
Lord will avenge this despite.

> Μηδαμῶς, ἀδελφέ, ἀποδώσῃς κακὸν ἀντὶ κακοῦ τῷ πλησίῳ
> σου, διότι κύριος ἐκδικήσει τὴν ὕβιν ταύτην.
>
> *Joseph and Asenath* 28.14. Ibid., 84.

It is not right for a man who worships God to return evil for evil.

> οὐ προσῆκόν ἐστιν ἀνδρὶ θεοσεβεῖ ἀποδοῦναι κακὸν ἀντὶ κακοῦ
>
> *Joseph and Asenath* 29.3. Ibid., 84-85.

Lev 19:18, Prov 17:13, 20:22, 25:21-22, Matt 5:39, 43-44, Luke
6:27-29, 35, 1 Thes 5:15, Rom 12:17, 1 Pet 3:9.

C32 / *Small to Great* _____

But you seek to increase from being small and (not) from greater to being
less. And when you have been invited to dine and you enter, do not sit in the
prominent places, lest someone more honored than you should arrive and the
host should say to you, "Go further down," and you be put to shame. But if
you sit down in the lesser place and a man lesser than you should come in,
the host will say to you, "Go higher up," and this will be advantageous to you.

ὑμεῖς δὲ ζητεῖτε ἐκ μικροῦ αὐξῆσαι καὶ (+ μὴ sy^c) ἐκ μείζονος
ἔλαττον εἶναι. εἰσερχόμενοι (-sy^c) δὲ καὶ παρακληθέντες
δειπνῆσαι μὴ ἀνακλίνεσθε εἰς τοὺς ἐξέχοντας τόπους, μήποτε
ἐνδοξότερός σου ἐπέλθῃ καὶ προσελθὼν (-sy^c) ὁ δειπνοκλήτωρ
ἔιπῃ σοι· ἔτι κάτω χώρει, καὶ καταισχυνθήσῃ. ἐὰν δὲ ἀνα-
πέσῃς εἰς τὸν ἥττονα τόπον καὶ ἐπέλθῃ σου ἥττων, ἐρεῖ σοι
ὁ δειπνοκλήτωρ· σύναγε ἔτι ἄνω, καὶ ἔσται σοι τοῦτο χρήσιμον.

Codices D, Φ, it, sy^c after Matt 20:28. Aland, *Synopsis*, 353.

PARALLELS

Luke 14:7-11, Mark 12:38-39, Luke 20:46, 11:43, Matt 23:6-7, Prov 25:6-7.

C33 / *Fasting, Prayer, Almsgiving*

Jesus said to them: If you fast you will beget sin for yourselves, and if you pray you will be condemned, and if you give alms you will do evil to your spirits. And if you go into any land and travel in the regions, if they receive you, eat what they set before you. Heal the sick among them. For that which goes into your mouth will not defile you, but that which comes out of your mouth, that is what will defile you.[1]

ⲡⲉϫⲉ
ⲓ̅ⲥ̅ ⲛⲁⲩ ϫⲉ ⲉⲧⲉⲧⲛ̅ϣⲁⲛⲣ̅ⲛⲏⲥⲧⲉⲩⲉ ⲧⲉⲧⲛⲁ
ϫⲡⲟ ⲛⲏⲧⲛ̅ ⲛ̅ⲛⲟⲩⲛⲟⲃⲉ ⲁⲩⲱ ⲉⲧⲉⲧⲛ̅ϣⲁ̅
ϣⲗⲏⲗ' ⲥⲉⲛⲁⲣ̅ⲕⲁⲧⲁⲕⲣⲓⲛⲉ ⲙ̅ⲙⲱⲧⲛ̅ ⲁⲩⲱ
ⲉⲧⲉⲧⲛ̅ϣⲁⲛϯ ⲉⲗⲉⲏⲙⲟⲥⲩⲛⲏ ⲉⲧⲉⲧⲛⲁⲉⲓ
ⲣⲉ ⲛ̅ⲟⲩⲕⲁⲕⲟⲛ ⲛ̅ⲛⲉⲧⲙ̅ⲡ̅ⲛ̅ⲁ̅ ⲁⲩⲱ ⲉⲧⲉⲧⲛ̅
ϣⲁⲛⲃⲱⲕ' ⲉϩⲟⲩⲛ ⲉⲕⲁϩ ⲛⲓⲙ ⲁⲩⲱ ⲛ̅ⲧⲉⲧⲙ̅
ⲙⲟⲟϣⲉ ϩⲛ̅ ⲛ̅ⲭⲱⲣⲁ ⲉⲩϣⲁⲣ̅ⲡⲁⲣⲁⲇⲉⲭⲉ
ⲙ̅ⲙⲱⲧⲛ̅ ⲡⲉⲧⲟⲩⲛⲁⲕⲁⲁϥ ϩⲁⲣⲱⲧⲛ̅ ⲟⲩⲟⲙ̅ϥ̅
ⲛⲉⲧϣⲱⲛⲉ ⲛ̅ϩⲏⲧⲟⲩ ⲉⲣⲓⲑⲉⲣⲁⲡⲉⲩⲉ ⲙ̅ⲙⲟ
ⲟⲩ ⲡⲉⲧⲛⲁⲃⲱⲕ ⲅⲁⲣ' ⲉϩⲟⲩⲛ ϩⲛ̅ ⲧⲉⲧⲛ̅ⲧⲁ
ⲡⲣⲟ ϥⲛⲁϫⲱϩⲙ̅ ⲧⲏⲩⲧⲛ̅ ⲁⲛ' ⲁⲗⲗⲁ ⲡⲉⲧⲛ̅
ⲛⲏⲩ ⲉⲃⲟⲗ' ϩⲛ̅ ⲧⲉⲧⲛ̅ⲧⲁⲡⲣⲟ ⲛ̅ⲧⲟϥ ⲡⲉ
ⲧⲛⲁϫⲁϩⲙ̅ ⲧⲏⲩⲧⲛ̅

Gospel of Thomas 14. CG II, 35.14-27.

PARALLELS

Luke 10:8-9, 1 Cor 10:27, Mark 7:15, Matt 15:11, Matt 6:1-8.

Notes

¹ These religious observances are treated also in *Thomas* 6 [A18] and *Thomas* 104 [A37].

C34 / *The True Father* _____

Jesus said: When you see the one who is not born of woman fall on your faces and worship him. That one is your father.

ΠΕΧΕ ΙC ΧΕ ϨΟΤΑΝ
ΕΤΕΤΝ̄ϢΑΝΝΑΥ ΕΠΕΤΕ Μ̄ΠΟΥΧΠΟϤ'
ΕΒΟΛ ϨΝ̄ ΤCϨΙΜΕ ΠΕϨΤ' ΤΗΥΤΝ̄ ΕΧΜ̄
ΠΕΤΝ̄ϨΟ Ν̄ΤΕΤΝ̄ΟΥΩϢΤ ΝΑϤ' ΠΕΤΜ̄
ΜΑΥ ΠΕ ΠΕΤΝ̄ϨΕΙΩΤ'

Gospel of Thomas 15. CG II, 35.27-31.

C35 / *The Apple of the Eye* _____

Jesus said: Love your brother as your soul; keep him as the apple of your eye.

ΠΕΧΕ ΙC ΧΕ ΜΕΡΕ
ΠΕΚCΟΝ Ν̄ΘΕ Ν̄ΤΕΚ'ΨΥΧΗ ΕΡΙΤΗΡΕΙ Μ̄ΜΟϤ
Ν̄ΘΕ Ν̄ΤΕΛΟΥ Μ̄ΠΕΚ'ΒΑΛ'

Gospel of Thomas 25. CG II, 38.10-12.

Parallels

A man's almsgiving is as a signet with him (the Lord), and he will keep a person's kindness as the apple of his eye.

ἐλεημοσύνη ἀνδρὸς ὡς σφραγὶς μετ' αὐτοῦ, καὶ χάριν
ἀνθρώπου ὡς κόρην συντηρήσει.

Sirach 17:22. Rahlfs, *Septuaginta* 2:405.

Love as the apple of your eye everyone who speaks the word of the Lord to you.

ἀγαπήσεις ὡς κόρην τοῦ ὀφθαλμοῦ σου πάντα τὸν λαλοῦντά
σοι τὸν λόγον κυρίου.

Barnabas 19:9b. Funk-Bihlmeyer, *Die Apostolischen Väter*, 32.

Mark 12:31, Matt 19:19, 22:39, Luke 10:27, Rom 13:9, Gal 5:14, James 2:8, Lev 19:18, Deut 32:10, Ps 17:8, Prov 7:2, Zech 2:8.

C36 / *Fasting to the World*

⟨Jesus said:⟩ If you do not fast in regard to the world, you will not find the kingdom. If you do not keep the Sabbath as Sabbath, you will not see the Father.

ⲈⲦⲈⲦⲘ̄ⲢⲚⲎ
ⲤⲦⲈⲨⲈ ⲈⲠⲔⲞⲤⲘⲞⲤ ⲦⲈⲦⲚⲀⲞⲈ ⲀⲚ' ⲈⲦⲘⲚ̄ⲦⲈ
ⲢⲞ ⲈⲦⲈⲦⲚ̄ⲦⲘⲈⲒⲢⲈ Ⲙ̄ⲠⲤⲀⲘⲂⲀⲦⲞⲚ Ⲛ̄ⲤⲀⲂ'
ⲂⲀⲦⲞⲚ Ⲛ̄ⲦⲈⲦⲚⲀⲚⲀⲨ ⲀⲚ ⲈⲠⲈⲒⲰⲦ'

Gospel of Thomas 27. CG II, 38.17-20.

PARALLELS

Jesus said: If you do not fast in regard to the world, you will not find the Kingdom of God. And if you do not keep the Sabbath (as) Sabbath, you will not see the Father.

λέγει
Ἰ(ησοῦ)ς· ἐὰν μὴ νηστεύση
ται τὸν κόσμον, οὐ μὴ
εὕρηται τὴν βασιλεί
αν τοῦ θ(εο)ῦ· καὶ ἐὰν μὴ
σαββατίσητε τὸ σάβ
βατον, οὐκ ὄψεσθε τὸ(ν)
π(ατέ)ρα.[1]

P. Oxy. 1.4-11. Fitzmyer, *Essays,* 390.

The new law intends that you keep Sabbath continually, and you consider yourselves pious when you are idle for one day, since you do not understand why this has been commanded of you.

σαββατίζειν ὑμᾶς ὁ καινὸς νόμος διὰ παντὸς ἐθέλει, καὶ
ὑμεῖς μίαν ἀργοῦντες ἡμέραν εὐσεβεῖν δοκεῖτε, μὴ νοοῦντες
διὰ τί ὑμῖν προσετάγη·

Justin, *Dial.* 12.3. Goodspeed, *Die ältesten Apologeten,* 103-104.

In the literal sense fasting is abstinence from food, but food neither makes us more righteous nor more wicked; however, in the spiritual sense it is clear that, as life comes from food for each of us and the lack of food is a symbol of death, so it is necessary that we fast from worldly things, in order that we might die to the world and after this, having partaken of divine nourishment, live to God.

Ἡ νηστεία ἀποχὴ τροφῆς ἐστι κατὰ τὸ σημαινόμενον, τροφὴ
δὲ οὐδὲν δικαιοτέρους ἡμᾶς ἢ ἀδικωτέρους ἀπεργάζεται, κατὰ
δὲ τὸ μυστικὸν δηλοῖ ὅτι ὥσπερ τοῖς καθ' ἕνα ἐκ τροφῆς ἡ ζωή,
ἡ δ'ἀτροφία θανάτου σύμβολον, οὕτως καὶ ἡμᾶς τῶν κοσμικῶν
νηστεύειν χρή, ἵνα τῷ κόσμῳ ἀποθάνωμεν καὶ μετὰ τοῦτο τροφῆς
θείας μεταλαβόντες θεῷ ζήσωμεν.

> Clement, *Eclogae proph.* 14.1. Stählin-Früchtel, *Clemens* 3²:140.

But blessed are those who have made themselves eunuchs, (free)
from all sin, for the sake of the kingdom of heaven; these are the
ones who fast from the world.

ἀλλ' οἱ μὲν εὐνουχίσαντες ἑαυτοὺς ἀπὸ πάσης ἁμαρτίας διὰ
τὴν βασιλείαν τῶν οὐρανῶν μακάριοι οὗτοί εἰσιν οἱ τοῦ κόσμου
νηστεύοντες.

> Clement, *Strom.* 3.15.99. Ibid., 2³:241-242.

Blessed are those who renounce this world, for they will be pleas-
ing to God.

μακάριοι οἱ ἀποταξάμενοι τῷ κόσμῳ τούτῳ, ὅτι αὐτοὶ
εὐαρεστήσουσιν τῷ θεῷ.

> *Acts of Paul and Thecla* 5. Lipsius-Bonnet, *AAA* 1:238.

From this we further understand that we always ought to observe
a Sabbath from all servile work, and not only every seventh day
but throughout all time.

Unde nos magis intellegimus sabbatizare nos ab omni
opera seruili semper debere et non tantum septimo quoque
die, ser per omne tempus.

> Tertullian, *Adv. Jud.* 4.2. Thierry, *Tertulliani opera* 2:1347-48.

For the honored soul does no work on the genuine Sabbath,
ceases from shameful and foul thoughts, observes genuine Sabbath, and has genuine rest, desisting and being free from all dark
deeds.

ἡ γὰρ καταξιωθεῖσα ψυχὴ τοῦ ἀληθινοῦ σαββάτου ἀργεῖ
καὶ ἀναπαύεται ἀπὸ τῶν αἰσχρῶν καὶ ῥυπαρῶν λογισμῶν,
καὶ ἀληθινὸν σάββατον σαββατίζει καὶ ἀληθινὴν ἀνάπαυσιν
ἀναπαύεται, ἀργοῦσα καὶ ἐλευθερουμένη ἀπὸ πάντων τῶν
σκοτεινῶν ἔργων.

> Symeon, *Hom.* 35.1. Dörries, Klostermann, and Kroeger, *Geistliche Homilien*, 262-263.

And whatever souls are persuaded and come near, he gives them rest from these burdensome, tiresome, and impure thoughts, and they desist from all lawlessness, observing genuine, delicate, and holy Sabbath.

καὶ ὅσαι ψυχαὶ πείθονται καὶ προσέρχονται, ἀναπαύει
αὐτὰς ἀπὸ τούτων τῶν βαρέων καὶ φορτικῶν καὶ ἀκαθάρτων
λογισμῶν, καὶ ἀργοῦσιν ἀπὸ πάσης ἀνομίας, σαββατίζουσαι
Σάββατον ἀληθινόν, τρυφερόν, ἅγιον·
Symeon, *Hom.* 35.3. Ibid., 263.

Brother, blessed are the holy and pure, for they see the Lord Jesus and are not ashamed in his presence, and they are free from all evil and fast from the world[2] and its attractions.

Frater, beati sunt sancti et mundi, quia vident Dominum Iesum nec eos pudet in conspectu eius et liberantur ab omni malo et ieiunant mundo et illecebris eius.
Liber Graduum 89.22-25. Kmosko, PatSy 1.3:90.

Therefore let us no longer keep Sabbath in the Jewish fashion, nor by rejoicing in idleness. For the sayings (of Scripture) indicate: Let the one not eat who does not work; for in the sweat of your face you shall eat your bread. But let each of you keep Sabbath spiritually, rejoicing in meditation on the laws, not in relaxation of the body.

μηκέτι οὖν σαββατίζωμεν Ἰουδαϊκῶς καὶ ἀργίαις χαίροντες·
ὁ μὴ ἐργαζόμενος γὰρ μὴ ἐσθιέτω· ἐν ἱδρῶτι γὰρ τοῦ προσώπου σου φάγῃ τὸν ἄρτον σου, φασὶ τὰ λόγια. ἀλλ᾽ ἕκαστος
ὑμῶν σαββατιζέτω πνευματικῶς, μελέτῃ νόμων χαίρων, οὐ σώματος ἀνέσει·
Ps. Ignatius, *Magnesians* 9. Lightfoot, *The Apostolic Fathers* 2:173.

The Masbothaeans say that Christ himself is the one who taught them to observe Sabbath in regard to everything.

Masbothei dicunt ipsum Christum esse qui docuit illos in omni re sabbatizare.
Ps. Jerome, *Indiculus de haeresibus.* Oehler, *Corpus Haeresiologicum* 1:283.

NOTES
[1] For νηστεύσηται read νηστεύσετε; for εὕρηται read εὕρητε.
[2] Other occurrences of the phrase "fast from the world" are found in 32.23, 373.18-24, and 828.13.

C37 / *The Keys of Knowledge*

Jesus said: The Pharisees and the scribes have received the keys of knowledge (and) have hidden them. They have not entered, nor have they permitted those to enter who wish.[1] But you be wise as serpents and innocent as doves.

ΠⲈⲬⲈ ⲓⲤ ⲬⲈ Ⲙ̄ⲫⲀⲢⲒⲤⲀⲒ
ⲞⲤ ⲘⲚ̄ Ⲛ̄ⲅⲢⲀⲘⲘⲀⲦⲈ'ⲨⲤ ⲀⲨⲬⲒ Ⲛ̄ⳍⲀⳍⲦ'
Ⲛ̄ⲦⲅⲚⲰⲤⲒⲤ ⲀⲨⳍⲞⲠⲞⲨ ⲞⲨⲦⲈ Ⲙ̄ⲠⲞⲨ'ⲂⲰⲔ
ⲈⳍⲞⲨⲚ ⲀⲨⲰ ⲚⲈⲦⲞⲨⲰⳍ ⲈⲂⲰⲔ' ⲈⳍⲞⲨⲚ Ⲙ̄
ⲠⲞⲨⲔⲀⲀⲨ Ⲛ̄ⲦⲰⲦⲚ̄ ⲆⲈ ⳍⲰⲠⲈ Ⲙ̄ⲫⲢⲞⲚⲒⲘⲞⲤ
Ⲛ̄ⲐⲈ Ⲛ̄Ⲛ̄ⳍⲞϤ' ⲀⲨⲰ Ⲛ̄ⲀⲔⲈⲢⲀⲒ̈ⲞⲤ Ⲛ̄ⲐⲈ Ⲛ̄Ⲛ̄
ⳠⲢⲞⲘ'ⲠⲈ

Gospel of Thomas 39. CG II, 40.7-13.

PARALLELS

Jesus said: The Pharisees and scribes have received the keys of knowledge and have hidden them. They have neither entered nor permitted those who would enter to go in. But you become wise as serpents and innocent as doves.

[λέγει]
['Ι(ησοῦ)ς· οἱ Φαρισαῖοι καὶ]
[οἱ γραμματεῖς ἀπ]
ἐλ[αβον τὰς κλεῖδας]
τῆς [γνώσεως καὶ ἀπέ]
κρυψ[αν αὐτάς· οὔτε]
εἰσῆλ[θον οὔτε τοὺς]
εἰσερ[χομένους ἀφῆ]
χαν [εἰσελθεῖν. ὑμεῖς]
δὲ γεί [νεσθε φρόνι]
μοι ὡ[ς οἱ ὄφεις καὶ ἀ]
χέραι[οι ὡς αἱ περιστε]
ρα[ί.

P. Oxy. 655. (i) 39-50. Fitzmyer, *Essays*, 413-414.

But you have not inquired whose is the time of the kingdom and whose is the seat of prophecy; although, he indicates it is himself saying: "The scribes and Pharisees sit on Moses' seat; listen to them in all things that they say to you." He spoke of them as entrusted with the key of the kingdom, which is knowledge, which alone is able to open the gate of life, through which alone there

is entrance to eternal life. Indeed, he says, they hold the key, but
they do not permit those who wish to enter.

ἀλλ᾽ οὐκ ἐζήτησας τίνος ἐστὶν ὁ τῆς βασιλείας χρόνος, τίνος
ἡ τῆς προφητείας καθέδρα, καίτοι αὐτοῦ ἑαυτὸν μηνύοντος τῷ
λέγειν· "Ἐπὶ τῆς καθέδρας Μωυσέως ἐκάθισαν οἱ γραμματεῖς καὶ
οἱ Φαρισαῖοι· πάντα ὅσα λέγουσιν ὑμῖν, ἀκούετε αὐτῶν."
αὐτῶν δὲ εἶπεν ὡς τὴν κλεῖδα τῆς βασιλείας πεπιστευμένων,
ἥτις ἐστὶν γνῶσις, ἣ μόνη τὴν πύλην τῆς ζωῆς ἀνοῖξαι δύνα-
ται, δι᾽ ἧς μόνης εἰς τὴν αἰωνίαν ζωὴν εἰσελθεῖν ἔστιν.
ἀλλὰ ναί (φησίν), κρατοῦσι μὲν τὴν κλεῖν, τοῖς δὲ βουλο-
μένοις εἰσελθεῖν οὐ παρέχουσιν.
Ps. Clem. Hom. 3.18. Rehm-Irmscher, *Homilien,* 63.

Be wise as a serpent in all things and innocent as the dove forever.

φρόνιμος γίνου ὡς ὄφις ἐν ἅπασιν καὶ ἀκέραιος εἰς
ἀεὶ ὡς ἡ περιστερά.
Ignatius, *Polycarp* 2.2. Funk-Bihlmeyer, *Die Apostolischen Väter,* 111.

R. Johanan said: The Holy One, blessed be He, said: "I call Israel
a dove, as it is written, And Ephraim is become like a silly dove,
without understanding (Hos. 7:11). To Me they are like a dove, but
to the nations they are like various kinds of beasts, . . ."
Cant. R. 2.14. Trans. from Simon, *Midrash Rabbah* 9:127-128.

R. Judah said in the name of R. Simon: With Me they are innocent
like doves, but with the nations they are cunning like serpents.
Cant. R. 2.14. Ibid., 128.

Matt 23:13, 10:16, Luke 11:52.

NOTES
¹ See *Thomas* 102 [W38] for an analogous criticism of the Pharisees which uses the
imagery of the dog in the manger.
² In line 47, read γίνεσθε for γείνεσθε.

C38 / *Passers-by* _____

Jesus said: Become passers-by.

ⲡⲉϪⲉ ⲓ̅ⲥ̅ Ϫⲉ Ϣⲱⲡⲉ ⲉⲧⲉⲧⲚⲢⲠⲀⲢⲀⲅⲉ
Gospel of Thomas 42. CG II, 40:19.

C39 / *Blaspheming the Spirit*

Jesus said: Whoever blasphemes against the Father will be forgiven, and whoever blasphemes against the Son will be forgiven, but whoever blasphemes against the Holy Spirit will not be forgiven, either on earth or in heaven.

ⲡⲉϫⲉ ⲓ̅ⲥ̅ ϫⲉ ⲡⲉⲧⲁϫⲉ
ⲟⲩⲁ ⲁⲡⲉⲓⲱⲧ' ⲥⲉⲛⲁⲕⲱ ⲉⲃⲟⲗ ⲛⲁϥ' ⲁⲩⲱ
ⲡⲉⲧⲁϫⲉ ⲟⲩⲁ ⲉⲡϣⲏⲣⲉ ⲥⲉⲛⲁⲕⲱ ⲉⲃⲟⲗ
ⲛⲁϥ' ⲡⲉⲧⲁϫⲉ ⲟⲩⲁ ⲇⲉ ⲁⲡⲡ̅ⲛ̅ⲁ̅ ⲉⲧⲟⲩⲁⲁⲃ
ⲥⲉⲛⲁⲕⲱ ⲁⲛ ⲉⲃⲟⲗ ⲛⲁϥ' ⲟⲩⲧⲉ ϩⲙ̅ ⲡⲕⲁϩ
ⲟⲩⲧⲉ ϩⲛ̅ ⲧⲡⲉ

Gospel of Thomas 44. CG II, 40.26-31.

PARALLELS

Mark 3:28-29, Matt 12:31-32, Luke 12:10.

C40 / *On Origins*

Jesus said: If they say to you: From where did you originate? tell them: We have come from the light, the place where the light came into being through itself alone. It stood, and it has revealed itself in their image. If they say to you: Who[1] are you? say: we are his sons and we are the elect of the living Father. If they ask you: What is the sign of your Father in you? tell them: It is a movement and a rest.[2]

ⲡⲉ
ϫⲉ ⲓ̅ⲥ̅ ϫⲉ ⲉⲩϣⲁⲛϫⲟⲟⲥ ⲛⲏⲧⲛ̅ ϫⲉ ⲛ̅ⲧⲁ
ⲧⲉⲧⲛ̅ϣⲱⲡⲉ ⲉⲃⲟⲗ ⲧⲱⲛ ϫⲟⲟⲥ ⲛⲁⲩ
ϫⲉ ⲛ̅ⲧⲁⲛⲉⲓ ⲉⲃⲟⲗ ϩⲙ̅ ⲡⲟⲩⲟⲉⲓⲛ ⲡⲙⲁ
ⲉⲛⲧⲁⲡⲟⲩⲟⲉⲓⲛ ϣⲱⲡⲉ ⲙ̣̅ⲙ̣ⲁ̣ⲩ ⲉⲃⲟⲗ
ϩⲓⲧⲟⲟⲧϥ' ⲟⲩⲁⲁⲧϥ' ⲁϥⲱϩ[ⲉ ⲉⲣⲁⲧϥ]
ⲁ̣ⲩⲱ ⲁϥⲟⲩⲱⲛϩ̣ ⲉ[ⲃ]ⲟ̣ⲗ ϩ̣ⲛ ⲧⲟⲩϩⲓⲕⲱⲛ ⲉⲩ
ϣⲁϫⲟⲟⲥ ⲛⲏⲧⲛ̅ ϫⲉ ⲛ̅ⲧⲱⲧⲛ̅ ⲡⲉ ϫⲟⲟⲥ
ϫⲉ ⲁⲛⲟⲛ ⲛⲉϥϣⲏⲣⲉ ⲁⲩⲱ ⲁⲛⲟⲛ ⲛ̅ⲥⲱⲧⲡ'
ⲙ̅ⲡⲉⲓⲱⲧ' ⲉⲧⲟⲛϩ ⲉⲩϣⲁⲛϫⲛⲉ ⲧⲏⲩⲧⲛ̅
ϫⲉ ⲟⲩ ⲡⲉ ⲡⲙⲁⲉⲓⲛ ⲙ̅ⲡⲉⲧⲛ̅ⲉⲓⲱⲧ' ⲉⲧϩⲛ̅
ⲧⲏⲩⲧⲛ̅ ϫⲟⲟⲥ ⲉⲣⲟⲟⲩ ϫⲉ ⲟⲩⲕⲓⲙ ⲡⲉ ⲙⲛ̅
ⲟⲩⲁⲛⲁⲡⲁⲩⲥⲓⲥ

Gospel of Thomas 50. CG II, 41.31-42.7.

Until baptism, they say, fate is actual, but after it the astrologers are no longer correct. But it is not only the washing which is liberating but also the knowledge of who we were, what we have become, where we were or where we have been placed, toward what we strive, from what we are redeemed, what is birth, and what is rebirth.

Μέχρι τοῦ βαπτίσματος οὖν ἡ Εἱμαρμένη, φασίν, ἀληθής,
μετὰ δὲ τοῦτο οὐκέτι ἀληθεύουσιν οἱ ἀστρολόγοι. ἔστιν
δὲ οὐ τὸ λουτρὸν μόνον τὸ ἐλευθεροῦν, ἀλλὰ καὶ ἡ γνῶσις,
τίνες ἦμεν, τί γεγόναμεν· ποῦ ἦμεν, [ἢ] ποῦ ἐνεβλήθημεν·
ποῦ σπεύδομεν, πόθεν λυτρούμεθα· τί γέννησις, τί ἀναγέννησις.
Exc. ex Theod. 78. Stählin-Früchtel, Clemens 3²:131.

NOTES
¹ Following the emendation **NIM** instead of **ⲠⲈ**, in 42.2, initially suggested by Guillaumont (Thomas, 28).
² For partly analogous instructions see the Gospel of Philip from Epiphanius, Haer. 26.13.2-3 and parallels [C6] and the First Apocalypse of James CG V, 33.11-34.20 and parallels [C47].

C41 / Hating One's Family

Jesus said: Whoever does not hate his father and his mother will not be able to be my disciple, and (whoever does not) hate his brothers and his sisters and take up his cross as I have[1] will not be worthy of me.

ⲠⲈⲬⲈ ⲓ̅ⲥ̅ ⲬⲈ ⲠⲈⲦⲀⲘⲈⲤⲦⲈ ⲠⲈϤⲈⲓⲰⲦ'
ⲀⲚ' ⲘⲚ̅ ⲦⲈϤⲘⲀⲀⲨ ϤⲚⲀⲰ Ⲣ̅ ⲘⲀⲐⲎⲦⲎⲤ ⲀⲚ
ⲚⲀⲈⲓ· ⲀⲨⲰ Ⲛ̅ϤⲘⲈⲤⲦⲈ ⲚⲈϤⲤⲚⲎⲨ· ⲘⲚ̅
ⲚⲈϤⲤⲰⲚⲈ Ⲛ̅ϤϤⲈⲓ ⲘⲠⲈϤⲤⲦⲀⲨⲢⲞⲤ Ⲛ̅ⲦⲀⲀⲆ
ϤⲚⲀⲰⲰⲠⲈ ⲀⲚ ⲈϤⲞ Ⲛ̅ⲀⲌⲓⲞⲤ ⲚⲀⲈⲓ
Gospel of Thomas 55. CG II, 42.25-29.

(Jesus said): Whoever does not hate his father and his mother as I do will not be able to be my [disciple]. And whoever does [not] love his [father] and his mother as I do will not be able to be my [disciple]. For my mother [. . .]² but my true [mother] gave me life.

ΠΕΤΑΜΕΣΤΕ ΠΕϤΕΙ[ΩΤ Α]Ν ΜΝ ΤΕϤ'
ΜΑΑΥ ΝΤΑϨΕ ϤΝΑΩ Ρ Μ[ΑΘΗΤΗ]Ϲ ΝΑΕΙ Α
ΑΥΩ ΠΕΤΑΜΡΡΕ ΠΕ[ϤΕΙΩΤ ΑΝ ΜΝ] ΤΕϤ
ΜΑΑΥ ΝΤΑϨΕ ϤΝΑΩ Ρ Μ[ΑΘΗΤΗϹ ΝΑ]
ΕΙ ΑΝ ΤΑΜΑΑΥ ΓΑΡ ΝΤΑ[   ]
[ΕΒ]ΟΛ [ΤΑΜΑΑΥ] ΔΕ ΜΜΕ ΑϹϮ ΝΑΕΙ ΜΠΩΝϨ
    Gospel of Thomas 101. CG II, 49.32-50.1.

And they fled to the aeon of the self-father, and they received the promise which had been promised them by the one who said: The one who leaves father and mother and brother and sister and wife and child and possessions and takes his cross and follows me will receive the promises I promised him. And I will give them the mystery of my hidden Father, for they have loved that which is theirs, and they have fled from the one who violently persecutes them.

ΑΥΩ ΑΥΠΩΤ ΕϨΡΑΙ ΕΠΑΙΩΝ ΜΠΑΥΤΟΠΑΤΩΡ ΑΥϪΙ ΝΑΥ
ΜΠΕΡΗΤ ΕΝΤΑΥΕΡΗΤ ΜΜΟϤ ΝΑΥ ϨΙΤΜ-ΠΕΤϪΩ ΜΜΟϹ
ϪΕ-ΠΕΤΝΑΚΑ-ΕΙΩΤ ϨΙ-ΜΑΑΥ ϨΙ-ϹΟΝ ϨΙ-ϹΩΝΕ ϨΙ-ϹϨΙΜΕ
ϨΙ-ϢΗΡΕ ϨΙ-ϨΥΠΑΡϪΙϹ ΑΥΩ ΝϤϤΙ ΜΠΕϤϹΤΑΥΡΟϹ ΝϤΟΥΑϨϤ
ΝϹΩΙ ϤΝΑϪΙ ΝΝΕΡΗΤ ΕΝΤΑΙΕΡΗΤ ΜΜΟΟΥ ΝΑϤ. ΑΥ‹Ω›
ΠΜΥϹΤΗΡΙΟΝ ΜΠΑΙΩΤ ΕΘΗΠ ϮΝΑΤΑΑϤ ΝΑΥ ϪΕ-ΑΥΜΕΡΕ-
ΠΕΤΕ-ΠΩΟΥ ΠΕ. ΑΥΩ ΑΥΠΩΤ ΕΒΟΛ ΜΠΕΤΠΗΤ ΝϹΩΟΥ
ϨΝ-ΟΥϪΙΝϬΟΝϹ.
    Untitled Gnostic Text from Codex Brucianus, ch. 15. Schmidt-Macdermot, *The Books of Jeu and the Untitled Text*, 256.

If one will not denounce all which he has and take up his cross and follow me and imitate me, he is not worthy of me.

Si quis non renunciaverit omnibus quae possidet, et tollat crucem suam et sequatur me et imitetur me, non est me dignus.
    Liber Graduum 3.5. Kmosko, PatSy 1.3:54-55.

He said: He who does not take up his cross and walk in my footsteps and in my manner is not worthy of me.

Qui non tollit, ait, crucem suam et incedit in vestigiis meis et in conversatione mea, non est me dignus.
    Liber Graduum 20.15. Ibid., 570.

And if you wish to attain this great portion and perfection and imitate me and be glorified with me, leave everything and take up your cross and follow me. And if you do not, you are not worthy of me.

Si autem ad hanc portionem magnam perfectionemque pervenire velis et me imitari et mecum conglorificari: relinque omnia et tolle crucem tuam et sequere me; et si non, non es me dignus.

Liber Graduum 30.26. Ibid., 923.

I left father and mother and brother and sister.
I became a stranger because of your name.
I took up my cross; I followed you.
I left the things of the body for the things of the spirit.
I despised the glory of the world because of
your glory which does not pass away.

ⲁⲓ̈ⲕⲁ ⲓ̈ⲱⲧ ϩⲓⲙⲉⲩ ϩⲓⲥⲁⲛ ϩⲓⲥⲱⲛⲉ
ⲁⲓ̈ⲣ̄ϣⲙ̄ⲙⲟ ⲉⲧⲃ̣[ⲉ ⲡ]ⲉⲕⲣⲉⲛ
ⲁⲓ̈ⲃⲓ ⲡⲁⲥⲧⲁⲩⲣⲟⲥ ⲁⲓ̈ⲟⲩⲁϩⲧ ⲛ̄ⲥⲱⲕ
ⲁⲓ̈ⲕⲁ ⲛⲁⲡⲥⲱⲙⲁ ⲉⲧⲃⲉ ⲛⲁⲡⲡ̅ⲛ̅ⲁ̅
ⲁⲓ̈ⲕⲁⲧⲁⲫⲣⲟⲛⲏ ⲙ̄ⲡⲉⲁⲩ ⲙ̄ⲡⲕⲟⲥⲙⲟⲥ
ⲉⲧⲃⲉ ⲡⲕⲉⲁⲩ ⲉⲧⲉ ⲙⲁϥⲟⲩ̣ⲓⲛⲉ

Manichaean Psalm-Book 175.25-30. Allberry, *Manichaean Psalm-Book,* 175.

Mark 8:34, 10:29-30, Matt 10:37-38, 16:24, 19:29, Luke 9:23, 14:26-27, 33.

NOTES

[1] Or, "in my way."

[2] Lambdin completes the lacuna to read, "gave me falsehood" (in Robinson, *Nag Hammadi Library,* 129).

C42 / *Renouncing Power*

Jesus said: Let him who has become rich become king, and let him who has power renounce it.

ⲡⲉϫⲉ ⲓ̅ⲥ̅ ϫⲉ ⲡⲉⲛⲧⲁϩⲣ̄ ⲣⲙ̄ⲙⲁⲟ ⲙⲁ
ⲣⲉϥⲣ̄ ⲣⲣⲟ ⲁⲩⲱ ⲡⲉⲧⲉⲩⲛ̄ⲧⲁϥ' ⲛ̄ⲟⲩⲇⲩⲛⲁ
ⲙⲓⲥ ⲙⲁⲣⲉϥⲁⲣⲛⲁ

Gospel of Thomas 81. CG II, 47. 15-17.

PARALLELS

Jesus said: Whoever has found the world and become rich, let him renounce the world.

ΠΕΧΕ ΙC ΧΕ ΠΕΝΤΑϨϬΙΝΕ [Μ]ΠΚΟCΜΟC
ΝϤϤ ΡΜΜΑΟ ΜΑΡΕϤΑΡΝΑ ΜΠΚΟCΜΟC
Gospel of Thomas 110. CG II, 51.4-5.

1 Cor 4:8.

C43 / *Inside and Outside* _____

Jesus said: Why do you wash the outside of the cup? Do you not know that
he who made the inside is also he who made the outside?

ΠΕΧΕ ΙC ΧΕ ΕΤΒΕ ΟΥ ΤΕΤΝΕΙϢΕ ΜΠCΑ Ν
ΒΟΛ' ΜΠΠΟΤΗΡΙΟΝ ΤΕΤΝΡΝΟΕΙ ΑΝ ΧΕ
ΠΕΝΤΑϨΤΑΜΙΟ ΜΠCΑ ΝϨΟΥΝ ΝΤΟϤ ΟΝ
ΠΕΝΤΑϤΤΑΜΙΟ ΜΠCΑ ΝΒΟΛ'
Gospel of Thomas 89. CG II, 48.13-16.

PARALLELS

As the Lord said: Blind Pharisee, wash the inside of the cup and
the dish in order that the outside might also be clean, for he who
made the inside also made the outside.

ὡς φησὶν ὁ κύριος· "Φαρισαῖε τυφλέ", "τὸ ἔσωθεν τοῦ ποτηρίου
καὶ τῆς παροψίδος πλῦνον," ἵνα "καὶ τὸ ἔξωθεν" ᾖ "καθαρόν."
"ὁ" γὰρ "ποιήσας τὸ ἔσωθεν καὶ τὸ ἔξωθεν ἐποίησεν."
Symeon, *Hom.* 8.1 (Type III). Klostermann and Berthold, *Neue Homilien
des Makarius/Symeon*, 38.

He said: Blind Pharisee, wash the inside of the cup in order that
the outside also might be clean.

φησίν· "Φαρισαῖε τυφλέ, τὸ ἔσωθεν τοῦ ποτηρίου πλῦνον,
ἵνα γένηται καὶ τὸ ἔξωθεν καθαρόν."
Symeon, *Hom.* 28.4 (Type III). Ibid., 168.

To which Jesus said: Woe to you scribes and Pharisees, hypocrits.
Why do you wash the outside of the cup and the dish, whereas
the inside is filled with impurity? Or, do you not know that he who
made the outside also made the inside?

ad quod Iesus ait: Vae vobis scribae et Pharisaei hypocritae, quare
quod deforis est catini et calicis lavatis; quod autem intus est

inmunditia plenum est? Aut nescitis quia qui fecit quod foris est
et quod de intus est fecit?

> Acts of Archelaus 24. Beeson, *Hegemonius Acta Archelai*, 35.

Let us wash and wipe the interior as the exterior and the exterior
as the interior.

interius ut exterius abluamus et extergamus et exterius ut
interius, . . .

> *Liber Graduum* 10.3. Kmosko, PatSy 1.3:254.

Matt 23:25-26, Luke 11:39-40.

C44 / *Give Your Goods*

[Jesus said]: If you have money do not lend at interest but give [it] to the one
from whom you will not get it (back).

[ⲡⲉⲭⲉ ⲓ̅ⲥ̅ ⲭⲉ] ⲉϣⲱⲡⲉ ⲟⲩⲛ̅ⲧⲏⲧⲛ̅ ⲍⲟⲙⲧ′
ⲙ̅ⲡⲣ̅ϯ ⲉⲧⲙⲏⲥⲉ ⲁⲗⲗⲁ ϯ[. . .] ⲙ̣̅ⲡⲉ[ⲧⲉ]
ⲧⲛⲁⲭⲓⲧⲟⲩ ⲁⲛ ⲛ̅ⲧⲟⲟⲧϥ

> *Gospel of Thomas* 95. CG II, 48.35-49.2.

PARALLELS

Exod 22:25, Lev 25:36-37, Luke 6:34-35.

C45 / *The House of the Father*

The Lord said to the disciples: [. . .] [. . .] come into the house of the Father,
but do not take (anything) in the house of the Father nor carry it away.

ⲡⲉⲭⲉ ⲡⲭⲟⲉⲓⲥ ⲛ̅ⲙ̅ⲙⲁⲑ[ⲏⲧⲏⲥ . . .]
[. . . . .] ⲙⲉⲛ ⲓ ⲉⲍⲟⲩⲛ′ ⲉⲡⲏⲉⲓ
ⲙ̅ⲡⲉⲓⲱⲧ [ⲙ̅]ⲡⲣ̅ⲭⲓ ⲟⲩⲇⲉ ⲛ̅ⲧⲟϥ′ ⲍⲛ̅ ⲡⲏ
ⲉⲓ ⲙ̅ⲡⲉⲓⲱⲧ ⲛ̅ⲧⲉⲧⲛ̅ϥⲓ ⲉⲃⲟⲗ′

> *Gospel of Philip* 18. CG II, 55.37-56.3.

NOTES
The lacunae cannot be completed with confidence. Most translators have left a
blank. Isenberg (in Robinson, *Nag Hammadi Library*, 134) has the following: "[Bring
out] from every (other) house. Bring into the house of the Father. But do not take
(anything) in the house of the Father nor carry it off."

C46 / *Joined with the Angels* ———————————

He said on that day in the thanksgiving: You who joined the perfect, the light, with the Holy Spirit, join the angels with us also, the images.

ΠЄϪΑϤ Μ̄ϷΟΟΥ ЄΤΜ̄
ΜΑΥ 2Ν̄ ΤЄΥϪΑΡΙCΤЄΙΑ ϪЄ ΠЄΝΤΑⲌⲌШΤΡ
Μ̄ΠΤЄΛЄΙΟC ΠΟΥΟЄΙΝ' ЄΠΠΝ̄Α ЄΤΟΥ
ΑΑΒ' 2ΟΤΡ̄ Ν̄ΑΓΓЄΛΟC' ЄΡΟΝ' 2ШШΝ ΑΝ
2ΙΚШΝ

Gospel of Philip 26. CG II, 58.10-14.

C47 / *Origin and Destiny* ———————————

But when you come to them, one of them who is their guard will say to you: Who are you or where are you from? You will say to him: I am a son, and I am from the Father. He will say to you: What kind of son are you, and what father are you from? You will say to him: I am from the Father who is pre-[existent], and (I am) a son in Him who is pre-existent. . . .

[For six lines the text is very fragmentary]

of alien things. You will say to him: They are not altogether alien but are from Achamoth who is the female. She created them as she brought this race down from Him who is pre-existent. Therefore they are not alien but are ours. On the one hand they are ours, for she who rules them is from Him who is pre-existent. On the other hand they are alien for this reason, that He who is pre-existent did not have intercourse with her when she created them. When he also says to you: Where will you go? you will say to him: I shall go again to the place from which I have come. And if you say these things, you will escape from their attacks.[1]

ЄϢШΠЄ
6Є ЄΚϢΑΝЄΙ ЄΤΟΟΤΟΥ' ΟΥΝ̄
ΟΥΑ ЄΒΟΛ Ν̄2ΗΤΟΥ ΝΑϪΟΟC
ΝΑΚ' ЄΥΡЄϤΑΡЄ2 Ν̄ΤΑΥ ΠЄ
ϪЄ Ν̄ΤΚ̄ ΝΙΜ Η̄ Ν̄ΤΚ̄ ΟΥЄΒΟΛ
ΤШΝ' ЄΚЄϪΟΟC ΝΑϤ ϪЄ ΑΝΑΚ
ΟΥϢΗΡЄ ΑΥШ ΑΝΟΚ ΟΥЄΒΟΛ
2Μ̄ ΠΙШΤ' ϤΝΑϪΟΟC ΝΑΚ ϪЄ
Ν̄ΤΚ̄ ΠΑΛШ Ν̄ϢΗΡЄ· ΑΥШ
Ν̄ΤΚ̄ ΠΑΝΙΜ Ν̄ЄΙШΤ· ЄΚЄ
ϪΟΟC ΝΑϤ ϪЄ ΑΝΟΚ ΟΥЄΒΟΛ

2M̄ ΠΙⲰΤ ЄΤΡ̄ ϢΟΡ︦Π [Ν̄ϢΟΟΠ]
ΟΥϢΗΡЄ ΔЄ Є4ϨΜ̄ ΠЄΤ[Ρ̄]
ϢΟΡ︦Π Ν̄ϢΟΟΠ [Є4ΝΑϪΟΟС]
ΝΑΚ ϪЄ ΑΥ[
ЄΚЄ Ϫ[ΟΟС ΝΑ4 ϪЄ
2Μ̄ ΠΗ[
ϪЄ ЄΪЄ[
[. .]ЄΤ[
[. . .]
[Ν̄]ΝΙϢΜ̄ΜΟ· ЄΚЄϪΟΟС ΝΑ4
ϪЄ 2Ν̄ϢΜ̄ΜΟ ΑΝ ЄΠΤΗΡ4 ΝЄ′
[Α]ΛΛΑ 2ЄΝЄΒΟΛ 2Ν̄Ν Α[ΧΑ]ΜⲰΘ
ΝЄ· ЄΤЄ ΤЄС2ΙΜЄ· ΑΥⲰ ΝΑΪ
ΑСΤΑΜΙΟΟΥ′ ЄСЄΙΝЄ Μ̄ΠΙГЄ
ΝΟС ЄΠЄСΗΤ′ ЄΒΟΛ 2Μ̄ ΠΗ ЄΤΡ̄
ϢΟΡ︦Π Ν̄ϢΟΟΠ· ΑΡΑ 2ЄΝϢΜ̄
ΜΟ ΑΝ ΝЄ· ΑΛΛΑ ΝЄΤЄ ΝΟΥΝ ΝЄ·
ΝЄΤЄ ΝΟΥΝ ΜЄΝ ΝЄ· ϪЄ ΤЄ
ΤΟ Ν̄ϪΟЄΙС ЄΡΟΟΥ· ΟΥЄΒΟΛ
ΤЄ 2Μ̄ ΠЄΤΡ̄ ϢΟΡ︦Π Ν̄ϢΟΟΠ′
2ЄΝϢΜ̄ΜΟ ΔЄ ΝЄ ΚΑΤΑ ΠЄΪ
ϪЄ ΠЄΤΡ̄ ϢΟΡ︦Π Ν̄ϢΟΟΠ Μ̄ΠЄ4
Ρ̄ΚΟΙΝⲰΝΙ ЄΡΟС ΤΟΤЄ ЄСΝΑ
ΤΑΜΙΟΟΥ′ Є4ΝΑϪΟΟС ΝΑΚ ΟΝ
ϪЄ ЄΚΝΑΒⲰΚ ЄΤⲰΝ· ЄΚЄϪΟ
ΟС ΝΑ4 ϪЄ ЄΠΜΑ ЄΤΑΪЄΪ ЄΒΟΛ
Μ̄ΜΑΥ ЄΪΝΑΒⲰΚ ΟΝ ЄΜΑΥ′
ΝΑΪ ΔЄ ЄΚϢΑΝϪΟΟΥ ΚΝΑΡ̄
ΒΟΛ ЄΝЄΥΠΟΛЄΜΟС·

First Apocalypse of James. CG V, 33.11-34:20.

PARALLELS

And they instruct them, when they come to the powers after they
have died, to say this: I am a son from the Father, the pre-existent
Father, a son in Him who is pre-existent. I came to see all things
which are mine and which are alien. However, they are not
altogether alien but belong to Achamoth who is female and made
these things for herself. For she brought down this race from Him
who is pre-existent. And I return to the things which are mine
from whence I came.

Et praecipiunt eis venientibus ad potestates haec dicere, postea-
quam mortui fuerint: Ego filius a Patre, Patre qui ante fuit, filius

247

autem in eo qui ante fuit. Veni autem videre omnia quae sunt mea et aliena; non autem aliena in totum, sed sunt Achamoth, quae est foemina, et haec sibi fecit: deducit enim genus ex eo qui ante fuit, et eo rursus in mea unde veni.

Irenaeus, *Adv. haer.* 1.21.5. Harvey, *Sancti Irenaei* 1:187.

I am a son from the Father, the pre-existent Father, a son in Him who is pre-existent.[2] I came to see all things, the things which are mine and those which are alien, though they are not absolutely alien but are of Achamoth who is female and made these things for herself. I derive my lineage[3] from Him who is pre-existent, and I go again to my own things, from whence I have come.

ἐγὼ υἱὸς ἀπὸ Πατρός, Πατρὸς προόντος, υἱὸς δὲ ἐν τῷ προόντι[2]· ἦλθον ‹δὲ› πάντα ἰδεῖν τὰ ἴδια καὶ τὰ ἀλλότρια, καὶ οὐκ ἀλλότρια δὲ παντελῶς, ἀλλὰ τῆς Ἀχαμώθ, ἥτις ἐστὶν θήλεια καὶ ταῦτα ἑαυτῇ ἐποίησεν. κατάγω[3] δὲ τὸ γένος ἐκ τοῦ προόντος καὶ πορεύομαι πάλιν εἰς τὰ ἴδια, ὅθεν ἐλήλυθα.

Epiphanius, *Haer.* 36.3.1-2. Holl-Dummer, *Epiphanius* 2²:46.

NOTES

   [1] The section quoted is part of a larger passage in which Jesus instructs James. For partly analogous instruction see the *Gospel of Philip* from Epiphanius, *Haer.* 26.3.2-3 and parallels [C6] and *Thomas* 50 and parallels [C40].

   [2] On the basis of the Latin rendering of Irenaeus and the Coptic of the First Apocalypse of James, I have emended the text to read ἐν τῷ προόντι, "in Him who is pre-existent," instead of ἐν τῷ παρόντι, "in the present."

   [3] The Latin and Coptic passages might suggest an emendation κατάγει here, and the clause would then refer to Achamoth, "she brings down the race." However, geneaological usage of καταγεῖν τὸ γένος is attested, "to derive one's lineage" (see Liddell-Scott-Jones, *A Greek-English Lexicon,* 888), so the phrase need not refer to producing a race or species, an activity understandable of figures such as Achamoth, though not of individual ascending souls. The geneaological usage in the first person may have been original in the Greek of Irenaeus and his source. Subsequent misunderstanding of the idiom may then have led to the change to the third person reference to Achamoth.

BIBLIOGRAPHY

Adriaen, M. *S. Hieronymi Presbyteri Opera* 1.2. CChrSL 73 (1963); 1.6. CChrSL 76 (1969) Turnhout: Brepols.

Aland, Kurt, ed. *Synopsis Quattuor Evangeliorum.* 2nd ed. Stuttgart: Württembergische Bibelanstalt, 1964.

Allberry, C.R.C. *A Manichaean Psalm-Book.* Manichaean Manuscripts of the Chester Beatty Collection 2.2. Stuttgart: W. Kohlhammer, 1938.

Altaner, Berthold. *Patrologie.* Freiburg: Herder, 1960.

Assemanus, J. S. *Sancti Ephraem Syri, Opera Omnia.* 6 vols. Rome: Vatican Press, 1732.

Baehrens, W. A. *Origenes Werke* 8. GCS 33. Leipzig: Hinrichs, 1925.

Batiffol, P. *Studia Patristica, Études d' ancienne Littérature Chrétienne.* Paris: E. Levoux, 1889.

Beeson, Charles Henry. *Hegemonius Acta Archelai.* GCS 16. Leipzig: Hinrichs, 1906.

Bell, H. Idris, and Skeat, T. C. *Fragments of an Unknown Gospel and Other Early Christian Papyri.* London: British Museum, 1935.

Bensly, Robert L. *The Fourth Book of Ezra.* TextsS 3.2. Cambridge: University Press, 1895.

Bernard, J. H. *The Odes of Solomon.* TextsS 8.3. (1912) Reprint ed., Nendeln/ Liechtenstein: Kraus Reprint, 1967.

Bert, Georg. *Aphrahat's des Persischen Weisen Homilien.* TU 3.3-4. Leipzig: Hinrichs, 1888.

Black, Matthew. *Apocalypsis Henochi Graece.* Pseudepigrapha Veteris Testamenti Graece 3, edited by A. M. Denis and M. De Jonge. Leiden: Brill, 1970.

Böhlig, Alexander. "Christliche Wurzeln in Manichaismus." *Bulletin de la Société d'archéologie Copte* 15 (1958-60).

Bonner, Campbell. *The Homily on the Passion by Melito Bishop of Sardis.* SD 12. London: Christophers. Philadelphia: University of Pennsylvania, 1940.

Bonwetsch, Nathanael, and Achelis, Hans. *Hippolytus Werke* 1. GCS 1. Leipzig: Hinrichs, 1897.

Bonwetsch, Nathanael. *Methodius von Olympus.* GCS 27. Leipzig: Hinrichs, 1917.

Borret, Marcel, S.J. *Origène Contra Celse I.* SC 132. Paris: Les Editions du Cerf, 1967.

Brandt, Samuel. *L. Caeli Firmiani Lactanti Opera Omnia.* Vol. 1. CSEL 19 (1890). Vol. 2. CSEL 27 (1893). Leipzig: G. Freytag, 1890-97. Reprint ed., New York: Johnson Reprint, 1965.

Brightman, F. E. *Liturgies: Eastern and Western 1. Eastern Liturgies.* Oxford: Clarendon, 1896.

Bruyne, D. Donatien de. "Epistula Titi, Discipuli Pauli, de Dispositione Sanctimonii." *RBén* 37 (1925): 47-72.

Bruyne, D. Donatien de. "Nouveaux Fragments des Actes de Pierre, de Paul, de Jean, d'Andri, et de l'Apocalypse d'Elie." *RBén* 25 (1908): 149-160.

Budge, E. A. Wallis. *Miscellaneous Coptic Texts in the Dialect of Upper Egypt.* London: British Museum, 1915.

Bultmann, Rudolf. *History of the Synoptic Tradition.* New York: Harper & Row, 1963.

Burnet, John. *Platonis Opera 1.* Oxford: Clarendon, 1900.

Buttenweiser, Moses. *Die hebräische Elias-Apokalypse.* Leipzig: Eduard Pfeiffer, 1897.

Casey, Robert Pierce. *The Excerpta Ex Theodoto of Clement of Alexandria.* SD 1. London: Christophers, 1934.

Casey, Robert Pierce, and Thomson, R. W. "A Dialogue Between Christ and the Devil." *JTS* 6 (1955).

Catanzaro, C. J. de. "The Gospel According to Philip." *JTS* (1962): 35-71.

Černy, Jaroslav. *Coptic Etymological Dictionary.* Cambridge: University Press, 1976.

Chadwick, Henry. *The Sentences of Sextus.* TextsS, N.S. 5. Cambridge: University Press, 1959.

Charles, R. H. *The Apocrypha and Pseudepigrapha.* Vol. 2: *Pseudepigrapha.* Oxford: Clarendon, 1913. Reprint ed., 1963, 1976.

Charlesworth, James H. *The Odes of Solomon: Syriac Texts.* Texts and Translations 13, Pseudepigrapha Series 7. Missoula, MT: Scholars Press, 1977.

Colson, F. H. *Philo.* 10 vols. LCL. Cambridge, MA: Harvard University Press. Vol. 3 (1930), Vol. 8 (1939).

Connolly, R. Hugh. "A Negative Form of the Golden Rule in the Diatessaron?" *JTS* 35 (1934).

Connolly, R. Hugh. *Didascalia Apostolorum.* Oxford: Clarendon, 1929. Reprint ed., 1969.

Cooper, James, and Maclean, Arthur John. *The Testament of Our Lord.* Edinburgh: T. & T. Clark, 1902.

Crossan, John Dominic. *In Parables: The Challenge of the Historical Jesus.* New York: Harper & Row, 1973.

Cureton, William. *Ancient Syriac Documents.* London, Edinburgh: Williams & Norgate, 1864. Reprint ed., Amsterdam: Oriental Press, 1967.

Danby, Herbert. *The Mishnah.* London: Oxford University Press, 1933.

Diercks, C. F. *Tertulliani Opera Omnia 1.* CChrSL 2. Turnhout: Brepols, 1954.

Dindorf, Guillaume. *Luciani Samosatensis Opera.* Paris: Firmin-Didot, 1867.

Dodd, C. H. *New Testament Studies.* Manchester: University Press, 1953.

Dörries, Hermann. *Symeon von Mesopotamien: Die Überlieferung der Messalianischen "Makarios" Schriften.* TU 55.1. Leipzig: Hinrichs, 1941.

Dörries, Hermann; Klostermann, Erich; and Kroeger, Matthias. *Die 50 Geistlichen Homilien des Makarios.* PTS 4. Berlin: de Gruyter, 1964.

Drower, Ethel Stefana. *The Canonical Prayerbook of the Mandaeans.* Leiden: Brill, 1959.

Egan, George A. *St. Ephrem, An Exposition of the Gospel.* CSCO 292, Scriptores Armenica 6. Louvain: Secretariat du Corpus SCO, 1968.

Emmel, Stephen. *Nag Hammadi Codex III,5: The Dialogue of the Savior.* NHS 26. Leiden: Brill, 1984.

Epstein, Isidore, gen. ed. *The Babylonian Talmud.* 34 vols. in 5 parts. London: Soncino Press, 1935-1952.

Finegan, Jack. *Hidden Records of the Life of Christ.* Philadelphia: Pilgrim, 1969.

Fitzmyer, Joseph A. *Essays on the Semitic Background of the New Testament.* London: Geoffrey Chapman, 1971.

Freedman, H., and Simon, Maurice. *Midrash Rabbah.* 13 vols. in 10 parts. 2nd ed. London: Soncino Press, 1951.

Funk, F. X., and Bihlmeyer, Karl. *Die Apostolischen Väter.* 2nd ed. Tübingen: J. C. B. Mohr, 1956.

Funk, F. X. *Didascalia et Constitutiones Apostolorum.* Paderborn: Schoeningh, 1905. Reprint ed., Torino: Bottega D'Erasmo, 1960.

Gasquet, Cardinale Francis Aidan, ed. *Biblia Sacra juxta Latinami Vulgatem Versionem.* 16 vols. Rome: Polyglot Press of the Vatican, 1926-1981. Vol. 12, 1964.

Gaster, M. *The Chronicles of Jerahmeel.* New York: Ktav, 1971.

Gearia, F. S. *Hieronymi Presbyteri Opera* 1.4. CChrSL 75. Turnhout: Brepols, 1964.

Gebhardt, Oscar von. *Das Evangelium und die Apokalypse des Petrus.* Leipzig: Hinrichs, 1893.

Gieseler, J. *Petri Siculi Historia Manichaeorum.* Göttingen: Vandenhoeck & Ruprecht, 1846.

Goodspeed, Edgar J. *Die ältesten Apologeten.* Göttingen: Vandenhoeck & Ruprecht, 1914. Reprint ed., Ann Arbor: University Microfilms International, 1976.

Grant, Robert M. *The Secret Sayings of Jesus.* London: Collins, 1960.

Grenfell, Bernard P., and Hunt, Arthur S. *The Oxyrhynchus Papyri,* Part V (1908) and X (1914). London: Egypt Exploration Fund.

Guillaumont, A., et al. *The Gospel According to Thomas.* Leiden: Brill, 1959.

Haenchen, Ernst. *Die Botschaft des Thomas-Evangeliums.* Berlin: Töpelmann, 1961.

Hall, Stuart George. *Melito of Sardis On Pascha.* Oxford Early Christian Texts. Oxford: Clarendon, 1979.

Halm, Karl. *Fabulae Aesopicae Collectae.* Leipzig: Teubner, 1852.

Harmon, A. M. *Lucian.* Vol. 2 (1919) and Vol. 3 (1921). LCL. New York: G. P. Putnam's Sons. Reprint ed. Cambridge, MA: Harvard University, 1969.

Harnack, Adolf von. *Marcion: Das Evangelium vom fremden Gott.* 2nd ed. Leipzig: Hinrichs, 1924. Reprint ed. Darmstadt: Wissenschaftliche Buchgesellschaft, 1960.

Harnack, Adolf von. *Der Pseudocryprianische Tractat de Aleatoribus.* TU 5.1. Leipzig: Hinrichs, 1888.

Hartel, G. *Cypriani Opera Omnia.* 3 vols. CSEL 3.1. (1868), 3.2 (1871), 3.3 (1871). Vienna: C. Gerald's Son.

Harvey, W. Wigan. *Sancti Irenaei Libros quinque adversus Haereses.* 2 vols. Cambridge: University Press, 1857.

Helmbold, W. C. *Plutarch's Moralia* 6. LCL. Cambridge, MA: Harvard University Press, 1939.

Hennecke, Edgar, and Schneemelcher, Wilhelm, eds. *New Testament Apocrypha.* Vol. 1: Gospels and Related Writings; Vol. 2: *Writings Relating to the Apostles; Apocalypses and Related Subjects.* Philadelphia: Westminster Press, 1963.

Henry, René. *Photius Bibliothèque* 3. Paris: Société d'Edition des Belles Lettres, 1962.

Hill, J. Hamlyn. *The Earliest Life of Christ.* Edinburgh: T. & T. Clark, 1894.

Hofius, Otfried. "Das Koptische Thomasevangelium und die Oxyrhynchus-Papyri Nr. 1, 654 und 655." *EvT* 20 (1960): 182-192.

Holl, Karl. *Epiphanius Werke.* 3 vols. GCS 25 (1915), 31 (1922), 37 (1933). Leipzig: Hinrichs, 1915-1933.

Howard, George. *The Teaching of Addai.* Texts and Translations 16, Early Christian Literature Series 4. Chico, CA: Scholars Press, 1981.

Hurst, D., and Adriaen, M. *S. Hieronymi Presbyteri Opera* 1.7. CChrSL 77. Turnhout: Brepols, 1969.

Iselin, Jacob Christoph. *Eine bisher unbekannte Version des ersten Teiles der "Apostellehre."* TU 13.1. Leipzig: Hinrichs, 1895.

Jaeger, Werner. *Gregorii Nyssenii Opera* 8.1. *Opera Ascetica.* Leiden: Brill, 1952.

Jaeger, Werner. *Two Rediscovered Works of Ancient Christian Literature: Gregory of Nyssa and Macarius.* Leiden: Brill, 1954.

James, Montague Rhodes. *Apocrypha Anecdota.* 2 vols. TextsS 2.3 (1893) and 5.1 (1897). Cambridge: University Press.

Jeremias, Joachim. *Unknown Sayings of Jesus.* London: S.P.C.K., 1958. 2nd ed., 1964.

Jülicher, Adolf; Matzkow, Walter; and Aland, Kurt. *Itala: Das Neue Testament in altlateinischen Überlieferung* 1. Berlin: de Gruyter, 1972.

Kasser, Rudolphe. *Compléments au Dictionnaire Copte de Crum.* Cairo: Imprimerie de l'Institut français d'archéologie orientale, 1964.

Klijn, A. F. J. *The Acts of Thomas.* NovTSup 5. Leiden: Brill, 1967.

Klostermann, Erich. *Apocrypha 2. Evangelien.* KlT 8. Bonn: Marcus and Weber, 1929.

Klostermann, Erich. *Eusebius Werke* 4. GCS 14. Leipzig: Hinrichs, 1906.

Klostermann, Erich. *Origenes Werke.* Vol. 3. GCS 6 (1901). Vol. 10. GCS 40 (1935). Leipzig: Hinrichs.

Klostermann, Erich, and Berthold, Heinz. *Neue Homilien des Makarius/ Symeon.* TU 72. Berlin: Akademie, 1961.

Kmosko, Michael. *Liber Graduum.* Patrologia Syriaca 1.3. Paris: Firmin-Didot, 1926.

Koetschau, Paul. *Origenes Werke.* Vol. 2. GCS 3 (1899). Vol. 5. GCS 22 (1913). Leipzig: Hinrichs.

Koester, Helmut. "One Jesus and Four Primitive Gospels," *HTR* 61 (1968).

Koester, Helmut. *Synoptische Überlieferung bei den apostolische Vätern.* TU 65. Berlin: Akademie-Verlag, 1957.

Krause, Martin, and Labib, Pahor. *Die drei Versionen des Apokryphon des Johannes.* Wiesbaden: Harrassowitz, 1962.

Kuhn, K. H. "The Sahidic Version of the Testament of Isaac." *JTS* n.s. 8 (1957).

Lagarde, P. de. *Agathangelus und die Akten Gregors von Armenien.* Abhandlungen der Königlichen Gesellschaft der Wissenschaften zu Göttingen 35. Göttingen: Dieterich, 1887.

Lauterbach, Jacob. *Mekilta de-Rabbi Ishmael.* 3 vols. Philadelphia: Jewish Publication Society, 1933. Reprint ed., 1949.

Leaney, A. R. C. *The Rule of Qumran and Its Meaning.* Philadelphia: Westminster, 1966.

Leipoldt, Johannes. *Das Evangelium nach Thomas.* Berlin: Akademie, 1967.

Leipoldt, Johannes, and Schenke, Hans-Martin. *Koptische-gnostische Schriften aus den Papyrus-Codices von Nag Hammadi.* Hamburg-Bergstedt: Herbert Reich, 1960.

Leloir, Louis. *Éphrem de Nisibe, Commentaire de l'Évangile Concordant ou Diatessaron.* SC 121. Paris: Éditions du Cerf, 1966.

Leloir, Louis. *Saint Éphrem, Commentaire de l'Évangile Concordant.* Louvain: L. Durbecq, 1954.

Leloir, Louis. *Saint Éphrem Commentaire de l'Évangile Concordant, Texte Syriaque.* Chester Beatty Monographs No. 8. Dublin: Hodges Figgis, 1963.

Lelyweld, Margaretha. "Les Logia de la Vie dans l'Évangile selon Thomas." Dr. Dis. Strasbourg, 1981.

Leutsch, E. L., and Schneidewin, F. G. *Corpus Paroemiographorum Graecorum* 1. Göttingen: Vandenhoeck & Ruprecht, 1831.

Lewis, Agnes Smith. *The Old Syriac Gospels or Evangelion da Mepharreshê.* London: Williams and Norgate, 1910.

Liddell, Henry George; Scott, Robert; and Jones, Henry Stuart. *A Greek-English Lexicon.* Oxford: Clarendon, 1961.

Lightfoot, J. B. *The Apostolic Fathers* 2.3. 2nd ed. London and New York: Macmillan & Co., 1889-1890.

Lipsius, Richard A., and Bonnet, Maximilian. *Acta Apostolorum Apocrypha.* 3 vols. Hildesheim: Olms, 1959.

Lofgren, Oscar. *Det Apokryfiska Johannesevangeliet.* Stockholm: 1967.

Malinine, Michel. *Epistula Iacobi Apocrypha.* Zürich: Rascher, 1968.

Mara, M. G. *Évangile de Pierre.* SC 201. Paris: Les Éditions du Cerf, 1973.

Marcovich, M. "Textual Criticism on the Gospel of Thomas." *JTS* 20 (1969): 53-74.

Martin, Joseph. *Commodianus, Claudius Marius Victorius.* CChrSL 128. Turnhout: Brepols, 1960.

Mayeda, Garo. *Das Leben-Jesu Fragment Papyrus Egerton 2 und seine Stellung in der urchristlichen Literaturgeschichte.* Bern: Haupt, 1946.

Ménard, Jacques É. *L'Évangile selon Philippe.* Paris: Letourney et Ane, 1967.

Ménard, Jacques É. *L'Évangile selon Thomas.* NHS 5. Leiden: Brill, 1975.

Migne, J. P., ed. *Patrologiae Cursus Completus.* Series Graeca. Paris: J. P. Migne, 1857-1866.

Migne, J. P., ed. *Patrologiae Cursus Completus.* Series Latina. Paris: J. P. Migne, 1844-1864.

Mommsen, Theodor. *Eusebius Werke* 2.1. GCS 9.1. Leipzig: Hinrichs, 1903.

Müller, F. W. K. "Handschriften-Reste in Estrangelo-Schrift aus Turfan, 2," *Abhandlungen der preussichen Akademie der Wissenschaften.* Phil-Hist. Kl., Abhandlung 2 (1904).

Mutzenbecher, Almut. *Aurelii Augustini Opera* 7.2. CChrSL 35. Turnhout: Brepols, 1967.

Neusner, Jacob. *Aphrahat and Judaism.* Leiden: Brill, 1971.

Oehler, F. *Corpus Haeresiologicum* 1. Berlin: Ascher, 1856.

Parisot, Johannes. *Aphraatis Sapientis Persae Demonstrationes.* Patrologia Syriaca 1.1. Paris: Firmin-Didot, 1894.

Parmentier, Léon. *Theodoret Kirchengeschichte.* GCS 19. Leipzig: Hinrichs, 1911.

Parrot, Douglas M. *Nag Hammadi Codices V, 2-5 and VI, 1 with Papyrus Berolinensis 8502.* NHS 11. Leiden: Brill, 1979.

Perry, Ben Edwin. *Aesopica* 1. Urbana, IL: University of Illinois, 1952.

Perry, Ben Edwin. *Babrius and Phaedrius.* LCL. Cambridge, MA: Harvard University Press, 1965.

Petschenig, Michael. *Iohannis Cassiani Conlationess XXIII.* CSEL 13. Reprint ed., New York: Johnson Reprint Corp., 1966.

Phillips, George. *The Doctrine of Addai, the Apostle.* London: Trübner, 1876.

Pick, Bernard. *Paralipomena: Remains of the Gospels and Sayings of Christ.* Chicago: Open Court, 1908.

Pietersma, Albert, and Comstock, Susan. *The Apocalypse of Elijah.* Texts and Translations 19, Pseudepigrapha Series 9. Chico, CA: Scholars Press, 1981.

Pines, Shlomo. *The Jewish Christians of the Early Centuries of Christianity According to a New Source.* Israel Academy of Sciences and Humanities Proceedings, Vol. 2, Nr. 13. Jerusalem: Central Press, 1966.

Pötscher, Walter. *Porphyrius Pros Markellan.* Philosophia Antiqua 15. Leiden: Brill, 1969.

Preuschen, Erwin. *Antilegomena: Die Reste der ausserkanonischen Evangelien und urchristlichen Überlieferungen.* 2nd ed. Giessen: Töpelmann, 1905.

Preuschen, Erwin. *Origenes Werke 4.* GCS 10. Leipzig: Hinrichs, 1903.

Quasten, Johannes. *Patrology.* Westminster, MD: Newman, 1951.

Rabin, Chaim. *The Zadokite Documents.* Oxford: Clarendon, 1954.

Rahlfs, Alfred, ed. *Septuaginta.* 2 vols. 6th ed. Stuttgart: Privilegierte Württembergische Bibelanstalt, 1952.

Rehm, Bernhard. *Die Pseudoklementinen.* Vol. I: *Homilien.* GCS 42 (1953). Vol. II: *Rekognitionen in Rufins Übersetzung.* GCS 51 (1965). Berlin: Akademie.

Resch, Alfred. *Agrapha: Ausserkanonische Schriftfragmente.* TU 15,3-4. Leipzig: Hinrichs, 1906. Reprint ed., Darmstadt: Wissenschaftliche Buchgesellschaft, 1967.

Resch, Gotthold. *Das Aposteldecret.* TU 13.3. Leipzig: Hinrichs, 1905.

Roberts, Alexander, and Donaldson, James, eds. *The Ante-Nicene Fathers.* Vol. 5. New York: Charles Scribner's Sons, 1926.

Robinson, James M., et al., eds. *The Facsimile Edition of the Nag Hammadi Codices*, Codex II. International Committee for the Nag Hammadi Codices. Leiden: Brill, 1974.

Robinson, James M., ed. *The Nag Hammadi Library.* San Francisco: Harper & Row, 1977.

Rousseau, Adelin. *Irénée de Lyon Contre les Hérésies.* SC 153 (1969); SC 264 (1979). Paris: Editions du Cerf.

Sachau, Edward, trans. *Albiruni's India 1.* London: Trübner, 1888.

Sande Bakhuyzen, W. H. van de. *Der Dialog des Adamantius.* GCS 4. Leipzig: Hinrichs, 1901.

Schaff, Philip, and Wace, Henry, eds. *A Select Library of Nicene and Post-Nicene Fathers of the Christian Church.* 2nd series, Vol. 13. New York: Christian Literature Company, 1898. Reprint ed., Grand Rapids: Eerdmans, 1956.

Schepss, Georg. *Priscillien, Opera.* CSEL 18. Vienna: Tempsky, 1889.

Schmidt, Carl. *Gespräche Jesu mit seinen Jüngern nach der Auferstehung.* Leipzig: Hinrichs, 1919. Reprint ed., Hildesheim: Olms, 1967.

Schmidt, Carl. *Gnostische Schriften in Koptischer Sprache aus dem Codex Brucianus.* TU 8,1 and 2. Leipzig: Hinrichs, 1892.

Schmidt, Carl. *Kephalaia. Manichäische Handschriften der Staatlichen Museen Berlin 1.* Stuttgart: Kohlhammer, 1940.

Schmidt, Carl, and Macdermot, Violet. *Pistis Sophia.* NHS 9. Leiden: Brill, 1978.

Schmidt, Carl, and Macdermot, Violet. *The Books of Jeu and the Untitled Text in the Bruce Codex.* NHS 13. Leiden: Brill, 1978.

Schwartz, Edward. *Eusebius Werke.* Vol. 2,1. GCS 9.1 (1903); Vol. 2,2. GCS 9.2 (1908). Leipzig: Hinrichs.

Smith, Joseph P. *St. Irenaeus, Proof of the Apostolic Preaching.* The Works of the Fathers in Translation 16. Westminster, MD: Newman, 1952.

Stählin, Otto. *Clemens Alexandrinus* 1. GCS 12. Leipzig: Hinrichs, 1936.

Stählin, Otto, and Früchtel, Ludwig. *Clemens Alexandrinus.* Vol. 2, 3rd ed. GCS 52 (1960). Vol. 3, 2nd ed. GCS 17.2 (1970). Berlin: Akademie.

Steindorff, Georg. *Die Apokalypse des Elias.* TU 2.3a (17). Leipzig: Hinrichs, 1899.

Stern, S. M. "'Abd Al-Jabbar's Book on the Signs of Muhammed's Prophecy." *JTS* 19 (1968).

Stone, Michael, and Strugnell, John. *The Book of Elijah, Parts 1–2.* Missoula, MT: Scholars Press, 1979.

Strack, Hermann, and Billerbeck, Paul. *Kommentar zum Neuen Testament aus Talmud und Midrash.* 4.1. Munich: Beck, 1928.

Swainson, C. A. *The Greek Liturgies.* London: C. J. Clay & Son, 1884.

Thierry, J. J. *Tertulliani Opera Omnia* 2. CChrSL 25. Turnhout: Brepols, 1954.

Till, Walter C. *Das Evangelium nach Philippos.* Berlin: de Gruyter, 1963.

Till, Walter C. *Die Gnostischen Schriften des Koptischen Papyrus Berolinensis 8502.* TU 60. Berlin: Akademie, 1955.

Tischendorf, Konstantin von. *Apocalypses Apocryphae.* Leipzig: Mendelssohn, 1866. Reprint ed., Hildesheim: Olms, 1966.

Tischendorf, Konstantin von. *Evangelia Apocrypha.* Reprint ed., Hildesheim: Olms, 1966.

Turner, John. *The Book of Thomas the Contender from Codex II of Cairo Gnostic Library from Nag Hammadi,* CG 2,7. Missoula, MT: Scholars Press, 1975.

Wendland, Paul. *Hippolytus Werke* 3. GCS 26. Leipzig: Hinrichs, 1916.

Whittaker, Molly. *Der Hirt des Hermas.* GCS 48. Berlin: Akademie, 1956.

Wilmart, André, and Tisserant, Eugène. "Fragments Grecs et Latins de l'Évangile de Bartholémy." *RB* 22 (1913).

Wilson, R. McL. *The Gospel of Philip.* New York: Harper & Row, 1962.

Wordsworth, John, and White, Henry. *Novum Testamentum Latine* 1. Oxford: Clarendon, 1889-1898.

Zahn, Theodor. *Acta Joannis.* Erlangen: Deichert, 1880. Reprint ed., Hildesheim: Gerstenberg, 1975.

Zahn, Theodor. *Geschichte des Neutestamentlichen Kanons.* 2 vols. Erlangen: Deichert, 1890. Reprint ed., Hildensheim: Olms, 1975.

INDEX OF SAYINGS AND PARALLELS

Headings of Sayings	Extracanonical Sayings of Jesus	Extracanonical Parallels, not as Sayings of Jesus	Parallel Canonical Sayings of Jesus	Canonical Parallels, not as Sayings of Jesus
A-5 On Procreation	Gospel of the Egyptians [2], in Clement, Strom. 3.9.66			
A-6 When the Two Will Be One	2 Clement 12.2 Gospel of the Egyptians [3], in Clement, Strom. 3.9.66 Gospel of Thomas 22 Martyrdom of Peter 9 (Acts of Peter 38) Ps. Linus, Martyr. Petri 14 Acts of Philip 140 (34) Gospel of Philip 69 CG II, 67:30-34	Acts of Thomas 147 Test. of Our Lord 1.28 Gospel of Philip 78 CG II, 70.9-17 Gospel of Philip 71 CG, II, 68.22-26 Hippolytus Ref. 5.7.14-15	Mark 10:13-16 Matt 9:13-15, 18:3 Luke 18:15-17 John 3:3, 5 Mark 10:6-8 Matt 19:4-6 John 17:11, 20-23	Eph 5.31 Eph 2:14-16 Gen 1:27 Gen 2:24-25 Gen 3:7, 10 Gal 3:28
A-7 Tribute to Kings	P. Egerton 2, 2r. 43-59		Mark 12:13-17 Luke 20:20-26 Matt 22:15-22 John 5:36 Luke 6:46 Matt 7:6-7, 21 Matt 15:7-9	Isa 29:13 (LXX) Ps 78:36-37 Luke 23:2 John 3:2 John 10:24-25
A-8 Jesus and the Lawyers	P. Egerton 2, 1v. 1-19		John 5:39, 45	John 9:29
A-9 Lambs in the Midst of Wolves	2 Clement 5.2-4 Prochorus' Acts of John Ps. Titus Epistle [1]		Matt 10:16, 28 Luke 10:3 Luke 12:4, 5	

Headings of Sayings	Extracanonical Sayings of Jesus	Extracanonical Parallels, not as Sayings of Jesus	Parallel Canonical Sayings of Jesus	Canonical Parallels, not as Sayings of Jesus
A-10 Jesus and the Tax-Collector	Clement, *Strom.* 4.6.35		Luke 19:1-10	
A-11 The Temple Tax	Codex 713 to Matt 17:24-27 Arabic *Diat.* 25:4-7		Matt 17:24-27	
A-12 Who Will See the Coming Kingdom	Hippolytus, *Comm. on Dan.* 4.60 Papias, in Irenaeus, *Adv. haer.* 5.33.4			
A-13 The Perishing of Weak Souls	Mani, *Bk. of Mysteries* [1]			
A-14 The Inanimate and the Living	Mani, *Bk. of Mysteries* [2]			
A-15 Faith to Move Mountains	Aphrahat, *Demon.* 1.17 *De fide*		Matt 14:28-31 Matt 17:20, 21:21 Mark 11:23 Luke 17:6	1 Cor 13:22
A-16 Work on the Sabbath	Codex D after Luke 6:4			
A-17 Jesus in the Temple	P. Oxy. 840		Matt 23:25-28 Luke 11:39	Mark 11:27-28 Matt 21:23 Luke 20:1-2 Mark 7:1-5 Matt 15:1-2

Headings of Sayings	Extracanonical Sayings of Jesus	Extracanonical Parallels, not as Sayings of Jesus	Parallel Canonical Sayings of Jesus	Canonical Parallels, not as Sayings of Jesus
A-18 Do Not Do What You Hate	*Gospel of Thomas* 6 P. Oxy. 654.32-42	*Liber Graduum* 20.10 *Liber Graduum* 15.16 *Didache* 1.2 *b. Sab.* 31a *Sent. of Sextus* 179	Mark 4:22 Matt 6:1-18 Matt 7:12 Matt 10:26 Luke 6:31 Luke 8:17 Luke 12:2	Tobit 4:15 Eph 4:25 Col 3:9 James 3:14 Lev 19:11
A-19 The Authority of James	*Gospel of Thomas* 12		Mark 10:43 Mattt 20:26 Matt 23:11 Luke 22:26	Mark 9:34 Matt 18:1 Luke 9:46
A-20 The Three Words Spoken to Thomas	*Gospel of Thomas* 13	*Acts of Thomas* 47 *Quest. of Barth.* 2.5 *Odes of Solomon* 11:6-7	Mark 8:27-30 Matt 16:13-16 Matt 23:8 Luke 9:18-21 John 4:10-14 John 7:37-38 John 15:15	John 8:59 John 10:31
A-21 The Beginning and the End	*Gospel of Thomas* 18	Clement, *Exc. ex Theod.* 78.2	Mark 9:1 Matt 16:28 Luke 9:27 John 8:51-52	
A-22 The Mustard Seed	*Gospel of Thomas* 20		Mark 4:30-32 Matt 13:31-32 Luke 13:18-19	

Headings of Sayings	Extracanonical Sayings of Jesus	Extracanonical Parallels, not as Sayings of Jesus	Parallel Canonical Sayings of Jesus	Canonical Parallels, not as Sayings of Jesus
A-23 Little Children in a Field	*Gospel of Thomas* 21a			
A-24 Light Within	*Gospel of Thomas* 24		John 14:4-5 John 13:36-37 John 11:10 Matt 6:22-23 Matt 5:14-16 Luke 11:34-35	
A-25 Undressing without Shame	*Gospel of Thomas* 37 P. Oxy. 655.17-23	Hippolytus, *Ref.* 5.8.44		Gen 2:25
A-26 Tree and Fruit	*Gospel of Thomas* 43		John 8:25	
A-27 The New World Is Present	*Gospel of Thomas* 51		Luke 17:20-21	
A-28 Concerning the Prophets	*Gospel of Thomas* 52 Augustine, *Cont. adv. leg. et proph.* 2.4.14			
A-29 The Value of Circumcision	*Gospel of Thomas* 53	*Tanchuma* B7 (18a) *Odes of Solomon* 11:1-3a		Rom 2:25, 29 Rom 3:1 Phil 3:3 1 Cor 7:19 Gal 5:6 Gal 6:15 Col 2:11 Deut 10:16 Jer 4:4

Headings of Sayings	Extracanonical Sayings of Jesus	Extracanonical Parallels, not as Sayings of Jesus	Parallel Canonical Sayings of Jesus	Canonical Parallels, not as Sayings of Jesus
A-30 The Samaritan and the Lamb	*Gospel of Thomas* 60			
A-31 Being Undivided	*Gospel of Thomas* 61b		Matt 11:27 Luke 10:22	John 3:35 John 13:3
A-32 Jesus Not a Divider	*Gospel of Thomas* 72 'Abd Al-Jabbar's *Book on the Signs of Muhammed's Prophecy*		Luke 12:13-14	Exod 2:14 Acts 7:27, 35
A-33 True Blessedness	*Gospel of Thomas* 79		Matt 12:50 Matt 24:19 Mark 3:35 Mark 13:17 Luke 11:27-28 Luke 8:21 Luke 23:29 Luke 21:23	Luke 1:28 (var) Luke 1:42, 48
A-34 Knowing the Times	*Gospel of Thomas* 91		Matt 16:1-3	
A-35 Jesus' True Relatives	*Gospel of Thomas* 99 *2 Clement* 9.11 Clement, *Ecl. pro.* 20.3 *Gospel of the Ebionites* [1], in Epiphanius, *Haer.* 30.14.5		Mark 3:31-35 Matt 12:46-50 Matt 7:21 Luke 8:19-21	
A-36 Tribute to Caesar	*Gospel of Thomas* 100 Justin, *Apol.* 1.17.2	*Sent. of Sextus* 20	Mark 12:13-17 Matt 22:15-22 Luke 20:20-26	Rom 13:7 Prov 24:21 (LXX) Luke 23:2

Headings of Sayings	Extracanonical Sayings of Jesus	Extracanonical Parallels, not as Sayings of Jesus	Parallel Canonical Sayings of Jesus	Canonical Parallels, not as Sayings of Jesus
A-37 Fasting and Prayer	*Gospel of Thomas* 104		Mark 2:18-20 Matt 9:14-15 Luke 5:33-35	
A-38 The Kingdom Spread Out on the Earth	*Gospel of Thomas* 113 Symeon, *Hom. B* 35		Luke 17:20-21	
A-39 Women Entering the Kingdom	*Gospel of Thomas* 114	Clement, *Exc. ex Theod.* 21.3		
A-40 Gifts of the True Mother	*Gospel of Philip* 34b CG II, 59.23-27			
A-41 Jesus in the Dye-Works	*Gospel of Philip* 54 CG II, 63.25-30			
A-42 Jesus' Love for Mary Magdalene	*Gospel of Philip* 55 CG II, 63.32-64.5	*Gospel of Mary* 10.1-3 *Gospel of Mary* 18.12-15 P. Rylands 463 (*Gospel of Mary*)		John 11:2, 5

PARABLES

P-1 The Talents	*Gospel of the Nazaraeans* [4], in Eusebius, *De theoph.* 19		Matt 25:14-30 Matt 24:49 Luke 19:12-27 Luke 12:45 Luke 15:13	

Headings of Sayings	Extracanonical Sayings of Jesus	Extracanonical Parallels, not as Sayings of Jesus	Parallel Canonical Sayings of Jesus	Canonical Parallels, not as Sayings of Jesus
P-2 The Fig-Tree	Apocalypse of Peter 2		Mark 13:28-29 Matt 24:32-33 Luke 21:29-31 Luke 13:6-9, 21:8 Mark 13:6, 22-23 Matt 24:5, 24	
P-3 The Date Palm	Apocryphon of James CG I, 7.22-35			
P-4 The Grain of Wheat	Apocryphon of James CG I, 8.16-27			
P-5 The Ear of Grain	Apocryphon of James CG I, 12.22-31		Mark 4:26-29	
P-6 The Wise Fisherman	Gospel of Thomas 8	Aesop's Fables [Babrius 4] Clement, Strom. 1.1.16 Clement, Strom. 6.11.95	Matt 13:47-50	
P-7 The Sower	Gospel of Thomas 9 Justin, Dial. 125.1 Memoria Apostolorum	1 Clement 24.5	Mark 4:3-9, 13-20 Matt 13:3-9, 18-23 Luke 8:5-8, 11-15	
P-8 The Weeds	Gospel of Thomas 57		Matt 13:24-30	
P-9 The Rich Fool	Gospel of Thomas 63		Luke 12:16-21	
P-10 The Banquet	Gospel of Thomas 64		Matt 22:2-10 Luke 14:16-24	

Headings of Sayings	Extracanonical Sayings of Jesus	Extracanonical Parallels, not as Sayings of Jesus	Parallel Canonical Sayings of Jesus	Canonical Parallels, not as Sayings of Jesus
P-11 The Wicked Tenants	Gospel of Thomas 65		Mark 12:1-8 Matt 21:33-39 Luke 20:9-15a	
P-12 The Pearl Merchant	Gospel of Thomas 76		Matt 13:45-46 Matt 6:19-20 Luke 12:33	
P-13 The Leaven	Gospel of Thomas 96		Matt 13:33 Luke 13:20-21	
P-14 The Woman with a Jar of Meal	Gospel of Thomas 97			
P-15 The Assassin	Gospel of Thomas 98			
P-16 The Lost Sheep	Gospel of Thomas 107		Matt 18:12-13 Luke 15:3-6	
P-17 The Hidden Treasure	Gospel of Thomas 109	*Mekilta de-Rabbi Ishmael,* *Beshallah 2* *Song of Songs,* r.4.12.1 *Lev. r.* 5.4 Philo, *Unchangeableness* *of God* 20.91 *Fables of Aesop,* 98a, 98b	Matt 13:44	

265

PROPHETIC AND APOCALYPTIC SAYINGS

Headings of Sayings	Extracanonical Sayings of Jesus	Extracanonical Parallels, not as Sayings of Jesus	Parallel Canonical Sayings of Jesus	Canonical Parallels, not as Sayings of Jesus
Pro-1 The Fruitfulness of the Kingdom	Papias, Fragments in Irenaeus, *Adv. haer.* 5.33.3	1 Enoch 10:18-19 2 Baruch 29.5 Apocalypse of Paul 22		Amos 9:13 Isa 25:6 Ezek 34:25-27
Pro-2 The Coming of the Son of God	*Apocalypse of Peter I* *Epistula Apostolorum 9* (Ethiopic 16)	*Apocalypse of Elijah* 31.19-32	Matt 24:4-5 Matt 24:23-27 Matt 24:30-31 Matt 26:64 Matt 16:27 Mark 8:38 Mark 13:5-6 Mark 13:21-22, 26-27 Mark 14:62 Luke 9:26 Luke 21:8, 27 Luke 17:23-24	Dan 7:13 2 Thes 1:7 Rev 1:17 Rev 14:14 Rev 2:23 1 Pet 4:5 2 Tim 4:1
Pro-3 The Punishment of the Wicked	*Apocalypse of Peter 7.9*	*Ps. Titus Epistle* [2] *Chronicles of Jerahmeel 14.4* *Chronicles of Jerahmeel 161.1-5* *Acts of Thomas 6.56* *Apocalypse of Paul 38-39* *Apocalypse of the Virgin Mary* 6, 9, 14		

Headings of Sayings	Extracanonical Sayings of Jesus	Extracanonical Parallels, not as Sayings of Jesus	Parallel Canonical Sayings of Jesus	Canonical Parallels, not as Sayings of Jesus
Pro-4 Keeping the Commandments	Gospel of the Nazaraeans [5] in Cod. N.T. 1424 2 Clement 4.5		Matt 7:23 Matt 25:12 Luke 13:27	Ps 6:8
Pro-5 Not All Will Be Saved	2 Clement 4.2		Matt 7:21 Luke 6:46	
Pro-6 Divisions and Factions	Justin, *Dial.* 35.3 *Didascalia* 6.5 Didymus, *De Trinitate* 3.22	Lactantius, *Div. inst.* 4.30	Matt 24:5, 7, 15 Matt 10:35 Matt 24:11 Luke 12:53 Mark 13:22	1 Cor 11:18, 19 Gal 5:20 2 Cor 11:13
Pro-7 The Circumstances of Judgment	Justin, *Dial.* 47.5 *Liber Graduum* 15.4 *Liber Graduum* 3.3	Clement, *Quis div. salv.* 40 Athanasius, *Quaestiones ad Antiochum* 36 Johannes Climacus, *Scala Paradisi* 7.16 *Vita S. Antonii* 15 Basil, Epistle 42, *Ad Chilonem* Cyprian, *De mortalitate* 17 Jerome, Letter 12, *To Rusticus*			Ezek 7:8 Ezek 18:30 Ezek 33:22

267

Headings of Sayings	Extracanonical Sayings of Jesus	Extracanonical Parallels, not as Sayings of Jesus	Parallel Canonical Sayings of Jesus	Canonical Parallels, not as Sayings of Jesus
Pro-8 Passion and Resurrection Predicted	Justin, *Dial.* 51.2	Ignatius, *Smyrnians* 3.3 Ps. Ignatius, *Smyrnians* 3 *Apostolic Const.* 6.30	Mark 8:31, 9:31 Mark 10:33-34 Matt 16:21, 17:22-23 Matt 20:18-20 Luke 9:22, 18:31-32 Luke 24:7	Acts 10:41
Pro-9 Called and Elect	Clement, *Exc. ex Theod.* 9.2		John 2:14-16 Mark 11:15-17 Matt 21:12-13 Luke 19:45-46	
Pro-10 White-washed Tombs	Naassene Exegesis, in Hippolytus, *Ref.* 5.8.23-24		Matt 23:27 John 5:28	
Pro-11 Crucifying the World	*The First Book of Jeu* 1			Gal 6:14
Pro-12 Weak and Strong	*Apostolic Church Ord.* 26			
Pro-13 The Children of Cain	Aphrahat, *Dem.* 16.8, *De gentibus*		John 8:37, 39-44	Matt 3:9 Luke 3:8 John 8:33
Pro-14 Beatitudes and Woes	Ps. Ephrem, *Sermo compunctorius*		Matt 5:4-7 Luke 6:21, 5	
Pro-15 The Purification of the Kingdom	Ephrem, *Commentary on the Diatessaron* 18.7		Matt 13:41	2 Pet 3:13

268

Headings of Sayings	Extracanonical Sayings of Jesus	Extracanonical Parallels, not as Sayings of Jesus	Parallel Canonical Sayings of Jesus	Canonical Parallels, not as Sayings of Jesus
Pro-16 Predictions of the End	*Ps. Clementine Homilies* 2.17		Mark 13:2, 6, 14, 22 Mark 13:26 Matt 24:2, 5, 11, 14, 15 Matt 24:23-25, 30 Luke 21:6, 8, 20, 27	
Pro-17 The Good Things to Come	*Ps. Clementine Homilies* 12.29 *Clementine Epitome* 96 Aphrahat, *Demo.* 5.1 "Of Wars" *Manichaean Ps. Bk.* Ps. 239.27-28		Matt 18:7 Luke 17:1	
Pro-18 Victory Prize	*Liber Graduum* 3.3			1 Cor 9:24-27 James 1:22 Rev 2:10
Pro-19 Worthy of the Paraclete	*Liber Graduum* 5.18		John 14:16-17 John 15:19	
Pro-20 Self-knowledge Is Blessed	*Psalms of Thomas* 13.19-20			
Pro-21 A Thief in the Night	Didymus, *De Trinitate* 3.22 Epiphanius, *Ancoratus* 21.2 Epiphanius, *Haer.* 69.44		Matt 24:43, 44 Luke 12:35-40	1 Thes 5:2, 4 2 Pet 3:10 Rev 3:3, 16:15

Headings of Sayings	Extracanonical Sayings of Jesus	Extracanonical Parallels, not as Sayings of Jesus	Parallel Canonical Sayings of Jesus	Canonical Parallels, not as Sayings of Jesus
Pro-22 Entering the Bridal Chamber	*Acts of Philip* 135		Matt 6:28 Matt 9:37-38 Matt 22:2-14 Luke 10:2, 12:27 Luke 14:16-24 John 4:35	James 1:12
Pro-23 Inheriting the Glory of Righteousness	Freer ms. to Mark 16:14-15			
Pro-24 Tribulations	*Prochorus' Acts of John*	*Barnabas* 7.11b Irenaeus, *Adv. haer.* 5.28.3 Symeon, *Hom.* 27.20		Acts 14:21-22 4 Ezra 7:14
Pro-25 Signs of the Anti-Christ	*Testament of the Lord* 1.11 *Test. of the Lord in Gal.* 6	*Codex Treverensis* 36 *Ms. Parisinus Graecus 4, fol. 228r* *Apocalypse of Elijah* 33-34 *Apocalypse of Esdras* *Apocryphal Apoc. of John*		
Pro-26 Unclean Souls	Ps. *Titus Epistle* [3]			
Pro-27 On Excesses	Ps. *Titus Epistle* [4]			
Pro-28 Inheriting Eternal Life	*Agathangelus* 65		Mark 10:29-30 Matt 19:29 Luke 18:29-30	

Headings of Sayings	Extracanonical Sayings of Jesus	Extracanonical Parallels, not as Sayings of Jesus	Parallel Canonical Sayings of Jesus	Canonical Parallels, not as Sayings of Jesus
Pro-29 The Unclosed Eye	Vita Schnudi			
Pro-30 Not Tasting Death	Gospel of Thomas 1 P. Oxy. 654.3-5		Mark 9:1 Matt 16:18 Luke 9:27 John 8:52	
Pro-31 The Kingdom Is Within and Outside	Gospel of Thomas 3 P. Oxy. 654.9-21 Gospel of Mary 8.12-19	Manichaean Psalm-Book, p. 160.20-21	Luke 17:20-21	Job 12:7-8
Pro-32	Gospel of Thomas 4 P. Oxy. 654.21-27 Hippolytus, Ref. 5.7.20	Pss. of Heracleides 192.2-3	Matt 11:25, 19:30 Luke 10:21, 13:30 Mark10:31	
Pro-33 The Hidden Will Be Revealed	Gospel of Thomas 5 P. Oxy. 654.27-31 Behnesa Grave Wrapping Mani, Kephalaia 65		Mark 4:22 Luke 8:17, 12:2 Matt 10:26	
Pro-34 Man	The Lion Will Become	Gospel of Thomas 7 Contender: CG II, 139.2-8	The Book of Thomas the	
Pro-35 Dead, Alive	Gospel of Thomas 11	Hippolytus, Ref. 5.8.32	Mark 13:31 Matt 24:35, 5:18 Luke 16:17, 21:23	Isa 51:6
Pro-36 Divisions, Fire, Sword	Gospel of Thomas 16		Luke 12:49 Matt 10:34-36	4 Ezra 6:24

Headings of Sayings	Extracanonical Sayings of Jesus	Extracanonical Parallels, not as Sayings of Jesus	Parallel Canonical Sayings of Jesus	Canonical Parallels, not as Sayings of Jesus
Pro-37 Becoming Disciples	Gospel of Thomas 19	Manichaean Psalmbook, p. 161.17-18		Jer 1:5; Ezek 47:12; Rev 2:7, 22:2; Gen 2:8, 9
Pro-38 The Watchful Householder	Gospel of Thomas 21b		Matt 24:43-44; Luke 12:35-40	
Pro-39 The Uprooted Vine	Gospel of Thomas 40; Gospel of Philip 126 CG II, 85.29-31	Ignatius, Trall. 11.1; Ignatius, Phila. 3.1a	Matt 15:13, 3:10; Matt 7:19; Luke 3:9	Isa 5:1-7; Ezek 19:10-14
Pro-40 Having and Not Having	Gospel of Thomas 41; Apocalypse of Peter CG VII, 83.26-84.6		Mark 4:25; Matt 13:12, 25:29; Luke 8:18, 19:26	4 Ezra 7:25
Pro-41 Greater than John the Baptist	Gospel of Thomas 46		Matt 11:11, 18:3; Luke 7:28	
Pro-42 Moving Mountains	Gospel of Thomas 48; Didascalia 3.6		Mark 11:23; Matt 17:20, 18:19; Matt 21:21; Luke 17:6	1 Cor 13:2; Eph 2:15
Pro-43 Blessed are the Single Ones	Gospel of Thomas 49		John 16:28	
Pro-44 Blessed are the Poor	Gospel of Thomas 54; Polycarp, Phil. 2.3		Matt 5:3; Luke 6:20	James 2:5

Headings of Sayings	Extracanonical Sayings of Jesus	Extracanonical Parallels, not as Sayings of Jesus	Parallel Canonical Sayings of Jesus	Canonical Parallels, not as Sayings of Jesus
Pro-45 Blessed Are Those Who Suffer	Gospel of Thomas 58	2 Clem. 19.3		James 1:12 1 Pet 3:14
Pro-46	Two on a Bed	Gospel of Thomas 61a		Luke 17:34-35 Matt 24:40-41
Pro-47 Blessed Are the Persecuted	Gospel of Thomas 68 Gospel of Thomas 69 Clement, Strom. 4.6.41 Mani, Unpublished Letter The Book of Thomas the Contender, CG II, 145.1-8		Matt 5:6, 10-11 Matt 10:22 Luke 6:21-22	1 Pet 3:14 1 Pet 4:14 Ps 107:9
Pro-48 What Is Within Will Save	Gospel of Thomas 70		Mark 4:25 Matt 13:12, 25,29 Luke 8:18, 19:26	
Pro-49 Many Are at the Door	Gospel of Thomas 75	Symeon, Hom. 4.6 Symeon, Great Letter Gregory of Nyssa, De instituto Christiano 83.9-12 Liber Graduum 19:36	Matt 25:10	
Pro-50 The Hidden Light	Gospel of Thomas 83			
Pro-51 Adam's Unworthiness	Gospel of Thomas 85	Gospel of Philip 80 CG II, 70.22-24 Gospel of Philip 83 CG II, 71.16-21		Gen 2:7

Headings of Sayings	Extracanonical Sayings of Jesus	Extracanonical Parallels, not as Sayings of Jesus	Parallel Canonical Sayings of Jesus	Canonical Parallels, not as Sayings of Jesus
Pro-52 The Wretched Body	*Gospel of Thomas* 87 *Gospel of Thomas* 112	Symeon, *Hom.* 11.1		
Pro-53 Angels and Prophets Will Come	*Gospel of Thomas* 88			
Pro-54 Knowing the Danger	*Gospel of Thomas* 103	Didymus, *De Trinitate* 3.22	Matt 24:43 Luke 12:39	1 Thes 5:2 2 Pet 3:10 Rev 3:3, 16:15
Pro-55 When Two Become One	*Gospel of Thomas* 106		Mark 11:23 Matt 17:20, 21:21 Luke 17:6	1 Cor 13:2 Eph 2:15
Pro-56 The Living Will Not Die	*Gospel of Thomas* 111		Mark 13:31 Matt 24:35 Luke 21:33 John 8:51	Isa 34:4 Heb 1:12 Rev 6:14
Pro-57 Blessed Is He Who Is	*Gospel of Philip* 57 CG II, 64.9-12	Irenaeus, *Proof of the Apostolic Preaching* 43 Lactantius, *Div. inst.* 4.8		Jer 1:5
Pro-58 Entering the Kingdom Laughing	*Gospel of Philip* 97 CG II, 74.24-26			
Pro-59 The Axe at the Root	*Gospel of Philip* 123 [1] CG II, 83.11-13		Matt 3:10	

Headings of Sayings	Extracanonical Sayings of Jesus	Extracanonical Parallels, not as Sayings of Jesus	Parallel Canonical Sayings of Jesus	Canonical Parallels, not as Sayings of Jesus
Pro-60 Truth Makes Free	*Gospel of Philip* 123 [2] CG II, 84.7-9	*Gospel of Philip* 110 CG II, 77.15-16	John 8:32	

WISDOM SAYINGS

Headings of Sayings	Extracanonical Sayings of Jesus	Extracanonical Parallels, not as Sayings of Jesus	Parallel Canonical Sayings of Jesus	Canonical Parallels, not as Sayings of Jesus
W-1 Pearls before Swine	*Didache* 9.5 *Gospel of Thomas* 93 Naassene exegesis, in Hippolytus, *Ref.* 5.8.33 Basilides' *Exegetica*, in Epiphanius, *Haer.* 24.5.2 *Liber Graduum* 30.11		Matt 7:6	
W-2 Seek, Find, Rule	*Gospel of the Hebrews* [1a] in Clement, *Strom.* 5.14.96 *Gospel of the Hebrews* [1b], in Clement, *Strom.* 2.9.45 *Gospel of Thomas* 2 P. Oxy. 654.5-9 *Pistis Sophia* 111 *Pistis Sophia* 102 *Pistis Sophia* 100	*Acts of Thomas* 136 *Pistis Sophia* 100	Matt 7:7-8 Luke 11:9-10	

Headings of Sayings	Extracanonical Sayings of Jesus	Extracanonical Parallels, not as Sayings of Jesus	Parallel Canonical Sayings of Jesus	Canonical Parallels, not as Sayings of Jesus
	Dial. of the Savior CG III, 129.14-16 The Book of Thomas, the Contender, CG II, 140.40-141.2			
W-3 Faithful in What Is Small	2 Clement 8.4-6 Irenaeus, Adv. haer. 2.34.3 Hilary, Epist. seu lib. 1		Luke 16:10-12 Luke 19:17 Matt 25:21, 23	
W-4 The Mind and the Treasure	Justin, Apol. 15.16 Clement, Strom. 7.12.77.6 Clement, Quis div. salt. 17.1 Gospel of Mary 10:13-16 Symeon, Hom. 43.3 Pistis Sophia 90 Manichaean Psalm-Book, Ps. 294.24-25 Mani, Kephalaia 89.3-4	Mani, Kephalaia 91.8-10 Sentences of Sextus 316 Sentences of Sextus 326a	Matt 6:21 Luke 12:34	
W-5 Alike and Different	Epistula Apostolorum 32		Matt 7:16-18, 12:33 Luke 6:43-44	
W-6 Seek Great Things	Clement, Strom. 1.24.158.2 Origen, Sel. in Ps. 4.4 Eusebius, In Ps. 16.2.4 Ambrose, Epist. 1.36.3, Ad Horantianus	Clement, Strom. 4.34.6 Origen, On Prayer 2.2 Origen, On Prayer 14.1 Origen, C. Celsum 7.44 Origen, On Prayer 16.2 Tertullian, De oratione 25.6	Matt 6:33	

Headings of Sayings	Extracanonical Sayings of Jesus	Extracanonical Parallels, not as Sayings of Jesus	Parallel Canonical Sayings of Jesus	Canonical Parallels, not as Sayings of Jesus
W-7 Skillful Money-changers	Origen, *Com. on John* 19.7.2 *Ps. Clem. Hom.* 2.51 Socrates, *Eccles. Hist.* 3.16 Jerome, Letter 119 *Ad Min. et Alex.* *Vita St. Syncleticae* 100 *Pistis Sophia* 134 Caesarius, *Dial.* 3, *Inter.* 140 Cassian, *Conlationes* 1.20 Cassian, *Conlationes* 2.9 Apelles, In Epiph. *Haer.* 44.2.6	Clement, *Strom.* 1.28 Origen, *Com. on Mt.* 17.31 Cyril of Alexandria, *Com. on Isaiah* 1.2 Dionysius of Rome, in Euseb. *Hist. eccl.* 7.7.3 Philo, *De spec. leg.* 4.77		1 Thes 5:21, 22
W-8 Wisdom's Children	Origen, *Hom. on Jeremiah* 14.5		Luke 7:35, 11:49 Matt 11:19	Prov 9:3 Jer 7:25, 25:4 Jer 26:5, 35:15 Jer 44:4 4 Ezra 1:32
W-9 Near and Far	Oxyrhynchus Papyrus 1224, 2r		Mark 9:40 Matt 12:30 Luke 9:50, 11:23	
W-10 The Rope and the Needle	Manuscript variants to Mark 10:25, Matt 19:24, Luke 18:25	*Apocryphon of James* CG I, 10.1-6		

Headings of Sayings	Extracanonical Sayings of Jesus	Extracanonical Parallels, not as Sayings of Jesus	Parallel Canonical Sayings of Jesus	Canonical Parallels, not as Sayings of Jesus
W-11 Illness and the Physician	Ephrem, *Com. on the Diatessaron* 17.1		Mark 2:17 Matt 9:12 Luke 5:31	
W-12 Opportunity for Satan	Ps. Clementine *Hom.* 19.2.4	*Gospel of Truth* CG I, 33.19-21		Eph 4:27 1 Tim 5:14
W-13 He Who Dies Will Live	*Manichaean Psalm-Book* Ps. 273.10-11	*Manichaean Psalm-Book,* p. 159.15-16	Mark 8:35 Matt 10:39, 16:25 23:12 Luke 17:33, 14:11 Luke 18:14	
W-14 Two Types of Shame	Jerome, *Com. on Ezekiel* (to Ezek 16:52)			Prov 26:11b Sirach 4:25 (LXX)
W-15 The Hand on the Plow	*Acts of Philip* 135	*Acts of Thomas* 147 *Teaching of Addai* [f 28b]	Luke 9:62	
W-16 The Prudent Farmer	*Gospel of Thomas* 21c		Mark 4:29	
W-17 Splinter and Beam	*Gospel of Thomas* 26 P. Oxy. 1.1-4	*b. 'Arakin* 16b	Matt 7:3-5 Luke 6:41-42	
W-18 Wealth amidst Poverty	*Gospel of Thomas* 29			2 Cor 8:9

Headings of Sayings	Extracanonical Sayings of Jesus	Extracanonical Parallels, not as Sayings of Jesus	Parallel Canonical Sayings of Jesus	Canonical Parallels, not as Sayings of Jesus
W-19 Prophet and Physician	Gospel of Thomas 31 P. Oxy. 1.30-35		Mark 6:4-5 Matt 13:57-58 Luke 4:23-24 John 4:44	
W-20 The City on the Mountain	Gospel of Thomas 32 P. Oxy. 1.36-41		Matt 5:14, Matt 7:24-25 Luke 6:47-48	
W-21 Lamps Are for Lampstands	Gospel of Thomas 33 P. Oxy. 1.41-44		Matt 10:27, 5:15 Luke 12:3, 8:16 Luke 11:33 Mark 4:21	
W-22 The Blind Leading Blind	Gospel of Thomas 34		Matt 15:14 Luke 6:39	
W-23 Binding the Strong Man	Gospel of Thomas 35	Clement, Exc. ex Theod. 52.1	Mark 3:27 Matt 12:29, 24:43 Luke 11:21-22, Luke 12:39	
W-24 Food and Clothing	Gospel of Thomas 36 P. Oxy. 655.i,1-17		Matt 6:25-34 Luke 12:22-31	
W-25 Grapes from Thorn Trees	Gospel of Thomas 45 Aphrahat, Demon. 14.48 Aphrahat, Demon. 9.11 Apoc. of Peter CG VII, 76.4-8 Dial. of Christ and the Devil 5		Luke 6:44-45 Matt 7:16 Matt 12:33-35	James 3:12 Sirach 27:6

Headings of Sayings	Extracanonical Sayings of Jesus	Extracanonical Parallels, not as Sayings of Jesus	Parallel Canonical Sayings of Jesus	Canonical Parallels, not as Sayings of Jesus
W-26 Serving Two Masters	Gospel of Thomas 47a	Clement, Strom. 3.26.2 Clement, Strom. 3.81.2	Matt 6:24 Luke 16:13	
W-27 Old and New Don't Fit	Gospel of Thomas 47b		Mark 2:21-22 Matt 9:16-17 Luke 5:36-38	
W-28 The World Is a Corpse	Gospel of Thomas 56 Gospel of Thomas 80 Gospel of Thomas 111b	Psalms of Thomas 17.24-25		
W-29 Left and Right Hands	Gospel of Thomas 62b		Matt 6:3	
W-30 The Rejected Stone	Gospel of Thomas 66	Hippolytus, Ref. 5.7.35	Mark 12:10-11 Matt 21:42 Luke 20:17	Ps 118:22 Isa 28:16 1 Pet 2:4-8
W-31 On Self Knowledge	Gospel of Thomas 67		Mark 8:36 Matt 16:26 Luke 9:25	
W-32 Laborers for the Harvest	Gospel of Thomas 73		Matt 9:37-38 Luke 10:2	
W-33 Many at the Cistern	Gospel of Thomas 74	Origen, C. Celsum 8.15.16		

Headings of Sayings	Extracanonical Sayings of Jesus	Extracanonical Parallels, not as Sayings of Jesus	Parallel Canonical Sayings of Jesus	Canonical Parallels, not as Sayings of Jesus
W-34 A Reed Shaken by the Wind	Gospel of Thomas 78	Acts of Thomas 136	Matt 11:7-8 Luke 7:24-25 John 18:38	
W-35 Seeing Living Images	Gospel of Thomas 84	Ps. of Thomas 1.14-17		
W-36 Foxes Have Holes	Gospel of Thomas 86		Matt 8:20 Luke 9:58	
W-37 Seek, Knock	Gospel of Thomas 94		Matt 7:7-8 Luke 11:9-10	
W-38 The Dog in the Manger	Gospel of Thomas 102	Lucian, Timon 14 Lucian, Adv. indoctum 30 Aesop's Fables 228	Matt 23:13 Luke 11:52	
W-39 Knowing Father and Mother	Gospel of Thomas 105	Origen, C. Celsum 1.28 Liber Graduum 22.11		

I SAYINGS

| I-1 Not a Bodiless Demon | Ignatius, Smyrnians 3.1-2
Origen, De princ. 1, preface 8 | | Luke 24:36-43
John 20:19-28 | |

Headings of Sayings	Extracanonical Sayings of Jesus	Extracanonical Parallels, not as Sayings of Jesus	Parallel Canonical Sayings of Jesus	Canonical Parallels, not as Sayings of Jesus
I-2 The Role of the Twelve	*Kerygma Petrou* in Clement, *Strom.* 6.6.48 in Clement, *Strom.* 6.5.43	Eusebius, *Eccl. hist.* 5.18.14	Matt 28:19-20 Mark 16:16 Luke 24:46-49	
I-3 The Most Worthy	*Gospel of the Nazaraeans* [6] in Eusebius, *De theoph.* 4.12		Matt 11:27 Luke 10:22 John 6:37, 39 John 17:2, 6, 9	
I-4 Jesus' Mother, the Holy Spirit	*Gospel of the Hebrews* [2] a. in Origen, *Com. on John* 2:12 b. in Origen, *Homily on Jer.* 15.4 c. in Jerome, *In Michaeam* 2 (to 7:6) d. in Jerome, *In Esaiam* 11 (to 40:9) e. in Jerome, *In Hiezech.* 4 (to 16:13)			Ezek 8:3 Bel and the Dragon 36
I-5 Cease Sacrificing	*Gospel of the Ebionites* [2] in Epiphanius, *Haer.* 30.16.4-5	Ps. Clem. *Recog.* 1.39 Ps. Clem. *Hom.* 3.56	Matt 9:13, 12:7	Hos 6:6 1 Sam 15:22 Ps 40:6 (LXX 39:7) Heb 10:5-6, 8
I-6 Choosing the Apostles	*Gospel of the Ebionites* [3] in Epiphanius, *Haer.* 30.13.2-3		Luke 5:27-28 Mark 1:16-20, 2:14 Matt 4:18-22, 9:9	Luke 3:23, 5:8-11 Mark 3:14-19 Matt 10:2-4
I-7 Jesus, the Vegetarian	*Gospel of the Ebionites* [4] in Epiphanius, *Haer.* 30.22.4		Matt 26:17-19 Luke 22:7-16	

Headings of Sayings	Extracanonical Sayings of Jesus	Extracanonical Parallels, not as Sayings of Jesus	Parallel Canonical Sayings of Jesus	Canonical Parallels, not as Sayings of Jesus
I-8 The Works of the Female	Gospel of the Egyptians [4] in Clement, Strom. 3.9.63 Dialogue of the Savior, CG III, 144.12-21			
I-9 Jesus' Triumph in Hades	Odes of Solomon 42.3-20			Gal 4:14
I-10 Hearing Jesus and the Father	Justin, Apol. 1.16.10 Justin, Apol. 1.63.5 Luke 10:16 in mss. Θ, Φ, it, sy^{s.c}		Luke 10:16 Matt 10:40 John 13:20, 5:23 John 12:44-45	
I-11 Words from the Cross	Gospel of Peter 5.19		Mark 15:34 Matt 27:46 Luke 23:46 John 19:30	
I-12 Feet on the Ground	Epistula Apostolorum 11 Commodian, Apol. 5.564-65	Acts of John 93.9	John 20:20, 25, 27 Mark 16:14 Luke 24:36-39	
I-13 Hope of the Hopeless	Epistula Apostolorum 21		Luke 4:18, 7:22 John 11:25-26	Isa 61:1-3
I-14 I Am You, You Are I	Gospel of Eve, in Epiphanius, Haer. 26.3.1 Pistis Sophia 96			

Headings of Sayings	Extracanonical Sayings of Jesus	Extracanonical Parallels, not as Sayings of Jesus	Parallel Canonical Sayings of Jesus	Canonical Parallels, not as Sayings of Jesus
I-15 Not Understood	*Acts of Peter* 10		Mark 8:17 Luke 18:34	
I-16 Desiring to Hear	Irenaeus, *Adv. haer.* 1.21.2 Epiphanius, *Haer.* 34:18		Matt 13:17 Luke 10:34	
I-17 My Love I Give	Clement, *Quis div. sal.* 37.4		John 13:34, 14:27	

I-18 Guarding the Mystery	Clement, *Strom.* 5.10
	Ps. Clem. Hom. 19.20
		St. John Chrysostom
		  In Epist. I ad Cor. Hom. 7
		Theodoret, *In Psal.* 65.16
		John of Damascus, *De sacra*
		  parallelis 9.1
			Mark 4:11
			Matt 13:11
			Luke 8:10
				Isa 24:16

I-19 The True Gate	Naassene Exegesis, in Hippolytus, *Ref.* 5.8.20 *Ps. Clem. Hom.* 3.52		John 10:7, 9 Matt 7:13-14	
I-20 Words of the Pre-existent Jesus	Naassene Hymn, in Hippolytus, *Ref.* 5.10.2			
I-21 Weak, Hungry, Thirsty	Origen, *Com. on Matthew* 13.2		Matt 25:35-45 John 19:28	Matt 18:7 1 Cor 9:22 2 Cor 4:3-4

I-22 As in a Mirror	Ps. Cyprian, *De montibus sina et sion*	*Eugnostos the Blessed*
		  CG III, 75.1-5
		The Sophia of Jesus Christ
		  CG III, 98.25-99.3
				1 Cor 13:2
				James 1:23

Headings of Sayings	Extracanonical Sayings of Jesus	Extracanonical Parallels, not as Sayings of Jesus	Parallel Canonical Sayings of Jesus	Canonical Parallels, not as Sayings of Jesus
I-23 I Am the Day	Fragment of Marcellus, in Eusebius, *Against Marc.* 1.2		John 8:12, 9:5 John 12:46	
I-24 Believing without Seeing	Eusebius, *Eccl. hist.* 1.13 (*Letter of Jesus to Abgar*) *The Teaching of Addai* [f 3b] *Epistle of Abgar* *Epistula Apostolorum* 25.1-7 (Ethiopic 29) *Apocryphon of James* CG I, 12:38-13.1		John 20:29 John 12:39-40 Mark 4:11-12 Matt 13:14-17 Luke 8:9-10	
I-25 No One to Whom to Speak	*Pss. Heracleides* 187.27-29 *Acts of John* 98		John 16:4-5	
I-26 Near as Clothing	*Manichaean Psalm-Book*, Ps. 239.23-24	Origen, *Hom. on Jer.* 18.9 Clement, *Paed.* 1.9.84 *Pseudo-Ezekiel*		Jer 13:11 (LXX) Ezek 23:14-16 Ezek 23:14-16
I-27 Chosen before Creation	Ephrem, *Com. on the Diatessaron* 4.18		Matt 25:34	Eph 1:4 2 Thes 2:13 Rev 13:8, 17:8
I-28 Jesus Tested	Ephrem, *Com. on the Diatessaron* 17.6		Mark 9:19 Matt 17:17 Luke 9:41	Ps 95:9-10 Num 14:22
I-29 Christ as Example	*Liber Graduum* 2.2		John 3:17, 9:39	

Headings of Sayings	Extracanonical Sayings of Jesus	Extracanonical Parallels, not as Sayings of Jesus	Parallel Canonical Sayings of Jesus	Canonical Parallels, not as Sayings of Jesus
I-30 Perfection Restored	*Liber Graduum* 9.12		John 14:3, 15:26 John 16:7	
I-31 Coming to Make Perfect	*Liber Graduum* 9.13			
I-32 To Destroy the Law	*Dial. of Adamantius* 2.5 Epistles of Isidore 1.371 b. *Shabbath* 116b 'Abd Al-Jabbar, *Book on the Signs of Muhammed's Prophecy* 70a		Matt 5:17	Rom 3:31, 10:4
I-33 Proclaim My Death	*Apostolic Constitutions* 8.12.37 *The Liturgy of St. Mark* *The Liturgy of St. Basil* Liturgy of the Coptic Jacobites	*The Liturgy of St. James*	Mark 14:22 Matt 26:26-29 Luke 22:15-20 1 Cor 11:23-26	
I-34 The Prophet Moses Foretold	Ps. *Clementine Homilies* 3.53			Deut 18:15, 18-19 Acts 3:22-23
I-35 Death and Resurrection Prophesied	*Acts of Pilate* 4.3	Justin, *Dial.* 106	Luke 24:44-46	
I-36 The Great Inheritance	Symeon, *Hom.* 12.17			

Headings of Sayings	Extracanonical Sayings of Jesus	Extracanonical Parallels, not as Sayings of Jesus	Parallel Canonical Sayings of Jesus	Canonical Parallels, not as Sayings of Jesus
I-37 I Am Here	Epiphanius, *Haer.* 23.5.5 Epiphanius, *Haer.* 66.42 Epiphanius, *Haer.* 41.3 Epiphanius, *Ancoratus* 53		John 5:17	Isa 52:6
I-38 Begotten from the Father	Epiphanius, *Haer.* 69.53.1-2	*Gospel of the Ebionites* [5] in Epiphanius, *Haer.* 30,13	John 8:42 John 14:10-11, 28 John 16:27-28	Ps 2:7 Luke 3:22 (var)
I-39 If Anyone Should Open	Epiphanius, *Haer.* 69.63 Epiphanius, *Haer.* 69.54 Epiphanius, *Ancoratus* 69.5		John 14:23	Rev 3:20
I-40 Not to Destroy But to Save	Luke 9:55b, 56a in mss. K, Θ, λ, Φ, al lat sy^c p bo^pt Marcion			
I-41 Not like Jesus	Sinaitic Syriac to John 12:44		Luke 10:16 Matt 10:40	
I-42 Growing in Service	Codex D to Luke 22:27, 28			
I-43 Loving the Father	Theodoret, *Ch. Hist.* 1.4.45		John 5:23, 8:42 John 12:44-45 John 13:20 Matt 10:40 Luke 10:16	1 John 5:1
I-44 The Living Water	Peter of Sicily, *Hist. of the Manichaeans* 29		John 4:10, 7:37, 38	Rev 21:6 Rev 22:17

Headings of Sayings	Extracanonical Sayings of Jesus	Extracanonical Parallels, not as Sayings of Jesus	Parallel Canonical Sayings of Jesus	Canonical Parallels, not as Sayings of Jesus
I-45 The Accomplishments of Christ	Melito, *Hom. on the Passion*			
I-46 The World on Fire	*Gospel of Thomas* 10 Curetonian Syr. to Matt 10:34b		Luke 12:49, 51 Matt 10:34	
I-47 Not Peace but a Sword	*Gospel of Thomas* 16a		Luke 12:51, 12:49 Matt 10:34	
I-48 What Eye Has Not Seen	*Gospel of Thomas* 17 *Martyrdom of Peter* 10 Turf. Manich. frag. M 789 *Dialogue of the Savior* CG III, 139.20-140.9 *Test. of the Lord in Gal.* 11 *Apocryphal Gospel of John*			1 Cor 2:9
I-49 One from a Thousand	*Gospel of Thomas* 23 *Pistis Sophia* 134	Irenaeus, *Adv. haer.* 1.24.6 Epiphanius, *Haer.* 24.5.4 *Mandaean Prayers,* 90	Matt 22:14	Eccl 7:28
I-50 All Are Drunken	*Gospel of Thomas* 28 P. Oxy. 1.11-21, i			John 11:14 1 Tim 3:16
I-51 Where There Are Three	*Gospel of Thomas* 30 P. Oxy. 1.23-27 Ephrem, *Comm. on the Diatessaron* 14.24	Clement, *Strom.* 3.10.68 *Mekilta, Bahodesh II* *Pirke Aboth* 3.2 *Pirke Aboth* 3.6 *b. Berakoth* 6a	Matt 18:20	

Headings of Sayings	Extracanonical Sayings of Jesus	Extracanonical Parallels, not as Sayings of Jesus	Parallel Canonical Sayings of Jesus	Canonical Parallels, not as Sayings of Jesus
I-52 Desiring to Hear	*Gospel of Thomas* 38 P. Oxy. 655.30-38, i	Cyprian, *Test. lib. tres ad Quirinum* 3.29	Matt 13:17 Luke 10:24, 17:22 John 7:34, 36 John 8:21, 13:3	Hos 5:6 Prov 1:28
I-53 Seeing the Living One	*Gospel of Thomas* 59		Luke 17:22 John 7:33-34, 36 John 8:21, 13:33	
I-54 Worthy of His Mysteries	*Gospel of Thomas* 62a	*Apocryphon of John* CG II, 7.29-30		
I-55 Destroy This House	*Gospel of Thomas* 71		Mark 14:58 Matt 26:61 John 2:19	Mark 15:29 Matt 27:40 Acts 6:14
I-56 Jesus the All	*Gospel of Thomas* 77 P. Oxy. 1.27-30	*Martyrdom of Peter* 10 Lucian, *Hermotimus* 81	John 3:19 John 8:12, 9:5 John 12:46	John 1:3-5,9 Rom 11:36 1 Cor 8:6, 11:12 Eph 4:6 Col 1:16 Heb 2:10
I-57 Near the Fire	*Gospel of Thomas* 82 Origen, *Hom. on Jer.* 3.3 Didymus, *In Ps.* 88.8 Ps. Ephrem, *Expos. of the Gospel* 83	*Paroimiai* of Aesop Diogenianus		

Headings of Sayings	Extracanonical Sayings of Jesus	Extracanonical Parallels, not as Sayings of Jesus	Parallel Canonical Sayings of Jesus	Canonical Parallels, not as Sayings of Jesus
I-58 The Easy Yoke	Gospel of Thomas 90		Matt 11:28-30	Sirach 21:23-27
I-59 Seek, Ask	Gospel of Thomas 92		Matt 7:7-8 Luke 11:9-10 John 16:4-5. 23-24	
I-60 Drinking from Jesus' Mouth	Gospel of Thomas 108	Irenaeus, Adv. haer. 1.13.3	John 4:10, 14	Rev 21:6 Rev 22:17
I-61 Things Above and Below	Gospel of Philip 69 CG II, 67.30-34			

COMMUNITY RULES

Headings of Sayings	Extracanonical Sayings of Jesus	Extracanonical Parallels, not as Sayings of Jesus	Parallel Canonical Sayings of Jesus	Canonical Parallels, not as Sayings of Jesus
C-1 Be Merciful	1 Clement 13.1-2 Polycarp, Phil. 2.3 Clement, Strom. 2.18.91 Didascalia 2.21.36, 42 Ap. Const. 2.21.36, 42 Symeon, Hom. 37	Manichaean Psalm-book, Ps. 239.3-4	Luke 6:31, 36-38 Luke 11:4 Matt 5:7, 6:12, 14 Matt 7:1-2, 18:32-35 Mark 4:24, 11:25	Col 3:13 James 2:13 Sirach 28:2
C-2 Pray for Enemies	Didache 1.3 Justin, Apol. 1.15.9	Polycarp, Phil. 12.3 Justin, Apol. 1.14.3	Matt 5:44-47 Luke 6:27-28, 32-33	Rom 12:14

Headings of Sayings	Extracanonical Sayings of Jesus	Extracanonical Parallels, not as Sayings of Jesus	Parallel Canonical Sayings of Jesus	Canonical Parallels, not as Sayings of Jesus
	Justin, *Dial.* 133.6 Justin, *Dial.* 96.3 *Didascalia* 5.14 P. Oxy. 1224 2r	Justin, *Dial.* 35.8 *Ps. Clem. Hom.* 12.32 *Manichaean Pss.* 239.33-34 *Didascalia* 1.2 *Apos. Const.* 1.2		
C-3 Bread for Tomorrow	*Gospel of the Nazaraeans* [7] in Jerome, *Com. on Mt.* 6.11		Matt 6:11 Luke 11:3	
C-4 Loving the Brother	*Gospel of the Hebrews* [3] in Jerome, *Com. on Eph.* 3.5			
C-5 The Brother's Spirit	*Gospel of the Hebrews* [4] in Jerome, *Com. on Ez.* 6			
C-6 The Soul Ascending	*Gospel of Philip*, in Epiphanius, *Haer.* 26.13.2-3	Irenaeus, *Adv. haer.* 1.21.5 Epiphanius, *Haer.* 26.10.9 Porphyry, *To Marcella* 10 Plato, *Phaedo* 67c		
C-7 Save Yourself	Clement, *Exc. ex Theod.* 2.2		Luke 17:28-33	Gen 19:17
C-8 Concerning Marriage	Clement, *Strom.* 3.15.97		Matt 5:31-32, 19:9 Matt 19:10-12 Mark 10:11-12 Luke 16:18	1 Cor 7:10-11, 1 Cor 7:27, 37-38

Headings of Sayings	Extracanonical Sayings of Jesus	Extracanonical Parallels, not as Sayings of Jesus	Parallel Canonical Sayings of Jesus	Canonical Parallels, not as Sayings of Jesus
C-9 Fellow Heirs	Clement, *Eclog. Prophet.* 20		Mark 3:33-35 Matt 12:49-50, 23:9 Luke 8:21	Rom 8:17 Eph 3:15
C-10 Unable to Enter	Naassene Exegesis, in Hippolytus, *Ref.* 5.8.11		John 6:53, 8:21 John 13:33, 18:11 Mark 14:36 Matt 20:22, 26:39 Luke 22:42	
C-11 Concerning Fasting	*Didascalia,* 5.14	*Apos. Const.* 14.20-21 *Didache* 8.1	Matt 6:16	
C-12 Christ the Head of Man	*Quest. of Bartholomew* 2.6-7			1 Cor 11:3 Eph 1:22, 4:15 Eph 5:23 Col 1:18, 2:19
C-13 Concerning Temptation	Cyprian, *De dom. orat.* 7 Cyprian, *De dom. orat.* 25 Arnobius Junior, *Conflict. de Deo Trino et Uno* 2.3 Augustine, *De ser. dom.* 2.9.30 Augustine, *De dono persever.* 6 Codices *Dub.* and *Rush.* of the Vulgate of Mt. 6:13 *Codex Bobiensis* to Mt. 6:13	*Ms. Rotulus Vaticanus* of The *Lit. of Alexandria* *Embol. of the Lit. of Alex.* *Embol. of the Lit. of St. James,* from Paris Ms. 476 *Syriac Lit. of St. James*	Matt 6:13 Luke 11:14	James 1:12-14

Headings of Sayings	Extracanonical Sayings of Jesus	Extracanonical Parallels, not as Sayings of Jesus	Parallel Canonical Sayings of Jesus	Canonical Parallels, not as Sayings of Jesus
C-14 Do Not Grieve the Spirit	Hilary, *On the Pss.* 118.15 Chromatius, *Trac.* 14 in *Ev. St. Mt.* Jerome, *Com. on Ez.* 48.16 Ps. Ambrose, *De sac.* 5.29 Ps. Augustine, *Serm.* 84 Ps. Cyprian, *De aleatoribus* 3	Shep. of Herm., *Mand.* 10.2 Hermas, *Mand.* 10.3 Clementine Epitome 146		Eph 4:30 1 Thes 5:19-20 Isa 63:10
C-15 Repentance	Manichaean Psalm-Book Ps. 239.19-22		Mark 1:15, 2:5 Matt 4:17	Matt 3:2
C-16 Possess Nothing	Ephrem, *Testamentum* Teaching of Addai [f30 a & b] Liber Graduum 3.6	Clement, *Strom.* 3.6.49	Mark 10:21, 6:8 Matt 19:21 Matt 10:9-10 Matt 6:19-21 Luke 18:22, 9:3 Luke 10:4 Luke 12:33-34	
C-17 Pray Unceasingly	Aphrahat, *Dem.* 4.16 (*De oratione*) Liber Graduum 29.8		Luke 18:1	

Headings of Sayings	Extracanonical Sayings of Jesus	Extracanonical Parallels, not as Sayings of Jesus	Parallel Canonical Sayings of Jesus	Canonical Parallels, not as Sayings of Jesus
C-18 Eliminating Faults	*Liber Graduum* 2.4.1		Matt 5:22, 29-30 Matt 7:3-5 Matt 18:8-9 Mark 9:43, 45, 47 Luke 6:41-42	
C-19 Sinners and Harlots	*Liber Graduum* 2.6.2		Mark 2:15-17 Matt 9:10-13 Luke 5:29-32, 15:1-2 Luke 19:1-10	
C-20 Leaving One's Family	*Liber Graduum* 19.14 *Liber Graduum* 30.25		Matt 10:37, 19:21, 29 Luke 14:26, 18:29-30	
C-21 Prayer for Sinners	*Liber Graduum* 20.13		Matt 5:44 Luke 6:27-28	
C-22 Separation from the World	*Liber Graduum* 25.4		Matt 19:21 John 15:19	
C-23 Sundown and Wrath	*Dial. of Adamantius* 13	Polycarp, *Philippians* 12.1 Clement, *Strom.* 5.5.27 *Didascalia* 2.53 *Apostolic Cont.* 2.53.1-3 Epiphanius, *Haer.* 61.1.10 Lactantius, *De ira Dei* 21 *Vita St. Syncl.* 63 *Vita St. Syncl.* 64		Eph 4:26b

Headings of Sayings	Extracanonical Sayings of Jesus	Extracanonical Parallels, not as Sayings of Jesus	Parallel Canonical Sayings of Jesus	Canonical Parallels, not as Sayings of Jesus
		Clementine Epitome 146 Photius, from *Com. of Jobius*, Bk. 9 1QS 5.24-6.1 Zadokite Documents 7.2b Testament of Isaac 19v-20r Plutarch, Moralia 6.488		
C-24 Come, Holy Spirit	Gregory of Nyssa, *De orat. dominica* 3 Maximus Confessor, *Exp. orat. dominicae* Variant to Luke 11:2 in codex 700 Marcion's version of the gospel 11:2	*Acts of Thomas* 27	Luke 11:2 Matt 6:10	
C-25 Receiving without Need	*Apos. Const.* 4.2-3	Didascalia 4.3 Didache 1.5 Hermas, *Mand.* 2.4-5		Acts 20:35
C-26 Commission to the Apostles	*Apos. Const.* 5.7		Matt 28:19-20 Mark 16:15-16 Luke 24:27	
C-27 The Tempter	*Ps. Clementine Homilies* 3.55		Mark 1:12-13 Matt 4:1-11 Luke 4:1-13	Heb 2:18, 4:15
C-28 Born Again	*Ps. Clementine Homilies* 11.26 Justin, *Apol.* 1.61.4		John 3:3, 5 Matt 28:19	

Headings of Sayings	Extracanonical Sayings of Jesus	Extracanonical Parallels, not as Sayings of Jesus	Parallel Canonical Sayings of Jesus	Canonical Parallels, not as Sayings of Jesus
C-29 Faith and Hope	Symeon, *Homily* 37.1	*Barnabas* 1.4 *Barnabas* 1.6		1 Cor 13:13 Gal 5:5-6 1 Thes 5:8 Col 1:4-5
C-30 Profaning the Eucharist	*Canonical Rule of the Holy Apostles* 3			
C-31 Evil for Evil	*Acts of Philip*, sec. 137	Polycarp, *Philippians* 2.2 1QS 10.17-18 *Slavonic Enoch* 50.2-4 *Joseph and Asenath*	Matt 5:39, 43-44 Luke 6:27-29, 35	Lev 19:18 Prov 17:13 Prov 20:22 Prov 25:21-22 1 Thes 5:15 Rom 12:17 1 Pet 3:9
C-32 Small to Great	Codices D, Φ, it, sy^c after Matt 20:28		Luke 14:7-11 Luke 20:46, 11:43 Mark 12:38-39 Matt 23:6-7	Prov 25:6-7
C-33 Fasting, Prayer, Almsgiving	*Gospel of Thomas* 14		Luke 10:8-9 Mark 7:15 Matt 15:11 Matt 6:1-8	1 Cor 10:27
C-34 The True Father	*Gospel of Thomas* 15			

Headings of Sayings	Extracanonical Sayings of Jesus	Extracanonical Parallels, not as Sayings of Jesus	Parallel Canonical Sayings of Jesus	Canonical Parallels, not as Sayings of Jesus
C-35 The Apple of the Eye	Gospel of Thomas 25	Barnabas 19.9b	Mark 12:31 Matt 19:19, 22:39 Luke 10:27	Rom 13:9 Gal 5:14 James 2:8 Lev 19:18 Deut 32:10 Ps 17:8 Prov 7:2 Zech 2:8 Sirach 17:22
C-36 Fasting to the World	Gospel of Thomas 27 P. Oxy. 1.4-11	Justin, *Dial.* 12.3 Clement, *Ecl. Proph.* 14.1 Clement, *Strom.* 3.15.99 *Acts of Paul and Thecla* 5 Tertullian, *Adv. Jud.* 4.2 Symeon, *Hom.* 35.1 Symeon, *Hom.* 35.3 *Liber Graduum* 89.22-25 Ps. Ignatius, *Mag.* 9 Ps. Jerome, *Ind. de haer.*		
C-37 The Keys of Knowledge	Gospel of Thomas 39 P. Oxy. 655 i, 39-50	Ps. Clem. Hom. 3.18 Ignatius, Polycarp, 2.2 Cant. R. 2.14	Matt 23:13, 10:16 Luke 11:25	
C-38 Passers-by	Gospel of Thomas 42			

Headings of Sayings	Extracanonical Sayings of Jesus	Extracanonical Parallels, not as Sayings of Jesus	Parallel Canonical Sayings of Jesus	Canonical Parallels, not as Sayings of Jesus
C-39 Blaspheming the Spirit	Gospel of Thomas 44		Mark 3:28-29 Matt 12:31-32 Luke 12:10	
C-40 On Origins	Gospel of Thomas 50	Clement, Exc. ex Theod. 78		
C-41 Hating One's Family	Gospel of Thomas 55 Gospel of Thomas 101 Untitled Gnostic Text 15 Liber Graduum 3.5 Liber Graduum 20.15 Liber Graduum 30.26	Manichaean Psalm-Book p. 175.25-30	Mark 8:34, 10:29-30 Matt 10:37-38, 16:24 Matt 19:29 Luke 9:23 Luke 14:26-27, 33	
C-42 Renouncing Power	Gospel of Thomas 81 Gospel of Thomas 110			1 Cor 4:8
C-43 Inside and Outside	Gospel of Thomas 89 Symeon, Hom. 8.1 Symeon, Hom. 28.4 Acts of Archelaus 24	Liber Graduum 10.3	Matt 23:25-26 Luke 11:39-40	
C-44 Give Your Goods	Gospel of Thomas 95		Luke 6:34-35	
C-45 The House of the Father	Gospel of Philip 18 CG II, 55.37-56.3			Exod 22:25 Lev 25:36-37

Headings of Sayings	Extracanonical Sayings of Jesus	Extracanonical Parallels, not as Sayings of Jesus	Parallel Canonical Sayings of Jesus	Canonical Parallels, not as Sayings of Jesus
C-46 Joined with the Angels	*Gospel of Philip* 26 CG II, 58.10-14			
C-47 Origin and Destiny	*First Apoc. of James* CG V, 33.11-34.20	Irenaeus, *Adv. haer.* 1.21.5 Epiphanius, *Haer.* 36.3.1-2		

299

SUBJECT INDEX

Light

A 24	Pro 16	Pro 47	W 12	I 44	C 14
A 31	Pro 21	Pro 50	W 21	I 56	C 46
	Pro 29				
	Pro 35				

Living One

I 53	A 25	Pro 11
	A 28	Pro 56

Love

A 1	P 16	Pro 47	I 9	C 4
A 26			I 17	C 2
A 42			I 43	C 22
				C 29
				C 35
				C 41

Male, Male–Female

A 6	Pro 3	C 7
A 39		

Marriage

C 8
C 20
C 22

Mary (Mother of Jesus)

A 2	(I 4)	C 41

Mary Magdalene

A 23	W 7	C 11
A 39		C 12
A 42		

Moses

A 8	I 32
	I 34
	I 35

Mystery

A 6	Pro 27	W 2	I 18	C 41
	Pro 33		I 20	
			I 49	
			I 54	

Passover

I 7	C 11
I 46	

Peace

Pro 1	I 40	C 1
Pro 37	I 47	
Pro 43		

INDEX OF BIBLICAL PASSAGES

Matthew (cont.)		9:19	I 28
28:19-20	C 26	9:31	Pro 8
		9:34	A 19
Mark		9:40	W 9
1:12-13	C 27	9:43	C 18
1:15	C 15	9:45	C 18
1:16-20	I 6	9:47	C 18
2:5	C 15	10:6-8	A 6
2:14	I 6	10:11-12	C 8
2:15-17	C 19	10:13-16	A 6
2:17	W 11	10:17-24	A 1
2:18-20	A 37	10:21	C 16
2:21-22	W 27	10:25	W 10
3:2	C 15	10:29-30	Pro 28
3:14-19	I 6	10:31	Pro 32
3:27	W 23	10:33-34	Pro 8
3:28-29	C 39	10:43	A 19
3:31-35	A 35	11:15-17	Pro 9
3:33-35	C 9	11:23	A 15
3:35	A 33	11:23	Pro 42
4:3-9	P 7	11:23	Pro 55
4:11	I 18	11:25	C 1
4:11-12	I 24	11:27-28	A 17
4:13-20	P 7	12:1-8	P 11
4:21	W 21	12:10-11	W 30
4:22	A 18	12:13-17	A 7
4:22	Pro 33	12:13-17	A 36
4:24	C 1	12:31	C 35
4:25	Pro 40	12:38-39	C 32
4:25	Pro 48	13:2	Pro 16
4:26-29	P 5	13:5-6	Pro 2
4:29	W 16	13:6	P 2
4:30-32	A 22	13:6	Pro 16
6:4-5	W 19	13:14	Pro 16
6:8	C 16	13:17	A 33
7:1-5	A 17	13:21-22	Pro 2
7:6-7	A 7	13:22	Pro 6
7:15	C 33	13:22	Pro 16
8:17	I 15	13:22-23	P 2
8:27-30	A 20	13:26	Pro 16
8:31	Pro 8	13:26-27	Pro 2
8:34	C 41	13:28-29	P 2
8:35	W 13	13:31	Pro 35
8:36	W 31	13:31	Pro 56
8:38c	Pro 2	14:12-16	I 7
9:1	A 21	14:22	I 33
9:1	Pro 30	14:36	C 10

INDEX OF SOURCES CITED

12.32	C 2
19.2.4	W 12
19.20	I 18
Recog. 1.39 [late 4th c.]	I 5

Ps. Cyprian
De aleatoribus, Ch. 3 [ca. 300]   C 14
De montibus sina et sion 13 [ca. 240]   I 22

Ps. Ephrem [5th c. or later]
Sermo compunctorius   Pro 14
Exposition of the Gospel 83   I 57

Ps. Ezekiel [1st c. BCE-1st c. CE]   I 26

Ps. Ignatius [late 4th c.]
Magnesians 9   C 36
Smyrnaeans 3   Pro 8

Ps. Jerome, *Indiculus de Haeresibus* [5th or 6th c.]   C 36

Pseudo-Linus, *Martyrium Petri* 14 [6th c.]   A 6

Ps. Titus Epistle [5th c.]
[1]   A 9
[2]   Pro 3
[3]   Pro 26
[4]   Pro 27

Questions of Bartholomew [3rd c.]
2.5   A 20
2.6-7   C 12

Qumran Scrolls, 1QS [1st c. BCE]
5.24-6.1   C 23
10.17-18   C 31

Sentences of Sextus [late 2nd, early 3rd c.]
20   A 36
179   A 18
316   W 4
326a   W 4

Shepherd of Hermas [mid 2nd c.]
Mand. 2.4-5   C 25
10.2   C 14
10.3   C 14

Slavonic Enoch 50.2-4 [late 1st c.]   C 31

Socrates [ca. 380-440]
Ecclesiastical History 3.16   W 7